I would like to share my deep and sincere thanks to everyone I have met on my travels for their time, wisdom, and wit in helping me on my personal and professional journey.

But I could not have done anything with it were it not for the patience, backing, guidance, and unfaltering love of my darling wife Sonya – she is the rock that I stand on, the confidant I depend on, and the greatest support I could ever wish for or have the good fortune to lean on.

Garvan Callan

Digital Business Strategy

How to Design, Build, and Future-Proof a Business
in the Digital Age

DE GRUYTER

ISBN 978-3-11-103179-8
e-ISBN (PDF) 978-3-11-103471-3
e-ISBN (EPUB) 978-3-11-103487-4

Library of Congress Control Number: 2023939769

Bibliographic information published by the Deutsche Nationalbibliothek
The Deutsche Nationalbibliothek lists this publication in the Deutsche Nationalbibliografie;
detailed bibliographic data are available on the internet at http://dnb.dnb.de.

© 2024 Walter de Gruyter GmbH, Berlin/Boston
Cover image: Hybert Design
Typesetting: Integra Software Services Pvt. Ltd.
Printing and binding: CPI books GmbH, Leck

www.degruyter.com

Change will not come if we wait for some other person, or if we wait for some other time. We are the ones we've been waiting for. We are the change that we seek. – Barack Obama

Acknowledgements

The insights, guidance, and practices that I provide in this book are thanks to too many to mention as they are the sum total of my experiences in business management and strategy over the past 31 odd years, and when we have seen the internet as the 'origin' of digital reshape just about every facet of business and life (not just as long as the internet itself, whose birthday is widely considered to be January 1, 1983).

So I would like to universally thank my former colleagues and the organisations I worked with, the clients and boards that I have served (and hope to continue to do so), and the educators and students whom I teach with – day in and day out they have listened to my ramblings where hopefully they at least pocketed a roughshod nugget or two, and they have taught me much more than I could ever impart by letting me into their ambitions, operations, and very often their hearts.

I interviewed close to 100 business and academic professionals in the run-up to the book's development, and their time, suggestions, and lessons were a most helpful resource which gave me great depth of direction, reflection, and often challenge and for that I am ever grateful.

This book could not have been possible without the belief, patience, and guidance of Steve Hardman, Lucy Jarman, and all the team at De Gruyter – thank you for persistence and instruction folks.

Mary Cummings who was with me every step of the way as the book's developmental editor put up with and compensated for my many writing flaws with a fuse of research skills and creative expertise – thank you Mary.

Thank you also to Lucky Beard for the support on research and their leader Adam Oberum who tested the early outlines of the work as did trusted confidants Alan Holmes and Aidan McCullen.

To Liam, Barry, and Sonya for your time and I dare say sufferance in reviewing all or parts of the work along the way, and finally to Alan McIntyre for being a most generous and wise counsellor and critique.

https://doi.org/10.1515/9783111034713-202

Foreword

In 1962, Thomas Kuhn published his book *The Structure of Scientific Revolutions*, which introduced the idea of a paradigm shift in the natural sciences. Kuhn described how science normally advances by the accumulation of new information, which then broadens and deepens our understanding of a particular topic within a generally accepted worldview. Kuhn's insight was that periodically science also experiences disruptive transitional stages when anomalous experimental results challenge that established worldview. The typical response from the scientific community is initial scepticism and increasingly strident efforts to force-fit the new data into the existing paradigm. Those who have built their careers and reputations within the old worldview have too much invested to just toss it aside and often see the new evidence as a personal affront. As the contrary evidence accumulates, alternative theories are proposed that better fit the data and this creative theorising then triggers a self-reflective crisis in the field. Eventually, the experimental evidence becomes overwhelming, and the scientific community is forced to adopt a new paradigm and the cycle begins again as the new theoretical framework is codified and expanded. One of the most famous examples of this type of transition was the attempt to keep adding complexity to Ptolemy's geocentric view of the solar system before the eventual acceptance that the Copernican heliocentric model had far better explanatory power. But even after this type of paradigm shift, many of the old guard find it difficult to accept the change. As physicist Max Planck famously observed, 'a new scientific truth does not triumph by convincing its opponents and making them see the light, but rather because its opponents eventually die, and a new generation grows up that is familiar with it'.

The World Economic Forum has described the current transition to a primarily digital economy as the Fourth Industrial Revolution because it has many hallmarks of the type of paradigm shift Kuhn described in the natural sciences. For many business leaders, the twentieth-century orthodoxy they grew up in was defined by ideas like using brand advertising to build differentiation and market share, digging competitive moats to protect their business via physical distribution partnerships, adding incremental growth through cautious international expansion, and managing the profitability of mature businesses through efficiency and pricing. Like Ptolemaic astronomers, these leaders built successful careers by executing playbooks grounded in these business truths and not surprisingly many have struggled as this orthodoxy has been challenged and upended by the digital revolution. We now live in a world where a new technology like ChatGPT can attract a million users within days of launch and a billion within a few months – a world in which traditional barriers to entry have collapsed and new business ideas can be brought to market in a matter of weeks. A world in which the established economics of supply and demand, of scale curves and marginal cost, and of protected intellectual property have been replaced by an attention-driven economy where many products and services are free at the point of use and instantly available. In many sectors like retail or entertainment, it feels like the paradigm has already

https://doi.org/10.1515/9783111034713-203

shifted, but the reality is we are still in the early days of this business revolution and the pace of change will continue to accelerate as we grapple with the impact of immersive augmented reality/virtual reality, generative artificial intelligence, scaled quantum computing, and many other exciting technological developments that are far from mature.

While the digital paradigm shift is far from over, we are now far enough into the transition to start the process of codification, take the lessons learned from the last couple of decades, and begin to write a new playbook that helps business leaders navigate this rapidly changing and often disorientating new environment. That is the daunting challenge that Garvan Callan has taken on in this comprehensive attempt to describe what good business strategy looks like in the digital age. Just as journalism is often viewed as a first draft of history, any attempt to impose a coherent framework on something as dynamic and fast changing as the digital business environment risks being proved wrong within months or even weeks. However, I believe what Garvan has done in this book will stand the test of time, as it focuses less on the answer and more on the questions to be asked and the processes that business leaders need to follow to build confidence in their strategic direction.

Garvan grounds his approach in a couple of key insights. One is that – regardless of the nature of the end product – every business is now a digital business. Even when the customer product is satisfyingly physical like Starbucks coffee or Warby Parker glasses, digital technology can have a transformative effect on the entire value chain, from sourcing and product design to payments and customer service. Only by decomposing a business into its component parts and then rigorously interrogating how better data, collaboration, and technology can improve each component can the true potential of digital be realised. While the revolutionary ideas will often grab the headlines, huge value can be created by disciplined evolutionary approaches that incrementally flesh out a new digital approach to seemingly mundane back-office processes and support functions.

Garvan's second key insight is that there is a huge difference between a digital start-up with no legacy, inertia, cultural baggage, or existing stakeholders and an established business looking to reinvent itself. The seduction of digital for many successful businesses is that it is something that can be done on the periphery without disrupting day-to-day operations. That digital can be a side project that will hopefully one day absorb the legacy organisation as it scales and evolves. Garvan rightly identifies that true digital transformation must happen at the heart of an established business to be truly successful. That is a harder, longer, and more complex endeavour than blank sheet of paper innovation because complex digital transformation isn't just about a new idea, it's also about a complex multifaceted process that needs to be managed, iterated, course-corrected, and appropriately governed to be successful. I would often comment to my clients that if they still had a 'chief digital officer' on the org chart, then they weren't truly a digital business, and Garvan does a great job of showing how digital thinking needs to permeate every part of an organisation to graduate from incremental change to true transformation.

While that challenge can be daunting in both its scope and complexity, Garvan provides a great roadmap that curates the very best frameworks, tools, and approaches developed over the last 50 years as he unpacks the strategy process from customer insight generation through enabling capabilities and competences to replicable execution. He also adds his own memorable and thought-provoking contributions to the digital corpus in the form of ideas like the 'Waltzer effect' and 'spin-out syndrome'. By necessity, there is a lot of theory in any attempt to comprehensively describe an approach to digital business strategy, but Garvan consistently leavens it with numerous corporate case studies (both successes and failures) that bring the theory to life, and which flesh out his archetypes of successful digital strategy.

A decade ago, the idea that every business was a digital business was still considered heresy by many leaders whose success, expertise, and personal identity were grounded in the physical business world. Thankfully the paradigm has now shifted as economic value has migrated to digital innovators across broad swathes of the global economy. As current and future generations of business leaders grapple with the implications of competing in a truly digital economy, I hope many of them turn to Garvan's 'digital business strategy' as a roadmap that can help them navigate the coming decades with confidence and success.

Alan McIntyre

Contents

Part IV: **People, Culture, and Digital DNA**

Part V: **Delivering Value Through Ambidexterity and Roadmapping**

Part VI: **Preparing for the Next Wave of Innovation**

Introduction

Scan the business landscape, and you will find examples of ambitious digital companies disrupting their industries. They are brave, bold, and highly innovative, with a laser-focused desire to change the world. Their reward? Astounding growth, five times more revenue than their competitors, and an enviable cult brand status.

Which companies immediately come to your mind when you think of a digital business? The handful of shining stars we have all come to know and love (or loathe): Amazon, Apple, eBay, Facebook, Google, Microsoft, PayPal, Tesla, Twitter?

Love or hate them, behind each success story is a transformed business model often cited to inspire other entrepreneurs to follow. The online website Jeff Bezos launched in 1994 to sell books is now a global e-commerce giant for consumers, sellers, and content creators, including a streaming and cloud service powerhouse worth a market value of $1.2 trillion and year-end profits at the time of writing of $33 billion.[1] Apple, now worth $2.4 trillion and raking in a profit of $94 billion, started life as three men and a 'baby' – Steve Jobs, Steve Wozniak, Ronald Wayne, and Wozniak's hand-built computer. The geeky computer scientists who developed Google[2] can now boast a revenue of over $200 billion. Facebook,[3] the social media website initially launched to connect Harvard University students, now has an annual revenue circling around $100 billion. I could continue; we know their stories well enough.

But while the dizzy heights of these companies are impressive, I aim to show how ordinary businesses in traditional sectors can successfully embrace today's digital technology and trends. I cannot think of any industry – agriculture, education, mining, retail, transportation, travel and hospitality, pharmaceutical, or others – where digital transformation will not improve the proposition, the business model and its operational processes to expand the physical customer base beyond the existing. I also want to show that a digital business isn't necessarily, by default, a company that sells digital products.

Throughout the years I have worked in digital, I have observed the diverse perspectives and approaches people have had in adopting it. To some, becoming digital is merely deploying new technology, for example, replacing legacy systems. To others, it is a way of connecting and engaging with customers. For the more ensconced, it is a new way of working, applying data and technology to create and capture new value or even defend it, with the intent of delivering a bold new vision.

---

1 Fortune 500, 2022, "Amazon," accessed April 7, 2023, https://fortune.com/company/amazon-com/fortune500/.

2 Fortune 500, 2022, "Alphabet," accessed April 7, 2023, https://fortune.com/company/alphabet/fortune500/.

3 Fortune 500, 2022, "Facebook," accessed April 7, 2023, https://fortune.com/company/facebook/fortune500/.

https://doi.org/10.1515/9783111034713-001

These perspectives show me that digital means different things to different people, and some still shy away from understanding it enough to take advantage of what it offers. According to the Salesforce Digital Index 2022, based on over 23,000 workers in 19 countries, nearly three-quarters of respondents (73%) do not feel equipped to learn the digital skills businesses need now, and (76%) do not feel prepared for the future. Despite 82% of survey respondents planning to learn new skills in the next 5 years, only 28% are actively involved in digital skills learning and training programs.[4] According to a separate McKinsey Report, 9 out of 10 companies think their business model needs to change in 2023, and 64% believe they need to build a new digital business model to remain economically viable.[5]

Digital Transformation Is Non-negotiable

I cannot help but wonder why more businesses are not digitally transformed and enabled when, after all, digital technology permeates every corner of society.

Instant messaging and global audio-visual communication connects us across the globe; voice recognition commands 'Alexa' or other smart devices to assist us in all manner of conveniences; online banking and mobile payment Apps facilitate bill payments; online retail shopping is now a faster and smoother experience made possible by storing payment preferences; we depend on cloud storage for documents and photos; smart technology for fitness, fashion, and homes and isn't life a tad more pleasurable with streamed music and entertainment?

The corporate world relies heavily on digital, too, with the cloud for productivity and task management, customer relationship management, digital platforms, and corporate banking solutions fused with enterprise resource planning systems.

It is no exaggeration to say digital transformation is non-negotiable, and crucially, given that digital is driving our rapidly evolving world, it will not wait for laggards. The Covid-19 pandemic has undoubtedly increased the transformation tempo and has left businesses little option but to leverage new technologies to survive its initial disruption. But it is becoming increasingly evident that the pandemic has presented unprecedented changes to the way we live and work and the need for businesses to embrace digital innovation to be digitally agile and resilient. While I will not unpick every other event that has had a macroeconomic impact on businesses today, it is

---

4 Salesforce, "Salesforce Launches Global Digital Skills Index: In-depth Insights from 23,000 Workers" (January 27, 2022), accessed April 7, 2023, https://investor.salesforce.com/press-releases/press-release-details/2022/New-Digital-Skills-Index-from-Salesforce-Reveals-76-of-Global-Workers-Say-They-Are-Unequipped-for-the-Future-of-Work/.

5 McKinsey, "The new digital edge: Rethinking strategy for the postpandemic era" (May 26, 2021), accessed April 7, 2023, https://www.mckinsey.com/capabilities/mckinsey-digital/our-insights/the-new-digital-edge-rethinking-strategy-for-the-postpandemic-era.

safe to say that our complex world will continue to serve up seismic challenges that we will all need to navigate, and in a landscape that encompasses an eclectic mix of incumbent legacy businesses competing for a slice of the consumer or business-to-business (B2B) pie alongside digitally transformed ones, only the latter will survive.

I like to use the iconic tale of David and Goliath as an analogy. The story is often told to celebrate the underdog's victory against the bigger bully. But to me, the story is as much about the swifter, skilled marksman who deftly topples a complacent, lumbering behemoth. Today, unwieldy, non-digitised organisations blinded by the success of their pre-digital glory days best beware lest they suffer Goliath's fate.

So, back to the more ensconced who apply digital, data, and technology to deliver a bold new vision. They have grasped that while value creation is the starting point (after all, the very concept of business), not all value is created equal. Their vision centres around the customer or end user, and invariably, it is a vision that solves a unique 'problem' in a unique way.

At the very dawn of digital creation, there was an intersection of innovative new pioneers who intuitively understood this and, when they came together, purposely recreated new customer experiences that were refreshing and regenerative. A simple example I can think of is how we now listen to music. If we wanted to listen to music in the pre-digital era, we bought vinyl records, cassettes, and later CDs. In the late 1980s and early 1990s, manufacturers rushed to bring a mobile experience to music lovers, releasing various iterations of the Walkman, Discman, and MP3 player. These devices at least solved the problem of turning music into a semi-mobile experience, but they were often bulky, had limited storage capacity, and weren't easy to use. In the case of MP3 players, one had to burn songs from a CD to a computer and then copy them from the computer to an MP3.

In 2001, Apple launched its iPod, with the accompanying music library iTunes. I remember the excitement at seeing this sleek, new-wave pocket-sized device with its user-friendly interface that integrated a CD with the player. One simply had to insert the CD into a computer and transfer it to iTunes. Once someone purchased music from the iTunes store, an entire compendium was available on the iPod within seconds.

Then came the launch of the social sharing site Myspace in 2003, allowing artists a new way of connecting with their fans globally without needing hardware. Hot on its heels in 2006 was Spotify, initially launching a file-sharing service that legally compensated the music industry, morphing into the streaming service we know and love today.

This handful of pioneers used digital capabilities to solve problems in new ways by reimagining their industry, and it is a mindset that I find truly inspiring, and grateful for as a lover of the experience and music.

Today, companies that do this just as well are the likes of Warby Parker, on a mission to make buying spectacles convenient, cost-effective, and fun. Their strategists and technologists have developed proprietary tools, such as a customised point-of-sale system called Point of Everything, with integrated data that makes it easier for customers to store their preferences. Customers can work with Warby Parker associates to find the perfect pair of glasses and pay via a tablet. The system also holds purchase history and which style of glasses the customer has browsed so that when they walk into a store, the adviser already knows what the customer might like. Other digital tools include their frame placement and fit system. Using Apple's ARKit and TrueDepth camera technology, the company has built an easy-to-use tool that uses AR and a selfie camera that enables customers to virtually try on glasses before they buy via the Warby Parker app.[6]

We also see new entrants in the car industry who want to change the way we buy cars, Cazoo in the UK and Carvana in 24 states around the United States. Both recognise that the typical car-buying experience is full of red tape for employees and customers. Users can now browse and find their ideal car online, choose how to pay, and have it delivered to their front door.

Mortgage provider Molo[7] could be the future of mortgages. The company is the UK's first fully digital mortgage lender to offer mortgages underwritten entirely online. Many of us can relate to the frustration of applying for a mortgage and trawling through paperwork, signatures, and long waiting times for approval. Molo's CEO and co-founder, Francesca Carlesi, faced the same frustration and decided to make the experience faster, affordable, and more efficient for consumers. The company uses AI to provide real-time decision-making and instant data validation, eliminating paperwork and speeding up the approval process.

IKEA, the conglomerate of ready-to-assemble furniture, has launched IKEA Kreativ, a virtual and mixed reality-powered app which allows customers to step into any of its 50+ virtual reality rooms. Shoppers can visualise and design a living space and, once happy with the design, purchase the items online or place an order to collect them from their local store.

The American National Football League is partnering with Amazon Web Services to use analytics, machine learning, and artificial intelligence (AI) to gain a deeper understanding of the game to create a better experience for fans, players, and teams.[8]

For the near future, advancements in 5G, AI, extended reality, and decentralised ledger technologies are forming the metaverse, an evolution of the Internet where people can move beyond browsing to 'inhabiting' and sharing person-to-person experiences in an extension of real life. Gaming, entertainment, and retail brands are already investing in the metaverse to develop and explore the opportunities it presents,

---

6 Fabric, "Warby Parker's Retail Playbook to Reach 900+ Stores," Patrick Young (March 8, 2022), accessed April 7, 2023, https://fabric.inc/blog/warby-parker-retail/.

7 Forbes, "15 Minute Mortgages? Meet Molo – The New Fintech Aiming to Shake Up the Market," Tiffany Young (February 5, 2019), accessed April 7, 2023, https://www.forbes.com/sites/tiffanyyoung1/2019/02/05/15-minute-mortgages-meet-molo-the-new-fintech-aiming-to-shake-up-the-market/.

8 TechCrunch, "Fueling the future of sports: How the NFL is using data to change the game on the field, in the stands, and in your home," accessed April 7, 2023, https://techcrunch.com/sponsor/aws/fueling-the-future-of-sports-how-the-nfl-is-using-data-to-change-the-game-on-the-field-in-the-stands-and-in-your-home.

which according to JP Morgan,[9] could be as much as $1 trillion per year. Companies of all shapes and sizes should consider whether they need to be there and if their customers will be there too.[10]

The common thread among these companies is a business model centred around the customer, using analytics and digital tools to provide a great experience that delights at every touch point. By homing in on what the customer wants (or needs), they have identified practical solutions that sell, often at a premium, using a fresh perspective with applied technologies and data to build them. It is as simple as that – or is it?

An Early Warning From Transformation Failures

For every success story, there are as many if not more tales of transformation woes.

You may remember 'A Kodak Moment', the Kodak Company's slogan throughout the 1980s and 1990s. The slogan became synonymous with ordinary people preserving life's celebrations – birthday parties, family holidays, sporting events, that first missing tooth – you name it, a Kodak Moment could capture it. Marketeers often oversimplify this case study, not only mistakenly attributing its demise to technology but, in my view, completely missing the point. When you look at what the company did right, you realise success or failure is often in the margins.

Kodak was founded in the late 1880s by Henry Eastman at a time when cameras were cumbersome, expensive, and mainly available to professional or movie photographers. Eastman consistently innovated simple and inexpensive products to make photography accessible to the mass market. The first 'Brownie Camera' cost a mere $1, and the film 15 cents a roll. In the decades that followed, Kodak's strength lay in catering to this new amateur market with well-targeted marketing and affordable products.

When digital showed promise in the early 1980s, the company was slow to invest in the technology (despite, ironically, pioneering the first digital prototype in 1975). Still, one could argue that it went on to launch a decent range of digital cameras, investing billions of dollars in its DC-, LS-, and Easy Share Series from 1991 until as late as 2004. It even bought a digital photography website Ofoto, in 2001, which it renamed Kodak Easy Share Gallery in 2005, for online photo storage, sharing, and digital prints.

Faced with disruptive changes in its market, Kodak did what many companies do. It took drastic action, heavily invested in technology, and even a new business model. With the benefit of hindsight, Kodak was achingly close to a billion-dollar idea with

---

9 JPMorgan, "Opportunities in the metaverse – How businesses can explore the metaverse and navigate the hype vs. reality," accessed April 7, 2023, https://www.jpmorgan.com/content/dam/jpm/treasury-services/documents/opportunities-in-the-metaverse.pdf.

10 Accenture, Fjord Trends 2022, "The new fabric of life," accessed April 7, 2023, https://www.accenture.com/content/dam/accenture/final/a-com-migration/r3-3/pdf/pdf-169/accenture-fjord-trends-2022-full-report.pdf.

its online sharing site only years before Zuckerberg's Facebook. Perhaps Kodak's challenge was determining which business model to ditch and which to defend. Or perhaps it was guided by the belief that its long-standing inner strengths and capabilities would continue to deliver value for its customers and move the brand forwards, the classic 'inside-out' strategy. Here lies the marginal decision that can often be the downfall – stay with what we know, love and profit from today, or transform to a new path and future. Perhaps the answer is in following the customer, and where the market is taking them.

Any form of transformation is challenging, and digital transformation is no less so. It requires a new mindset and an entirely new worldview. I will go so far as to say that Kodak's executives will have benefited from a team of disruptive, visionary thinkers who were armed with customer insights, prototyping, and a willingness to dig down to the real problem users were trying to solve. If it had adopted the 'outside-in' approach and used insights to engage with customers deeply enough, it might have discerned why they were online: to share images with friends and family, not as Kodak assumed, to store photos to later print off as digital prints. Kodak has since reinvented itself as an imaging specialist and perhaps learned some invaluable lessons, but not before filing chapter 11 bankruptcy and undergoing significant executive fallout.

Sony had a similar fate in its failure to modify its business model. Like Kodak, it wasn't simply a case of failing to innovate. Its brand name had always been synonymous with cutting-edge technology and beautifully designed products – Trinitron, Betamax, the Walkman, and PlayStation, to name a few – and as for digital technology, it launched its digital MiniDisc players in 1999, 2 years before Apple's iPod. As with Kodak, this case study isn't about technology. It's about failing to focus on customer value and, crucially, being willing to innovate *for* the customer. Where Sony focused on developing stunning hardware (and lots of it), Apple created hardware and software, and not just any mediocre software, but one that delivered an exceptional experience for its users.

A case in point is that Apple proactively encourages developers to build and submit their apps to the Apple store for approval. Each app is rigorously tested (developers must go through extensive checks and procedures), and if approved, it is marketed and then curated in the store for users to purchase and download. The value exchange is experience for access. Apple smartphone users are buying *mini-experiences* created especially for them, perhaps one of the defining features of the digital era. Sony's downfall was both classic myopia and a lack of agility. In defending its product-based business model, it only narrowly missed an opportunity: the difference in mobile phone operating system and a change from button handsets to swipe screen technology.

But this is not to say that technology or hardware is unimportant. In the digital era, choosing the best system for the organisation's core processes is vital, and as some organisations have found, transforming legacy, industrialised systems to digital is no mean feat. The Co-operative Bank in the UK built its core banking system in the 1970s. Like many UK banks, its IT was antiquated and organised into silos, with more components added over the decades as the bank developed new products and services.

New regulatory requirements in the UK (the Faster Payments scheme in 2007) and a merger with Britannia Bank in 2008 forced the bank to consider upgrading its core IT infrastructure. But the cost and complexity of the project were too ambitious for the bank for several reasons. Firstly, its merger and proposed transformation co-incided with The Subprime Mortgage Financial Crisis of 2007 and the subsequent collapse of Northern Rock Bank in the UK, for which the Co-operative Bank was a clearing house. The Co-operative Bank was a retail bank also supporting SMEs, so the scale of transactions it would have been clearing, given the limitations of technology at the time, would have been crippling. Of note, according to Sir Christopher Kelly, tasked with conducting an independent review of the debacle, no other bank at that time had attempted an IT transformation of its kind, comparing it to 'changing engines on an airliner at 30,000 feet'.[11] Other problems that exacerbated the failure of the transformation were redundancies, lack of agreement between colleagues and stakeholders, lack of training, and no cohesive planning.[12]

Transformation is not impossible, but like a great recipe, it needs planning, a careful blend of ingredients in the right quantities, and care and attention while executing. One even needs to check the 'oven' occasionally, never mind the diner (the end consumer); in the case of transformation, a constant evaluation of goals and their alignment with purpose, vision, and mission.

A failed transformation may seem like a temporary setback, but it does not necessarily signal doom. Nike launched Nike Digital Sport in 2010 to take the lead on digital initiatives across the company. Two years later, the company released its innovative wearable FuelBand, which provided wearers with analytics, making Nike a leader in wearable devices. In 2014, Nike cut back the Digital Sport workforce and discontinued FuelBand after being unable to exploit the data, along with poor margins and difficulty finding enough skilled engineers. Nike eventually stopped manufacturing hardware in-house and focused on its software offering to continue building the Nike Plus digital brand.[13]

These unsuccessful examples demonstrate that digital transformation is not just about the technology, backing it into the organisation like a module, and it is not just about capturing data. Attempting to integrate digital capabilities without buy-in from the entire organisation and stakeholders, without changing the organisation's mindset and culture, considering its unique structure, strengths, weaknesses, competitors, and a host of other contributory factors sets the transformation to failure. It is also important

---

11 Forbes, "Replacing Legacy Core Banking Systems – SAP Has Limited Success," Tom Goroenfedlt (December 18, 2012), accessed April 7, 2023, https://www.forbes.com/sites/tomgroenfeldt/2012/12/18/replacing-legacy-core-banking-systems-sap-has-limited-success.

12 The Co-operative Bank, "The Kelly Review, An Independent Review of the Co-Operative Bank", accessed April 7, 2023, https://www.co-operative.coop/investors/kelly-review.

13 Raconteur, "How Five Brands Learned From Digital Transformation Failure," Finbarr Toesland (September 26, 2018), accessed April 7, 2023, https://www.raconteur.net/digital/digital-transformation-failure/.

to understand that digital transformation is not a linear, single event. It is an iterative transition of repeatable iterations where we constantly learn and find the right equilibrium through trial and error.

In this book, we will circumnavigate the business world, looking at where digital touches consumers and, in the case of B2B end users, across a supply and demand spectrum. We will ascertain, extract, and make sense of where and how it can deliver organisational and end-user efficiency, smarter risk management, and get the most value from an organisation's precious asset, its people. After all, people make a difference and make digital all it can be. The code is only as good as the coder.

What has drawn me to work with, and in digital, is my constant awe at our ability to evolve and develop a better life, a better place to live, and the means for the next generation to step forwards again. While that may not be true for everyone, and one could argue we have become lost in consumerism, I believe those innate instincts are alive and well, and they are what excites me.

From an early age, I was fascinated by invention, something my father passed down to me. When I was a kid, he would speak of how electricity fundamentally changed his generation. As the internet became widespread in his later years, he would nod to what he called the 'next electrification'. Tied to his wonderment for innovation, he also had an insatiable appetite for understanding the natural world around him. I believe this type of curiosity is the foundation of the scientists, engineers, and entrepreneurs who are patrons of much of the world's innovation today.

Who This Book Is Written for

Taking these worldviews, I have written this primarily as a business guide for senior leaders to first-line management and domain leaders across every sector responsible for shaping their teams, companies, service, or proposition in markets that are rapidly becoming digital. My hope is that it will share guidance, insights, and methods to navigate the gauntlet, and embrace digital for all it can be. It should also serve as a perspective on leadership in this digital era, given the strategic nature of the content and the emphasis on equipping leaders to understand how to unpack and build the capabilities to build a digital enterprise and sustainable value.

Entrepreneurs building, scaling, or selling their company will also benefit from understanding what is new and different about strategy and entrepreneurship in a digital world, as will professional advisers looking to bolster their approach, toolbox, and methodologies.

Finally, students in professional or degree-level education can use this to enhance their studies in digital, business, and strategy to get a real-life perspective to accompany their academic pursuits.

How to Get the Most From This Book

As we move through the book, I will share practical step-by-step guides with frameworks, examples, tools, and techniques for designing and delivering a digital business ready to operate and thrive in our digital era. The book covers six substantive parts:

1. **The evolution of innovation**
   What has given rise to the digital age, and why is it essential to master digital methods, mindsets, and technologies? We will discuss the evolution of digital innovation and why it matters in relation to where we are today.

2. **Developing a digital business strategy**
   How do you link digital and strategy? Which comes first, and how do they support each other? This chapter shows you how to develop a compelling digital business strategy.

3. **Capability building to deliver a digital business strategy**
   We will unpack the core capabilities, tools, and platforms you need to deliver a comprehensive digital business strategy.

4. **Developing digital leadership and a new digital culture**
   We will define and develop the skills you need to lead a digital business and how to deliver value with a new digital culture.

5. **Delivering value through ambidexterity and roadmapping**
   We will see how building for or adopting digital in business is a complex endeavour, so we will share approaches and experiences to maximise success and master the often elaborate undertaking.

6. **Preparing for the future**
   Finally, with the five cornerstones of building a digital business covered above, we will discuss how to prepare for the next dawn of disruption that will emerge sooner rather than later.

I have structured this book in a way that allows you to either read through each chapter chronologically or, alternatively, head directly to the ones that interest you using the index as a guide. I have referenced salient points to surrounding chapters wherever possible, so you should find it easy to navigate. I also continually reference 'jobs to be done',[14] which refers to the philosophy or putting the customer or end user at the heart of strategy and design and references back to the influential writing of Clayton M. Christensen and his colleagues at Harvard Business School where I had the honour of attending 10 or more years ago now.

---

14 Clayton M. Christensen, Taddy Hall, Karen Dillon, and David S. Duncan, "Know Your Customers, Jobs to Be Done," Harvard Business Review (September, 2016), accessed April 7, 2023, https://hbr.org/2016/09/know-your-customers-jobs-to-be-done.

My final words before we begin are for you to be brave, bold, and persistent. Return to this book time and again as you progressively perfect each part. Utilise my experience and the valuable insights I have been fortunate enough to obtain from CEOs, CDOs, COOs, and founder/entrepreneurs through years of practice, teaching, and research. In all, it is a broad tapestry of real-world thought leadership and approaches that will enrich your diagnosis and conclusions.

Transformation is uncomfortable, but it is inevitable in an era where complexity is the new norm. Use this book to shape your organisation to thrive now and in the future. Step out to see the art of what is possible.

Digital will be your new toolset of competencies to make the seemingly impossible possible.

Part I: **The Evolution of Innovation**

You cannot connect the dots looking forward,
you can only connect them looking backwards. – Steve Jobs

What driving factors led to the digital era, and how does it impact businesses today?

We see the future with greater clarity when we reflect on our past. We can then join the dots, make sense of the world, and glean insights to help us prepare for what lies ahead. In this part, we will skim the history of technological innovation from early, rudimentary endeavours to the first industries, computer science and digital technology that we know and utilise today.

We will dive deeper into understanding the nature of accelerating change and its impact on our era of unpredictability. Finally, we will conclude with the lessons we must learn as a business response and how to prepare for the next wave of innovation.

https://doi.org/10.1515/9783111034713-002

Chapter 1
Harnessing the Earliest Technologies Through to Industry 4.0

Give me but one firm spot on which to stand and I will move the Earth. – Archimedes

Since the dawn of time, we have crafted raw, natural materials, then later machine-made and softer substances to create value. The earliest records of *Homo sapiens* date back to circa 300,000 years or so (give or take 50,000 years). We differed and succeeded from other *Homo* species (e.g. Neanderthals and Denisovans), in that our brains appear to have evolved faster, facilitating greater intelligence and stronger survival. This enabled innovation in areas such as language, sustenance, and warfare, which in many respects can be laterally associated with the art of company management today – engagement, funding, and competition.

As depicted in Figure 1, from roughly 2.5 million years ago to 10,000 BC (the Stone Age), we were hunter-gatherers living in simple caves or canopies in equilibrium with the natural world around us. We used tools of stone, wood, or bone for survival, and with such a simple lifestyle, we didn't need to pursue wealth or riches.

As prey became scarce, we sought more stable forms of longevity, transforming to farming and forging metals for hand axes or adzes for the more arduous tasks of ploughing and tending to crops each season. We also made advancements in home construction by building simple huts and devised barter systems to facilitate trade and specialism.

By the Bronze and Iron Ages (between AD 500 and 1500), we evolved in how we defined professions, living, and socialising at a much faster pace than before. We discovered how to heat and forge metals – bronze, copper, tin, alloy, and later steel – blending them with wood to create mechanical machinery for lifting and light manufacturing. We leveraged specialist skills, such as weaving textiles, pottery, and other crafts, to supply a demand for growth and began exploring in pursuit of riches and territories. By AD 1600, we expanded from villages and towns to hamlets, cities, and ports and began trading internationally. It was also an era of scientific revolution with Galileo, Newton, Déscartes, Copernicus, and Kepler, to name a few.

Each significant era, from 10,000 BC to the First Industrial Revolution, saw slow, steady periods of innovation spurred by our need to expand and our desire to explore. But when we exploited soft resources, i.e. up to the First Revolution (Industry 1.0), steam, we saw rapid changes in innovation, leading to greater prosperity and accelerated wealth, as indicated by the Global World Product Line in Figure 1.

The invention of the steam-powered water pump, for example, in 1698 by Thomas Savery (c. 1650–1715), led to refinements that triggered significant economic growth. Savery designed the pump to draw water from the bottom of coal mines and serve water to

https://doi.org/10.1515/9783111034713-003

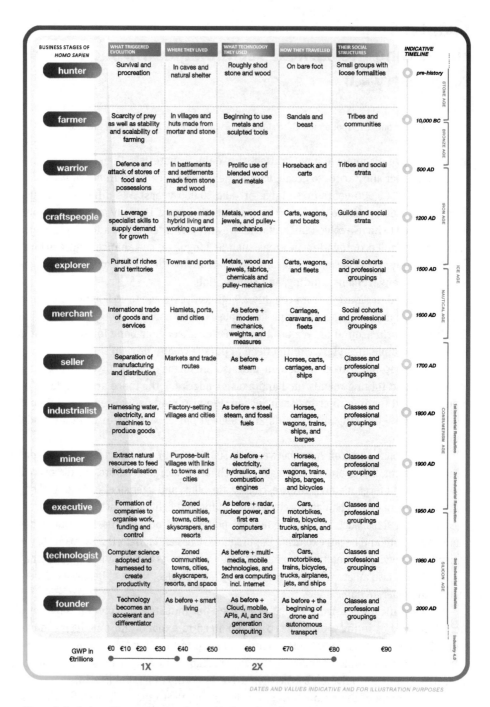

Figure 1: Evolution of innovation from humankind's early endeavours.

towns for mills. Thomas Newcomen (1664–1729) and later James Watt (1736–1819) refined the design to create the steam engine.

Steam-powered machines soon replaced human or horse power to fuel factories and mills that employed larger communities. While there were social ills around factory work, such as appalling conditions and child labour, and steam was initially expensive to run, its later adoption by larger mills and the manufacture of textiles created new industries and prosperity.

Steam invigorated farming, leading to the large-scale production of wool, providing new fibres for manufacturing clothes. Farmers mass-produced food, selling it to local cities, which by then were 'urbanised' with people living near the local factories that employed them.[15] Transport became faster, with steam-powered ships and locomotives carrying new resources across cities nationwide and later Europe and the Globe.

Conditions were not perfect for everyone, particularly the so-called lower classes, and this glance over the history of early innovation is not intended to gloss over the harm to the environment caused by exploitative mining and coal-powered steam. Ignorance regarding the relentless use of the Earth's natural resources undoubtedly played a role, and we must now draw back to repair the damage. But underlying this innovation – from pump to water wheel to steam engine – was a process of enablement. Each pioneer saw where there were bottlenecks and solved them with the tools and materials of their time. In so doing, they pushed technological innovation forwards to merge with industry.

Incidentally, value creation came from a place of genuine problem-solving, which is the essence of customer-centricity. Customer-centricity refers to putting your customer at the core of every decision you make in developing your proposition (whether it is a product or service) and creating your proposition based on the value it brings to your customer. It is a term you will often see throughout the book.

We will now see how innovation continued from Industry 2.0 to early computer technology, leading to the genesis of digital technology.

Reflection

- Early innovators used the rudimentary tools and machinery of their time to solve problems, create new value, and realise possibilities ahead.
- Underlying this chain of innovation was a process of enablement and empowerment. By bettering each predecessor's invention, they yielded the skills for the

---

15 Robert C. Allen, *The British Industrial Revolution in Global Perspective* (Cambridge University Press, 2009).

next and, in so doing, developed new technologies, new industries, and as a by-product, new wealth.

–   As equally as important was the pace of accelerating change. Once people harnessed new devices and power sources, tens of thousands of years of early evolution initially achieved in thousands of years became hundreds and then mere decades, accelerating prosperity and wealth.

Industrialisation to Early Computing

Never doubt that a small group of thoughtful, committed citizens can change the world. Indeed, it's the only thing that ever has. – Margaret Mead

The Second Industrial Revolution, also called the Technological Revolution, was characterised by rapid scientific discovery, mass production, and industrialisation. It was highly profitable, with rapid development in vital industries: railroads, steel and iron production, increased use of steam power, the invention of the internal combustion engine, widespread manufacturing, and the beginning of electrification.

Steam-powered locomotives carried resources further afield, across Europe, the United States, and into new territories in the East and Southern hemispheres. Railway networks became the catalyst for developing regional, continental, and later global economies. Businesses increased profit margins as it became easier to access new markets, facilitating faster communication and, consequently, the birth of the telegraph.

With large-scale manufacturing came large-scale factories and state-of-the-art machinery, which led to the formation of corporations to raise capital. For the first time, professional managers oversaw hundreds, if not thousands, of workers dedicated to production, assembly, selling, and shipping products from plant to public. In tandem, people used simple calculating machines to track costs, leading to one of the first successfully mass-produced calculators, the Arithmometer, by Charles Xavier Thomas de Colmar (1820). The arithmometer and machines like it used gears to perform calculations (an operator would crank the handle of the machine to rotate the gears). So began an early form of computer science.

Construction, finance, banking, shipping, insurance, engineering – any industry that needed calculations – relied on printed tables prior to this, which operators copied and typeset by hand. These tables often contained errors, which could either be costly or, in the case of shipping, disastrous. They also took time to make, couldn't be changed once printed, and time to use, which necessitated training. Users needed reliable, easy-to-use solutions, and the story told of Charles Babbage, often referred to as 'the grandfather of computing', is that he was so exasperated by arduous, error-ridden tables that he set out to design a mechanical machine that could eliminate human error.

In 1821, with funding from the British government, Babbage designed a series of analytical engines to calculate and tabulate complex mathematical functions automatically. His designs were ahead of his time. The analytical machine, for example, has features found in modern digital computing: the engine was 'programmable' (using punched cards); it had a 'Store' for numbers and intermediate results, and a separate 'Mill' for arithmetic processing. Today, one could say that the Store was the memory, separated from the processor 'Mill'. It was also capable of functions for which we have modern names: conditional branching, looping (iteration), microprogramming, parallel processing, latching, polling, and pulse-shaping.[16]

Augusta Ada Lovelace (1815–1852), mathematician and daughter of poet Lord Byron, met Babbage and supported his work. Notably, she wrote extensive notes in one of her papers detailing the steps Babbage's analytical engine took in solving mathematical problems. We would probably call her notes algorithms or early programming code.

Of course, there were drawbacks to using mechanical gears for 'computing'. The arithmometer was the size of a desk, and Babbage never completed his 5-tonne, 5-foot-high (1.52 m) analytical engine with its 8000 moving parts, such was the complexity and cost of building such a gargantuan machine. As we will see in our next chapter, the technology to reduce the size of computers and speed up their processing power came much later in the twentieth century.

In 1880, the US Census Bureau collected more data than it could manually tabulate and held a competition to find the most efficient way to process and tabulate the data. A young engineer Herbert Hollerith designed a tabulating machine that allowed the US government to tally the census in 6 months, compared to almost 7 years before its use.

The mid-1880s also saw the work of English mathematician George Boolean (1815–1864), who wrote various essays on the connection between logic and algebra to represent a form of 'reasoning'. His descriptions became the basis of Boolean algebra on which (once refined by others) computer switching theory is based, i.e. directing a signal or data to a hardware destination.

In the early twentieth century, Alan Turing used the electromechanical Turing-Welchman Bombe to decipher Enigma-enciphered messages about German military operations during the Second World War, well chronicled and central to the movie 'Enigma'. Turing improved the wartime code-breaking effort by developing faster and more efficient techniques with the machine he co-invented with Gordon Welchman,[17] and his work underpins much of computer science today. For instance, his code breaking during the war focused on cryptanalysis, which pertains to internet security

---

16 Computer History Museum, "The Babbage Machine," accessed April 7, 2023, https://www.computer history.org/babbage/.
17 The National Museum of Computer, "The Turing-Welchman Bombe," accessed April 7, 2023, https://www.tnmoc.org/bombe.

and data protection. His research into whether 'computers can think' ('Computing Machinery and Intelligence' published in 1950[18]) has influenced artificial intelligence today in a world where artificial, digitally intelligent software influences every aspect of our lives.

I realise I have only selected a handful of notable names who contributed to the foundations of computer technology. However, once again, we see a theme of *problem-solving* underlying the work of these visionaries and their desire to use the materials of their time to *create and release* value, whether that meant inventing a tangible new product or visualising new possibilities for the future.

Their work collectively proved to be a precursor to computer and digital technology breakthroughs that would set the scene for the next wave of innovation, Industry 3.0.

Reflection

- The second industrial revolution saw rapid advancement and growth in innovation and technology, with pioneers using the materials of their time to build upon their predecessor's work.
- No single person was responsible for developing computer technology. Its evolution was incremental, with fits, starts, and iterations from the early developments of Babbage's work down to Turing's and many others in between.
- These nineteenth- and twentieth-century scientists, mathematicians, and entrepreneurs, our 'computer founders', unleashed incredible applications for new technology that cumulatively changed the course of history forever.

Computer Science and the Foundations of Industry 4.0 – Impact

> Technology goes beyond mere tool making; it is a process of creating ever more powerful technology using the tools from the previous round of innovation. – Ray Kurzweil

In the twentieth century, an amalgam of math, engineering, and electronics came together to form the birth of the computing age, Industry 3.0.

Developers, scientists, engineers, and entrepreneurs continually sought ways to collate data to make it more efficient and available to the masses. This new industry saw the birth of systems that enabled connections to a global audience on a much deeper, more integral level than ever before, creating the digital economy we have today.

---

18 The Alan Turing Institute, "Artificial Intelligence," accessed April 7, 2023, https://www.turing.ac.uk/.

The number-crunching machines of previous industries were limited to just that – number crunching.

Mathematicians, scientists, and engineers were beginning to realise the limitations of this naïve view of mathematical calculations. If they wanted to collate data and perform not just math but numerous complex problems for their industries, machines had to compute by solving complex equations. Developers would need to create a programming language, and the devices running them would need to be capable of running automated processes.

As these early-day disruptors honed their crafts and gradually realised the technology for their ideas, they began laying the foundation for first-, second-, and third-generation computing. In turn, much of the technology that underpinned computer technology spawned other inventions that either had applications for business use or gradually made their way into everyday lives.

For example, in 1937, physicist and inventor John Atanasoff became interested in solving partial differential equations with computers. With assistance from one of his students, Clifford Berry, he developed the first digital computer, the ABC, a machine to store data in binary form and electronic logic circuits, with no Babbage-like gears, belts, or shafts.

In 1939, David Packard and Hewlett founded their garage start-up Hewlett Packard. They went on to become one of the cornerstones of Silicon Valley with notable digital innovations that included a high-speed frequency counter (1951) used by radio stations to meet FCC requirements, the caesium-beam standard clock (1964) that sets international time standards, the first desktop calculator (1968), the first scientific hand-held calculator (1972), and the first desktop mainframe computer (1982).

In 1944, Howard Aiken and colleagues at IBM developed the Harvard Mark I, the first entirely electronic computer that processed data primarily by switching (remember Boolean?). Electronic computers thereafter became the bedrock of modern computing, built around the Vacuum Tube Multiplier, the basis of all computers until the invention of the microchip in the 1960s. They were modular in fashion, built with interconnected circuits and transistors, and due to their delicacy and sheer scale, were costly, unpredictable, and slow.

Microchip technology facilitated faster, cheaper, and more reliable data processing, pioneered by Jack Kilby and Robert Noyce. In 1959, Kilby of Texas Instruments received a US patent for a miniaturised electronic circuit, and Noyce of Fairchild Semiconductor Corporation received a patent for a silicon-based integrated circuit. Their inventions were interdependent, and their companies were at first in conflict over the right to progress, but they later cross-licensed their technologies, creating the trillion-dollar silicon microprocessor industry we know today and the benefits of it.

The speed at which chips could relay data and code using these new micro-scale integrated circuits was a game changer. When you consider that computers are fundamentally conductors for data and associated instructions, the success formula is in the speed at which they can relay this data and execute instructions. Microchips put computers on warp speed.

By the early 1960s, microchips were becoming the 'engines' of computing. Processing power was making significant strides, and in parallel to this, significantly reduced production costs. In 1965, Gordon Moore, a director of Research and Development at Fairchild and a peer of Noyce, observed that the number of transistors on a chip doubled every 2 years, and he forecasted that this would continue for at least 10 years[18] (this exponential growth pattern was later coined 'Moore's law'). That growth rate was, in fact, later refined to doubling every 18 months.

During his time at Fairchild, Moore realised there would always be an art-like skill associated with the production of silicon chips. Excited by the prospect of pushing the boundaries further, Moore and Noyce formed Intel in 1968 to merge science, theory, and practice, allowing research scientists to work directly on the production of the chips.[19]

Their mission was to drive perpetual innovation, and it is a culture that has served them well to this day. In parallel with similar initiatives, a team at Intel pioneered the microprocessor. In essence, this engineering moved computing onto a single chip and was instrumental in fuelling the exponential growth of the computer. It also paved the way for the personal computer, the tablet, the mobile, and smartphone, and then later, 'smart' technology such as the smartwatch.

To put this exponential growth in context, one way to measure the comparative processing power of a computer processor (or CPU) is floating operations per second (FLOPS). While there are many estimates and no one absolute, a useful illustration was developed by Experts Exchange in 2015, illustrating that between 1956 and 2016, processing power increased a trillion-fold. This gives us a bellwether of the comparative power difference between the first mainstream machines and the kind of computers in everyday use today, including gaming consoles and the more powerful mobile devices. To give you an idea of the speed of microprocessors, Intel's first microprocessor, the 4004, released in 1971, had 2300 transistors. It was the size of a fingernail and delivered as much computing power as the gargantuan electronic computers of 1946.[20] Apple recently announced its M1 Ultra microprocessor, which packs a powerful 114 billion transistors, the most in a personal computer to date.[21]

---

19 Britannica, "Gordon Moore," accessed April 7, 2023, https://www.britannica.com/biography/Gordon-Moore.

20 Intel, "The Store of the Intel 4004 – Intel's First Microprocessor," accessed April 7, 2023, https://www.intel.com/content/www/us/en/history/museum-story-of-intel-4004.html.

21 Apple, "Apple Unveils M1 Ultra, the World's Most Powerful Chip for a Personal Computer," Apple Press Release ((March 8, 2022), accessed April 7, 2023, https://www.apple.com/newsroom/2022/03/apple-unveils-m1-ultra-the-worlds-most-powerful-chip-for-a-personal-computer/

So, computing power has increased by up to a trillion times. As importantly, the associated hardware such as memory (RAM), batteries, screens/interface, and software have also multiplied in capability at a phenomenal rate.

Let's also observe another aspect of Moore's law that the cost of computing to the end user would halve every 2 years, resulting in the inverse effect that production costs have reduced exponentially. There is also Rock's law (Moore's second law) that the cost of a semiconductor chip fabrication plant doubles every 4 years, a direct consequence of the ongoing growth of the semiconductor industry. In other words, innovative and popular products mean more profits, which in turn means more capital available to invest in ever higher levels of large-scale integration. This then leads to even more innovative products.

While there is debate about when we will reach the taper points for growth in computing power (and that will be the case for silicon-based solutions), we are already working on the next generation of computing engineering. Quantum computing, biologically inspired computing, nanocomputing, and optical computing all show the potential to bring about a variety of challenging new applications. Understanding, mastering, and applying these kinds of emerging, innovative approaches will empower us to chart the future course of computing. So, we can work on the assumption that what we have is here to stay and that we will continue to see exponential innovation as we look forwards.

While I will not delve into the breadth and depth of computer adoption in business and society in detail, the potency of computers is well understood.

There are over 6.92 billion smartphones[22] in active use today and north of 2 billion computers, including servers, desktops, and laptops. As of January 2023, there were 5 billion internet users worldwide, which is 63% of the global population.[23] There are 14.1 billion connected devices, projected to be 25 billion by 2025,[24] including sensors and smartthings (cloud and internet-based connected devices that we can interact with, such as Amazon's 'Alexa').

The exponential growth of computing and reduced production costs have only partly led us to where we are today. The other factors that accelerated the jump from Industry 3.0 to the digital age, Industry 4.0, namely, are the cornerstones of the digital age and best remembered by the acronym IMPACT – Internet, Mobile, Platforms, Artificial Intelligence, and Cloud Technology.

We will start with the internet, the highway upon which computing unleashed multiple waves of communications, content, and service innovations.

---

22 Exploding Topics, "How Many People Own Smartphone," Josh Howarth (January 26, 2023), accessed April 7, 2023, https://explodingtopics.com/blog/smartphone-stats.

23 Statista, "Number of Internet and Social Media Users Worldwide as of July 2022," accessed April 7, 2023, https://www.statista.com/statistics/617136/digital-population-worldwide/.

24 Techjury, "How Many IoT Devices Are There in 2023?" accessed April 7, 2023, https://techjury.net/blog/how-many-iot-devices-are-there/.

Chapter 2
The Cornerstones of the Digital Age

The Evolution of the Web

The first manifestation of the internet began in the 1960s by government researchers looking for easier ways to share information between two facilities (instead of shipping around the actual machines or large magnetic tapes). This evolved into the ARPANET (Advanced Research Projects Agency Network), a closed loop used by many academic and research organisations with contracts with the Defense Department. Demand grew for this innovative means of communication, which led to a new protocol to unify connectivity called Transfer Control Protocol/Internet Protocol (TCP/IP). ARPANET and the Defense Data Network officially changed to the TCP/IP standard on January 1, 1983, the date on which the internet was officially born.

The internet was initially envisaged and utilised as an academic and research communications service until, on August 6, 1991, at a CERN facility in the Swiss Alps, a 36-year-old physicist Tim Berners-Lee published the first-ever website. His vision was to make life a little easier, a philosophy central to the digital doctrine which we will revisit many times. Unsurprisingly, it was a basic site, but it contained instructions on creating web pages and using HTML, HTTP, and URLs, the building blocks for creating websites. This was Web 0.0 and from there began a wave of change that has gone on to power and disrupt business, engagement, and consumption patterns in ways we could not have foreseen. There were 10 websites in 1992, 3000 websites in 1994, and 2 million by the time the search engine Google made its debut in 1996. Today, there are nearly 2 billion sites, growing at an astonishing rate of 500,000 every day.

The web as we know it has evolved through three epochs, illustrated in Figure 2, ready to blossom onto a fourth.

Web 0.0 was not interactive. Other than the novelty of email messaging, web pages were static, somewhere to load content. But where people gather, trade follows, and the web soon became a medium for e-commerce and the dot.com era, Web 1.0.

Web 1.0 was fully interactive, but its potential was not fully realised until mobile technology and the rise of platforms, Web 2.0, which led to harnessing analytics and cloud technology to create the era of engagement today.

I have left Web 3.0 until Part VI, as it has yet to fully materialise. However, its evolution is rapidly emerging, driven by the motivation to decouple users and platforms and liberate the web back into the control of the end user to decentralise it.

The drivers of Web 2.0 were mobile technology that put the power of purchasing into the hands of consumers, and later, platforms that launched mobile purchasing power globally.

https://doi.org/10.1515/9783111034713-004

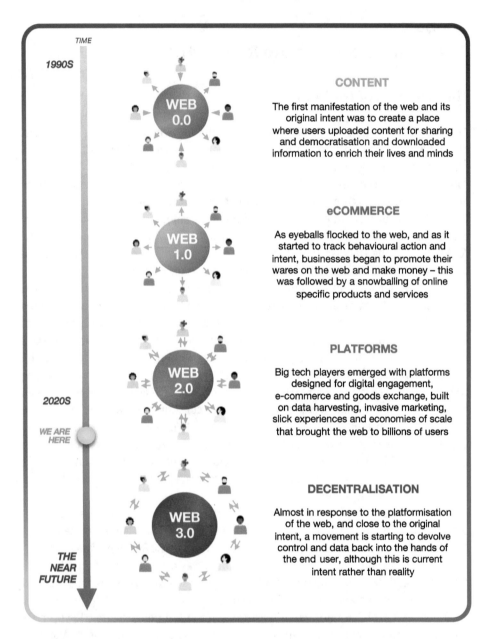

Figure 2: The evolution of the web.

Mobile and the Pivot to Platforms

Two-way hand-held communication has been a staple of science fiction for centuries. It became a reality when Heinrich Rudolf Hertz, a German physicist, proved the existence of electromagnetic waves in the late 1880s. World War II saw the introduction of the 'walkie-talkie' for field communications, and later, various iterations went into public consumption, starting in 1946 and including the iconic Motorola DynaTAC in 1984. This first commercially available cell phone became the symbol of a new genre of elitist technophiles – at almost $10,000 at today's prices – despite the limitations of connectivity at the time.

These first-generation or 1G phones used cellular networks and analogue frequency transmission, first enabled by Bell Laboratories in the 1970s. The 2G networks introduced in the 1980s utilised Global System for Mobile Communications standards as a new global protocol. Handset and network technologies progressed through the 1990s, and cell phones became mainstream, connecting to the internet in 2001, thanks to the move to 3G.

Then in 2007, Steve Jobs launched the iPhone, which granted users unencumbered access to the internet through a touchscreen display, a 2-megapixel camera, messaging, and a fully functional phone complimented by boastful battery life, weather apps, and an alluring design. These signalled a new status symbol, an accelerator of internet adoption. The internet was now accessible from the palm of consumers' hands. Crucially, Apple had pre-seeded the iPhone with iTunes (launched in 2001) and the iPod (launched in 2002), and with it, millions of loyal music lovers. Apple opened the digital store to the developer community in 2008, through which developers worldwide could launch an App-based service using the software development kit and Apple's iOS, which maintained strong quality marks.

Apple was not alone in disrupting industries like music. Anyone could pay a developer to re-imagine or create new industries. The App Store launched with 500 apps; there are now 3.8 million.

Innovators launched new apps and paid to access these users, while advertisers paid to be in front of them. Google followed in 2008 with its open-source Android OS powering Samsung, HTC, Huawei, and countless others, and platforms were born enabling any time, any place access to the internet via mobile devices.

Platforms Explained

Now that we have laid out the evolution of the web, the emergence of the mobile web and platforms, and where platforms sit on that continuum, we need to unpack them as they are central to the digital age and the digital businesses that inhabit it. It is important to understand the difference between technology platforms and end user platforms. These are the two primary platform types; as we will see, each has a subcategory.

1. Technology platforms enable digital services, and can either help end users directly or help businesses to help their end users. Their function is to help people get jobs done, digitally, and they get paid directly for it if being used by an end-user, or indirectly if they are enabling a business to help an end-user through enterprise service contracts. Microsoft Office is a great example.
2. End user platforms start with a job and end users and curate services, products, communities, and content. Amazon and eBay are great examples that most of us will know, and they make money by 'intermediating' services and users, or businesses trying to reach and serve end users.

Both kinds of platforms, particularly end user categories, benefit from what is called 'network effects'. The more users on the platform, the more valuable the platform is as it will attract more services. This in turn will attract more users – and so a self-perpetuating cycle in itself begins. Think about the quantum of community platform users – 4.48 million,[25] 93% of internet users and 56% of the world's population are now active users of social media. That was 0% before 1997 when the first platform, a short-lived Six Degrees profile uploading service, was launched, and followed by the titans we know of today such as LinkedIn in 2002 and Facebook in 2004.

As we will see later, digital businesses utilise both platform types, and in some cases multiple categories in some shape or form. Digital businesses can therefore occupy multiple platform positions at the same time. For example, Amazon is both a marketplace that intermediates buyers and sellers, while in parallel, it provides cloud environments and software to businesses in a B2B model and so is also a technology platform. Google provides its search utility to end users, and provides advertising services to businesses to reach those users. Platforms are monetised in three ways, and Amazon is a great example of all three in action: (1) businesses pay for services from technology platforms, e.g. Amazon Web Services; (2) businesses pay for the right to access the end user network, e.g. Amazon Marketplace; and (3) end users pay to access services from the platform, e.g. Amazon Prime.

I have shared some further classifications in Figure 3.

It is impossible to explain every aspect of the platform economy on a single page, and we will explore them further in Part III. What I have tried to do here is to give a basic understanding of what they are and their role as one of the parallel drivers of the digital age. I encourage you to read more and explore for yourself. Resources include 'The business of Platforms' by Cusumano, Gawer, and Yoffie, and 'Fightback' by Staeritz and Torrence.

---

25 Backlinko, "Social Network Usage & Growth Statistics: How Many People Use Social Media in 2022?" Brian Dean (October 10, 2021), accessed April 7, 2023, https://backlinko.com/social-media-users.

EXAMPLES

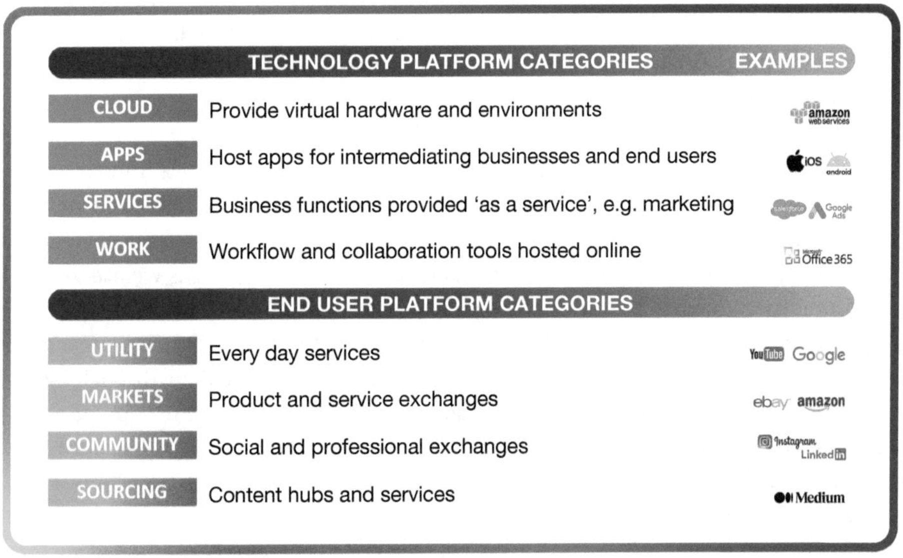

Figure 3: Platforms unbundled.

Analytics and the Emancipation of Digital Data

Data powers platforms; analytics enables insights and predictions, and now with Generative AI assistive services.

In the analogue world, there was no indisputable record. Storytellers defined history, and decision-making was intuitive. In business, asides from basic accounting, we used acumen and observation for strategy, action, and allocation of resources. Computer science has changed that. We can now capture the patterns of the world with digital data records, which has given rise to an era of insight through the use of measurement and understanding by algorithms.

In 2018, we created an astonishing 2.5 quintillion (2,500,000,000,000,000,000) bytes of data every day.[26] (What does that figure even mean? In an attempt to conceptualise it, one quintillion words would fill 11 trillion books, apparently.[27]) By 2025, our

---

26 Seed Scientific, "How Much Data Is Created Every Day? +27 Staggering Stats," Branka Vuleta (October 28, 2021), accessed April 7, 2023, https://seedscientific.com/how-much-data-is-created-every-day/.
27 Pointless Large Number Stuff, "One Quintillion," accessed April 7, 2023, https://sites.google.com/site/pointlesslargenumberstuff/.

daily data consumption will be 463 exabytes (463 followed by 18 zeros), and 175 zetta-bytes (175 followed by 21 zeros) of data in the global 'datasphere'.[28]

These numbers are what one might call 'big data', and now that we can capture, categorise, and interrogate the flow of life and businesses, there is a new game in town. With digital data underpinning it, we can now use analytics to drive far more refined decisions.

At its most basic, analytics is the ability to understand and make decisions using code (algorithms) to extract, interpret, and communicate data. We use it to communicate back to users or machines programmed to make decisions and perform tasks based on the intelligence received. Artificial intelligence (AI) has brought us to new, unforeseen levels. It uses vast datasets and algorithms to analyse patterns we use to either build predictive models or to automate and optimise tasks. You could think of AI as a digital and superior version of the nineteenth-century number-crunching machines used to calculate complicated tasks. Today, automated decision-making through techniques like machine learning is commonplace, powered by the proliferation of data. I have illustrated the maturity model for data analytics in Figure 4.

The world now operates at a prescriptive level. Here are some prescriptive analytics services that you might already have used today:
1. Email – Your spam filter will have blocked out unwanted and unsolicited contact.
2. Online shopping – Recommendations on your favourite site, such as 'You might like [this] because you bought [that]'.
3. GPS and route management – Personal travel planning and public route management.
4. Weather – Locality-based prediction and dynamic live forecasting.
5. Biometrics – Fingerprint, facial, or retina recognition to unlock physical or digital access to your personal devices.
6. Search – Browser and robot assistant support on the web, as well as voice, e.g. Alexa, and most recently the introduction of assistive services such as ChatGPT.
7. Streaming – Personalised feeds of music, video, and content, e.g. Spotify.
8. Social – Recommended content, connections, and advertising feeds.

While these services are visible, the data science behind them is invisible, such is its diffusion and propagation. Like the web, apps, and social media, it surfaces to provide or extract data from the end user to power automated services and experiences.

But analytics reaches back into the belly of the organisation. We use analytics in finance to gather and drive real-time cash-flow optimisation. In HR, it identifies coaching performance indicators. It reduces supply chain waste in manufacturing and automates high-risk, low-motivational repetitive work. In legal and risk functions, it filters vast amounts of documentation for attention and intervention. As we can

---

28 Seed Scientific, "How Much Data Is Created Every Day? +27 Staggering Stats."

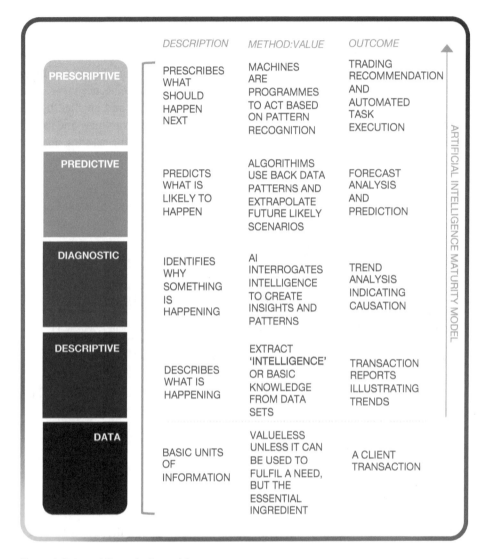

	DESCRIPTION	METHOD:VALUE	OUTCOME
PRESCRIPTIVE	PRESCRIBES WHAT SHOULD HAPPEN NEXT	MACHINES ARE PROGRAMMES TO ACT BASED ON PATTERN RECOGNITION	TRADING RECOMMENDATION AND AUTOMATED TASK EXECUTION
PREDICTIVE	PREDICTS WHAT IS LIKELY TO HAPPEN	ALGORITHIMS USE BACK DATA PATTERNS AND EXTRAPOLATE FUTURE LIKELY SCENARIOS	FORECAST ANALYSIS AND PREDICTION
DIAGNOSTIC	IDENTIFIES WHY SOMETHING IS HAPPENING	AI INTERROGATES INTELLIGENCE TO CREATE INSIGHTS AND PATTERNS	TREND ANALYSIS INDICATING CAUSATION
DESCRIPTIVE	DESCRIBES WHAT IS HAPPENING	EXTRACT 'INTELLIGENCE' OR BASIC KNOWLEDGE FROM DATA SETS	TRANSACTION REPORTS ILLUSTRATING TRENDS
DATA	BASIC UNITS OF INFORMATION	VALUELESS UNLESS IT CAN BE USED TO FULFIL A NEED, BUT THE ESSENTIAL INGREDIENT	A CLIENT TRANSACTION

ARTIFICIAL INTELLIGENCE MATURITY MODEL

Figure 4: Data analytics maturity model.

now train algorithmic programmes to take action when we observe certain criteria, we can automate far more, making human intervention less necessary.

We are now witnessing another era of rapid automation, much like prior industrial revolutions. But this one is different. This time around, algorithms can use the latest data science methods of machine and deep learning to self-train and perpetuate. They can do this because they have vast quantities of data on which to train their predictions. Computing power and algorithm sophistication are such that we can run calculations and processes that replicate intelligence in nano-time and to degrees of detail far superior to human cognitive capacity. AI (a branch of data analytics) will lead us to a new era and industry, the Intelligence Age, just as the internet, mobile, and platforms bridged us from Industry 3.0 to Industry 4.0.

When we delve into this realm as a strategic enabler and core digital capability later in the book, we will discuss the risks associated with the intelligence inherent in this new form of automation. The intelligence emerging from and enabled by the learning models incumbent in machine and deep learning is still very new and reliant on data sciences to control and guide its output so that it is value-creating and not value-destroying.

Side Bar – Debunking Algorithms and Advanced Analytics

ALGORITHMS – Essentially, the instructions you give a computer to work with data and deliver a result. We can also think about them as being equations, given they involve deep statistical mathematics.

ARTIFICIAL INTELLIGENCE – This is the science devoted to making machines think and act like humans, and is a broad categorisation as opposed to a specific method under the theme of data analytics.

MACHINE AND DEEP LEARNING – Machine learning uses algorithms and programmes to do what it says on the tin – learn. They do this by using vast amounts of data to inform inherent decision-making functionality built into the algorithms. Sometimes the algorithms are 'supervised' by humans, and sometimes are 'unsupervised' – they are programmed to self-learn. Deep learning is a branch of machine learning that uses networks of algorithms that mimic the structure of the human brain, which allows for significantly scaled results at the cost of scaled processing demand.

The final cornerstone of our digital economy is the cloud. Everything needs something to run on to work and perform. We need fuel; digital services need hardware, software, and data. The cloud provides these three components via the internet instead of housing them in a physical location.

Cloud Technologies and Liberation

Although the term has become synonymous with the digital age, the idea that virtual machines would act as networking nodes and extensions for computing tasks has been around since computers in the 1950s. This idea of distributed computing was a concept of the internet itself. The name 'cloud' is attributed to the symbol that engineers used to notate virtual or web-based services. There is a public cloud where access to services is open to everyone and a private cloud which offers restricted or closed-loop access. Hybrid is a blended model most adopted in enterprise settings where the path to the cloud is gradual.

Utilising cloud services moves the heavy lifting of data storage, retrieval, processing, and attribution to a virtual space, which has multiple benefits. On the demand side, it offers agility, scalability, and access to resources on a global scale from anywhere via a PC or mobile device at a lower cost. It also provides access to enhanced data protection and backup. However, some industries where data trust is at a premium (for instance, banking and health) have been slow to adopt the cloud, given the lack of direct control. In addition, many data centres where cloud services are routed to/from are operated on foreign soil, bringing about legal and regulatory barriers or concerns.

On the supply side, the provision of cloud services captures all the trappings of scale efficiencies, specialism, and access to the biggest growth market ever. Although many companies can take credit for originating the cloud, it is unsurprising that ownership is disputed territory. The cloud is an amalgamation of computing services accessed virtually and, therefore, a fusion of numerous items. Salesforce, however, was the first company to offer software as a service in 1999, one of the three main pillars of cloud services available today.

The three pillars of cloud services:

1. Software as a service – The distribution of specific software applications over the internet, and central development model (e.g. Salesforce).
2. Platform as a service software – the development of tools and hardware (a technology platform) provided from virtual environments (e.g. Oracle).
3. Infrastructure as a service – The provision of server, storage, and computing infrastructure from virtual centres delivered via the internet (e.g. Amazon Web Services).

Before the cloud, the internet-based tasks we take for granted and easily access – building websites, accessing the internet, data, analytics models, and the software and hardware they run on – were burdensome and expensive. Cloud technologies and services have liberated the utilisation of these digital capabilities and put them into the hands of everyone, allowing access to a global market.

If you have a good idea, you can spin up a website, plug in AI and payment services, craft your SEO and media strategy, and theoretically, be ready to start 'selling' within hours. That is a far cry from the narrow entry point of 50 years ago when opening for trade meant finding premises, paying key money, hiring staff, buying on-premise servers, and installing software on disks. We have leapt forwards a long way and have the ancestors of digital to thank.

Chapter 3
Joining the Dots – Technology-Enabled Ancestors to Digitally Enabled Pioneers

So, we have seen that computer science gave us the internet, liberating access through mobile devices and connectivity, giving rise to platforms that harnessed analytics to build services on cloud technologies: IMPACT. These are the dots that we want to connect by reflecting on our past so that we can look forwards and make sense of the digital age with more certainty. With certainty comes clarity and confidence in what to do and how to act.

Previous industrial revolutions focused on automating processes and tasks, 'jobs to be done', which pivoted around manufacturing and selling to the customer. But in each case, this meant the company's jobs. The inherent motivation was to drive business growth and delivery prowess. Borne out of this were business-to-customer (B2C) or business-to-business (B2B) marketing models. As this concept of doing and selling scaled ferociously through Industries 1.0 and 2.0 with the rise of automation and consumerism, the buying process was also industrialised and, frankly, less personal. Customer service was a way to keep trade personable in an impersonal setting, but it was papering over the cracks as businesses built their strengths around the mass proliferation of products and services.

In contrast, the digital age has changed the game. Businesses that have harnessed the IMPACT ingredients have rethought how they will connect with their customers or end users and, by extension, how they will innovate propositions to serve them solutions to the jobs they are trying to do. Before digitalisation, entrepreneurs were perhaps a rarer breed. Today, IMPACT has democratised these powerful tools, putting explosive capabilities into the hands of the many and empowering a new era of entrepreneurs, including a new type of digital pioneer: social media creators, influencers, and brand ambassadors.

I dig a little deeper into innovation as a strategy in Part II, but for now, we will consider how the IMPACT factors have played out and how digital pioneers mastered what I call 'the Waltzer effect'.

Reflection

- Computer science developed as an independent discipline in the late twentieth century. Mathematicians, scientists, and engineers saw the limitations of early number-crunching machines and computing and continually sought ways to push the boundaries further.
- Computer science gave us the internet, liberating access through mobile devices and connectivity, which gave rise to platforms that harnessed analytics to build cloud technologies – the foundation of IMPACT, the Internet, Mobile, Platforms, Artificial Intelligence, and Cloud Technologies.

https://doi.org/10.1515/9783111034713-005

- Underpinning this computer technology has been our ability to collect and process significantly more data, enabling us to glean insights, drive far superior decision-making, and use it to create new value.
- Digital has, in fact, proven to be a disruptor, as businesses that have learned how to harness the IMPACT factors have rethought how to connect with their customers, sought ways to create new value, and by extension, created new disruptive industries.

The Waltzer Effect – A Fusion of 'IMPACT'

Coming together is the beginning. Keeping together is progress. Working together is success.
– Henry Ford

Each IMPACT cornerstone is an amplifier with a connecting and compounding effect on the other, creating what I call 'the Waltzer effect'. This compound configuration is what has set digital leaders apart from the laggards.

The Waltzer is a fairground ride often found at British and Irish Summer Fairs. Invented in Cheshire, England, in the 1920s, originally and aptly labelled 'The Whirligig', it is one of the most exhilarating rides you'll find. Ten cars rotate in free fall on a revolving carousel that spins around a centre point on an undulating floor. Operators walk the floor, further propelling the already swirling cars to create the 'jerk' and maximise the thrill. These wild and random g-force effects are exhilarating and are a collective manifestation of three engineering forces and one human.

I like to use the Waltzer effect as an analogy for how the IMPACT cornerstones have created a remarkable combination of g-forces. Think of the rotating floor of the ride as computer science and its exponentially increasing capacity, the basis of all digital, which delivers the first foundational force. The IMPACT cornerstones are each of the cars and how they individually revolve as the rotating floor begins to turn – the second force. The third force is the undulating floor, which unpredictably accelerates the spin of each car, and the overall effect is the culmination of all three engineering forces combining simultaneously.

The fourth, the human force, is the lightning conductor and what makes the magic happen (or fear, as you may well have experienced). Operators closely watch each car as the ride peaks into a concoction of speed and screams as the three engineering forces kick in. Using their experience and freedom to act, they pull and push the cars to make the passengers' experience tip from mild thrill to heart-stopping mini-panic with the gentlest of interventions.

This Waltzer effect is one way to understand the combinator effect or the gut-wrenching pace of change we have all felt in the accelerating shift from Industry 3.0 to 4.0 and more recently industry 5.0, with digitally enabled innovators creating new industries and disrupting existing ones as a result. Here are some examples:

- Digital marketing: Traditional marketing is restricted by geography and location, making international campaigns expensive or labourintensive. Today, businesses with a modest budget can launch a campaign to a global audience. We also see marketeers using cloud platforms (marketing as a service) provided by companies such as Adobe or Salesforce, which incorporate progressive AI to build predictive messaging campaigns for specific segmented audiences and deliver them on social, mobile, and the internet. Sensors are used in physical locations to detect devices and present 'in the moment' targeted messaging or 'wow' moments.
- Digital supply chains: The Covid pandemic has highlighted how unexpected global events can adversely impact supply and demand and hamper efforts to plan or meet delivery schedules. Manufacturers can now use digitised processes to automate the manual steps usually involved in the manufacturing and supply chain process (e.g. design and logistics). Many manufacturers including mass fashion houses use digital and engineering tools to design and manufacture products using virtual reality and 3D printing, automating the process, reducing waste and cost, and increasing speed and efficiency. AI is perpetuated throughout to drive continuous iteration and innovation.
- Autonomous vehicles: Sensors and 4/5G networks collect and create real-time digital replicas of the surrounding terrain. AI engines calculate and instruct the vehicle on the correct driving strategy (using the internet of things and digital twinning). Tesla and the major car brands are pushing the boundaries here. However, we are seeing manufacturers push the boundaries even further. Notably, on December 22, 2021, digital freight company TuSimple launched the world's first fully autonomous freight truck operating on a public road while naturally interacting with motorists and traffic.[29]

Pioneering technologists have grasped that by combining the IMPACT cornerstones, they do not just evolve the existing game; they can create new ones. These combined factors have led to what I call 'nine digital delights', as illustrated in Figure 5, and have become firmly embedded in our lives.

The Nine Digital Delights

It is perhaps easier to see how customers or end users experience these digital delights in the real world, so here are some examples. You may know these companies well, but if not, hopefully, you will see how they have gained prowess and unique positioning.

---

29 TechCrunch, "TuSimple Completes Its First Driverless Autonomous Truck Run on Public Roads," Rebecca Bellan (December 29, 2021), accessed April 7, 2023, https://techcrunch.com/2021/12/29/tusimple-completes-its-first-driverless-autonomous-truck-run-on-public-roads/.

00 protect me
Make it safe for us to engage, protect my data, and look out for threats

01 know me, understand me
Be personable, and be personalised – serve me based on what I think or may need

02 be where I expect you
I want to get access when I want, how I want, and where I want – be there for me

03 improve quickly and invisibly
Fix bugs, don't repeat mistakes, and upgrade me and my systems without any hassle

04 be easy, easy, easy
Don't make me work hard – do it for me through simple steps, the less the better

05 make it happen now
I want what I want now – don't make me wait, just make it happen

06 link your price to my benefits
Make your pricing, and the value exchange transparent by giving me tiered options

07 have a reason for being
Stand for a purpose that we both care about and can connect on

08 bring me new stuff
Surprise me, extend the offer, think about it for me. In fact, do the thinking for me

Figure 5: The nine digital delights.

Protect Me – Apple

Apple is a champion of security and privacy in an industry that voraciously consumes user data: from protecting internet users from threats, and providing the most secure operating systems available for business use, to enforcing strict privacy rules among technology companies. A study by NordVPN revealed that smartphone users trust Apple over Samsung, where security and privacy are concerned. Apple's history of standing firm against third-party companies is a major reason for this. Despite frequent challenges from the likes of Meta and Google, the tech giant has stuck to its privacy policy, safe in the knowledge that iPhones have established a monopoly of sorts. Notably, Apple's recent new operating system offers users greater privacy control, and blocks Facebook's app and advertising tracking feature. Unsurprisingly, Meta (Facebook's holding company) is not happy, reportedly having lost $10 billion in advertising revenue.[30] While Apple continues to strengthen privacy controls for its customers, Google, Microsoft, and Meta struggle to follow suit as their business models are based around ads and collecting user data for revenue. Other Apple protection features are:

–   Apps on the App Store must provide privacy labels upfront.
–   Safari, one of the most privacy-friendly browsers out there, includes intelligent tracking prevention.
–   Tracking blockers built into email.
–   Health, passwords, and messages are end-to-end encrypted on iCloud.

Apple is also previewing a ground-breaking security capability called Lockdown Mode, which offers additional specialised protection to users at risk of highly targeted cyberattacks. The company recently announced details of a $10 million grant to bolster research into preventing cyberattacks, which it says will continue to strengthen Lockdown Mode[31] and is reportedly offering a bug bounty of up to $2 million to hackers who can find a way to bypass its security.[32]

30 Forbes, "Apple's Stunning $10 Blow to Facebook," Kate O' Flaherty (November 6, 2021), accessed April 7, 2023, https://www.forbes.com/sites/kateoflahertyuk/2021/11/06/apples-new-iphone-privacy-features-cost-facebook-10-billion/.
31 Apple Insider, "Apple Debuts New High-Security Lockdown Mode, $10M Cybersecurity Grant," Mike Peterson (July 6, 2022), accessed April 7, 2023, https://appleinsider.com/articles/22/07/06/apple-debuts-new-high-security-lockdown-mode-10m-cybersecurity-grant.
32 Forbes, "Apple Offers $2M to Hackers Who Can Break Its New Lockdown Mode," John Koetsier (July 7, 2022), accessed April 7, 2023, https://www.forbes.com/sites/johnkoetsier/2022/07/07/apple-offers-2m-to-hackers-who-can-break-its-new-lockdown-mode/.

Know Me, Understand Me – Grammarly

Grammarly, the online writing assistant that prompts as you write, uses the data it collects from the end user and delivers weekly reports to them, providing an analysis of their writing technique. This allows the user to see how their writing has improved since using the Grammarly app, pinpointing areas that need improvement.

Be Where I Expect You – Walgreens

Walgreens' pharmaceutical store chain has created an omnichannel pharmaceutical experience by using its mobile app as a primary tool for brand communications. Customers can use the app to check and refill prescriptions without calling their pharmacy. They can also set up reminders to renew and collect their prescriptions.[33]

Improve Visibly and Quickly – Android

Android seamless updates almost eliminate the downtime associated with the standard over-the-air update technique, as software is downloaded and installed in the background.[34]

Be Easy, Easy, Easy – Lemonade

Lemonade brings insurance to the mobile-first, digitally native world. Its playful bots have become synonymous with making a fun, fast, and interactive app-based experience across every step of the insurance process.

Make It Happen – Foxtrot

Foxtrot operates a 30-min delivery or 5-min pickup service featuring trendy snacks and items from leading brands and local companies, including cafes and coffee shops.

---

33 HubSpot, "What Is Omni-Channel? 20 Top Omni-Channel Experience Examples," Clint Fontanella (December 13, 2022), accessed April 7, 2023, https://blog.hubspot.com/service/omni-channel-experience.
34 Hexnode – "Android Seamless Updates: Everything You Need to Know," Lizzie Warren (November 9, 2022), accessed April 7, 2023, https://www.hexnode.com/blogs/android-seamless-update-everything-you-need-to-know/.

The company serves customers around the clock, using leading technology and a strong in-person experience.[35]

Link Your Price to My Benefits – Slack

Slack is an instant messaging and workflow programme. Its free tier gives teams the flexibility to get started (besides acting as the perfect acquisition model) with voice, video calls, and file sharing. Its premium tiers bring more features to the table, such as file archiving, unlimited apps, search intelligence, and more options to upgrade to either Business Plus or Enterprise. In each case, Slack clearly defines the pricing structure and benefits to the user. Its pricing also aligns with its value metric. The more often teams use the system, the more valuable it becomes to easily search for files or messages. For larger companies, compliance reports and support become more important. Each tier fuels growth and provides the precise value needed by that level of customer.

Have a Reason for Being – Patagonia

Patagonia's mission statement is, 'We're in the business to save our home planet'. The company exemplifies a purpose-led brand and is a key leader in sustainability. Its purpose centres around producing the best product – in this case, outdoor clothing – while not causing unnecessary harm to the planet, using the business to inspire and implement solutions to environmental crises. What differentiates the brand is its well-known activism to drive positive social and environmental change.

Here I would note that when thinking about the exemplars that I have studied or worked with, that reason for being can be a defining force in driving businesses and their teams to achieve great things – so this is not just a customer delight, but also a colleague one.

Bring Me New Stuff – Chewy

Online pet retailer Chewy uses surprise and delight to console grieving pet parents. When a customer's pet companion passes away, the company will refund money from unused food and send flowers with a note of condolence from the customer's Chewy representative. They will also suggest a local shelter for the food to be donated.

---

35 LinkedIn – "No Need to Wait: 5 Examples of Instant Gratification," Blake Morgan (November 18, 2021), accessed April 7, 2023, https://www.linkedin.com/pulse/need-wait-5-examples-instant-gratifica tion-blake-morgan.

Businesses like those outlined here have experimented with and mastered the Waltzer effect. They are the digital operators that combine the forces around them to build a new era of industry: Industry 4.0. An era where the pioneer starts with the customer's job to be done uses the IMPACT cornerstones to build solutions that create, unlock, and defend value, and the principles of the nine digital delights to guide them in making the entire experience digital.

I recognise, however, that the transformation to become a digital business will not be the same for everyone. You may need to build a digital business from the ground up. Others will spin one out of their existing pre- or part-digital business to develop parallel or 'greenfield' offshoots, and others will need to make the arduous trek from a traditional legacy model.

Whatever the starting point, there are stages that a business will often go through to get to the destination. Here is a mental model that will help compartmentalise how digital thinking and technologies are deployed to make part or all of the trip.

Digitisation, Digitalisation, and Digital Transformation Explained

Digitisation, digitalisation, and digital transformation are often confused as meaning the same thing, but they are very different stages and processes that result in very different outcomes.

Digitisation

To digitise something means to transfer it from an analogue version to a digital copy. A simple example is a scanned letter converted into a PDF document. It is an important process in today's digital era, and just think, many analogue products will be lost forever if they are not preserved. A compact disc player or video cassette player lurking somewhere in your living room chest of drawers might suffer that fate.

With digitisation, the contents or information remain the same; a PDF copy of an analogue book is still a book. But the storage of onward use of that product is now different. In the case of the book, the analogue version is only available to you unless you are kind enough to loan it to someone else. Your digitised book, however, is potentially available to a wider audience if you provide a link to your Dropbox folder or send it as a PDF file to your WhatsApp group, and so on. Digitisation facilitates democratisation, much like how the knowledge held in encyclopaedias was liberated when published on Web 0.0. Their contents were liberated and accessible to the masses, which changed the analogue business model entirely, as you will recall. Do paper versions exist outside libraries and schools?

Digitalisation

Digitalisation builds or, in the case of an existing business, recreates business processes and customer journeys through digital channels. They are then automated and fulfilled using digital technologies. Take customer onboarding as an example. You will have digitised (as explained above) some of the processes by using, for example, an online form instead of a paper one to collect customer details.

However, digitalising the onboarding experience requires even further adaptation to recreate and automate the journey. This involves considering the sequence of steps involved and then building a digital stream to facilitate end-to-end execution; for example, collecting and processing client data in realtime, ID verification using biometric measures, and so on. To make the journey a pleasurable, customer-centric one for the on-boarder, you would use tools such as journey mapping (which we will cover later in the book) to apply the principles of the nine digital delights.

Digital Transformation

Digital transformation involves employing and deploying digital practices and tools holistically throughout the entire organisation to enable strategy. In this regard, it is holistic and complete, not focusing on one thing (digitisation) or one process or journey (digitalisation).

The Digital 360° depicted in Figure 6 illustrates how digital is utilised in various layers of an organisation to enable strategy, with an explanation for each. Digital is not the strategy itself but enables the strategy to drive the organisation's goals in delivering, creating, or defending value across each of these layers which span the breadth and depth of business. Look out for this model as we walk through this and later parts.

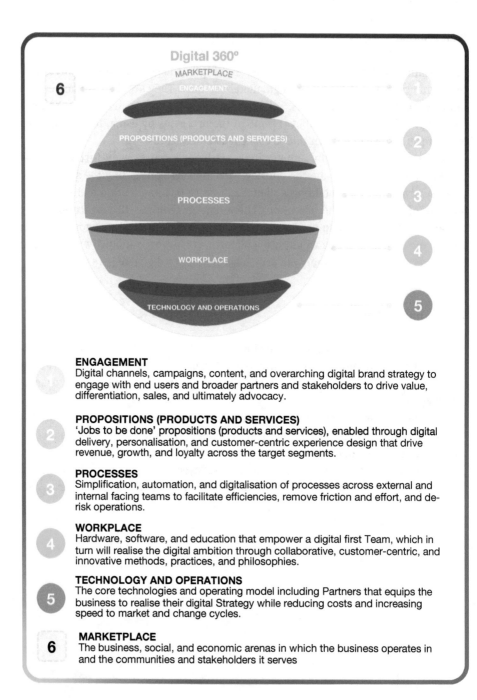

ENGAGEMENT
Digital channels, campaigns, content, and overarching digital brand strategy to engage with end users and broader partners and stakeholders to drive value, differentiation, sales, and ultimately advocacy.

PROPOSITIONS (PRODUCTS AND SERVICES)
'Jobs to be done' propositions (products and services), enabled through digital delivery, personalisation, and customer-centric experience design that drive revenue, growth, and loyalty across the target segments.

PROCESSES
Simplification, automation, and digitalisation of processes across external and internal facing teams to facilitate efficiencies, remove friction and effort, and de-risk operations.

WORKPLACE
Hardware, software, and education that empower a digital first Team, which in turn will realise the digital ambition through collaborative, customer-centric, and innovative methods, practices, and philosophies.

TECHNOLOGY AND OPERATIONS
The core technologies and operating model including Partners that equips the business to realise their digital Strategy while reducing costs and increasing speed to market and change cycles.

MARKETPLACE
The business, social, and economic arenas in which the business operates in and the communities and stakeholders it serves

Figure 6: Digital 360°.

A Case Study on the Journey of Digital Transformation

Take the image illustrated in Figure 7 as an example, around for millennia in physical format. When French scientist Joseph Nicéphore Niépce took the first photograph in 1826, the image was catapulted from analogue to digital. While the process was chemical rather than computer science, it was a digital genesis in that what was in a physical format was converted into a non-physical format. This is digitisation.

Soon after, cameras and cinema industrialised the photograph to bring the image to the masses in creative, replicative ways, much like Turing and Lovelace created the first automated calculators and algorithms. The innovation of computers led to digital cameras, allowing consumers to capture, convert, and print photos using digital technology. This is digitalisation. The smartphone, with its embedded camera, has, in turn, empowered a social media creator economy which, according to HubSpot, is worth a staggering $104.2 billion.[36]

We are now witnessing new business models facilitated by digital innovation and emancipated thinking, creating new pools of value. This is digital transformation and the genesis of Digital Business. Other examples include:
- Digital art enabled by AI and distributed in a digital format called Non-Fungible Tokens, which use distributed ledger technologies such as blockchain to secure lineage, a pre-Web 3.0 move, but more on that later.
- Cameras and sensors are used on top of autonomous vehicles to survey their landscapes, much as we do as humans today in analogue vehicles to navigate and detect danger.
- Super-cameras such as the Hubble telescope can help us see across galaxies and help answer the big questions of the universe, and micro-cameras have aided a new era of surveillance.
- Virtual and augmented reality, one of the most promising emerging business opportunities, will create new realms of media, education, and operational sophistication.

We will next discuss how these phases of digital deployment are affecting our world today and how businesses are responding.

Reflection

- The Waltzer Effect is one way to understand the combinator effect of the gutwrenching pace of change felt in the accelerating shift from Industry 3.0 to 4.0.

---

36 Hubspot.com, "The Creator Economy Market Size Is Growing: How Brands Can Leverage It," Erica Santiago (January 21, 2023), accessed April 7, 2023, https://blog.hubspot.com/marketing/creator-econ omy-market-size.

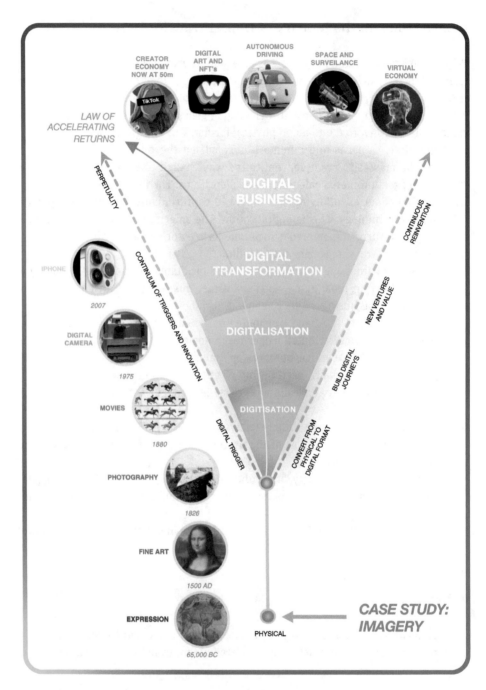

Figure 7: From digitisation to the digital transformation of imagery.

- Digitally enabled innovators have created new industries and disrupted existing ones with new, innovative business models. Our digital exemplars experimented with and mastered the Waltzer Effect, using the forces around them to build customer-centric business models.
- The journey to digital transformation will not be the same for everyone, as some will need to build a digital business from the ground up, and others will spin one out of their existing pre- or part-digital business to develop parallel models. But the lessons are clear. Businesses must transform or be left behind.

The Spin-Out Syndrome – The Complexity of Business in the Digital Age

The greatest thing in this world is not so much where we stand as in what direction we are moving. – Johann Wolfgang von Goethe

The result of exponential technological growth, the Waltzer effect, and the need to be digitally transformed to capture or create value has presented a new era of complexity, particularly for businesses that are historically well-established but at the risk of being left behind.

In the diagram illustrated in Figure 8, you'll see that pre-2000 and before the adoption of the internet, conducting and managing a business was 'straightforward'. The business model was linear; companies created value through products and services and sold them in supply chains to their customers.

The internet has enabled companies a multitude of ways to market, run their operations, and manage their resources and stakeholders. The digital age has created cognitively challenging and resource-hungry complexity, and we are beginning to see what the next wave of considerations will look like as we hurtle toward 2030.

I call this the spin-out syndrome, after the process of a spider building its web. It begins with the anchoring frame of the web (the spokes), then lattices it with sticky silk, moving from the centre out. As the spider grows from the nourishment captured by the first waves of silk near the centre, she needs more sustenance, so she spins more cross-spoke threads to capture more food, and so it continues. In the same way, companies build foundations (propositions, operations, and people) and develop capability, which over time multiplies to create and capture value.

But the degree to which companies build capability and the resulting complexities will continue to multiply exponentially. The spin-out syndrome illustrates why we are exploding complexity in a compressed period and why digital transformation equates to business transformation. This is why we feel like we're on the Waltzer.

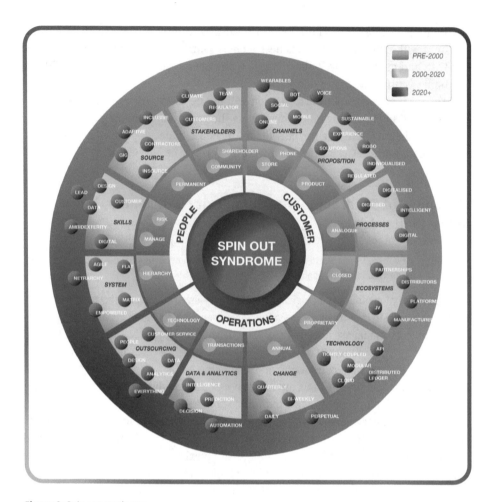

Figure 8: Spin-out syndrome.

Keeping pace with customer expectations is where we first see the spin-out syndrome take hold and become the driving force for the remainder of the web:

- Engaging customers requires the management of physical and digital channels that need to work in seamless synchronisation (what is called omni- or opti-channel) and a new brand strategy.
- Propositions need to centre around the customer on an individualised basis, deliver brilliant experiences through digital and human advice, and provide a value exchange built on transparency, sustainability, and authenticity.
- The underpinning processes to deliver the experience need to be digitally transformed, which must go through the process of being digitised, then digitalised, end-to-end.

- Businesses must put in place an ecosystem of partners to solve these unique experiences to ensure that the solution is comprehensive, holistic, and complete.

A new realm of sophisticated operational and technical capabilities is necessary to keep pace with this customer-driven transformation:
- Businesses need to apply new technology and data infrastructures to deliver these experiences and routes to market.
- They must invest in managing big data foundations and develop analytics muscles.
- Management must meet the newfound velocity of change and consider outsourcing, as there may not be the capability or capacity to manage this internally.

To move faster while using new tools to deliver new value to a broader community, organisations need to evolve their talent and stakeholder management strategies:
- The organisation's work needs to shift from top-down hierarchies to self-propelling and empowered teams who work across disciplines to put the customer at the centre by leveraging new technologies and data.
- Organisations need new ways of working and new operational dimensions in technology, ecosystems, design, and data. These all require new skills that are often not inherent and in high demand (posing attraction and retention factors).
- Companies now consider hybrid talent sourcing, given that people want control over how they work. The Covid pandemic of 2020 accelerated this change in the way we work. In 2021, the Harvard Business Review presented the observation that the project-oriented economic activity would grow to $20 trillion in 2027, forecasting that projects would become the primary way we work.[37]
- Organisations are also shifting back to their roots of serving the community after a phase of shareholder-centric dominance. This includes people and the planet and is a further level of complexity.

Transformation Hope Not Fear

At this point, you would be forgiven for thinking there is too much to decipher and the transformation journey too hard to travel. But there is hope and much of it. Many existing businesses have successfully embraced what it means to be a digital business, as I show in the examples below.

---

[37] The Harvard Business Review, "The Project Economy Has Arrived – Use These Skills and Tools to Make the Most of It," Antonio Nieto-Rodriguez (December, 2021), accessed April 7, 2023, https://hbr.org/2021/11/the-project-economy-has-arrived.

As indicated at the outset of this book, I have chosen a cross-selection of examples from traditional sectors to show you how feasible it is to digitally transform a business that falls outside the scope of selling digital products and services:

IKEA – Around since 1943. About 80% of its journeys now start online. Stores are 'the' personification of Phygital (where digital and physical are blended), facilitating experience with order efficiency and digital workflow to support. Employees help at every step. AI is implemented throughout the value chain to identify market trends and optimise materials and manufacturing. VR/AR is used to help customers visualise products at home, boosting store footfall by 19%.

AUDI – The Audi City stores are digital showrooms based in high-end locations where prospective buyers are hosted by personal shopping concierges. Through skilled engagement, visitors can visualise advanced internal and external configurations through giant interactive screens. Stock and prime real estate are minimised, while these locations reportedly boast 60% better conversion and upsell over traditional forecourts.

DISNEY – This 99-year-old company continues to purvey magic and diversify its business using digital technology throughout. Apps guide visitors, manage queues, and upsell. Many of its theme park rides now embrace the latest digital engineering to deliver ground-breaking experiences such as Rise of the Resistance. Through its acquisition of Pixar from Steve Jobs in 2006, it became the frontrunner in 2–4D digital animation, a capability it missed, needed, and acquired. Disney+, launched in 2019, is giving Netflix and other content subscription services a good run for their money and boasts a market-leading user experience.

STARBUCKS – The ultimate physical product, coffee, is perfectly accompanied by an app that stores cash and rewards, remembers orders, and facilitates pre-ordering and fast collection. Starbucks deploy AI and digital inventory management throughout its network of c. 35,000 stores worldwide. The amount of cash stored in the app equates to a large regional bank offering certainty and cash flow benefits.

These companies have embraced digital as the opportunity it should be. We are living in an era in which we must rethink value creation and the transformational sustainability of enterprise, which is what these companies have done. For them, digital isn't a list of things to do to the organisation. It is a new way of thinking, a culture that drives new value propositions.

Through my advisory work and research, I have observed the common characteristics of leading digital organisations and have summarised them below.

The Nine Attributes of a Leading Digital Organisation

Regardless of whether it is B2C, B2B, or any other type of franchise, this is what great digital companies do:

1. Guiding light: A strong and defining purpose drives the agenda, and every digital differentiator is compelled by a magnetic and deeply motivational North Star, spanning monetisable as well as social themes.
2. End-user value: Delivering value to the end user is the most important KPI. There is an absolute belief that if value is delivered, the rewards will follow.
3. Technology is an enabler: It is not the destination. Beware the zealous technologist who starts with the code, as they will have missed the point and invariably fail.
4. Data rules: Data, leveraged through analytics, guides decision-making and resource management in every corner of the organisation. They do not come to meetings without facts and insights.
5. Innovation is implicit: Testing and learning in short cycles, constantly testing with the end user, is a must. This brings a new meaning to economies. It is economies of growth, not scale.
6. Ruthless discipline: Focus and discipline are irrefutable. Distractions are not tolerated, and progress is baselined and measured every step of the way. If it is not working, it is killed quickly.
7. Adaptable: Agile is not just a way of working. It is a philosophy, and results in being able to respond to opportunity, switch path quickly, and manage resources (time, money, and people) smartly.
8. Risk is a strategy: Risk is managed as an asset, and regulation is interpreted advantageously. Risk appetite is about playing to win and playing not to lose.
9. Constructive discontentment: Leaders live in a state of perpetual constructive discontentment. They always look for the angles and believe there is a better way, but perfection is the enemy of progress, so progress trumps.

Reflection

- Our exponential technological growth, combined with the Waltzer effect and the need to be digitally transformed or risk being left behind, has created a new era of complexity. The internet has given companies access to a global market, with new ways to take products or services to market, run their operations, and manage their resources and stakeholders.
- The effect is challenging and resource-hungry, leaving businesses in an unfamiliar business landscape. Whereas the traditional, pre-digital business model was linear (although not necessarily more efficient) with a defined chain and supply

channel, businesses today will only survive if they merge with others in a business ecosystem.

- I call this spin-out syndrome, as it is much like the spider slowly spinning out its web to capture nourishment. Companies similarly build their centre foundations – their propositions, operations, and people – and spin out by developing capability, which over time multiplies to create and capture new value.
- But the complexity of this era means businesses must continue evolving while they develop their own capabilities to keep pace with customer expectations.
- And finally, we have seen that leading digital organisations have nine common attributes:
  - They have a guiding light, a motivational North Star.
  - They start with the end user to deliver value.
  - They use technology as an enabler.
  - Data rules; they drive intelligent decision-making through leveraged analytics.
  - Innovation is implicit; they test and iterate in short cycles.
  - Focus and discipline in creating value propositions are key.
  - Agile is a philosophy that takes time, money, and progress to heart.
  - Risk is not a negative; it is managed as an asset.
  - They lead in a state of perpetual constructive discontentment, constantly progressing and looking forwards.

What Can We Learn From the Pace of Technological Change

We can only see a short distance ahead, but we can see plenty there that needs to be done.
– Alan Turing

In this opening part of the book, we uncovered the theme of exponential growth, how innovation cycles shorten at every subsequent step, and the complexity that is presenting itself as businesses seek to respond.

It took tens of thousands of centuries of what now seems like slow progress using ordinary raw, hard materials to craft mechanical inventions to empower early societies. As those societies formed, learned, scaled, and specialised, they built on previous innovations with confidence, resilience, and exploration. In turn, the change cycles accelerated, and a multiplier effect took hold. We achieved tens of thousands of years in mere thousands, then hundreds to mere decades.

We often view the harnessing of steam and electricity as the foundational technologies of the first and second industrial revolutions. But other underlying innovations became significant enablers: science, physics, chemistry, mathematics, and engineering. The important reflection to draw here is that no single technology has created this pace of change but a multidimensional combination of technologies and disciplines that, when applied together, have given rise to fundamental shifts in innovation.

Seismic changes are not usually the result of one sweeping or stellar intervention. They emerge from the culmination of many more minor, frequent, and incremental progressions. And as we look forwards, we should digest and reconcile that the pace of change we have experienced thus far will not just continue but accelerate and accelerate again. This expectation and my experience from observing the world is that there is little time to ponder, and the time to act is now.

Ray Kurzweil's seminal essay, 'The Law of Accelerating Returns',[38] presents how exponential growth stretches beyond computers to fields such as brain scanning, DNA sequencing, innovation measured by patents, and economic development.

A key point early in Kurzweil's essay is that we are only at the very beginning of the next iteration of exponential change and are unprepared for the pace of what is to come. Our natural intuition when considering the future is to assume the current rate of progress will continue. However, Moore's law (that the number of transistors doubled every 2 years, and the cost of computing to end users would decrease) and Kurzweil's law of accelerating change shows us that innovation will double, double again, and so on. We need to think beyond our natural preconditions. Kurzweil illustrates this through the old fable of 'The Rice and the Chessboard'.

A servant asks a ruler for a grain of rice for the first square on a chessboard and to double the allocation for each of the subsequent 63 squares as a reward for a good deed done. That would equate to two grains for the second square, four for the third, and so forth. As illustrated in Figure 9, by the time the emperor arrives at the 64th square, the allocation will equate to 9,223,372,036,854,775,808 grains of rice – over 1500 times the annual world production of wheat in today's terms. So the rewards would have been impossible, illustrating our inability to calculate exponential progress.

The red line across the image illustrates that halfway along the exponential growth line, we can observe that while growth is stellar, it is consumable. At square 33, the grain count stands at 4.29 billion (the letters used are the abbreviations for the SI metric prefixes). Therefore, the illustration also has the purpose of sharing that it is not in the first half of the exponential journey that creates the impact; it is the second half. The 33rd square contains more rice than the entirety of the first half of the board, and it in itself is a meek and miniature digit compared to what follows.

Kurzweil puts forwards the argument that we are only in the first half of the chessboard of technology-enabled growth based on his backwards and forwards observations. If we think about it, that is intuitively true. As we progress with technology, we create more resources and capabilities, which we pour back into innovation

38 The Law of Accelerating Returns, "Kurzweil, Tracking the Acceleration of Intelligence," accessed April 7, 2023, https://www.kurzweilai.net/the-law-of-accelerating-returns.

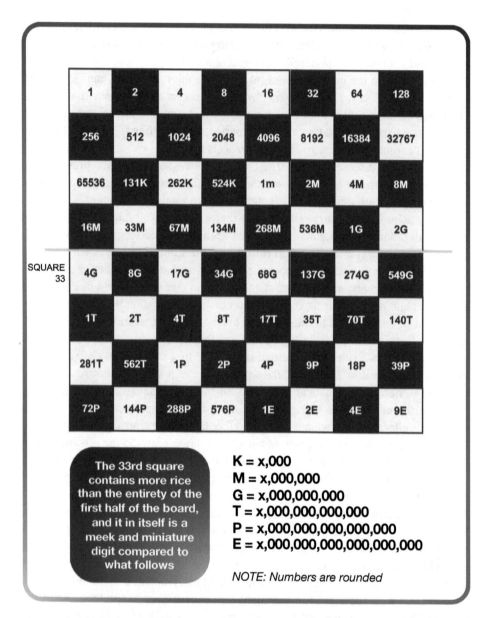

1	2	4	8	16	32	64	128
256	512	1024	2048	4096	8192	16384	32767
65536	131K	262K	524K	1m	2M	4M	8M
16M	33M	67M	134M	268M	536M	1G	2G
4G	8G	17G	34G	68G	137G	274G	549G
1T	2T	4T	8T	17T	35T	70T	140T
281T	562T	1P	2P	4P	9P	18P	39P
72P	144P	288P	576P	1E	2E	4E	9E

SQUARE 33

> The 33rd square contains more rice than the entirety of the first half of the board, and it in itself is a meek and miniature digit compared to what follows

K = x,000
M = x,000,000
G = x,000,000,000
T = x,000,000,000,000
P = x,000,000,000,000,000
E = x,000,000,000,000,000,000

NOTE: Numbers are rounded

Figure 9: The rice and the chessboard.

and technology, as described in the spin-out syndrome. This triggers further progress, resulting in a double exponential growth, where the exponential growth rate itself grows exponentially. Hence, the importance of the reflection. It should serve as a calling card to determine how to prepare for our era and beyond.

Preparing for Complexity

Now that we have uncovered that we usually expect our future growth to be similar to our past we can understand that exponential development and these new permutations we are experiencing jar with our assumptions and expectations. This new era of complexity has given rise to a unique expression, VUCA or VUCA World.

VUCA is an acronym for volatility, uncertainty, complexity, and ambiguity. Economists first used it in 1985 to observe the challenges of modern corporate leadership in the face of significant external forces. The US Army later used it to describe the post-Cold War landscape. Today it is used to indicate the necessity for leaders to adopt extreme agility to deal with increasing unforecastable dynamics and to be prepared to make the undetectable detectable.

We all feel the uncertainty of the world we are experiencing. The 2020 Corona Virus Pandemic was uniquely difficult, forcing us to re-evaluate all aspects of our lives, work and personal. VUCA is a world of ever-shifting operating requirements that puts considerable strain on organisations and will continue if not accelerate.

The challenge is determining how to embrace and navigate VUCA. Crucially, it is important to understand that you cannot manage VUCA. It requires an open mind, making new connections, and imagining new solutions to new problems. VUCA is about learning how to respond and react with agility – the hallmarks of a digitally transformed business. Businesses need to understand there are no rules in the way that rules existed before VUCA. They will need to adopt a creative mindset, particularly one who, as we have seen from unsuccessful transformations, understands the consumer's appetite for digital change and customer-centricity. It is a mindset that embraces complexity and one that accepts and turns into the expectation that we are at the start of the next era of exponential development.

These are themes we will deal with as we continue to unravel what it takes to build a digital business.

Summary – Part I

- **Learn from history:** Look back to look forwards – you can only join dots with dots that have been joined to create something bigger than dots.
- **Innovation is constant:** Since the dawn of time, we have utilised tools, resources and technologies to create value.
- **Progress multiplies:** The innovations of today are built on the inventions of yesterday, so we must be able to command current technologies possess prowess in the future.
- **Industry 3.0 to 4.0:** Computers created Industry 3.0. The internet, mobile, platforms, AI, and cloud are the cornerstones of Industry 4.0; everything else is an amplifier.
- **Waltzer effect:** The combination of technologies and innovators is what creates the seismic forces of change, and double exponentialism.
- **The age of the customer:** The digital age is really the customer age; the fundamental doctrine is to start with the job to be done and deliver to a higher purpose.
- **Spin-out syndrome:** The force and pace of exponential change has compressed normal business evolution such that transformation is necessary.
- **Learn from pioneers:** Organisations have commanded digital to drive purpose, commerciality, and sustainability; we can learn from these pioneers.
- **Tipping point:** We are in the first half of the chessboard, so we are only at the very beginning of the very start of exponential change.

https://doi.org/10.1515/9783111034713-006

Part II: **Developing a Digital Business Strategy**

You don't need a digital strategy. You need a business strategy for the digital age. – Judy Goldberg

This opening quote highlights a challenge for many organisations embarking on the journey of digital transformation. You would think starting with a digital strategy makes sense – on the contrary, it makes little sense.

I was motivated to write this book as a business owner, business adviser, board member, and educator with over 18 years of experience working with digital as a strategic asset to share my experiences and help others on what is a difficult journey. One of the most disturbing yet consistent themes that I've found to this day is that many organisations, particularly traditional successful ones, treat digital as a side project. And there it is exposed to failure.

They establish digital teams and locate them out with the customer-facing teams, at the engagement layer of Digital 360 – this is a good place to start, and natural to the less mature as digital is often all about marketing and sales isn't it! I don't believe so as strategy is developed in the heart of the organisation, in the board room and down through the executive team. I then often find that those in the channels are at the receiving end of the organisation's strategy. This has the effect of teams attempting to 'reverse engineer' digital to fit the ambitions formulated far away, with no linkage and no opportunity to inform the strategy. I believe strategy should be heavily informed by what's happening in the front line and in the market, but not solely as again I bring us back to our Digital 360 – successful digital businesses think about digital as an inherent trait, with the power to drive value and outcomes universally across the organisation – how it goes to market, what it brings to market, how it operationalises and fulfils it, and how its people are enabled by it.

Other organisations start the digital journey by growing an agenda in the heart of the house to use digital to build propositions, to automate operations. Some organisations develop their digital strategy right back in the technology teams with good intent but unfortunately this can be the tail wagging the dog.

I have also seen organisations establish an 'innovation team' to take some scarce time and resources and 'experiment'. They do this on the basis of not wanting to distract the team from running the business and the value that they are measured on today. But they realise that developing digital capability and insights is a necessity so they attempt to give it safe space: a noble approach, but for when the innovation team comes to try and find problems to solve and resources to solve them. Why would anyone want someone else 'running their business', and they get the 'we already have too much to do here to hit our KPIs' response – understandably.

What's happening here is 'digital dislocation', putting digital in a pocket somewhere so it can be learned, solve operational level problems, or deliver tactical business results. None of that is wrong, but the failing tends to be it's not thought of collectively as in we need to ensure that we are engaging the end users where they are (often in digital channels), with propositions that are digitally crafted (think about and solve jobs to be done), enabled by digital journeys (end-to-end journeys and processes that are digitalised), served by digitally savvy and enabled people all with the right technology and data underpin.

https://doi.org/10.1515/9783111034713-007

Failing to take this holistic 360 approach leads to failure, transformation failure. BCG writes that digital transformations are only likely to succeed in 30% of cases, based on a comprehensive study of 895 transformation programmes across the globe and sector. In that study, they identified the successful outliers, who were 80% successful, and identified six key traits:

- Define an overarching purpose that links to clear competitive value and value creation.
- Embed digital in the overall business strategy.
- Align leadership and create a change agenda.
- Develop a clear roadmap that is prioritised, measurable, and funded with dynamic governance.
- Concentrate on releasing discrete business use cases and value – don't bet on black as it's too complex and immeasurable.
- Enable your strategy with a clearly linked and with enabling tech and data strategy.

The failure dynamics I have outlined, and the treatments espoused for by BCG would be well embraced at the start of any discussion on strategy pertaining to digital.[39]

Digital transformation must, therefore, start with strategy, and in this part, I share tried and tested approaches to developing it with an array of tools and frameworks to guide you, from insight and analysis through to a clear picture of what you want to deliver.

As each business has unique individual goals and ambitions, you will find a kaleidoscope of frameworks that you can apply across any business scenario for your unique circumstances and to help you build a multidimensional view of your digitally enabled strategy. The tools and approaches that I have shared are based on my experiences across sectors, and amalgamated to be applied to all and every industry and business size and maturity.

Becoming digital isn't something you do to the business. While utilising digital technology is part of the process of becoming digital, the technology is only part of the picture. The essence of becoming digital is a way of thinking, a culture that enables your proposition to be delivered in the smartest, most competitive, and efficient way possible to digitally enabled end users.

It's also important to understand that organisations in traditional sectors can be digital, so this isn't limited to companies that deliver digital products or services. A digitally transformed business is one that operates competitively, efficiently, and effectively in our digital era by applying digital across the five layers of the business as

---

39 BCG, "Flipping the Odds of Digital Transformation," Patrick Forth, Tom Reichert, Romain de Laubier, and Saibal Chakraborty (October 29, 2020), accessed April 7, 2023, https://www.bcg.com/publica tions/2020/increasing-odds-of-success-in-digital-transformation.

I shared in our Digital 360. It's one that by definition can swiftly adapt to the rapidly changing needs of its users and stakeholders.

Habit 2 of Stephen Covey's '7 Habits of Highly Effective People'[40] is, 'begin with the end in mind', and it's an appropriate concept for building a digital business because as a habit, begin with the end means start with the task or project with a clear vision of your desired destination and then, as Covey says, 'flex your proactive muscles to make things happen'. In building digital capabilities into the organisation, we'll do the same; we'll start with the end user, we'll unravel what it is we're delivering to them (our proposition), how we're going to deliver it (and remember, value must be paramount), then we'll flex our digital muscles to extend that value.

Every strategy, as we will see, must start with a clear departure point, and a clear end in mind. Every strategy, in my view, needs a digital underpin that spans building core competencies and using digital to create new strategic value. Or in the case of many strong, and historically fit organisations unlock existing latent value, or at a minimum protect value already beholden. For all organisations, new and existing, digital is also a means to find and create new pools of value. I say pools as that's just the identification of the value. Strategy needs to identify that new value, but strategic execution needs to release and capture it.

Therefore, before we go on to building a digital business, we need to understand how to build a digitally enabled strategy which a digital business can serve and empower.

That leads us to take an expansion of the brief, developing business strategy (that is digitally enabled), which you will hopefully find critical for our core theme, but I hope also more generally stimulating.

---

40 Stephen R Covey, *The 7 Habits of Highly Effective People: Restoring the Character Ethic.* [Rev. ed.] (Free Press, 2004).

Chapter 4
What Is Strategy and How Do We Work With It to Drive Purpose and Digital

If you have built castles in the air, your work need not be lost; that is where they should be. Now put the foundations under them. – Henry David Thoreau, Walden

The dictionary definition of strategy is *a plan that is intended to achieve a particular purpose.*

There are many definitions of business strategy, but perhaps the simplest is: *a deliberate search for a plan of action that will build a business's competitive advantage and monetise it.*

The root word is derived indirectly from the Classic and Byzantine (AD 330) Greek 'strategos', which means general. It was linked to the wisdom and wit of Generals and their 'stratagems', which literally translates 'to tricks of war' or the general game plan one wishes to pursue to win. Strategy employs tactics, the manoeuvres adopted to achieve the desired objective. The word 'tactic' originated from 'orders', so we can see how strategy and tactics enjoy an intertwined existence.

Business strategy, as we think of it today, is a much newer art. Peter Drucker is an iconic name in the field of management-centred strategy focused on the customer. His insight on management and leadership was profound, with sometimes deceptively simple reasoning. 'Who is your customer?' 'What have you stopped doing lately (so as to free up resources for the new and innovative)'.[41] This is type of questions that should underpin strategy and is crucial if the business is truly to be customer-centric.

Other academics began the discourse of business strategy and using frameworks for market opportunity. In the spirit of our theme of pioneers building on their predecessors, some noteworthy names were Igor Ansoff; Alfred D. Chandler Jr; Harvard Business School Professors E.P. Learned, C.R. Christensen, K.R. Andrews, and W.D. Guth; and Bruce Henderson.

Although originally anchored in planning, strategic thought moved towards corporate growth and industrial/sector analysis, with strategists more focused on competitive differentiation and innovation. Today, strategy is a constant process of evaluation, decision-making, and execution. This is the manifestation of:
- Exponential technologies and a new breed of pioneering entrepreneurs enabling market disruption
- Globalisation, competitive scaling, and free market funding that creates new playing fields

---

41 Drucker Institute, "About Peter Drucker," accessed April 7, 2023, https://www.drucker.institute/about/.

https://doi.org/10.1515/9783111034713-008

– Business theory being no longer just for academics or the higher echelons. It is a widely understood and practised, empowering accelerated market dynamics

Today strategy is an ever-evolving pursuit of finding value, differentiation, and enablement through business levers such as digital and data, and also responding to new considerations such as ESG and competition from non-traditional sectors.

Strategy Fundamentals

Strategy must be grounded in understanding who you are as an organisation, the special place in the world you take, and to whom you matter the most. This will lead to either creating value (revenue through something entirely new), capturing it (the ability to extract further value from the business you already operate), or protecting it (making sure that your business is staying with a rapidly changing world, and not exposed to decline).

Strategy development usually follows a cognitively linear process to enable a business to create value in achieving its purpose. The basic steps are (1) understanding the circumstances in which you are operating, (2) making associated prioritisation calls to drive growth and differentiation in the achievement of the purpose, and (3) a plan for execution

Finance should not drive strategic thinking. It is a consideration, and the result of a good strategy is financial value creation and sustainability, but it is not the end in itself. Strategy should, instead, be in pursuit of value, which is often articulated through a defining purpose, a guiding North Star. At the heart of purpose will be the end user (consumer, stakeholders, partners, and other businesses) and, of course, other stakeholders, partners and the ecosystem dynamic I highlighted at the start of the book (shareholders, the community, and the environment).

You need a business strategy, not a set of goals. I often see strategies that revolve around financial targets, customer satisfaction or experience, and employee engagement. These goals or KPIs are how you measure the success of your strategy and how well you deploy financial and human capital. At the other end of the scale, strategy is not a collection of nice words and ideas. It can be beautifully narrated, but if it lacks the substance of research, a plan to deliver, resources to execute and governance, then it is likely to remain nothing other than nice words and intent.

Strategy can exist at multiple levels within an organisation (1) at an overarching or enterprise level, (2) at a business line level, i.e. products and services, and (3) at a functional or team level. If there is a misalignment between these levels, if they are not cross-enabling and add up to a cogent plan, then we have 'strategy dysfunction' – an organisational disaster.

Strategy Schools of Thought

Because strategy is unique to every organisation, with each operating within its own context, we can employ a variety of strategy processes. In the book *The Strategy Safari – The Guided Tour Through the Wilds of Strategic Management*,[42] the authors, Henry Mintzberg, Bruce Ahlstrand, and Joseph Lampel, give a crash course on the 10 schools of thought in strategic approaches and critique each one.

I will not go into significant detail about each school of thought, but here is a summary of each style. The first three are considered prescriptive approaches in that they are guided by analysis, the following six are descriptive meaning they are guided by engagement, and the final one is a combination or the two.

1. The Design School approach is a simple premise that views strategy as a process of design to fit between the external environmental threats/opportunities alongside internal capabilities. A typical tool used is SWOT analysis.
2. The Planning School is an analytical approach and focuses on procedure. It usually follows a three-step process of (1) conduct analysis, (2) make a plan based on the analysis, and (3) move to action.
3. The Positioning School formulates strategy based on the company's position in the marketplace and its industry. Practitioners iterate through an analyse-act-analyse cycle, often used for research and development.
4. The Entrepreneurial School is the first of the subjective approaches and is a visionary, intuitive approach with strategy shaped and driven by an enigmatic, charismatic leader. Think CEOs of rapidly scaling start-ups.
5. The Cognitive School uses mental models and interpretation to filter circumstances and drive ideas. The more challenging part of this model is turning ideas into action.
6. The Learning School is an emerging process with strategy developed through rapid ideation, trial, and iterated through cells of empowered teams. It is driven by learning as it is ideated and executed in almost real time. Alignment to a guiding North Star is critical.
7. The Power School approaches strategy as a negotiation process between 'power holders'. This approach is practical when multiple parties collaborate to achieve a win-win between them. You will find this in network strategies such as banks collaborating on payment or ATM systems.
8. The Culture School approaches strategy as a collaborative process based on collective beliefs or values. This approach caters for multiple or diverse stakeholder groups through consultation and reconciliation. Government strategies often follow this route.

---

42 Henry Mintzberg et al., *Strategy Safari – A Guided Tour Through the Wilds of Strategic Management* (Free Press, 1st Edition, September 25, 1998).

9. The Environmental School shapes strategy based on external environmental factors, with biology as its basis. While environmental factors are a consideration in business, they are not the only force at play. This school of thought is used in logistic projects in response to the natural world.
10. The Configuration School approaches strategy as a process of transformation. Multinational corporations often use this approach, as they adopt multiple strategies in tandem and need to maintain cohesion across strategies within a multi-model or evolving organisation.

In practice, strategists may use a combination of approaches, as strategy is a living, breathing thing. It needs to be. Remember its links with war and the general's game? Your strategy will evolve as you learn through patterns, processes, and experience. However, Strategy Safari is a valuable guide for new managers and students to teach the fundamentals.

Reflection

-   Business strategy is a method of approaching business activity and formulating a direction for the organisation.
-   It is grounded in understanding who you are as an organisation and to whom you matter the most, clearly understanding your uniqueness in the marketplace and the environment you are operating in and making associated prioritisation calls to drive growth.
-   Ten nuanced approaches to developing strategy allow for different perspectives to defining your path in the context of your market, industry, and competitors.
-   While an organisation's goal is to foster growth, which revenue will follow, finance should not drive strategic thinking. It should, instead, be in pursuit of value, articulated through a defining purpose, with the end user at the heart of that purpose.
-   Now that we have a summary of these approaches, we can move on to the basics of modern business strategy as a foundation for developing a digitally enabled one.

The Base Model for Modern Strategy

> Excellence is never an accident. It is always the result of high intention, sincere effort, and intelligent execution; it represents the wise choice of many alternatives – choice, not chance, determines your destiny. – Aristotle

Digital is not the strategy. Digital enables it, which is why it is helpful to understand how the two support each other.

Strategy is a perpetual process that involves making sense of the landscape you are operating in and then making bets on the best course of action.

The base model for modern strategy that I share in Figure 10 iteratively knits together the external and internal dynamics of an organisation, sometimes called their ecosystem. We will use it to diagnose where to focus your resources to create value and how best to deliver it, and use the power of digital to propel it.

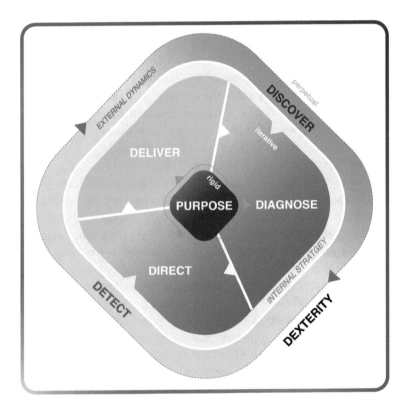

Figure 10: The 6D model for modern strategy.

The 6Ds are six sequenced steps that you can take in developing and refining your strategy:

1. Discover: understanding the market, how one's business is positioned and the social or cultural fabric you are operating in, in addition to the internal ambitions and business performance.
2. Detect: looking further out so you can future-proof your thinking, identify impending or possible external trends that can shape the future market or any internal signals that you need to consider.

3. Diagnose: assessing external and internal knowledge gathered from the first two steps, and extracting the critical themes for consideration, including how and where to create value.
4. Direct: prioritising strategic themes for development and nailing down the required drivers, the desired objectives and the target outcomes.
5. Deliver: translating the chosen strategic themes into actionable delivery plans supported by governance.
6. Dexterity: ongoing internal and external evaluation and recalibration using the discover to delivery steps 1–5.

Working with these six steps in a cyclical manner will enable strategic adaptability or what I call 'stradaptability, which is critical in the exponentially changing world that we live in today (see Figure 11). The final D, Dexterity, is essential in enabling you or your strategist to perpetually assess your choices, and your organisation's ability to create value from these choices, and recalibrate where appropriate.

The other dynamic we capture and cater for with dexterity is the ability to use various tools and nuanced approaches within the base 6D flow. It will allow you to follow a logical method and improve the strategic process by selecting the most appropriate from the range of tools available for each step.

At its heart, strategy should be guided by a compelling purpose, a higher-order intent to deliver value to end users and stakeholders. This purpose is fixed and serves as the touchstone for you to constantly shape intent.

Revolving around this purpose are three fundamental steps of strategy; diagnosis, direction setting, and delivery. These are iterative, anchored by purpose, yet assisting evolutionary change guided by delivery and outcomes.

The iterative internal cycle is informed by constant internal, and external monitoring in the outer discover and detect activities, which is also perpetually active. This involves constantly interrogating big trends, competitive dynamics, and market innovation to detect opportunities and threats given the rapidly changing landscape. This three-tier approach can be complemented and augmented.

For instance, if you are operating with a partnership or as part of an ecosystem, you may jointly develop the diagnose, direct, and deliver components, with all parties bringing their respective discover and detect inputs. This is reflective of the Culture School of thought as it caters for multiple stakeholders.

In the diagnose phase, you might find it helpful to adopt frameworks from the Cognitive School, as this approach interrogates and filters out ideas to help drive strategic analysis and choice.

If the path is less well known, for instance, in the case of a new venture, you might approach the delivery component using the Positioning School approach, as this formulates strategy based on your position in the marketplace. I often see startups using this approach, successfully getting to market with minimum viable products and iterating quickly to find the sweet spot of proposition demand.

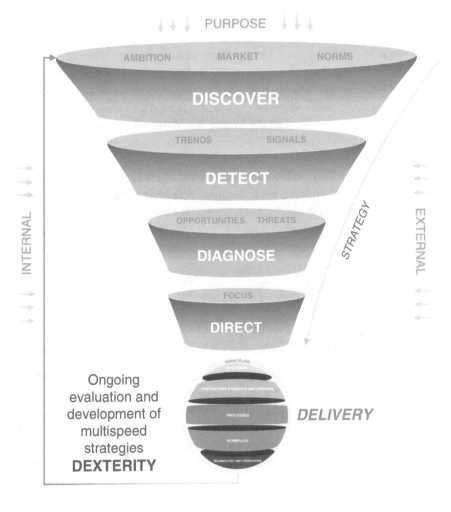

THE 6D FLOW OF DIGITAL STRATEGY
THROUGH TO DELIVERY

Figure 11: The 6D flow of strategy.

The other variable is frequency. While your purpose will be constant, the time intervals for the internal and external cycles will adapt to fit with the business need. Finally, the sixth dimension, dexterity, allows ongoing recalibration or a twin-track/multi-speed strategy, something we will discuss later in the book.

Each business has its unique set of circumstances and personalities, so a context-fit combination should be adopted. The 6D model enables a holistic analysis to decision approach, alongside iterative adjustment. But as with my experience in life, there is no better way to learn strategy than to actually do it, so I will now walk you through the key steps you can use within the 6D process.

Reflection

- The Base Model for Modern Strategy knits together the internal and external dynamics of an organisation's strategy. We will use this to help you determine how best to focus resources to create value.
- The 6Ds of this model – discovery, detect, diagnose, direct, deliver, and dexterity – intertwine with your overarching strategy to inform and serve it.
- Using this approach and underlying tools will help you assess your company in the context of its market, internal knowledge and ambitions, future trends, and resulting themes to develop a robust business strategy to enable digital capabilities.
- Each business has a unique set of circumstances and context in which it is operating, so the 6D model is not designed to be a 'one size fits all'. Instead, it should be viewed as a master model to enable the development of your overarching strategy, alongside iterative adjustment as your strategy matures through execution.

How to Develop a Purpose-Led Strategy

> The heart of human excellence often begins to beat when you discover a pursuit that absorbs you, frees you, challenges you or gives you a sense of meaning, joy, or passion – Terry Orlick

When we have a purpose in life, we give more to the world and get more out of life. Studies even show we stay healthier and live longer.[43]

It is essential in business. Consumers have more choices and are passionate about the causes they believe in. They are concerned about the environment, climate change, and other socio-economic issues. They fully understand the connection between fair trade and modern slavery and know which companies are committed to these issues versus which companies are greenwashing or paying lip service. Therefore, companies that drive their business through a meaningful purpose for customers and stakeholders prosper in a committed, authentic manner.

Conversely, when 'digital' companies misuse data and their propositions, it fosters mistrust, forcing consumers to re-evaluate their alignment and expectations away from brands whose purpose does not align with theirs. A global survey of

---

[43] Harvard Health Publishing, Harvard Medical School, "Will a Purpose-Driven Life Help You Live Longer?" Kelly Bilodeau (November 28, 2019), accessed April 7, 2023, https://www.health.harvard.edu/blog/will-a-purpose-driven-life-help-you-live-longer-2019112818378.

30,000 consumers by Accenture found that 62% want companies to take a stand on current relevant issues. About 47% said they would walk away in frustration if they were disappointed by a company's social actions, and 17% said 'they would never come back. Ever!'[44]

Purpose is also vital in the workplace. It fosters pride and engagement among employees, as they can see the link between the company's values and its impact on stakeholders (other businesses, the community, and the environment). In turn, pride and engagement enhance employee recruitment and retention, as purpose-driven employees often become willing (i.e. voluntary) brand ambassadors who are connected and motivated intrinsically.

Purposeful organisations are also proven to be far more innovative, as the internal culture fosters a feeling of empowerment. According to Ernst and Young, employees in innovative companies have a problem-solving, value-creation mindset. Ernst and Young found in a global survey with Harvard Business Review Analytics that 62% of respondents from purposeful companies described their companies as focused on innovation and continuous transformation, compared with 26% from companies without a well-articulated purpose.[45]

Figure 12 illustrates how purpose acts as the spine around which you can build the nucleus of your business. You will see the connection between the vision and mission statement, including how they link with strategy.

People confuse purpose, vision, and mission, often using them interchangeably. While they are closely related, there are subtle differences. I like to think of them in terms of 'why', 'what', and 'how':

- Why = Your Purpose: Why you as an organisation exist, why you do what you do, why you play this role in the world. This is the central tenet of your organisation, acting as a centre of gravity.
- What = Your Vision: What you want to achieve by delivering your purpose. What do you want to be known for, and the legacy you want to leave behind.
- How = Your Mission: The big moves that will be made to live up to the aspired Vision and Purpose.

Strategy is informed by the Purpose, Vision, and Mission, and breaks the big moves down to plays to make them happen. Values are the traits the organisation wishes to live by, underpinning its purpose, vision, mission, and strategy. Together, they inform the very essence of your business and are critical for your brand.

---

44 Accenture Strategy, "From Me to We: The Rise of the Purpose-Led Brand," Rachel Barton, Kevin Quiring, Bill Theofilou (December 5, 2018), accessed April 7, 2023, https://www.accenture.com/gb-en/in sights/strategy/brand-purpose.
45 Ernst & Young, "How Purpose Can Help You Transcend Disruption," Ernst & Young Global (March 10, 2020), accessed April 7, 2023, https://www.ey.com/en_gl/purpose/how-purpose-can-help-you-transcend-disruption.

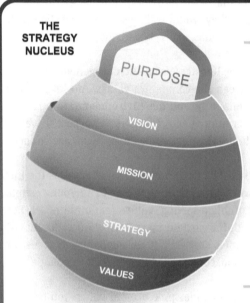

THE STRATEGY NUCLEUS

PURPOSE

VISION

MISSION

STRATEGY

VALUES

BRAND

These factors, in addition to how well you execute on them, will play a large role in defining your brand essence

A compelling and solid brand will have these factors in tight formation

The factors will also be defining on the organisations culture

Above we have illustrated and articulated how Purpose acts as the spine around which we build the nucleus of our business, including strategy.

We have also shared a definition and the associations that Vision and Mission statements have with Purpose, and how they link with strategy. Values are the traits that organisation wish to live by, and are underpinning for all segments of we call the Strategy Nucleus.

Purpose acts as the centrepiece, with Vision, Mission, Strategy and Values providing further layers of definition. Together they inform the very essence of a business and are critical inputs for Brand

YOUR ORGANISATION'S PURPOSE DEFINES WHY YOU EXIST – what role you play in the world at large

YOUR ORGANISATION'S VISION DEFINES WHAT YOU WANT TO ACHIEVE BY DELIVERING YOUR PURPOSE – what legacy or impact will you leave on the world

YOUR ORGANISATION'S MISSION DEFINES WHAT BIG MOVES YOU WILL MAKE TO DELIVER THE VISION – what will you be known for

YOUR ORGANISATION'S STRATEGY DEFINES WHAT WILL BE REQUIRED TO ENABLE YOUR BIG MOVES – the key plays that you will make to

YOUR ORGANISATION'S VALUES DEFINES HOW YOU WILL BEHAVE – the attributes that you will display

Figure 12: Purpose and the strategy nucleus.

Purpose Development

Purpose is the guiding North Star that your organisation has permanently fixed in front of it, articulating one's existence, boiled down into a single, clear, and resonating statement.

Your purpose statement should be a bold, audacious one, a stretch that is both inspirational and aspirational.

If you do not have a purpose statement or at least a compelling one, I encourage you to craft one. Ideally, your purpose will be holistic and cater not just for your digital capabilities but also for the organisation in general, expressing a deeper meaning for operating.

The following are guiding steps you can use to create a purpose statement. This is not a conclusive, prescriptive list. Remember, crafting a strategy for your organisation is unique, so your purpose should feel right for you in the context of your business, the market you are operating in, the value proposition you present to it, and, most importantly, what defines you as the leader.

1. Gather in a creative setting with trusted colleagues, and explain why you want to develop or even revisit your purpose (hopefully, what you will read in this book will help).
2. Have everyone think about your end users, whether they are consumers, businesses, communities, peers, or society, and lay out what problem you are trying to solve for them and, perhaps more importantly, what 'jobs do they want to get done'. It is a term coined by Clay Christensen in his book *Competing Against Luck: The Story of Innovation and Customer Choice.*[46] His notion, a simple yet clever one, is that when customers buy a product, they hire it to solve a problem that they have. If the product does a good job, the consumer will 'hire' it again. If not, they will fire it and look for something else that will. This applies equally to a service of course. So, think – what job would your end users hire your product or service to do for them?
3. If you can, ask your end users what they think too, or gather up brand reviews, the voice of the customer, etc., and pluck out the essence words. You could also research relevant social, economic, political, or environmental issues if appropriate for your organisation and the market you are operating in. This keeps your finger on the pulse of topics your end users might be interested in.
4. Reflect on what makes you and your colleagues tick, what makes you get out of bed in the morning, and what will make this tangible for your employees to embrace. If a purpose statement seems vague, there is nothing to hold on to or take pride in. Jot ideas down as short, action-oriented statements.

---

46 Clayton M. Christensen et al., "Competing Against Luck: The Story of Innovation and Customer Choice," HarperBus (November 3, 2016).

5. Do the *New York Times* test. Write the headline for what you would like to be lauded for on the front page in 10 years' time.
6. Work in pairs or small groups to select the most resonating results and assemble a number of drafts. Share and begin to whittle down to a chosen proposal as a collective group.
7. Once again, if you can, test with stakeholders and collect feedback; even test in real time with passers-by.
8. Use time and feedback to iterate, but do not let procrastination defer you from creating a unifying purpose that unites and inspires the team.

I always find it useful to look at examples for inspiration, and here are some of my favourites:

–   'To create a better everyday life for the many people' – *Ikea*
–   'Inspire builders of tomorrow' – *Lego*
–   'To create healthy eating habits that last a lifetime' – *Ella's Kitchen*
–   'To inspire the limitless potential in every girl' – *Barbie*
–   'To empower every person and every organisation on the planet to achieve more' – *Microsoft*
–   'We want to entertain the world' – *Netflix*
–   'Bring inspiration and innovation to every athlete* in the world. *If you have a body, you are an athlete' – *Nike*
–   'Our ambition is lasting impact. We make a difference by being part of a global movement for social justice' – *Oxfam*
–   'Accelerating the World's Transition to Sustainable Energy' – *Tesla*

As you can see, they are short, emotive, and highly ambitious statements of intent. They should be, and here are some tips for you and your team when crafting your final version:

–   Be inspiring – your aim is to unlock intrinsic motivation.
–   Be sure to craft a statement that delivers a big, audacious outcome.
–   Keep it simple – often, the simplest of statements are the most sophisticated.
–   Keep it short – ideally, less than a dozen words.
–   Do not be commercial – money comes as a result of delivering on your purpose.
–   Make sure that it connects with a job your target audience is trying to do; otherwise, it is not relevant.
–   Be aspirational – your intent should feel stretching, almost out of reach, as that is the tension you are trying to create and the greatness you are trying to achieve.

Vision and Mission Development

Whereas your organisation's purpose is your North Star and the direction in which you are heading, your vision is the lodestar that guides and inspires you towards that North Star.

Like your purpose, it guides your strategy, defining and setting goals for the future. But unlike your purpose, which is static, your vision may change as business needs or the external environment may require. There is, however, a complementary construct that comes with developing a purpose and vision.

Here are some examples from the samples already shared above:

Microsoft
Purpose: 'To empower every person and organisation on this planet to achieve more'.
Vision: 'Build best-in-class platforms and productivity services for a mobile-first, cloud-first world'.

Tesla
Purpose: 'To accelerate the world's transition to sustainable energy'.
Vision: 'To create the most compelling car company of the 21st century by driving the world's transition to electric vehicles'.

Microsoft's purpose will likely remain unchanged, to empower every person and organisation on this planet to achieve more – after all, we can always 'achieve more'.

However, its vision might change as dictated by, for example, technology. Currently, the focus is on building best-in-class *platforms* with *mobile* and *cloud* because that is the technology we all rely on today. But when future technology evolves, Microsoft's vision may evolve to suit whatever is applicable at the time.

Similarly, Tesla's vision currently reflects the world's focus on transitioning to electric vehicles. But when the next wave of innovation in the automobile industry takes hold – fully autonomous cars, perhaps? – I expect Tesla will adapt their vision accordingly.

To create your vision statement, follow similar steps to collaborating and crafting your purpose, as I have outlined above. Here are some further tips:

1. Your vision should be aspirational, conveying a sense of excitement and enthusiasm for the future your company is working towards. How do you want your organisation to make a difference in the world? How can you achieve it in a way that no other organisation can? Answers should be closely aligned with your organisation's strengths, culture, values, and strategic goals.
2. Create a short, pithy statement focused on outcomes, as in the examples cited; in other words, not what your proposition is but how you deliver it. Microsoft builds computers and software, but their outcome is to help you achieve more.

3. As with your purpose, a vision statement should be feasible, something tangible that everyone in the company can visualise and embrace.

This brings us to your mission. This conveys how you will achieve your vision and has three main components:
1. Your target audience
2. Your proposition
3. What makes you unique

Here is IKEA's mission, publicly displayed on their website[47]:

> to offer a wide range of well-designed functional home furnishing products at prices so low as many people as possible will be able to afford them.

From this mission statement, we see that IKEA's audience is 'as many people as possible' (you may take the view that this is not a targeted niche, but it obviously serves IKEA's purpose). Its proposition is 'home furnishing products', and what makes the company unique is furnishing that is 'well-designed, functional and affordable'.

Incidentally, purpose and vision are sometimes combined, which is fine if more appropriate for your organisation.

Take your time in crafting your purpose, vision, and mission. They take careful consideration that cannot be rushed nor created in isolation from invested colleagues and stakeholders. Once crafted, however, it will keep your organisation focused and motivated or at least that's the idea, but doing so requires adoption and ongoing revisit and calibration of business decisioning.

The strategy nucleus depicted in Figure 13 demonstrates how all these components work together to formulate a compelling brand that is authentic with each aim. But while strategy ebbs and flows as a consequence of external and internal factors, purpose anchors the organisation to its core origins and intents while markets and trends shift around it. Hence, purpose sits at both the centre of the strategy nucleus and the 6D model, delivering purpose-led value for your organisation's customers, end users, and stakeholders.

Reflection

– Weaving purpose into the strategic direction of your company is critical to success.

---

47 IKEA, "The IKEA Vision, Values and Business Idea," accessed April 7, 2023, https://www.ikea.com/ie/en/this-is-ikea/about-us/the-ikea-vision-and-values-pub9aa779d0.

- Companies that have a clear, compelling purpose empower their teams internally, motivating them to work with the organisation in creating value for end users with pride. By extension, this enables a deeper human connection with end users (and the wider community of stakeholders), fostering trust and authenticity. Purpose-led organisations are also more cohesive, innovative, and profitable.
- When you have a clear purpose-led strategy, you understand why you matter and to whom you matter.
- It anchors you as an organisation with a genuine articulation of intent that runs far deeper and more meaningful than profit. Hence the expression, 'purpose over profit'.
- You will notice that digital is not inherent in the purpose examples or discussions we have had here – it only emerges in vision, mission, and strategy underpinning our point that digital itself is not the driving force, rather the means to get there.

In many organisations where I have worked to develop strategy, those where there was or we created clear purpose/vision/mission were much more likely to succeed in developing a solid, actionable and fluent strategy. Without it I have found it often harder to nail down the things to focus on and prioritise. Equally though, let us not be fooled that putpose/vision/mission denotes good strategy – they do not, they are merely good bedfellows. So let us go on now to step through the phases of strategy development.

Chapter 5
Making Sense of the Landscape – Looking Out

> The main role of strategy is to chart the course of an organisation in order for it to sail cohesively through its environment. – Henry Mintzberg

Once you have a clear purpose, the next step is to move on to the discovery and detect phase.

This is to understand what is happening in the realm of your end users, the competition, your stakeholders, and what patterns of business and consumption might be emerging or fading away.

The discovery and detect stages will help you draw inspiration to identify opportunities or strategic threats. It is also where you will begin to incorporate digital capabilities as part of the broader strategy process.

In Figure 13, I share a round of discover and detect questions that map back to the layers we presented in Digital 360°.

You can use these questions to:

(a) determine what is happening in your businesses (discovery),
(b) compare what signals you should be paying attention to (detect), and
(c) analyse the market across the five layers of your organisation (engagement, proposition, processes, people, technology, and operations).

What might an overview look like? I have shared a sample industry-level perspective in Table 1, which are an amalgamation of insights from interviews conducted for this book, my client work, desktop research, and forecasts based on decades of market practice.

As with all forecasting, it is not an exact science, so departure from suggested future realities could take place in ways that you might not foresee (i.e. trends, pace, etc.); however, I hope it is a valuable starting point.

I encourage you to explore other tools that can help you evaluate a broader context. They include:

PESTLE frameworks, which look at the impacts of political, economic, social, technology, legislative, and environmental forces, often through a local and global perspective, and weights them applicability to an organisation's footprint or context. Other filters can be helpful such as the time frame of potential impacts and, of course, size.

Constructing trend radars, which are useful for mapping market and technology trends back to business focus, although their use is multidimensional. In example Figure 14, we share a generic example – the centre ring articulates the core business objectives, with the next ring out describing known market-level

https://doi.org/10.1515/9783111034713-009

360° Layer	DISCOVER	DETECT
Engagement	What brands are resonating and why? Which competitors are enjoying growth in which segments, and how? What channels are delivering most impact? Which of our Partners are having the best success? Who and what is setting the bar in CX? What other industries can we learn from?	What are end users expecting from brands of the future, e.g. ESG? What demographic shifts are forecasts, and what will that bring? What role will technology play in shaping the patterns of end users? What startups are appearing in our sphere? How could other industries move adjacently into ours?
Proposition	What jobs are our target segments/end users trying to do? Who is really good at getting those jobs done, and why? What stories, features and benefits are most compelling to end users? What gaps are not being served in the market?	What will be the jobs of the future for end users, and what will shape them, e.g. AI, urbanisation, climate action, food and longevity? What industry boundaries will extend and constrict as Ecosystems reshape the landscape? Will regulation open or constrict markets? Are there shocks?
Processes	What does the best onboarding, service delivery, and offboarding process look like and what's different? What are the comparative cycle times and cost:income ratios for executing business? Which of our competitors it easiest to do business with? What other industries emulate best practice?	What automation levers are likely to create synergies in operational processing, e.g. AI, 5G? Will nano or industrial robotics create new fields for product development? Will decentralised systems create a new playing field, e.g. smart contracts, DeFi?
People	What do the worlds best employers look like? What values do they emulate, and how? What kind of leadership qualities are the preserve of winners? How are leading businesses developing the skills of the future?	How will AI change the shape of work, e.g. displacement, augmentation? What roles are the yet to be designed e.g. social engineers? What will reward look like post the 'future of work' and the gig economy?
Technology & Operations	What does a future-proofed technology strategy look like? How do winning organisations organise and execute progressive change and transformation? Who are the standard-bearers for optimal risk and finance management? What different types of operating models are being employed by growth stars?	What does web 3.0 mean – in general and for our business? Will technology innovations create threat or promise, e.g. IoT, 3D printing? What will the central functions of the future look like, e.g. Risk, Finance, Operations? Will autonomous organisations feature on the landscape?

Figure 13: Digital 360 discovery and detection question bank.

developments (e.g. the discovery prompt) and on the very outer ring you can observe the macro-trends relating to the various core themes. Radars come in various shapes and sizes, and with other components, e.g. start-ups or tech companies that are active and worth tracking against the various themes can be plotted or 'maturity markers' that indicate how hot or cold a specific theme may be at that point in time.

Table 1: Industry-level sample perspective: digital discovery and detection trends.

Sector	Value: Latest figures available or estimated for 2021	Discovery trends: What's going on right now	Detection signals: What signals should we pay attention to	Outlook
Financial services	$22.5 trillion across banking, insurance, asset management, and leasing	A mass shift from physical to digital in the last 20 years, and rise of Fintech AI and automation in wide-scale deployment to support claims, decisioning, monitoring, and process optimisation	Decentralised finance (DeFi) undergoing significant development AI will be the most significant disruption area Web 3.0 is not understood but will have as much impact as Web 2.0	Significant shift across industry underpins anticipated in coming decade
Travel and tourism	$9.6 trillion across transport, accommodation, food and beverage, entertainment, sports, and some retail	Online promotion, research, and booking a mainstay – VR/AR starting to emerge as a supporting research and augmentation tool Reputation management and service quality require closer attention	Autonomous travel and sharing economy will shape new services VR/AR and Web 3.0 will provide most opportune areas for augmentation, but threaten existing businesses	Major shifts in access and delivery of services

Table 1 (continued)

Sector	Value: Latest figures available or estimated for 2021	Discovery trends: What's going on right now	Detection signals: What signals should we pay attention to	Outlook
Retail	$20.3 trillion across all categories of independent and franchise operators	eTailing and Creator Economy now a must for most B2C, Research to delivery value chains being rapidly automated across the board Drone and autonomous delivery investment significant	Gaming, VR/AR, Web 3.0, and Creator Economy are growth areas 3D printing and AI with IoT including autonomous logistics will reset supply chain management and investment	Access and delivery of products to radically change
Manufacturing and agriculture	€14.8 trillion (manufacturing) and €3.7 trillion (agriculture) across all products, goods, and beast categories	Analytics and IoT widely deployed across value chains to drive efficiency Robotics used in scale facilities to drive efficiency and safety 3D printing, VR/AR, and digital twinning all emerging as next-gen tooling	Material innovation and 3D manufacturing will renew sector (N.B. 3D manufacturing is the combination of AR/VR, digital twinning, and 3D printing in design and production value chains) Robotics and AI will see significant investment and adoption IoT and VR/AR to rejuvenate product/beast life cycle management	Production and life cycle management to be significantly augmented

Table 1 (continued)

Sector	Value: Latest figures available or estimated for 2021	Discovery trends: What's going on right now	Detection signals: What signals should we pay attention to	Outlook
Property	$3.3 trillion across all property services and classes	Online research, letting and booking a mainstay robotics, AI and 3D printing rising in design, building, and certification IoT and 5G starting to emerge as research and monitoring supports	3D manufacturing and material innovation will accelerate shifts IoT and AI will change asset lifecycle management/ optimisation Smart Contracts to create new realm for asset ownership/sharing	Production and life cycle management to be significantly augmented
Health care	$6.6 trillion across all categories of public and private care	Insurance and first consultation services moving online (Covid accelerated) Scanning, analysis, and diagnosis widely supported by IoT and AI VR/AR, IoT, and AI undergoing significant investment across all categories	VR/AR, nano-robotics, and AI will play a most significant role in research and delivery of precautionary and intervention services IoT and AI to drive increase in wellness services	Robotics, AI, and IoT will create new ecosystem of service provision
Technology	$8.3 trillion across IT services, hardware, telecom, and software	Wholesale move to the cloud, alongside move to low code/no code Cyber the fastest growing category, and significant investment in 5G Sustainable technology and next gen hardware and AI in focus	Next generation networking to support adoption/ decentralisation Race for next-gen hardware and AI is on Cyber will continue to be a significant growth area	Industry will continue to be at the heart of innovation, and therefore transformation

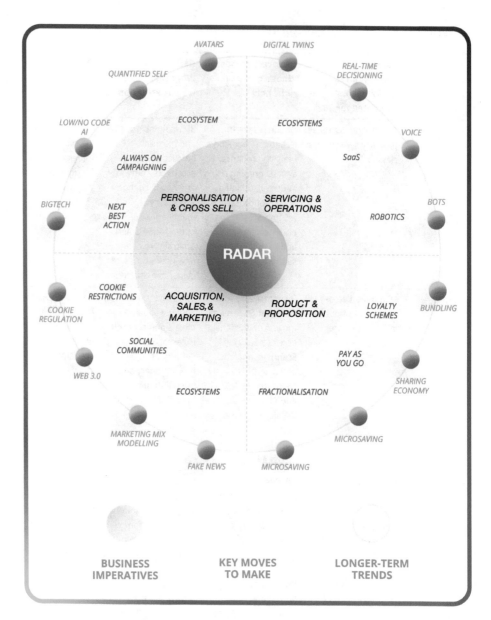

Figure 14: Sample trend radar.

A regular strategic endeavour in politics and war is scenario planning (also known as war gaming), if not a mainstay.

As the pace of change and disruption in industry increase, scenario planning has become or at least should be more than a business continuity exercise. In Figure 15, you will see a two-step approach that my consultancy often uses with clients. The dual dynamic of imagining the range of potential desired or feared scenarios (in this case, volatile economic and competitive forces – the result of asking what is predictable, probable, and potential) and the associated preparatory positions (that could be pursued based on a range of options – those in the various quadrants) brings order to disorder, confidence, and often-needed preparation.

I also find external resources such as the '11 Sources of Disruption' from the Future Today Institute are handy, where you will find a range of frameworks and long-term trend analyses.[48] We will cover this further in the final part of the book.

Now that we have outlined methods and tools to explore and synthesise the macro picture, both present and potential, the next step is to start assessing circumstances closer to home: the local market and competitive positioning.

Competitive Landscape Mapping

A cornerstone of any strategic analysis is competitive benchmarking. An analysis tool is illustrated in Figure 16. This tool is versatile in that it can be populated with qualitative market observations and quantitative analysis, such as market surveys, if available. It has the following advantages:
- A visual layout helps to illustrate and amplify relative positioning across a busy landscape.
- The vectors spanning the dimension 'polarities' help to depict relativity, differentiation, and strategic considerations.
- As it is completed using qualitative perspectives and business knowledge (readily available in most instances), rather than deep field research, it can be constructed in a short multi-hour workshop and be sufficiently accurate for strategic analysis.
- As a tool, it can be kept updated and, over time to illustrate shifts across the competitive landscape and market.

The sample detail shared in Figure 16 is extracted from a real-life market analysis (anonymous to save any blushes) to give you a sound and practical illustration of how the tool can be used.

As you can see, the company undertaking the analysis (represented by the dark blue triangle) ranks broadly in the middle of several fellow incumbent competitors (competitors 1 and 2), all of whom are challenged by a digital challenger (competitor 3).

But even though the challenger is a leader in harnessing digital and has a differentiated market proposition, they have a weakness: a lack of access to advisors, which

---

[48] Future's Today Institute, "What We Create," accessed April 7, 2023, https://futuretodayinstitute.com/tools/.

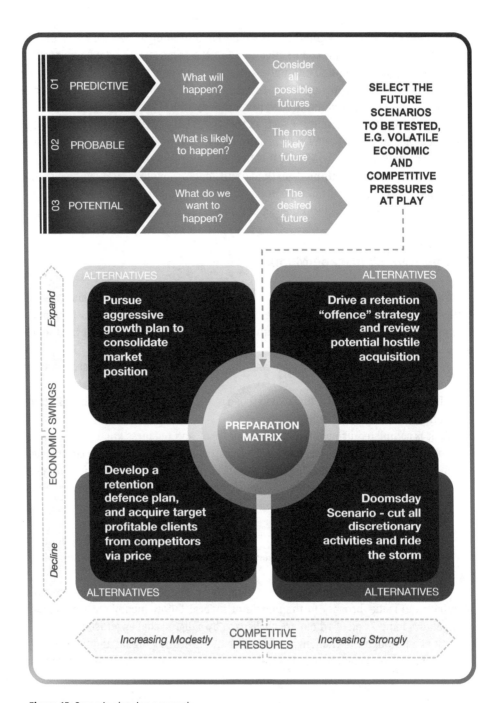

Figure 15: Scenario planning approach.

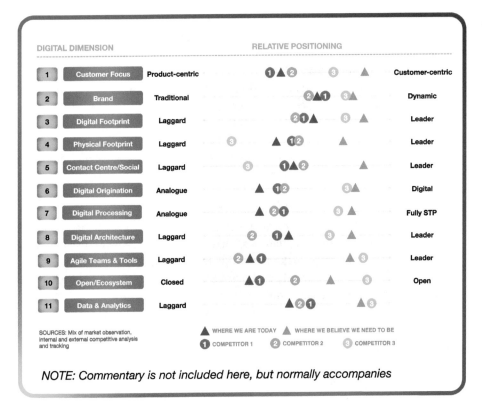

Figure 16: Competitive landscaping tool.

is critical when it comes to more complex products in this sector. This weakness has the risk of overshadowing a solid focus on customer-centricity.

The perspective that this analysis illuminates for the business in question is: if they are going to successfully respond to digital challengers (there may be more than one on the horizon), they will need to invest in digital thinking, engagement, proposition, processes, and capability – a digital operating model.

This correlates nicely with Digital 360°, which I usually find to be the case for incumbents. Making these investments will help to offset the challenger's attack on the market and defend value. (The other incumbents are likely doing the same.) However, seeing the challenger's weakness will also encourage the organisation to consider creating a uniquely blended digital and human proposition to make the best of both dynamics, creating a new territory that no one else has considered, presenting a distinctive competitive advantage.

When significant divergence or areas of interest emerge from this type of holistic analysis, it is often a good idea to 'double click' on the vector to analyse at a deeper level and highlight key drivers.

For instance, in Figure 16, we might observe that competitor 3 has a chink in the armour of digital processing, and we may wish to understand why. To pursue this we may decide to investigate both the markets and the competitor's own view with a more detailed set of questions such as:

- What is the impact of digital processing on customer experience?
- What is competitor 3's process competence?
- What degree of potential improvement is there in competitor 3's processes?
- How different are these processes versus the market, and what are they?
- Where are the manual aspects of competitor 3's processes, and how could they damage their delivery and brand attributes?

When you collate relative views, the market's and competitor's views will be useful in identifying plans to close gaps or create potential competitive gaps. But here is where I prescribe caution, as gathering detailed, factual, and 100% reliable insight can be limited. I suggest you simply make and validate a high-level view, then move forwards. The idea is to simply identify competitive or market gaps that can be exploited, and focus on how when you get to the delivery stage.

Evaluating Rarity

This takes us to another analysis method, which is complementary to the competitive analysis above; understanding how unique and difficult you or your competitor might be to replicate, and if not, why not.

VRIN (valuable, rare, inimitable, and non-substitutional) analysis is ideal for this task. It helps to illuminate what makes your business competitively and sustainably unique. Take the example of Disney+ in Figure 17. As you can see on dimensions such as e-commerce or user experience, while Disney+ has advantages, some are easy to imitate or substitute. Factors such as customer experience, price leadership, and content quality, however, are much harder to replicate and, given their competitiveness and value to the end user, should be carefully guarded. Their brand, of course, is a jewel in the crown, in case anyone needs reminding.

It is also useful for analysing your own and your competitor's organisation, particularly if threats are coming from a single or small number of them. Determining your uniqueness and those of your competitor to calculate what is competitively valuable in the seams in-between prepares you to defend the valuable or expose potential risk.

The frameworks and examples illustrated on external discovery and detection are not exhaustive. Remember, strategy is a process and a journey. The way to go about it will be commanded by the nature of your business, its participants, and the

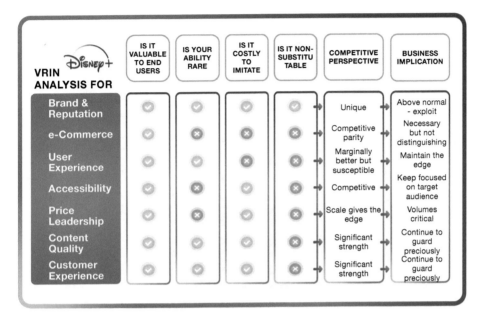

VRIN ANALYSIS FOR	IS IT VALUABLE TO END USERS	IS YOUR ABILITY RARE	IS IT COSTLY TO IMITATE	IS IT NON-SUBSTITUTABLE	COMPETITIVE PERSPECTIVE	BUSINESS IMPLICATION
Brand & Reputation	✓	✓	✓	✓	Unique	Above normal - exploit
e-Commerce	✓	✗	✗	✗	Competitive parity	Necessary but not distinguishing
User Experience	✓	✓	✗	✗	Marginally better but susceptible	Maintain the edge
Accessibility	✓	✗	✓	✗	Competitive	Keep focused on target audience
Price Leadership	✓	✗	✓	✗	Scale gives the edge	Volumes critical
Content Quality	✓	✓	✓	✗	Significant strength	Continue to guard preciously
Customer Experience	✓	✓	✓	✗	Significant strength	Continue to guard preciously

Figure 17: VRIN analysis (valuable, rare, inimitable, and non-substitutional).

environment in which it operates. What I have shared is what I find helpful as a starting point in my work, but I often find that I will swap in and out different approaches, blend them, or create new situational-specific approaches, and I encourage you to do that too.

SWOT (strengths, weaknesses, opportunities, and threats) analysis (see Figure 18) is perhaps the most renowned tool for analysing the overall strategic position of the business and its environment. Although it has limitations, including the potential to be too generic, it is always a foundational departure point for beginning the internal analysis phase.

It is sometimes overlooked as a tool and considered too simplistic or used too broadly with little action resulting from using it. I agree that in isolation it is simplistic. But if used in the 6D model, it can be a pivot between external and internal thinking as it helps to frame conclusions from the external analysis and force the same from the internal point of view – and it's internal thinking that we go to next.

Reflection

–   Once you have a clear purpose, use a variety of tools to analyse the market in the context of your end users, your competition, and your stakeholders.
–   I encourage you to initially use the discovery and detect interrogation bank, as it is a comprehensive source of questions to analyse each of the five layers of your

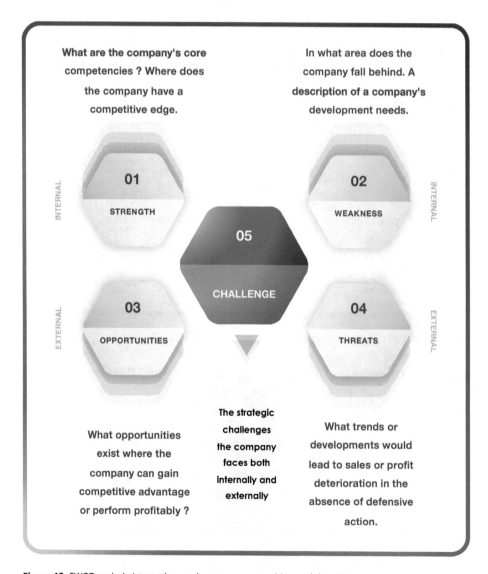

Figure 18: SWOT analysis (strengths, weaknesses, opportunities, and threats).

organisation in the context of what is happening now and what signals you should be paying attention to for the future.

- Other tools for broader analysis are:
  - PESTLE, to identify external influences on your organisation
  - Multidimensional radars to detect macro- and micro-level threat
  - Scenario planning for long-term analysis

- Competitive landscape mapping for both qualitative market observation and quantitative analysis
- VRIN analysis to evaluate how unique you are
- SWOT analysis to identify internal capabilities versus external dynamics

The aim of using the discovery and detect question bank is to identify where gaps may arise and draw inspiration on where and how to implement digital capabilities into your strategy going forwards.

Chapter 6
Business Evaluation and Crafting Priorities –
Looking In

> An organisation's ability to learn, and translate that learning into action rapidly, is the ultimate competitive advantage. – Jack Welch

Once you have determined the external dynamics, perhaps using SWOT as a starting point, you can begin to investigate the mechanics of your organisation to diagnose your current strategy.

The test card in Figure 19 is a helpful diagnostic to use in understanding the current strategy of the business, the currency of the underpinning operational components of the business, as well as evaluating the performance across a balanced scorecard of customer, financial, operations/risk, and organisation/people components.

This helps us to understand the overarching strategic plans and associated purpose, assuming both are in place, and we can also assess through the business and operating model blocks, what needs to be considered throughout the business. This helps us build a bottom-up picture of demand, opportunity, and threat areas. Finally, by reviewing the performance components, we can understand the drivers of success we need to work towards.

You can work across the test card in three steps as follows.

Strategic Focus, Performance, Opportunities, and Challenges

Working with Figure 19 and taking the four dark blue boxes under the heading 'Strategic Plans' across the top, there are a set of four consistent questions, which I have set out below with heading-related guidance points:

Overarching strategy (and purpose):
- What is our current focus? Here we want to establish the core focus of the strategy, its pillars and outcomes, and the guiding purpose.
- How are we performing strategically? How do we measure strategic performance? What are the objectives and key results, and what is the status? How do we validate strategic outcomes against the purpose?
- What are the opportunities? Where do we see an untapped competitive advantage or latent opportunity?
- What are the threats? Are we exposed competitively, commercially, or culturally? Where is our Achilles heel?

https://doi.org/10.1515/9783111034713-010

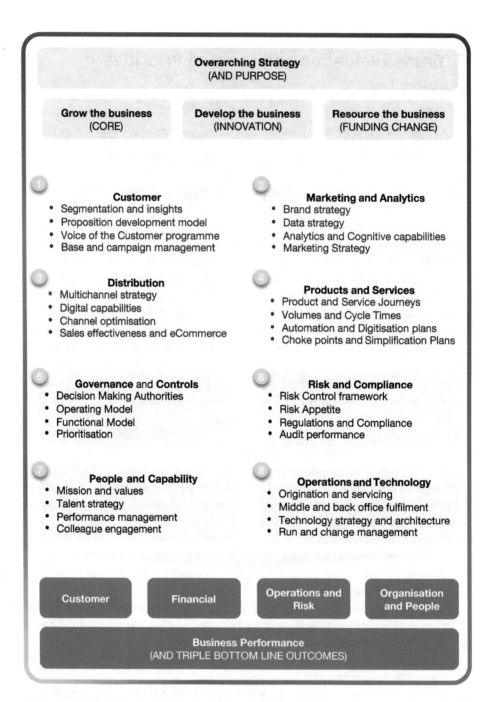

Figure 19: Business analysis test card.

Grow the business (the focus of the core):
- What is our current focus? What are the business plans for growth in the core? Is it a scale play, margin game, or cost play? All three or more? What segments and sectors are we focused on?
- How are we performing? How are we performing against stated objectives? What are the key deliveries and why? Why are we focused on specific sectors and segments, and what is our right to win?
- What are the opportunities? Why are we strong where we are strong, and what do we capitalise on competitive advantage?
- What are the threats? Why are we weak, where, and how do we defend against exposure?

Develop the business (the innovation agenda):
- What is our current focus? To what degree is the business innovating across all three horizons (more on horizons later in the book)? What is the development and execution model? How are themes identified, validated, and monitored?
- How are we performing on building for the future? What does the product and service pipeline look like across the three portfolios? How is the backlog created? What are the KPIs (key performance indicators) and rewards, and how are people participating?
- What are our opportunities? Have we identified where the market growth opportunities are and put a commercial or brand value on them?
- What are the threats? What is stopping us from innovating, and where do we see a weakness in our innovation agenda and themes?

Resourcing the business (funding and resourcing):
- What is our current method of funding? How are growth and innovation funded? Is there a central brain to manage the portfolio? Are people and processes in place?
- How are we performing? Who is involved in growth, change, and innovation? How are they rewarded? What is the payback formula? Are there strong links between change and BAU?
- What are the opportunities? What unutilised capital and resourcing is there on hand, and what headroom for growth or asset optimisation do we see?
- What are the threats? What funding restrictions do we need to consider: capital, people, regulations, etc.?

How Are the Business and Operations Set Up to Deliver Strategy?

We then focus on the eight components of business and operations. Four are externally focused:
- customer,
- marketing and analytics,
- distribution, and
- products and services.

Four are internally focused:
- governance and controls,
- risk and compliance,
- people and capability, and
- operations and technology.

Digging into these components under the headings I have shared in Figure 19 or using headings that are more specific to your context helps to cement and gather a more operational perspective in support of the broader strategic evaluation.

Again there are four questions I encourage you to ask of each component and their sub-headings:
- How capable are we in this component? For example, under customer, do we have a strong voice in the customer programme where we gather, analyse, and present insights on our customers' preferences and needs?
- What is the current focus in this component? For example, under products and services, do we have a product roadmap, are there specific journeys that we would like to build or improve?
- What opportunities should we consider? For example, do we have several manual processes in our back office, and are there sources of cost and risk we could eliminate?
- What threats should we consider? For example, do we have skill shortages in certain parts of our organisation that are critical for growth, such as data science?

How Are We Performing Against Our Existing Goals?

Here it is harder to prescribe the exact dimensions and metrics you should ascertain other than to say there are some core pillars of performance that I see alive and measured in most organisations, informative towards strategic focus. They include:
- Customer experience – How well are we solving the jobs for customers or end users, and what is it like to experience those solutions? This can come in the format of strategic measures such as Net Promoter Scores, Customer Satisfaction Surveys (CSAT), and others such as Ease (ease of doing business). Often an organi-

sation will also include waiting times, query handling times, and turnaround times as supplemental operational measures to supplement the strategic scores to build an overall customer experience perspective.

- Sales and service – How efficient are we at converting opportunities to paying customers, and how efficient are we at delivering our propositions to those paying customers? Here we see the measurement of conversations from awareness to sale in funnels, market/segment penetration, as well as cost to acquire, cost to fulfil, and cost to serve.
- Operations and risk – How efficient, effective, and risk-free is our core operational machine? Here we look to identify process cycle times, percentage of process automation, pass/fail rates, fraud, complaints, and redress.
- Organisation and people – How well organised and resourceful are we? The aim here is to highlight the capacity for run and change activities, skills, decision-making, productivity, and engagement. We can then identify whether we are tapping into discretionary motivation and equipping teams to win.
- Commercial/financial – How efficient are we at deploying capital to create value and extracting value from operations? Here we are looking for the usual financial measures such as return on capital employed, earnings, costs, profit, equity, and cash flow but as mentioned, the mix will be driven by the business type and context.

In brackets you will see that I have indicated the strategic focus area at the top and bottom of the scorecard, and below business performance which is the culmination of business metrics I have referred to triple bottom line outcomes. Triple bottom line reporting is a relatively recent reporting approach that covers three categories of business outcomes – people, planet, and profit. And should directly correlate to an organisation's purpose (see top line indication to close the loop).

You can gather this insight for both internal and external analyses in several ways, depending on the time and resources you have available. For example, in larger organisations, I often see small teams sourced from a consultancy, leveraging a mix of qualitative and quantitative intelligence, i.e. building 'fact books' of analysis, trends, and insights. Or, where this amount of intelligence is not required or in smaller businesses, a member of the leadership team with support from colleagues (or a consultant) carries out the project in a workshop format.

You can glean much of the data points from existing documents (public and private), but perhaps the richest insights and perspectives will come from internal interviews and views shared by business leaders. I encourage you to be as comprehensive and inclusive as possible with the breadth of people and sources you include. So, in addition to the usual candidates like the CEO and strategy teams, I suggest the following:

External

– End users – Any strategy work should, first and foremost, start by walking in the shoes of the end user. This establishes the real value exchange measures, experience, but also needs, competitive perspectives, and desires. Believe it or not, this is seldom undertaken and risks missing major blind spots.

– Partners and exemplars – As with end users, the best perspectives are often found at your front door. Partners know the market and your stance in it better than anyone. Exemplars are those you admire, in and outside of your sector, and they are surprisingly often very willing to talk. By their nature, they are curious and want to hear your story too.

– Consultancies and research firms – Whether you work with them, and regardless of whether you would, this group uses perspective and thought leadership as their calling card, so a lot of knowledge is freely available. Beware expensive research briefs unless exploring a significant market move and managing it tightly to maximise value.

– Incubators and academia – You can often get a glimpse of what is coming down the tracks and the latest thinking by visiting the start-up and academic community. You will also find willing conspirators and collaborators for proposition and research initiatives but beware of the 'one-way street' dynamic.

Internal

– Other business leaders and local strategy owners – This is particularly relevant in large enterprises where strategy is developed centrally and without engaging with those who own the execution and live the market and operations. Those closest to the business always have the true end user, delivery, and financial perspective, although you sometimes need to help them frame it.

– Change, digital, and innovation leaders – Change leaders have their finger on the pulse of what a business is trying to do, how it is trying to do it, and its ability to execute. This group can act as an important 'reality test'. Digital and innovation leaders (who may be sitting in various pockets of an organisation) do see a bigger picture and have a good sense of market forces and opportunities/threats.

– Boards and executives – This group has the broadest perspective on what an organisation is trying to achieve and how it is positioned to achieve it; from investment and risk appetite perspectives, as well as being the ultimate arbitrators so, this community is key.

– Finance and risk leaders – The finance and risk functions often have the broadest view across what is working and what is not in an organisation, and therefore should be engaged. Both roles are also important decision-makers/approvers of investment and change delivery. Hence, it is always good to have them in the tent.

The range of questions, frameworks, and sources will give an excellent perspective on where your strategic goals can be supported by digital capability, and why.

But these discover and detect activities are merely the build-up to the main event, the diagnosis, where you can assess the relevance of this data and extract priorities. This is our next step.

Reflection

We learn much about your existing strategy by delving deeper into the business and operating model of the organisation.

Using the business analysis test card, we can uncover where your current focus is and how well you measure up to your existing goals, keeping the following four questions as principal themes under which we collate the data:
–   How capable are you in this component?
–   What is your current focus of this component?
–   What opportunities should you consider?
–   What threats should you consider?

The ultimate aim of this analysis is to help you draw a comprehensive picture of opportunities or highlight potential blocks for your digital capabilities.

Diagnosis – Extracting the Priorities

> Take time to deliberate, but when the time for action comes, stop thinking and go in. – Napoleon Bonaparte

After using the discover and detect elements to gather external and internal intelligence, we can move down the strategy funnel and begin diagnosis.

Diagnosis Part 1 – Consolidation

The first step is to cluster the analysis into themes, filtering out what may be many items into fewer key items for deeper evaluation.

This process will help you assimilate the insights and chart emerging themes, which can be a mix of opportunities or challenges. You can see how this is illustrated in Figure 20a: part 1 – consolidation. The objective here is to extract the first crystallisation of focus areas to pursue strategically.

Diagnosis Part 2 – Interrogation

Depending on the context of your organisation (size, time available, etc.), you may gain sufficient clarity from the consolidation stage to bring the key themes forwards as priorities. However, I often conduct a deeper level of interrogation, using the methods illustrated in Figure 20b: part 2 – interrogation.

As you will see here, the themes are put side by side on a scoring mechanism called an interrogation matrix. As outlined in steps 1 and 2, criteria are chosen for assessment, and the themes are scored against that criteria to give a first-level prioritisation.

You can run further rounds of interrogation as described in steps 3 and 4, where merits and alternatives are debated and/or criteria weighting is applied. These steps can give a more robust set of focus areas as a result of the additional stress testing and challenge. You may need several rounds of this process to develop a more qualified plan for each theme, which I actively encourage.

Diagnosis Part 3 – Categorisation

Assuming you have debated and validated the strategic themes, you can begin to map them back to business objectives.

As with the clustering activity from the consolidation step, we are focused on the proposed outputs of priority initiatives, sometimes called 'currencies'. Our goal here is to begin allocating measurable objectives and key results that we expect to see from the execution of the strategic themes. This will be useful in ultimately tracking and monitoring, but first, we will use it to help with final prioritisation. This is outlined under part 3 – categorisation in Figure 20c.

Diagnosis Part 4 – Prioritisation (Effort:Impact)

Whether you follow steps 2 and 3 (remember these processes are suggested but may not always be applicable), this step 4 is a must (see Figure 20d). Bringing the identified strategic themes back into the lens and the currencies of the business is an important step. Currencies are success measures that are valuable to business leaders in the organisation, and correlate with either what they are measured on (money, risk, etc.) or what they passionately care about (such as brand and reputation). If we are not trading in these currencies, we are unlikely to 'buy in' across the decision-making community and convince them to part budgets and resources.

Visually displaying these initiatives helps the decision-making process and the development of a balanced portfolio. It pinpoints potential digital opportunities and brings them into laser-sharp focus so you can decide what is tangibly beneficial (aligned with your strategy) or not, and what to discontinue (if that is to be the case).

Each step should be tested to ensure your proposal aligns with the overarching purpose, and perhaps, more importantly, a digital lens continually applied throughout the waterfall. Allow digital market dynamics to inform the initial themes as they emerge. In other words, identify how digital can be used to enable the opportunities you want to pursue or any challenges you want to address and defend against. You cannot solve everything with digital capabilities; many initiatives will stand on their own. But I dare say digital will play a part in most.

What I have set out here is classic prioritisation, and you can adopt several alternative approaches to effort:impact mapping, including:

– The MoSCoW approach: Often used in roadmap planning, and as useful in strategy or any project that splits initiatives into the categories of 'Must', which takes first-order priority, then 'Should' (second-order priority), 'Could' (third-order priority), and finally 'Won't' (to be excluded).

– The three-part desirable, feasible, viable approach: Often used in proposition sizing activities. This can be extended to simpler strategy processes where desirable assesses how appealing or aligned themes are with end users, and where feasible assesses the business's ability to execute it and viability tests the commerciality of pursuing. I have also seen 'ethical' added as a fourth dimension, which assesses ethics as the name suggests but also extended to a purpose check, which should be carried out regardless of the process.

We have now prioritised themes to work with and can begin formulating our strategy. Our next step is to use digital to enable and deliver value.

Reflection

This diagnosis exercise extracts themes for you to work with, and points you towards what you need to do.

Consolidating, categorising, and prioritising themes will display core initiatives to determine whether to invest in highlighted capabilities closely aligned with your strategy or discard them.

If necessary and appropriate to your organisation, interrogate again, and categorise them into themes to map back to the business objective.

Simpler approaches may be used, such as 'MoSCoW' or 'desirable, feasible, viable', if more suited to your business needs. But overall, whichever method you use, you now have core themes you can work with to apply digital to enable and deliver value.

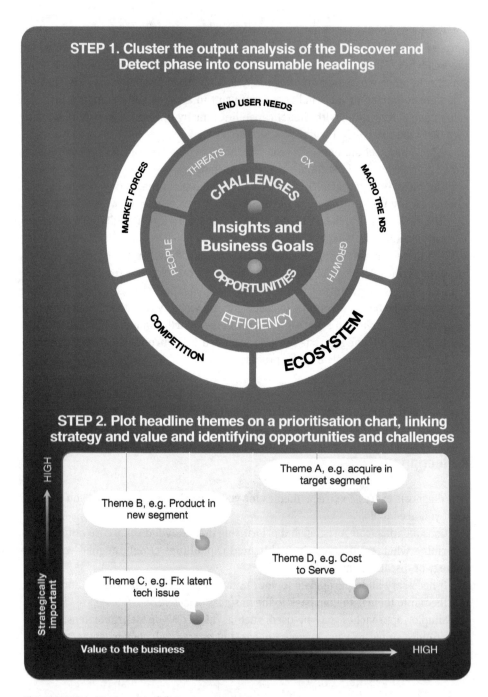

Figure 20a: Prioritisation waterfall step 1 – consolidation.

Across the themes prioritised, second-level prioritisation can further refine our focus and 'return on effort'

Interrogation Matrix	Theme A	Theme B	Theme C	Theme D
Strategic alignment	5	2	5	4
Market size/ growth forecast	3	1	3	3
Business case/ NPV/IRR	4	3	3	1
Wow factor/ Concept value	2	4	2	3
Technical feasibility	3	2	1	4
Manufacturing feasibility	1	5	5	1
Delivery feasibility	2	1	1	1
Competitive advantage	1	2	2	2
Column Total	21	20	22	19

STEP ONE

Create the criteria against which the strategic themes will be assessed and compared.

STEP TWO

Score each of the initiatives in line with the assessment criteria identified. and tally the results to give a prioritisation.

STEP THREE (optional)

Rate them against each other and then debate and challenge findings, and propose alternatives for a next round.

STEP FOUR (optional)

Consider adding a weighting to the criteria as a stress test, or to unlock 'tight' scoring (example in Tools supplement).

NOTE: FINANCIAL ANALYSIS WHILE PREFFERED MAY NOT ALWAYS BE FEASIBLE AT A DETAILED LEVEL, E.G. NPV/IRR

Figure 20b: Prioritisation waterfall step 2 – interrogation.

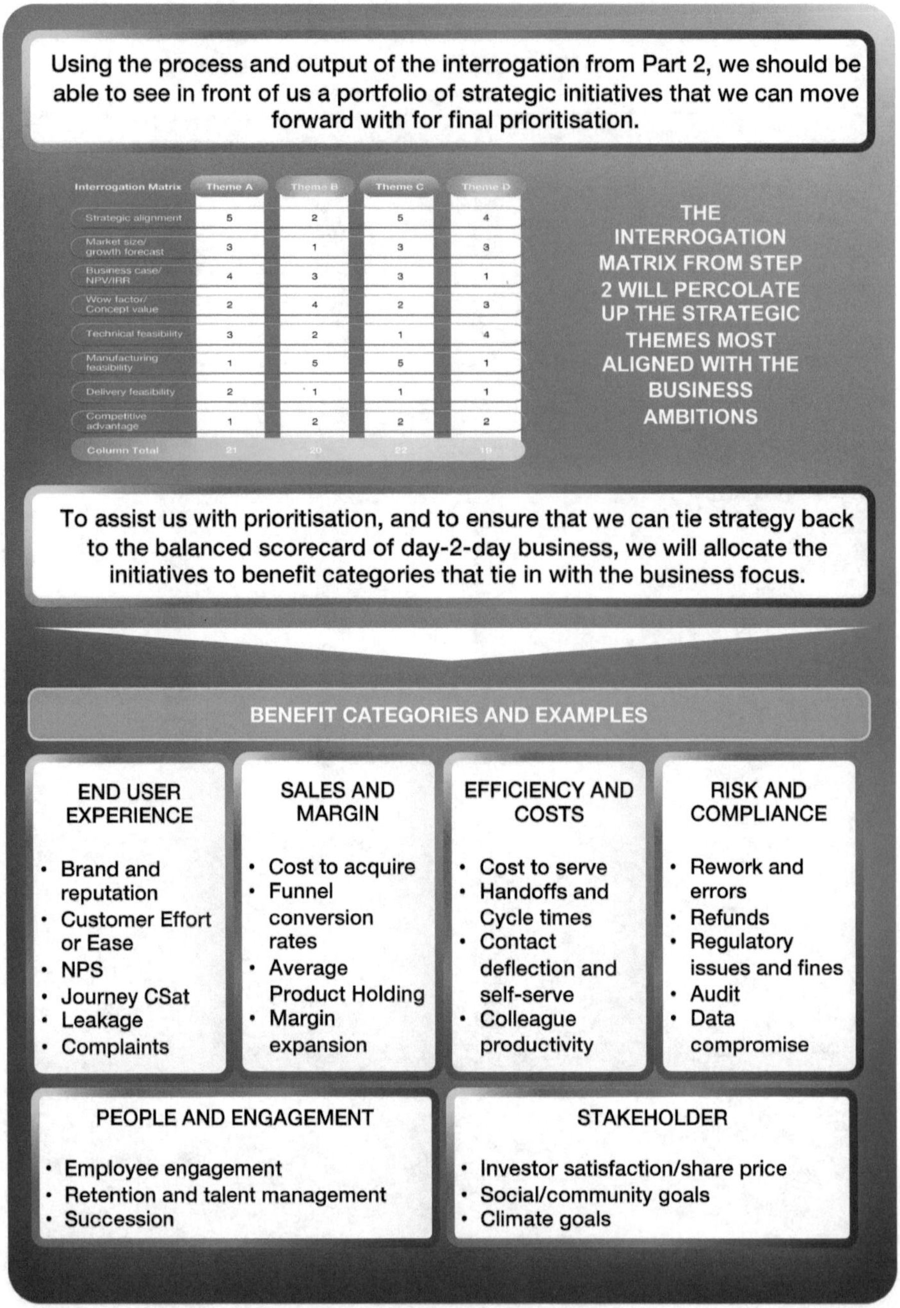

Using the process and output of the interrogation from Part 2, we should be able to see in front of us a portfolio of strategic initiatives that we can move forward with for final prioritisation.

Interrogation Matrix	Theme A	Theme B	Theme C	Theme D
Strategic alignment	5	2	5	4
Market size/ growth forecast	3	1	3	3
Business case/ NPV/IRR	4	3	3	1
Wow factor/ Concept value	2	4	2	3
Technical feasibility	3	2	1	4
Manufacturing feasibility	1	5	5	1
Delivery feasibility	2	1	1	1
Competitive advantage	1	2	2	2
Column Total	21	20	22	19

THE INTERROGATION MATRIX FROM STEP 2 WILL PERCOLATE UP THE STRATEGIC THEMES MOST ALIGNED WITH THE BUSINESS AMBITIONS

To assist us with prioritisation, and to ensure that we can tie strategy back to the balanced scorecard of day-2-day business, we will allocate the initiatives to benefit categories that tie in with the business focus.

BENEFIT CATEGORIES AND EXAMPLES

END USER EXPERIENCE

- Brand and reputation
- Customer Effort or Ease
- NPS
- Journey CSat
- Leakage
- Complaints

SALES AND MARGIN

- Cost to acquire
- Funnel conversion rates
- Average Product Holding
- Margin expansion

EFFICIENCY AND COSTS

- Cost to serve
- Handoffs and Cycle times
- Contact deflection and self-serve
- Colleague productivity

RISK AND COMPLIANCE

- Rework and errors
- Refunds
- Regulatory issues and fines
- Audit
- Data compromise

PEOPLE AND ENGAGEMENT

- Employee engagement
- Retention and talent management
- Succession

STAKEHOLDER

- Investor satisfaction/share price
- Social/community goals
- Climate goals

Figure 20c: Prioritisation waterfall step 3 – categorisation.

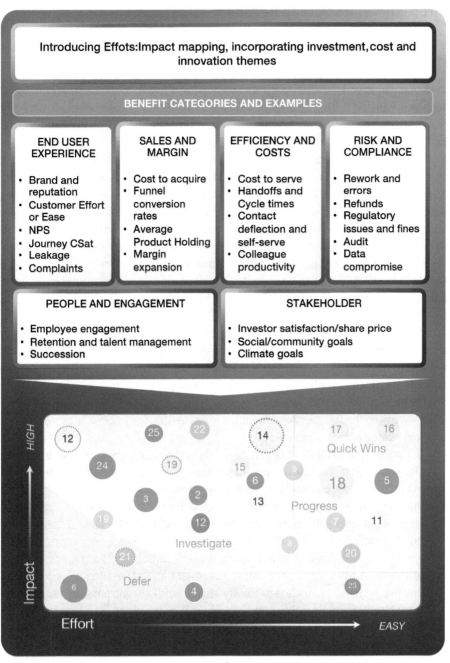

Introducing Effots:Impact mapping, incorporating investment,cost and innovation themes

BENEFIT CATEGORIES AND EXAMPLES

END USER EXPERIENCE

- Brand and reputation
- Customer Effort or Ease
- NPS
- Journey CSat
- Leakage
- Complaints

SALES AND MARGIN

- Cost to acquire
- Funnel conversion rates
- Average Product Holding
- Margin expansion

EFFICIENCY AND COSTS

- Cost to serve
- Handoffs and Cycle times
- Contact deflection and self-serve
- Colleague productivity

RISK AND COMPLIANCE

- Rework and errors
- Refunds
- Regulatory issues and fines
- Audit
- Data compromise

PEOPLE AND ENGAGEMENT

- Employee engagement
- Retention and talent management
- Succession

STAKEHOLDER

- Investor satisfaction/share price
- Social/community goals
- Climate goals

 SIZE OF BUBBLE DENOTES INVESTMENT COST

DOTTED OUTLINE DENOTES INNOVATION THEME

Figure 20d: Prioritisation waterfall step 4 – prioritisation.

Direction – The Strategy House

> Change is hard at first, messy in the middle and gorgeous at the end. – Robin S. Sharma, from *The Monk Who Sold His Ferrari*

Now that you have worked through the discover, detect, and diagnose phases of the 6D approach, you can craft the direction. This is a cohesive and comprehensive articulation of the strategic path to follow. It is one of the least complex of the steps, but just as important, a culminating narrative that acts as a ceremonial closure point and an essential communication tool. It also serves as a touchstone for ongoing recall and calibration. The strategy house is one way I like to capture and summarise the strategic direction visually. It begins with purpose, cascades down to vision (a summary statement that articulates what you want to achieve by delivering your purpose), into mission (a summary statement that encapsulates the bold moves that you will make), and finally, the strategic pillars (the outputs of the diagnose phase) and what you are going to focus on in execution.

Underpinning these are values that summarise the behaviours you believe are essential to model in pursuing your strategic endeavour. We will dive into values later, but for now, I have illustrated what the strategy house looks like in Figure 21 using my advisory firm ONEZERO1 as an example.

As you will see, it brings the core components of the strategy nucleus together to a single page with the purpose and values bookending (top and bottom, respectively) the vision, mission, and five strategic pillars. For cohesion and illustration, I have categorised the strategic pillars under the five headings from Digital 360° as ONEZERO1 is a digital business, and digital delivery is implicit.

I have used the full palette of modules from the strategy nucleus (purpose, vision, mission, strategic pillars, and values):
- Our purpose at ONEZERO1 is to leave every organisation we work with in a better place than we found it. This and our strategic pillars are the mainstay of our consultancy (and maybe should be for any organisation).
- Our vision, to leverage our experience to build better businesses and a better world for us to live in, is a direct extension of our purpose, and helps make it tangible.
- Our mission clearly shows how we will achieve our vision, by delivering strategy, innovation, and transformation results through consulting, change, and coaching services that will make a demonstrable, substantial, and sustainable impact.
- Our five strategic pillars, again closely aligned with our purpose but tangible, deliverable, measurable, show how we will achieve our vision, and how we will fulfil our strategic goals across the five layers of our agency.
- Finally, our values guide us and help us work towards a common goal.

As you can see, the strategy house articulates a clear direction of what you wish to be, and showing how you will fulfil your strategic goals. More importantly at this point you can see at this point where and how digital will play a role in delivering your

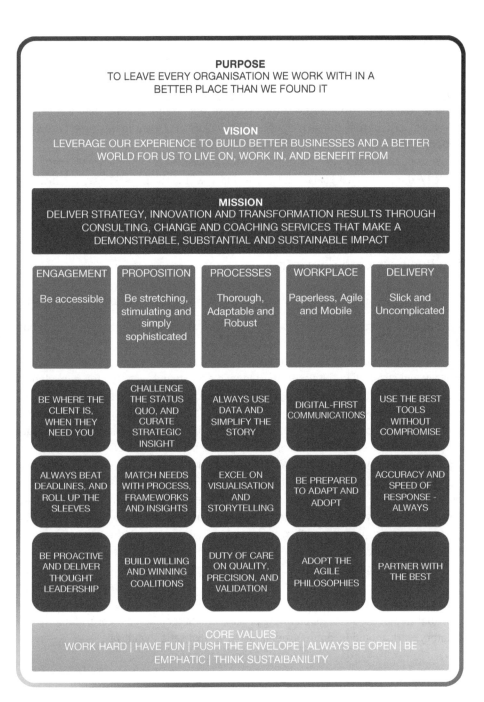

PURPOSE
TO LEAVE EVERY ORGANISATION WE WORK WITH IN A
BETTER PLACE THAN WE FOUND IT

VISION
LEVERAGE OUR EXPERIENCE TO BUILD BETTER BUSINESSES AND A BETTER
WORLD FOR US TO LIVE ON, WORK IN, AND BENEFIT FROM

MISSION
DELIVER STRATEGY, INNOVATION AND TRANSFORMATION RESULTS THROUGH
CONSULTING, CHANGE AND COACHING SERVICES THAT MAKE A
DEMONSTRABLE, SUBSTANTIAL AND SUSTAINABLE IMPACT

ENGAGEMENT	PROPOSITION	PROCESSES	WORKPLACE	DELIVERY
Be accessible	Be stretching, stimulating and simply sophisticated	Thorough, Adaptable and Robust	Paperless, Agile and Mobile	Slick and Uncomplicated
BE WHERE THE CLIENT IS, WHEN THEY NEED YOU	CHALLENGE THE STATUS QUO, AND CURATE STRATEGIC INSIGHT	ALWAYS USE DATA AND SIMPLIFY THE STORY	DIGITAL-FIRST COMMUNICATIONS	USE THE BEST TOOLS WITHOUT COMPROMISE
ALWAYS BEAT DEADLINES, AND ROLL UP THE SLEEVES	MATCH NEEDS WITH PROCESS, FRAMEWORKS AND INSIGHTS	EXCEL ON VISUALISATION AND STORYTELLING	BE PREPARED TO ADAPT AND ADOPT	ACCURACY AND SPEED OF RESPONSE - ALWAYS
BE PROACTIVE AND DELIVER THOUGHT LEADERSHIP	BUILD WILLING AND WINNING COALITIONS	DUTY OF CARE ON QUALITY, PRECISION, AND VALIDATION	ADOPT THE AGILE PHILOSOPHIES	PARTNER WITH THE BEST

CORE VALUES
WORK HARD | HAVE FUN | PUSH THE ENVELOPE | ALWAYS BE OPEN | BE
EMPHATIC | THINK SUSTAIBANILITY

Figure 21: Strategy house example ONEZERO1.

strategy, and most importantly the value it brings, creates or defends. This is how we develop a strategy where digital is implicit – a strategy for the digital age.

Purpose and strategic pillars are the mainstay of any strategy house. Vision, mission, and values are discretionary and at times you will see them used interchangeably. There is no right or wrong combination. What matters is that you are comfortable with the construct and that the strategy house articulates the core intent as it permeates across the narrative for your organisation.

You will also notice that the strategy is action-oriented, a dynamic we will return to. While I did mention that goals should be included within the house, I have not included my own in the example shared, for the obvious reasons, but they would normally appear in the internal and private versions.

The Business Case Check-In

> However beautiful the strategy, you should occasionally look at the results. – Winston Churchill

A sustainable business model with a solid business case should be the output of a robust strategy.

Just as I champion digital as an implicit part of strategy, I favour the approach that strategy and strategic initiatives supported by digital should be tested for return on investment and meet internal and, if required, external investment return hurdles. These hurdles will be specific to your business. They will reflect factors such as your sector profile, cost, or capital, which can be evaluated by investment assessment models, such as those below, on either a standalone or aggregate basis.

While most organisations will look at adding up the sum of the parts across the strategic plan to create a holistic value from the total of potential investments (including digital), I promote breaking down the business plan into a series of investment cases. This ensures that you allocate sufficient resources and focus to each initiative and KPIs to guarantee transparency of effort and reward. It also means that relative returns for non-value-adding cases are rooted out pre-investment or through execution.

Sometimes a below-hurdle initiative will be accepted 'as the cost of doing business' or on the basis that learning is as important as commercial returns where measuring learning seems difficult. But I still suggest that this business case check-in is an essential step in the strategic planning process and best completed here, albeit the calculatory work should be done throughout the prioritisation waterfall.

Business Case Assessment Models

– PAYBACK – In this simpler model, we look at the investment against the net, cumulative, and discounted cash flow to illustrate the payback period – put simply, how long does it take to get an initial investment back. This does not take into account the cost of capital or time but does provide an easily understandable effort to impact analysis.

- NET PRESENT VALUE – Net present value or the NPV of a project gives us the value of future cash flows reflected in today's terms by discounting those cash flows by anticipated inflation. Essentially this gives us a financial return that we can correlate and benchmark against current values.
- INTERNAL RATE OF RETURN – Internal rate of return or IRR calculates the percentage investment return from a project, which like NPV uses discounted cash flow analysis and equates the NPV to 0. So it gives a true annual percentage return forecast of the initiative and a reflection of what the yield will be in today's terms.

Non-financial participants involved in this process may require support to build and validate the assessment models, and an emphasis should be made on the assumptions being used. The old adage 'paper never refuses ink' was never truer when it comes to business cases.

Forecast accuracy often comes down to testing and 'curbing' the enthusiasm that often lives within the cost, benefit, and timeline assumptions adopted. So, adding contingency and evaluating low/medium/high-probability scenarios are a useful way to spur debate and manage expectations. How many projects do you know cost more, take longer, and suffer lower than anticipated take-up? Help everyone to make transformation more successful by lowering anticipation.

Investment Cycles

Digitally enabled strategies need repeatable investment cycles. This is particularly true of digital companies, as they witness significantly shortened product development cycles. But I would say that this is true for any company as there is also an ever-present need to reinvent in line with exponentially increasing customer expectations, technological advancements, and evolving business models. So, they must allocate sufficient resources (money, time, and people) to build the next wave of proposition and capability while enjoying the present spoils of their labour.

Therefore, I suggest that it is wise to apportion profits from where value is generated in the current portfolio, along with the resources that created them, to explore and build the next generation of value. By value, I mean (1) the products or services that deliver propositions and income, (2) the capabilities that support operations to deliver those propositions, and (3) reducing costs and effort of delivery. These all equate to delivering value internally and, by extension, externally to the end user.

Investments and the value they deliver have a life cycle, which is not always apparent from the assessment models mentioned in the Prioritisation Waterfall and which tend to look at launch and success but not decline and retirement. To demonstrate the lifecycle and the need to invest in the next generation of value amid the current one, I have illustrated an example in Figure 22.

On the top of the illustration, we see the investment life cycle. Investment in development is required to bring a new proposition to market (the first phase), which results in negative cash flow, the j-curve. Once the product is in production (whether a proposition in the market or a capability in the business), we start to see the cash flow turn positive (this is the growth phase). But every dog has its day and as demand or utilisation for the proposition declines (normally due to new competition), business models and alternative technologies present better ways to solve the job.

Cash flow will decline as demand wanes (the transition from the maturity to the decline phase), which may mean retiring a proposition before it enters a loss-making or value-destroying era it is unlikely to ever recover from. This end-to-end cycle is called the s-curve and merely draws out of the j-curve to reflect the full cradle-to-grave cycle. Waiting too late to begin replacement is an unnecessary risk and one that will come around faster in the digital age as velocity quickens in the race for value. The antidote to this risk is to begin reinvestment and reinvention in the 'profit zone' where value is still being created, deploying part of that value towards the next era and beginning a new s-curve. This is what we call jumping the s-curves and is the business of innovation, an inherent aspect for strategy and digital today.

Perpetual Digital Value Portfolio Management – Managing the S-Curves

Investments and s-curve cycles are seldom in isolation and are usually one of many in a portfolio of existing, known, upcoming, and under consideration initiatives. I, therefore, recommend that digital businesses have a line of sight across such a portfolio and manage their investments through these phases. To help us visualise portfolio management, I have used a twist on the BCG growth matrix at the bottom of Figure 22 to help plot and track a balanced portfolio of digital initiatives. I have replaced the growth and market share axes from the original with digital disruption and market need, and used the car manufacturing and refurbishment industry to bring it to life and play out how it might work.

In the low-disruption, high-need territory, we can observe that vintage cars will become rarer as the vehicle is electrified, but with more wealth around and less supply, refurbishment of vehicles will be in demand and at a premium, resulting in this line being a cow that can be 'milked' for cash. There may be some opportunities to digitalise diagnostics and body-making, but it will mainly be a manual endeavour and lacks scaling as fewer cars are around. Premium manufacturers could make a limited digital investment to maintain brand, loyalty, and nostalgia, but it would be wise to

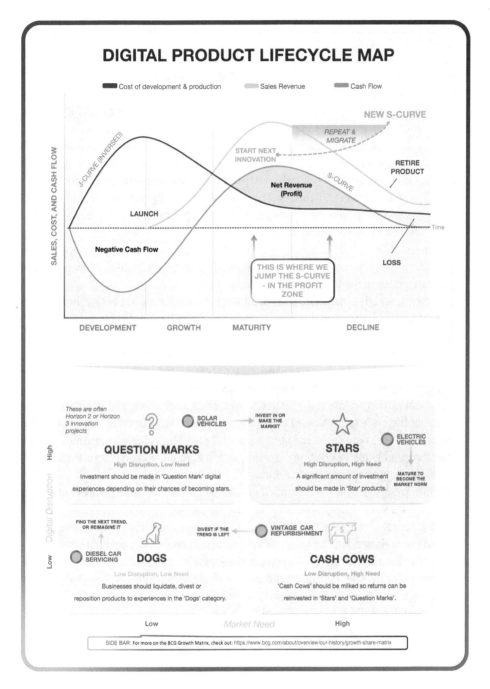

Figure 22: The investment life cycle and portfolio management.

use the rewards of this 'cash cow' for reinvestment elsewhere on the grid and therefore jump the s-curve.

In the low-disruption, low-need territory, we could say that diesel vehicles are first in line for decommissioning, and therefore investment should be avoided even though there are digital opportunities in non-engine innovation, e.g. autonomous systems. We say, liquidate, divest, or reposition these 'Dogs', e.g. a market for diesel-2-electric refit. Again a callout to jump the s-curve.

On to the high-disruption, low-need territory, where, we might observe that demand for electric vehicles will increase. But electricity costs or battery components could also increase or suffer supply constrictions which could tilt solutions towards self-fuelling, solar-powered vehicles. The thought here is to carefully consider which investments will likely see the most significant potential for future value creation (remember the detect phase in our market analysis to help these decisions). Understanding these trends allows us to invest in or discard these 'question marks' to ensure that we are placing our bets on high future potential so that we see them grow and enter the mature phase in the life cycle and exist as 'stars'.

Finally, the high-disruption, high-need territory where we know that in the automobile industry, disruption is already underway as vehicles evolve from mechanical to electric, and legislation alongside social trends will accelerate it further. This is where the current investment focus would most likely be. This is the 'star' territory, and will in time become the 'cow' and may perhaps need retirement in due course (but might be a little far down the road for now).

You can now correlate the question marks, stars, cash cows, and dogs back to the investment life cycle (as indicated along the timeline on the life cycle map) and, hopefully, begin to welcome the concept of perpetual portfolio value management. This is a craft that also helps to position how innovation is today a centrepiece for strategic renewal in many businesses and sectors.

Before we discuss that, it is important to mention that the time frames and length of value cycles vary widely across sectors. In the car sector example, cycles can happen over decades, compared to the fashion industry, where cycles are seasonal. But the fundamentals remain the same, as is the phenomenon that cycles continue to get shorter. Car manufacturers typically introduce new models to the market every 6–8 years, occasionally – depending on the make and model – making minor changes halfway through the life cycle but this too is becoming more frequent.

Incidentally, Tesla is challenging the market with as many as 177 'modifications' within a 4-year period. These modifications include software releases and a range of maintenance updates. The study was conducted by the London School of Economics, which collated data from various sources relating to Tesla's S model. The number of modifications made effectively equates to a 'new' S model every 11.5 days! It is an interesting study that shows how, with digital components and functionality, a product once considered ''completed' (on manufacture) can now be open, with options to continually upgrade (and even upsell).[49]

Innovation as an Investment Strategy

While we will deal with innovation at a more practical level in the next part of the book, now is a good time to introduce the concept of innovation strategy. Increasingly more organisations are turning to establishing innovation agendas, teams, and portfolios. This is a direct response to needing a faster development of propositions and harnessing digital capabilities to stay on top of the dynamics discussed previously: customer demands, business models, and technological advances.

This brings me to the topic of business models. There are variations in understanding that sometimes stretch into operating models or financial models, so for the sake of clarity, here are the three models side by side.

– Operating models: How we organise and orchestrate resources (people, data, assets, partners, etc.) to complete the work operationally to deliver the value that strategy dictates we pursue. Operating models translate strategy into execution.
– Financial models: How we account for the assets that are employed in the operating model and the value that is realised as a result.
– Business models: How an organisation charges its customer for the proposition or promise that it offers. It defines who the customer is, what is on offer, and how that offer is paid for once it is consumed.

For centuries, the prime business model was traded exchange; you agree to sell me a product for a specified price that I agree to pay. We then exchange money or goods (as was the case in the barter system) to settle that price and for me to receive the product. The trade is complete, and the business model works because there is a fair exchange of desired value.

While there have been business model adaptations and evolutions over the centuries, such as the membership model (pay a fixed fee for ongoing consumption of a product or service during the membership tenure) and brokerage (fees for introducing buyers to curated sellers), the digital age has given rise to a whole host of new business model variants, including:

– Freemium and premium: Receive a basic level of services for free and access to enhanced services for a premium fee. Players like Spotify have been very successful in building audiences by offering them free content and then enticing their

---

49 London School of Economics, "How Tesla Is Changing Product Life Cycle in the Car Industry," Antti Lyyra and Kari Koskinen (February 5, 2018), accessed April 7, 2023, https://blogs.lse.ac.uk/management/2018/02/05/how-tesla-is-changing-product-life-cycle-in-the-car-industry/.

'freemium' customers (yes, they call them customers, even though they do not pay) to unlock 'premium' benefits for a premium fee with the premium fees offsetting the cost of free services to deliver aggregated profit.

- Bundling: Packaging complimentary goods and services together to enhance margins. Restaurants and fast food are simple examples of this done well by offering drinks produced by wineries, breweries, and soda companies that complement the core. Digital banks and insurance companies are following suit with 'Bancassurance', a partnership where an insurance company sells insurance to a bank's customers. According to McKinsey and CB Insights, $700 billion in premiums is sold annually through this route.[50]

- Fractionalisation: A product or service is broken up into parts and sold in allocations. Think time-share (Airbnb) or purchasing a fraction of a stock market share on a digital trading platform when you cannot or do not wish to buy the entire asset. For the business, the model is to charge fees to secure access to assets that are otherwise unavailable.

I could continue, as there are many permutations of business models, but suffice it to say business model innovation has been a dominant feature of digital innovation, liberated by technologies and platforms.

This brings us back to innovation, which some organisations see as a strategic imperative. Different sectors see different patterns in innovation. In some, it is a mainstay where creativity and product are front and centre, such as in FMCG (fast-moving consumer goods), but also pharma and engineering firms. In other, more static, service and knowledge-based industries such as financial services and education, innovation has been more incremental. But it exists everywhere and will continue to be important across all sectors. I suspect we will particularly see this in established industries to manage a 'digital duality' that exists today, i.e. defend against tech-powered pioneers who have democratised digital tools to recreate and redefine value by solving jobs in new ways.

As a result, many businesses are now rightly allocating space and strategic resources for innovation to flourish. Within their strategies, they are allocating time and effort to multiple horizons of innovation using the likes of McKinsey's three horizon models (see top of Figure 23) to delineate between core, adjacent, and transformational innovation (all happening in parallel). Others like to use the innovation matrix (see bottom of Figure 23), which differentiates innovation activity on the basis of sustaining versus disrupting. Both, as you'll see, present a realm where improving what exists today to capture incremental value runs alongside creating new value for tomorrow, which doesn't exist today.

---

50 CB Insights, "How Fintechs Are Tapping Insurtechs to Bundle Services," (December 10, 2020), accessed April 7, 2023, https://www.cbinsights.com/research/insurtech-fintech-business–relationships/.

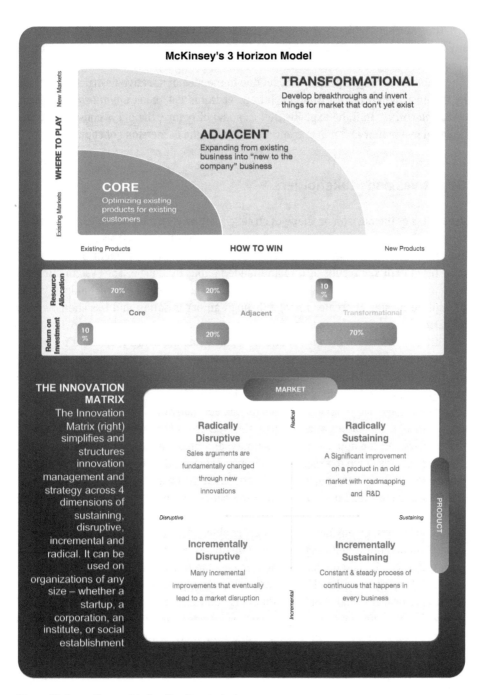

Figure 23: Innovation models for allocating strategic resources.

This mindset and its operationalisation is what we call 'ambidexterity', the necessity to extract (or exploit) value from what exists today while exploring new means to create value that can be exploited tomorrow.

Ambidexterity emerged as a model due to the idea of 'creative destruction', coined by the Austrian economist Joseph Schumpeter in his 1942 book *Capitalism, Socialism, and Democracy*.[51] In it, he explains that as a law of nature, the old is constantly being replaced by the new and that entrepreneurialism is the cornerstone of capitalism.

Objectives and Stakeholders

Regardless of the horizon or shape of strategy, setting clear, measurable, and strategically attributable objectives is imperative. I like to use the objectives and key results approach, the roots of which go back to Peter Drucker's management by objectives, later fused with key results at IBM and made famous by Google. The system attempts to tie tasks at an individual level to strategic goals in a cascade mechanism. While difficult to master, it creates lineage through an organisation and has the power to knit strategy and daily work together.

Strategy belongs to the board, and the chair holds the board to account for directing the organisation towards its purpose. As purpose is the starting point of strategy, the chair and, by extension, the board should push, pull, approve, and ultimately drive strategic initiatives, including digital. Many board members want and need more education on engagement with exposure to digital. For many of them, it is new, but for the organisation, it is pressing, and few deny this. It is critical to close any gaps by ensuring they understand the application, opportunity, and potential risks that digital presents. This also extends down to executives who may not sit on the board but have the day-to-day responsibility of carrying out the direction that the board has set.

Working with the board is only half the battle – strategy is a team sport, not one for elite squads or hero-like mavericks. That is generally true but even more so for digital strategies, given that digital is an enabler to delivering business strategy or through innovation redefining strategy. Equally, as digitalisation is still considered a 'new initiative', if stakeholders are not engaged and brought in on the journey, the chances of rejection by the old order are naturally high (disruption always is).

It is critical that stakeholder mapping is embraced at the beginning, during, and in the closing rounds of agreeing on strategy. Understanding who the stakeholders are, mapping their needs and interests, and ultimately testing that the strategy ticks the box for each facilitates alignment, all of which assume there is a stakeholder engagement plan running throughout strategy development. It also ensures there are no

---

51 Schumpeter, Joseph A., 1883–1950, *Capitalism, Socialism, and Democracy* (New York: Harper & Row, 1962).

overlooked or unmet needs and that the very essence of strategy and the drive for competitive differentiation is satisfied – solving the jobs to be done by the end users.

Reflection

–   This business check-in is an opportunity to test the return on investment to check whether your strategy is supported by a sustainable, solid, and potentially profitable business model.
–   It ensures initiatives are clearly allocated the resources, effort, and investment they require, and of course, to weed out any that will not add value. It is best to arrive at this decision pre-investment.
–   Tools and frameworks you can use to test whether the strategy themes you have consolidated are viable for your business model are:
    –   business case assessment models,
    –   investment cycles,
    –   perpetual digital portfolio management, and
    –   innovation as an investment strategy.
–   Whichever tool or framework you use, close any engagement gaps by ensuring your board and/or key stakeholders understand the application, opportunity, and potential risks that are inherent.

Moving to Delivery With Dexterity

Around here, however, we don't look backwards for very long. We keep moving forward, opening up new doors and doing new things, because we're curious . . . and curiosity keeps leading us down new paths. – Walt Disney Company

We have walked through the first four D's of the 6D model; discovering and detecting the key inputs from external and internal analysis to inform realities, potential circumstances, opportunities, and threats; then to diagnosing where to focus resources to protect and create value in line with purpose; and finally to crafting the direction including initiatives and their underpinning business/investment cases that the strategic plan should entail in order to deliver that value. This is the essence of strategy.

We can now move on to delivery, which is the more detailed steps required to build a tested and robust plan for strategy execution. This is an important transition as it means that strategy is formulated, and planning to execute can begin.

It is worth saying at this point that you or your business may already have a strategy, and if that is the case, understanding what we have walked through this far presents a benchmark for ensuring it has been robustly prepared. If not, it might spur a revisit. However, if it is fit for purpose, one can then work through the purpose, discovery/detection, and diagnosis through to the initiatives that are envisioned, test and extract the role that digital can play in delivery. Remember this should span the five layers of Digital 360°. It should span building capability to deliver propositions or a smarter organisation.

This 'side car' test both flushes out implicit opportunities that may have gone untapped or exposes explicit gaps that went unnoticed and will go to inform the digital components of the strategy. Business/investment cases can be reverse-engineered to test value or developed from scratch if not, which is good practice.

Alternative Strategy Exercises

Sometimes we do not have the time, the need, or the inclination to complete a full 6D strategy process. That could be because we are working as a team and not at an enterprise level or because the business is smaller, and scaling needs to conserve energy and resources. In these circumstances, we often run micro-planning exercises across 1- or 2-day workshops with key participants.

There is no secret sauce to such events, as they work in the same pattern:

Define purpose:
- What is our defining purpose?
- What strategic imperatives do we wish to pursue and achieve?

Develop strategic themes and initiatives:
- What are the key themes that need to be executed to deliver on the purpose and strategic imperatives?
- What value will we be executing on the themes delivered?

Build a roadmap:
- What will we deliver this year?
- What needs to be on the agenda for the next 2 years (looking beyond 2–3 years these days is becoming a rarity due to the pace of change)?
- What does an integrated, ambidextrous roadmap look like, and what are associated budgeting/resourcing requirements?

Assess what is required in the operating model to execute:
- What works need to be done, who does it, and what skills do we need to have in place?
- How do we measure and drive results?
- How do we work across business and support teams or individuals to play their part?

Define the execution model and how to measure success:
- What defines our delivery as a team – what are our OKRs (objective and key results)?
- How will stakeholders benefit from our existence?

As mentioned earlier, with planning and preparation activities such as gathering external insights, such exercises can be completed by small teams in rapid time. For some, there may be too much to consume in a single sitting, and if so, space it out across three 3-h sessions, but do give it a go – it is surprising what can be done when you set a deadline.

In other circumstances, we work with teams that have a solid strategy in place, but because of the passage of time or changing internal or external circumstances, it needs to be reviewed. In these cases, we use a rapid assessment method called the pulse check. The focus of this process is threefold.

Pulse Check

1. Look in: Review the original departure point and current direction of travel – test the execution performance and identify winning and challenging dimensions.
2. Look out: Observe the market and future trends to see what might have changed since the original strategy development.
3. Test the strategy: Test against the execution learnings and new market normal.
4. Develop a refined strategic plan that is presented back to board with rationale and fresh priorities ready for the delivery phase.

This approach is being adopted as an annual planning approach as increasingly more organisations leave fixed-term strategy behind (3–5 years) and move to an 'organic' strategy in response to change velocity (usually annually).

Play to Win

Matthew E. May, serial and bestselling author known for sharing the lessons from Toyota's innovation approach, has designed and shared a play-to-win[52] strategy canvas that we find useful to inspire teams. It follows the five traditional play-to-win strategy steps (the first 5), and adds two adjoined sections to unearth and test the assumptions that the strategic approach is being built on.

---

52 Matthew E May, "Play to Win Strategy Canvas," accessed April 7, 2023, https://matthewemay.com/wp-content/uploads/2015/08/A3-P2WCanvas.pdf.

As any financial professional will attest, understanding and testing the assumptions, very much like the risk assessment in the business case guidance I shared, is an important step. We like these builds and again this is a good step-by-step method for teams to adopt and use to define their digital strategy.

Digital Strategy Canvas

There are surprisingly (at the time of writing) few canvas or digital-specific frameworks freely available for digital strategy. There is a lot of writing and guidance from big consultancies, which are all very valuable and collectively help to build intellectual muscle, but finding the 'business model canvas' for digital is difficult. The Digital Strategy Canvas from Cogapp, a UK Digital Agency that specialises in digital strategies for museums, is helpful as a consolidation and audit tool.[53] There is also a helpful Digital Marketing Canvas published by Jeremy Corman from Marketing Makers, a French Digital Agency.[54]

The 5C Digital Challenge Board

A useful mechanism for self-evaluation is a twist on the 5C framework, which I outline below. There are a number of variations on the 5Cs, but the baseline approach is marketing-centric and funnels step-back analysis of the company, collaborators, customers, competitors, and climate. Ask the 5C digital challenge questions with this thought in mind: 'Is this the right strategy, and is digital playing the role we need?'

Competitive lens
–   How will competitors respond to your strategy?
–   What is your VRIN, and your competitors' VRINs
–   Where is there new territory that no one owns, and is it, or should it be yours?
–   How can you make sure this strategy stays ahead of the competition?

Concentration lens
–   How do you avoid concentration risk: internal and external?
–   What would Porter's 5-forces tell you?
–   How can you play in other ecosystems?
–   How do you get others to play in your ecosystems?

53 Cogapp, "Digital Strategy for Museums," accessed April 7, 2023, https://www.cogapp.com/r-d/digital-strategy.

54 Digital Marketing Canvas, "The Digital Marketing Canvas," accessed April 7, 2023, https://digitalmarketingcanvas.co.

Value creation lens
-   What is your competitive differentiation, and for whom; what jobs are you solving for which stakeholder?
-   What are the profit pools, and what will it take to unlock them?
-   With whom and how are you creating new demand?
-   What are the critical capabilities required to create value?

Value capture lens
-   How do you command a premium; what is the value enhancer?
-   What is the measure of value: brand, income, margin, market share, etc.?
-   What value do you already enjoy, and could this strategy erode it?
-   What are the accelerators: M&A, price, etc.?

Cooperation lens
-   Have you built an internal willing coalition; who is on or off the bus?
-   What partners will you need to work with, and are they aligned?
-   Do you need new partners? Who are they, and how do you secure them?
-   How do you build win-win relationships?

These guidelines are not exhaustive. The unique nature of your organisation – its style, structure, culture, and the market in which you operate – will craft your strategy to determine where you can embed and weave digital capabilities into it. In general, you should find this a useful part to help you craft your strategy for other themes, such as the ever-present and pressing environmental, social, and governance.

Reflection

-   If you do not have the resources to complete a fully comprehensive 6D analysis, alternative exercises are just as useful.
-   The 'play-to-win' framework, the 'Digital Strategy Canvas', and 'pulse check' can be used to:
    -   define your purpose with key strategic themes,
    -   develop a roadmap to determine what should or should not be implemented,
    -   assess how to measure and drive results,
    -   identify key business and support themes,
    -   review the original departure point and current direction of strategic travel,
    -   observe the market and future trends, and
    -   test the strategy against the execution data gleaned.

Summary – Part II

You can talk all you want about having a clear purpose and strategy for your life, but ultimately this means nothing if you are not investing the resources you have in a way that is consistent with your strategy. In the end, a strategy is nothing but good intentions unless it's effectively implemented. – Clayton M. Christensen,

We have covered extensive ground, from learning how to formulate a strategy to building and developing a strategy using a variety of frameworks and examples. The big message – digital doesn't stand on its own – develops strategy with digital within as the means to propel and excel.

The guidance in this book is aimed at an enterprise level because this is where it is toughest, but the principles can be adapted to businesses of all shapes and sizes. That includes family businesses, small and large, and partnerships. In Table 2 you will find some guidance on how this book can be utilised in different firms. (The designation of micro, small, and medium is defined by the European Commission.)

Table 2: Tailoring digital business strategy for the context.

Micro (1–9 employees)	Small (10–49 employees)	Medium (50–250)
– You may not need to be so comprehensive, but follow the fundamentals – The end user is the starting point for you – Think big, it is the only way to craft a breakthrough – You may need outside help, such as facilitators, mentors, and investors – Seek out support from public, private, and academic support services – Visit small- or medium-sized enterprises/businesses to get a feel for what works, or how to work with them – seek out partnerships with them if appropriate	– Expand your board and advisory partners – they will bring insights and thinking power, and the right participants will want to see you do well – Don't be afraid to get sophisticated and think big – you will not be unless you do – Purpose is really important as you pivot through scaling – Seek out support from public, private, and academic support services – Be careful about scope – knowing what not to do is more important now than ever – Partnerships are very tempting – think it through as they take effort and can be hard to reverse	– If you do not have divisions, do not make them, include everyone to get a broad perspective – If you are already operating in different territories, make sure to share and learn – Even go as far as to try different approaches in different locations – Be sure to consider market-leading competitors – think like a billion-dollar business – Consultants can be helpful – you can probably afford them now, and most of this or their playbook should be for you, but manage them tightly – Be sure to think through how you could be disrupted now that you have scale

https://doi.org/10.1515/9783111034713-011

These pointers are just as appropriate for not-for-profit and social enterprises of similar sizes. My experience working with both is that they are great at adopting strategic processes efficiently, so if this applies to you, I hope this helps. Equally, the strategy guidance outlined is appropriate for B2B businesses, but note that the stakeholder set is more complex and, therefore, the stakeholder assessment and engagement plan is even more necessary.

My final words to summarise this part and an observation from owning or working as a consultant on digitally enabled strategy are that strategy is an open, engaging process. It can be hard to include everyone, but the sum is always greater than the parts, so include the team and incorporate all perspectives within the context of the approaches mentioned at the outset of this part. Inclusion also begets support. It is easier to do what you know than what you don't. Think community games, not an elite sport.

Summing it up:
- **Strategy is distinct:** Every strategy should be different, and every strategy process will be different – spend a little time figuring out what approach is for you.
- **Crafting your unique role is crystallised through purpose:** A guiding North Star that inspires, drives, and guides our existence.
- **Digital is 360°:** It reaches every part of a business and has the potential of adding value across the board.
- **Outside in:** Strategy starts with looking out – making sense of the world around us is necessary to find our unique place within it.
- **Build radars:** Use diagnostics to synthesise information to insight and see the trends, opportunities, and threats – these are the three prime ingredients.
- **Good things take time:** The team needs time to think, reflect, and listen. Time is getting harder to secure as the world is spinning faster (we've seen that with the pace of change and our technological advancements). But if we do not make time, we do not make progress – real, substantial, and cut-through progress. Time allows us to weigh up options, consider alternatives, and learn from ourselves and others. Without it we are severely hampered. Go slower in the present to go faster in the future.
- **Prioritise and articulate:** Picking key themes and prioritising initiatives are fundamental – articulate your choices and direction to keep everyone with you.
- **Bind strategy to task:** Use methods such as strategy houses and OKRs to disseminate strategy into everyone's daily work to make strategy real.
- **'Think-do-think-do':** Some businesses do then think. Some just think. Far better to use a think-do-think-do approach as the basis for your strategy. View it as an activity of continual flow of analysis, testing, and seeing what fits, as opposed to a time-bound exercise. One of the hardest challenges you or your strategist may face is the counter view. When the strategic analysis and direction are set with the team roused for the action, I expect that the last thing you want is to be chal-

lenged. However, I would suggest that the counter view should be embraced. Building in an anti-view in the strategy process is grounding, enables testing and diverse thinking, and is a feature of going slower to go faster.

We will now delve into unpacking the capabilities you need to deliver your digitally enabled strategy.

Part III: **Capability Building to Deliver a Digital Business Strategy**

If we did all the things we are capable of doing, we would literally astound ourselves. – Thomas A. Edison

My experience of executing new digital transformation and building digital businesses is that we often need to learn new or at least enhance existing capabilities, in other words, the skills, tools, and methods we use to execute strategy and deliver value.

We need to be confident in our ability to build these capabilities. They are fundamental, not just for strategic delivery, but for business longevity and renewal. Developing them will also give confidence in the future and empower teams to work towards the organisation's ambitions and commitment to that future.

In this part, we unpack the 10 capabilities required to deliver a digital-enabled strategy, how to build them, and what support you need to enable them.

The 10 Critical Capabilities

In my work as a digital leader and more recently as an executive adviser, I have identified 10 critical capabilities that businesses must possess to deliver a digitally enabled business strategy.

Seven of these are what I call core competencies, which are the critical skills, knowledge, and tools that teams need to possess. The competencies are interlinked and cross-dependent on an organisation's ability to be:
1. Customer-centric – delivering great customer experience
2. Efficient
3. Digitally engaging
4. Analytical
5. Agile
6. Innovative
7. Open through partnering and ecosystems

Surrounding the seven, and attributable to them all individually or in their combinations, are three enabling platforms. I call them platforms because they provide the footing underneath and scaffold surrounding the seven core competencies to allow them to mature and prosper. They are:
8. Technology
9. Risk
10. People

One thing a strategy does not do is inform on what it will take to deliver the intended outcomes in the form of skills (people), investment, and roadmap. That is typically left up to strategy execution and governance. We will cover people in the next part of this book and then delivery and roadmapping in the following part as both are so important, they deserve additional attention.

https://doi.org/10.1515/9783111034713-012

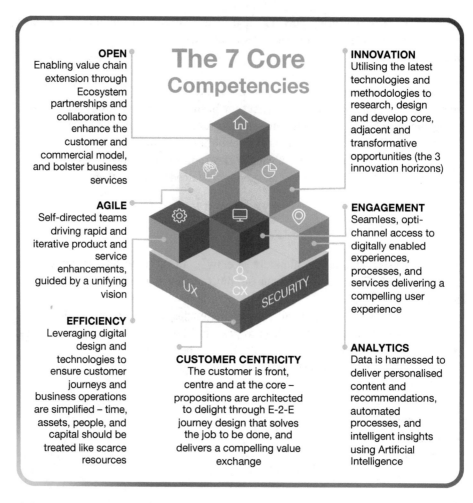

The 7 Core Competencies

OPEN
Enabling value chain extension through Ecosystem partnerships and collaboration to enhance the customer and commercial model, and bolster business services

INNOVATION
Utilising the latest technologies and methodologies to research, design and develop core, adjacent and transformative opportunities (the 3 innovation horizons)

AGILE
Self-directed teams driving rapid and iterative product and service enhancements, guided by a unifying vision

ENGAGEMENT
Seamless, opti-channel access to digitally enabled experiences, processes, and services delivering a compelling user experience

EFFICIENCY
Leveraging digital design and technologies to ensure customer journeys and business operations are simplified – time, assets, people, and capital should be treated like scarce resources

CUSTOMER CENTRICITY
The customer is front, centre and at the core – propositions are architected to delight through E-2-E journey design that solves the job to be done, and delivers a compelling value exchange

ANALYTICS
Data is harnessed to deliver personalised content and recommendations, automated processes, and intelligent insights using Artificial Intelligence

UX CX SECURITY

Figure 24: Seven core competencies.

First then we will work through the seven competencies as well as the technology and risk platforms. The ultimate goal is to ensure that when we do get on to people and roadmapping, we have a clear strategic direction (the 'what' that is taken from the strategy work), and a clear set of capabilities (the 'how' that we take from this chapter) to ensure that our strategic execution through ambidextrous roadmap management is effective, robust, and without gaps.

These seven core competencies are an interconnected matrix of proficiency sitting at the centre of a digital business.

Before we jump into the meat of this part, I have shared a high-level articulation of each of the seven core competencies in Figure 24. Digital leaders build from the customer back, or the purpose of the illustration I should say from the customer up.

Hence, customer-centricity is at the base to represent its foundational role, and why we build from there up. Open through partnering and ecosystems sits at the apex of the seven, as this is where the competencies of business reach out to and connect and collaborate with other businesses. The intervening five knit together between these two, and with each other; together they facilitate digital prowess.

Chapter 7
Customer Centricity – Delivering Great Customer Experience

> The key to good decision-making is not knowledge. It is understanding. We are swimming in the former. We are desperately lacking in the latter. – Malcolm Gladwell, Blink: The Power of Thinking Without Thinking

I have already stated that I believe the digital age should be called the customer age, as it is marked by a customer-centric instead of a product or production-centric focus for business supremacy.

Since trade began, there has always been a company-to-customer or company-to-company interaction. As this was scaled ferociously through the first and second industrial eras with the rise of automation and consumerism, the buying process was also industrialised and became less personal. Hence, customer service became a commodity, a way to keep trade 'personable' in an 'impersonal' setting. Until the emergence of digital, the focus was on making it easier to manufacture and sell. It was only when the internet and digital emerged that the wholesale philosophy of business rebalanced to making it easier to buy and consume products and services, to build those products from user needs back as opposed to business needs forwards. Simple in theory, but difficult to pivot into, as we will see.

Customer centricity is the state of being perpetually obsessed with delivering a job-solving solution, through a great experience, regardless of what stage the customer relationship is at. Gartner[55] defines it as, 'the ability of people in an organisation to understand customers' situations, perceptions, and expectations. Customer centricity demands that the customer is the focal point of all decisions related to delivering products, services and experiences to create customer satisfaction, loyalty and advocacy' (see: https://www.gartner.com/en/marketing/glossary/customer-centricity).

It is well reported that organisations that put customers at the centre of their edict command superior commercial returns. Research from Forrester and Qualtrics, two leaders in the area, reports that companies that lead in customer experience (CX) outperform laggards by nearly 80%.[56] This extends across dimensions such as revenue growth, acquisition costs, brand management, retention, loyalty, cost-to-serve reductions, employee productivity, and complaint management.

---

55 Gartner Glossary, "Customer Centricity," accessed April 7, 2023, https://www.gartner.com/en/marketing/glossary/customer-centricity.

56 Forbes, "50 Stats That Prove the Value of Customer Experience," Blake Morgan (September 24, 2019), accessed April 7, 2023, https://www.forbes.com/sites/blakemorgan/2019/09/24/50-stats-that-prove-the-value-of-customer-experience/.

https://doi.org/10.1515/9783111034713-013

In Part I, I identified the nine expectations that are firmly embedded in our psyche as a result of the adoption of the levers of the digital age to solve customer jobs. This is what lies at the heart of being customer-centric, companies and leaders who embed customer solutions as their purpose. It runs through the proposition and the way that the organisation thinks and acts. This latter point is crucial. Does everyone in your organisation truly believe their role is to understand the customer, and improve their lives by solving pain points, or leave them feeling happier, valued, understood, and better off?

The following are eight core winning traits of a customer-centric organisation:

1. Continually listen and test for what makes the customer tick, or ticked – never resting on their laurels, as the world and expectations change fast these days.
2. Connect with the customer to understand the value of CX by translating it to currencies or KPIs (key performance indicators) for their own businesses – this supports an important dynamic called 'mutual motivation'.
3. Connect executives with colleagues and ultimately end users on the front line so that decision-makers and the stewards of strategy and resources 'feel' friction or delight, and so will be minded to tackle or enhance it.
4. Use visual mapping techniques to identify and bring the customer journey to life – a picture paints a thousand words but also summons clarity, directs to action, and facilitates speed to act.
5. Prioritise by extracting the moments that have the best ROI (return on investment) in delivering CX – as they say 'go big or go home'.
6. Align cross-functional groups, both internally and externally, to solve for friction, or build new solutions – the customer should not see the seams of the organisation – they do not want to, do not expect to, and if they do, they will feel it, and witness it, in the experience.
7. Continually test and refine options and opportunities, and do so led by data; data is quantitative and qualitative, and by qualitative, I mean anecdotal as long as it is from the customer or the person closest to the customer (colleague or partner).
8. Embed CX as THE reward, from the top down, and celebrate the excellence that results from it.

There is an implicit ninth trait: CX leaders do more than focus on the customer as the end user; they incorporate colleagues and partners as end users complicit in delivering great CX; and their experience is listened to, mapped, and worked on throughout CX management to create a multi-layered game plan.

Putting the customer at the heart of the organisation is an easy thing to say but it is challenging to achieve and requires years of perseverance to craft, especially if an organisation comes from a pre-digital, product-centric stance. It may be easier when an organisation starts up afresh, but we need to be mindful that as it grows, it needs to introduce checks and balances to retain customer centricity as an antidote to complexity and bureaucracy which can follow scale, to offset the risk of losing the customer anchor.

Customer-Centric Framework

Here are the practices and activities to consider when adopting a customer-centric stance:

1. Customer Insight

Who are your customers and what pain points are you addressing? A clear articulation can be gathered in the methods outlined below:
– Segmentation and persona mapping: Breaking the market down into 'Janes' and 'Joes' (personas) that represent the life and times that sit behind the names. This helps you understand who you are dealing with, and by understanding this, ascertain what your customers are dealing with in life. As a result, you can extract the 'jobs' that the customer is trying to do to get on and move forwards.
– Ethnography: If personas are inadequate, I recommend extending customers' knowledge to include ethnography, which is a deeper look at individual cultures. This adds a rich layer of qualitative insight, and as we all know to be the case, if you want to know somebody, 'go and live with them for a little while'.
– Customer analytics and insights: To complement the mainly qualitative insight from ethnography and persona mapping, put insight specialists and analysts to work to extract customer patterns, pain points, and problems to solve from the data available. They can extract channel and product or service engagement data which will offer deeper perspectives.
– Competitive and partner intelligence: Understand what customers and end users are experiencing and doing with your competitors to add knowledge and round off an insight set.
– Creating this level of intelligence about your customers and end users (the same approach should be applied to both) will help to define their true needs, and from true needs come powerful solutions.

2. Value Proposition

What is the value proposition and what experience will you deliver? In response to understanding customer needs, craft propositions through:
– Design principles: This is the first point of departure towards developing compelling propositions. Many organisations craft a set of design principles to use as guidance wires to ensure that what they are developing is in direct response to the needs identified under the customer insights steps above.
– Design thinking: Using a range of tools such as experience maps and problem-solution fit canvases (to name but a few), design teams follow a systemised approach to

defining the most important and valuable problems to solve, before generating ideas for the most compelling solutions.

– Iterative testing and learning using MVPs (minimum viable products): Often, teams do not go headlong into complete proposition design and preparation before going to market. They create prototypes and test them in market to fast-track identification of failure in the wild, and the true solution characteristics that do the trick. Speed is of the essence, so, design teams will bring to the market what we call minimal viable products, which are essentially the base case solutions. There is no better way to validate and firm up requirements than through live feedback with customers. Once a solid course is set, continued testing happens with the customer and a perpetual cycle of improvement begins. This requires agile ways of working and product management practices which we will cover later in this part of the book.

– CX design: Once prototypes and MVPs identify the path forwards for product development and delivery, teams are set to work on designing end-to-end customer journeys using experience maps and service blueprints. These artefacts illuminate the process, systems, and human architectures required to deliver deep, meaningful, and commercially attractive delivery at each step of the fulfilment journey, and you can find many samples online.

One of the main criticisms of journey maps, and proposition and experience design in general, is the lack of clarity around operational requirements. Service Model Blueprints have been developed to resolve this tension, a tension I often find between artistry and engineering. Service Model Blueprints facilitate the phase and journey steps in the upper half of the artefact, above the line. Below the line, designers and architects (business and technology) capture corresponding channels, people, processes, technology, and critically the data enablers.

3. Route to Market

What is the best way to reach customers and leverage partners? Based on the job to be done and corresponding propositions garnered from the two steps above, customer-centric leaders craft the brand and marketing strategies to tell the world how their problems can be solved:

– Brand, marketing, and communication plans: We will work on the assumption here that the launch of new propositions would be catered for by comprehensive, composite brand market, and communication plans that leverage all touch points. Specifically, target those that are known to be the most likely places to encounter the target market in question. This necessitates the deep insights gathered in the customer insight module above, and planning should be driven to match those insights.

- Go-to-market strategies: Making a splash and using viral marketing strategies is a well-trodden and successful path for digital businesses with a particular focus on social channels but also leveraging multi-channel influencers and high-profile events. Digital businesses understand the power of social channels, and how to leverage them for amplification.
- Channel strategy: To bring propositions to market, and working effectively, customer-centric leaders will have crafted a channel architecture embedded in the experience design maps. These allow the customer and organisation to be guided (including people who may be required to support) to complete each step in the chain in the most efficient and pleasing way. This is what we call opti-channel design, making a call on what is most likely the best channel to facilitate and fulfil each step in the journey, and is extracted from the experience design process. For instance, when someone is making a general enquiry about a holiday package, we might design on the basis that they will browse options via a digital channel.

   For pre-packaged holiday experiences, designers may present an easy, efficient, and fast-to-book set of digital steps which both the booker and the holiday provider will find efficient to complete. However, in the case of a more complex bespoke holiday design, it may be appropriate for the booker to be handled by a booking agent and directed to a booking centre, at which they may purchase a more luxurious package.

4. Operating Model

How are you organised and what capabilities do you need to deliver the experiences you engineer? To support efficient, consistent delivery of the value proposition, what are the roles and measures for success that you need to be designed? While we will not dive into operating models here, for the purposes of customer-centric organisations they ensure:

- Whether the role and intervention points for people and partners (within and external to the organisations, respectively) are understood, each actor knows what is expected of them at each step in the journey, and is equipped to deliver it with the right tools, and importantly in the right manner with the right values.
- Whether it is the customer's self-serving or being supported in the service experience by a person or a partner, there will be clear processes and procedures in place that have been designed to deliver first and foremost a positive easy and encouraging set of customer success steps. Where possible, those processes will be automated with intelligent decisioning implicit to ensure that human intervention on either side of the proposition is minimised where it can.
- Human engagement can and should be prioritised for when it is needed most to ensure the customer has what and 'who' they need to get to through process steps.

– Innovation is crucial to delivering a customer-centric proposition, so there must be an implicit mandate to liberate innovators – one cannot happen without the other. Intrapreneurs or customerpreneurs – employees with entrepreneurial behaviour and the ambition to develop new propositions or ventures within the existing structure of an organisation – can play a vital role here, yet they are often a forgotten tribe who lay dormant in organisations and teams.

– To enable the customer and supporting people and partners to do the job they have been asked in the journey, core infrastructure and technologies need to be deployed as a process mechanism, and also as the data store, transmitter, and insight giver.

5. Change and Execution

Getting to market is one thing but staying, competing, and winning in market are just as tough, if not tougher. Customer-centric leaders continually enhance the proposition and effervescently track and seek to refine the experience. Here are some of the crucial ways you can make that happen:

– Experience delivery at every point across the channel: An experience map tracked with insights provided back to a self-perpetuating digital product team or a forum of cross-representative decision-makers so that they can identify and prioritise where the experience is not delivering on the ambition (e.g. the design principles). Identify where improvements can be made so that the experience can be improved and further value can be extracted.

– If into a digital product team, by their very nature they should be interrogating the friction points and improvement opportunities to identify solutions that are then put on the development backlog and prioritised alongside all the other features to be developed. If into a forum, there needs to be an execution machine that sits behind it and again identifies improvements and solutions and ensures development goes into prioritisation and ultimately build.

– There is an underpinning assumption here that the prioritisation and improvement mechanisms are established and working on an agile basis, which means that small deliveries are planned and developed in rapid succession using digital tooling and secure deployment methods.

– Build for adaptability, which requires continuous learning, recalibration, and facilitate fluidity, a way to shape-shift and match focus to what's right in front.

– Use customer-based data to make decisions in all deployment, evaluation, and scheduling activities. Therefore, the fundamental underpinning for customer-centric teams is the ability to track and extract insights on how customers or end users are adopting and using their digital propositions.

– Not satisfied with continually improving the customer's experience, customer-centric teams also recognise the need for motivation and pride in self-improvement.

Customer-centric teams systematically use ceremonies such as retrospectives and feedback loops to encourage and capture perspectives on how they can work better in order to make the experience better.

6. Culture

What is the role of people and partners, and how do they add value to digital-first propositions? To drive customer centricity throughout the proposition, journey, and operations, and enhance it with human intervention, a digital business will put in place several cultural foundations:

- North Star: The motivating guiding light that unites individuals and teams towards delivering value for all stakeholders. This means working towards a single focus of value creation to unlock discretionary effort, often required when defining and winning new ground.
- Design principles and customer promise: Design principles are an essential building block for guiding the creative effort of the organisation to ensure that it is fused to meet the needs of the customer and solve the job they are trying to do. I also encourage that a set of design principles catered for an internal audience is translated to a customer promise or charter that is published to the external audience, and is a concrete means to hold the organisation's intent to account.
- Values: A pedestal to assist the North Star design principles and customer promise is a stated set of values for the organisation. These values are only effective if they are truly owned by the organisation at an individual level, assuming they align with the beliefs and assumptions that underpin the North Star. I often see values printed on walls and in presentations which are the only places they are mentioned or witnessed, and if that is the case, they are not worth the paper or brick they are written on.
- Rewards: A final, often forgotten yet fundamentally critical component of building a customer-centric digital business is ensuring recognition, and reward methods are in place for employees who deliver exceptional CXs. This includes listening to and resolving concerns employees raise about the barriers they face in preventing them from delivering great experiences. Employees (especially customer-facing ones) often see these barriers long before company leaders. As with values, I will visit this in detail in the next part where I share a panorama of hard and soft motivational cogs that can be put into gear.

These guidelines presented above are not rigid – they can be simplified, enhanced, or refined but in their totality represents what I believe, based on my experience and observations, is necessary to build a customer-centric business, and are the methods and manifestations of the CX Leaders I have had the pleasure of knowing and regarding.

Customer-Centricity Toolbox

Now that we understand what customer-centric businesses do to add and build value to the end user, we can unpick the tools and methods that are fundamental to embedding these traits and intentions.

To enable consistency and fluidity, in addition to setting and maintaining the highest standards, I encourage investment in developing tools and techniques. This investment can ensure that 'the way we do this' is systemised and repeatable. With interim review 'pit-stops' and retrospectives, organisations can industrialise the approach.

The following are prime artefacts, tools, and methods to support this 'repeatability' and potential 'reusability'.

Data insight reporting: This includes brand, marketing traffic, channel and funnel measurement, and experience tracking (which is usually relationship net promoter score), customer satisfaction, and customer ease reporting. This intelligence is put to work to identify problems and opportunities for development teams to solve. In sophisticated digital businesses, this reporting is often broken down to a segment or persona level, which, if feasible, gives an intimate and rich source of guidance to ensure effort to impact is maximised.

Persona maps: These are used to identify the specific traits, patterns, and needs of specific target customer groups, and translate into journey maps, epics, and user stories. These are used to illustrate what a current or intended end-to-end journey looks like in steps and pinpoints the intended emotion of delight to be delivered. Development teams break journeys down into epics, which are job-centred frames within a journey (e.g. making an enquiry or making an application would be epics in the onboarding journey).

Epics are further broken down into user stories, which describe what the user wants at various steps in the epic (e.g. downloading a form, or submitting an application).

Journey maps, broken down into epics, are further segmented into stories, and in language representing what the customer is trying to do. They are utilised to inform developers on design for the customer, not for the business. Service blueprints translate the resulting journeys into systems, processes, and people support that enable the final experience.

A word of caution: Journey mapping is an extraordinary tool, used in the right hands and with the full commitment of the organisation behind it to turn the narrative into reality. However, I have often seen cases where time, talent, and ambition were wasted on the inputs (the journey map) as due consideration was not given to the outputs and the investment that needs to be in place for implementation.

Journey maps are only effective if you are going to see them through from A to Z. Their effectiveness will also depend on the business maturity and whether they can be driven self-sufficiently or require a partner to supplement, as there are several variants, broadly classified as follows:

- Industrial consultancy: Appropriate for large-scale, transformational projects where true end-to-end proposition and process reengineering is required.
- Visual strategising: Particularly useful when developing a macro-journey (such as a market map) or employee experience and utilises visual and facilitation methods.
- Design thinking and innovation: Appropriate to more focused projects where innovative reimagination of a proposition or the business model is required.
- Proposition design and wireframing: Often used by agile start-up teams and fits well where a team is in the early stage of a discreet proposition concept evaluation. Best deployed where pace, design excellence, and end-to-end proposition development are required.

Once the commitment and resources are in place to use journey mapping, it is important to understand which map to use and where.

Grandiose versions that illustrate a desired North Star or an ambitious future state are excellent for visual motivation and direction setting. However, they are almost always unusable for design and delivery teams. Breaking out signature phases of an end-to-end journey into epics helps root out work in a prioritised way for designers and developers. Epics are further broken down into (user) stories, and at this level we get into process mapping.

User Experience (UX) and User Interface (UI) Design

These complementary fields of practice are important components of customer-centric design and could be said to have a parent-child relationship. UX is the art of looking at the journey map and designing the touch points and interfaces for where the customer engages in the journey, whether through digital, human, or physical means. User interface (UI) has the narrow focus of designing the digital (essentially screen-based) interactions. UX and UI practices adopt tools and house guidelines to ensure consistency with brand, overarching experience design, and commercial requirements. This is often where we see the design principles being wielded. UX and UI designs also importantly incorporate accessibility requirements for the disadvantaged (historically discretionary but soon becoming mandatory – thankfully!).

Rapid Proposition Ideation and Development

The primary, fast-sequenced steps associated with such a practice, more often used in start-ups and growth companies, are rapid proposition development and can be adopted in large organisations just as easily through cross-functional teams. Decision rights and authority are critical for participants, as checking back with the boss can be detrimental to progress and motivation.

When developing new propositions, a rapid customer-centric design approach to proposition development is used to drive out proposition blueprints that include journey maps, which are then utilised to begin proposition build.

Rapid Research and Proposition Design Activities Enabled by Cross-Functional Teams

Often Completed in a Weekend, 1 Week, or 2 Week Sprint. The steps normally followed are as follows:

- Customer and market insight: what's the 'job' or 'problem' to be solved
- Idea generation and concept development
- Concept testing with customers, often using concept boards
- Feature design
- CX: end-to-end journey and experience maps
- Capabilities: requirements to develop the proposition
- Lo-fi prototype: bring the proposition to life
- Customer testing: iterate proposition based on customer feedback
- Move to proposition design

These steps are often iteratively repeated before certain stage gate criteria are met, and the proposition is released for development.

Value Reports

Identify the customer and the organisational value (income, cost + risk) to support feature prioritisation.

Backlogs

These are used by proposition owners to identify the sequence of development of proposition features, driven by value reports.

These guidelines are based on utilisation in both large transformation programmes and in organisations where CX and digital teams work across organisational boundaries to employ enterprise consistency.

These tools are not exhaustive, and reference should be made back to the customer-centricity framework for an indication of the activities against which a full array of tools and methods should be developed and deployed, for example, design thinking.

The Canvas Collection

I am a big believer in the use of the 'Canvas'. There are many, but the most notable is the Business Model Canvas.[57] I have a preference for a variation called the Lean Canvas, often used by start-ups to assess their unique potential corner in a market and for building a business or a central proposition 'on a page'. In the Lean version, a number of segments have been altered to focus on the problem to be solved, the solution, and the uniqueness of the proposal (and the unfair advantage sought). I think this forces sharper thinking compared to the more generic Business Model version.

The Value Proposition Canvas is a double-click on the Value Proposition segment of the Lean Canvas. Working from the right across to the left, users identify the job(s) the customer is trying to do, and the corresponding pains and gains (the demand side). Moving left, users ideate the proposed associated solutions (products and services) that will do the job, ease the pain, and deliver the gain. This then goes into the heart of the Lean or Business Model version to build the surrounding business. Both are illustrated in Figure 25, and I encourage experimentation with both as a means to have fun and initiate lean digital thinking. Personas are useful for orientating the Value Proposition Canvas.

Digital Technology and Customer Experience

Digital and CX is a hand-in-glove coordination and collaboration. Digital, whether part of the CXO (customer experience officer) role or separate, is a core enabler of a business's CX strategy, in the same way that digital is a core part of overall business strategy.

Again, digital sits side by side with CX leadership to ensure delivery is being realised, and that the CX design principles are being adopted to realise benefits where there is a mandate to champion CX culture. Digital works hands on with CX in the design and delivery of channels, journeys, user experience, and digital fulfilment, often as the delivery leader. Digital design and development are integrated and sometimes lead the coding and delivery of digital solutions to enable the CX goals and the CX.

In Figure 26, I have shared a sample CX governance model that you would often find in large organisations, but the principles can (and should) be applied to any business size. The board challenges leadership and brings inspiration with external views and thought leadership to set the vision for CX and approve single CX strategy in line with the broader group strategy. It also monitors the consistency of CX implementation,

---

57 Strategyzer, "Business Model Canvas," accessed April 7, 2023, https://www.strategyzer.com/business-model-canvas/key-resources.

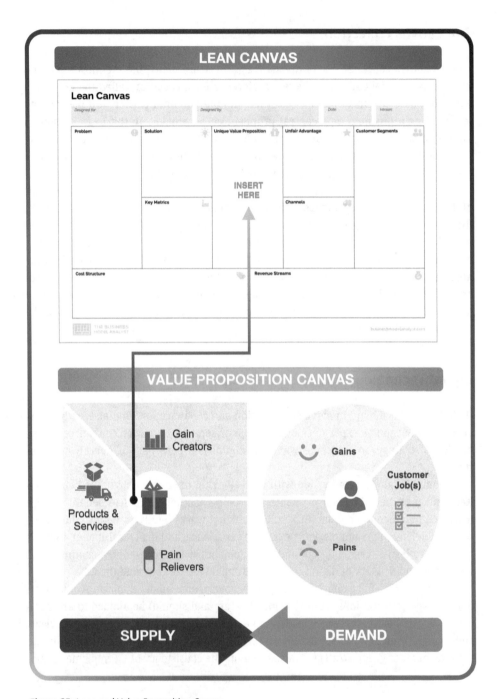

Figure 25: Lean and Value Proposition Canvas.

reviews KPIs for CX, sales and service, finance and risk, and sponsors new areas/products for investigation.

Group leadership defines CX strategy and budgets through resourcing and prioritisation of CX projects. It also manages the consistent implementation of CX strategy, and sponsors a customer-centric culture programme and stakeholder communication.

The business leadership working with the CX team validates proposed projects or solutions suitable for achieving the stated CX business benefits. It oversees projects across the six components of the customer-centric framework to ensure a coordinated strategy is implemented, resources are optimised, and consistent standards are met.

The business and projects team working with the CX team define requirements and business cases that align the CX strategy with the overall business strategy. It tracks the end-to-end delivery of CX initiatives responsible for implementing change in line with CX standards and design principles.

As the business transforms digitally, its success will depend on the new organisational culture and risk management, and hence I believe that a robust and tightly integrated CX governance model is required.

In summary, I began with customer centricity as that is where digital leaders start – with the customer. Digital transformation does not start with digital technol-

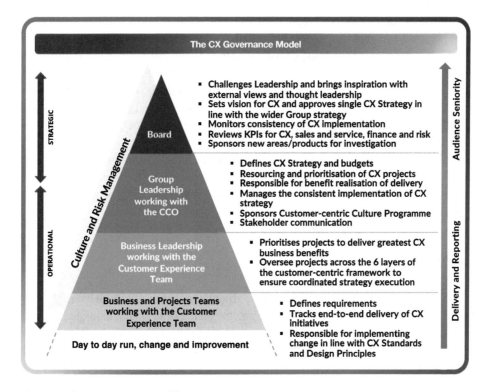

Figure 26: The CX governance model.

ogy. In fact, digital transformation is a philosophy, not a technology. The exemplars use digital to deliver great experiences, and profit from the endeavour.

Before we move on to the next core competency of efficiency, let's pause to reflect on an exemplar of customer centricity.

Case Study: Rail Europe's B2C Journey Design

B2C e-commerce travel provider Rail Europe allows customers to book rail tickets on-line easily. Their on-site UI is strong, but the company wanted to go deeper to understand the customer journey across all touch points.

Mapping the customer journey produced a full-spectrum CX map that illustrates the buyer's journey before, during, and after a purchase. It reminded their team that the buyer journey starts long before a customer lands on the website to book a ticket – and continues after the trip, through touch points like post-trip refunds, sharing recommendations, or publishing photos on social media.

Rail Europe's customer journey map also shows the transition between stages or channels to accurately visualise what is often a nonlinear journey. For example, in the initial research, planning, and shopping phases, customers often move back and forth between comparison pages, checking timetables, and website chat and planning features.

Mapping the journey like this helps Rail Europe understand different customers' channel preferences, see which touch points aren't working as they should, and which aspects of the user experience need more attention from design teams, marketing, and customer support. They visualised actions, thoughts, feelings, and experiences and rated the customer satisfaction of each stage, as well as the relevance and helpfulness of Rail Europe, to home in on areas for improvement.

The map doubles down on customer empathy by identifying travellers' overall concerns and frustrations while on the trip, even those unrelated to their rail journey – the overall travel experience is still connected with the company brand in customers' minds. You can read more on this case study at https://www.hotjar.com/customer-journey-map/.

Reflection

Customer centricity is the state of being perpetually obsessed with delivering a job-solving solution, through a great experience, 'the ability of people in an organisation to understand customers' situations, perceptions, and expectations. Customer centricity demands that the customer is the focal point of all decisions related to delivering products, services and experiences to create customer satisfaction, loyalty and advocacy'.

Eight core traits of customer-centric organisations are:

1. continually listen and test to truly understand the customer;
2. connect with the customer to understand the value of CX by translating it to currencies or KPIs for the organisation;
3. connect executives with colleagues and ultimately end users on the front line so that they will enhance CX;
4. use visual mapping techniques to identify and bring the customer journey to life;
5. prioritise by extracting the moments that have the best ROI in delivering CX;
6. align cross-functional groups, both internally and externally, to solve the friction, or build new solutions;
7. continually test and refine options and opportunities led by data; and
8. embed CX as THE reward, from the top down, and celebrate the excellence that results from it.

Do invest in the tools, technology, and techniques to enable consistency and fluidity of great CX and digital design. However, customer centricity is far more than just the technology, although it is an excellent enabler.

Customer centricity must be embedded throughout the organisation.

- North Star: The motivating guiding light that unites individuals and teams towards delivering value for all stakeholders.
- Design principles and customer promise: A customer promise or charter which guides your design principles to meet the needs of your customer.
- Values: How your organisation behaves to work towards your North Star design principles. Your values are only effective if truly owned by the entire organisation.
- Rewards: Recognition and reward methods for employees who deliver exceptional CXs.

Chapter 8
Efficiency

It is often the mastery of the seemingly unimportant details, the careful execution of the tedious tasks, and the dedicated work done outside of the public eye that make the changes we seek possible. – Kamala Harris

Hopping from customer centricity to efficiency may seem entirely random. But it is not; it is completely connected and linear.

Firstly, digital businesses focus on vigorously eliminating burden and waste from the customer journey, making only the minimum effort necessary. This is to maximise the customer experience, as that is where digital businesses start. But secondly, these businesses also manage time, assets, people, and capital like a scarce resource. An inefficient burden in the customer journey is also a waste in operation. A third dynamic of efficiency relates to transformation. Efficiency creates the capacity for existing businesses to digitalise and for new companies to emerge from building transformative experiences. These factors are about winning the right.

At the heart of efficiency lies simplicity. Its counterpart is complexity, and with complexity comes cost, waste, friction, and, ultimately, inefficiency. As inefficiency costs the end user in frustration, the organisation in costs, and opportunity foregone through waste, simplification must be a cornerstone of digital businesses. Through its endeavour, it does tackle cost, which is universally attractive as less cost means more funding to support investment or indeed, just good old-fashioned profit. But it also results in removing risk and value-destroying enterprise.

Here is my recommended approach to simplification.

The 10 Levers of Simplification

To optimise your assets (customers, people, operations, etc.), ruthlessly and perpetually remove the 'fat' that can creep in over time. This is what the great organisations I have worked with do – they spring clean, clear out the clutter and make sure the decks are clear for experience design and delivery.

Starting with customer experience, the ultimate objective is to make it easier to do business with you. In other words, reduce the spend and time it takes to fulfil customer and end-user journeys so that they get to do their job easier. These steps will likely be more applicable to larger, older enterprises, as due to the passage of time, unnecessary steps, features, functionality, and oversight can creep in. This is not abnormal, and is a cost of growth. The simplification exercise is a bit like the spring cleaning we all need to do every now and then to clear out the clutter that is just not

https://doi.org/10.1515/9783111034713-014

valuable anymore. A smaller business would, however, do well to look forwards to ensure they do not build a business that requires simplification further down the line.

What to Focus on at the Front of House

– **Product simplification:** Here the task is to eliminate the 80% of products that drive 20% of the profit. This sounds like a harsh exercise, and believe you me, in the trenches of simplification it is. Businesses build up their processes, inherent steps, features, and functionality overtime for a reason, because these had value. Now the source and degree of original value can always be challenged, but to the owner it is rarely disputable. Asking to remove that which is loved is tantamount to cannibalism. However, it is merely good housekeeping, and entirely necessary to ensure that in line with jumping the s-curves, you create capacity for renewal. Teams can kick start the work by undertaking data-driven Pareto principle analysis, and evaluating the cost-to-keep versus cost-to-build desired journeys and propositions you wish to get into market. Data is your friend, and the activity can be systemised with the introduction of product life cycle management where ongoing monitoring and cleansing becomes a routine exercise.

– **Process simplification:** Remove product-level journey friction through end-to-end process mapping, elimination, simplification, and automation. The sequence is important here, as the intention is to automate and digitalise processes where possible. However, I would like to introduce an important philosophy: 'don't code bad processes'. The journey to automation starts with simplification. I often see journey maps that have included unnecessary steps and asks along the way. This is either because they have crept in over time to alleviate some tactical necessity or often because the designer hasn't challenged themselves on the true need or value those steps bring to the customer experience.

Lean methods should be explored and we love and endorse the 'five why's' in this endeavour – the five why's are an interrogation method, developed by Sakichi Toyoda, the Japanese industrialist and founder of Toyota, whereby asking why five times of something that has happened will bring you back to root cause. If the process step stays after the fifth why, move on as it is valid and you will definitely find opportunity in the next round, but few processes survive this interrogation. Journey mapping existing processes, albeit an overhead, can become an asset if you couple the process with interrogation, discipline, and challenge by removing steps that add friction or no value. By no value, I mean unnecessary cost, risk, and poor customer experience which usually result in lost value. Simplified processes are then ready for digitalisation or transformation as may be dictated, but also release immediate value.

– **Customer and service simplification:** Undertake a review of current and lifetime value to identify sub-profitable segments and services for exit. Much like product simplification, here we are attempting to identify the cohort that utilises 80% of your effort to acquire and serve but only delivers 20% of the value. Once this analysis is complete, there are various courses of action from the more extreme such as seeking to conclude customer relationships unless a new value exchange can be found, to using the analysis to create service protocols whereby a more efficient digital servicing can be used to reduce the burden and rebalance the value exchange. This happily also has the effect of improving customer experience and importantly service team experience as they also free up time to pursue more value-adding relationships and business.

– **Distribution simplification:** Analyse distribution channels to identify sub-optimal routes to market for elimination or service revision. This is very often an activity that is conducted in strategy review cycles particularly when there are significant physical distribution franchises and real estate assets at play. Given the rapid adoption of digital, many organisations are proactively assessing how this rebalance is playing out in physical stores and footprints. We see this on our high streets every day with more stores closing as businesses move online. Once again, a word of caution. Digital is not the answer for everything and phygital experiences where digital blends with physical is a key element of digital business architecture, driven by understanding where physical engagement is necessary for delivering experiences and value. The complexities of real estate redirection and disposal need careful consideration.

– **Budget simplification:** Revise, reprioritise, or govern sprawling budgets to lower spend and increase return on investment. I often see organisations hire multiple teams, with an array of agencies and consultancies supporting them. This risks causing inefficiencies of scale and a lack of consistency of customer experience; both are unnecessary forms of waste. While I understand that different parts of an organisation will want to push ahead, particularly if there is no aligning team or mechanism, the cost usually outweighs the benefit. Ideally, businesses should combine budgets and effort to maximise stretch, and at worst, use aligning mechanisms to move towards part-unified budgets and partner management to remove waste.

Some Areas to Work on at the Back of House

– **Resourcing simplification:** Sweat your organisation's skills and hierarchy cross-divisionally to fuel capacity and recycle skills. Waste is often in the hierarchical constructs of the business, as with budget simplification mentioned above, in overlaps. A 'spans, layers, and overlaps' assessment will identify resources that you can potentially liberate if work is optimised. The latter is the challenge for many teams, or at least the expectation of it. But an assessment of capability is also helpful in identifying key talent that may support simplification, and the broader digitally enabled strategy to release it from constraint.

– **Sourcing simplification:** Lower the number of sourcing partners and increase the services outsourced to achieve economies of scale and service. While it may seem counter-intuitive at first (including from a risk-dispersion perspective), spreading out-sourcing can bring overheads that are sometimes unnecessary, and risks diseconomies of scale. So optimising existing outsourcing arrangements is worth a visit, albeit contract and migration considerations need to be factored in. More broadly, it is worth considering what can be outsourced to enable strategy, whether for existing in-house activity that can be managed more efficiently in an outsourced relationship or freeing up capacity for digital business capability, and harnessing partners to support building new digital business capability.

– **Corporate entities simplification:** Review legal entities and corporate structures to identify unnecessary overhead, complexity, and log jamming. One of the greatest anchors on progress is a lack of alignment and slow decision-making. It is a death knell. Time and energy are wasted, and opportunity cost amplified, while organisations shepherd decisions from one decision body to the next, or fail to share data across boundaries. I recently uncovered a case where a relatively minor decision on a new proposition made its way across 11 different committees! Not only did the process take months, but the final approval was also binned as the ongoing and outcoming proposal changed so dramatically in an attempt to appease the plethora of stakeholders along the way. Breaking down structures and corporate entities where separated decision-making is hard-wired is brave but I would say a necessary pursuit in siloed organisations for this reason.

– **Project delivery simplification:** Assess project management processes, prioritisation, and benefits realisation to lower cost and increase impact. How many times have we seen projects go 'into the hopper' and disappear down enterprise prioritisation processes to come whimpering back due to restrictions of budget and resourcing, if it even does? Project management should be assessed as should journey mapping, pain points identified, and end-user experience benefits isolated to build a perspective on where waste lies and how to go about killing it. This stretches right through a value chain from submission to mobilisation, to design and test, past deployment, and post-implementation reviews. My experience is that these experiences must be added (they are a rare breed, and hence the need to suggest simplification). I also see the sledgehammer:nut syndrome alive and well in some organisations; small and medium size change programmes undergoing enterprise-level governance, causing unnecessary reporting and process overhead. With some clients, we have established small teams who work with autonomy, under certain decision authority protocols, and this has made significant headway outside of the industrial processes. Size matters when it comes to change; it can choke velocity. The cycle of business case and benefit realisation, like post-implementation reviews, again is rare to see working fluidly. But where it does, a discipline can be brought into an organisation where only the best-cased change goes forwards, proven by look-backs that improve submission and review quality control, maximising those rare change budgets and windows.

– **Technology simplification:** Assess application maintenance, development, infrastructure, and security costs. We will come back to this area a little further when we visit the technology platform section, but for now and in preparation, the currency and infrastructure of a technology estate should always be under observation and pruning. Even pre-digital, application numbers, and complexities were exploding as a result of Industry 3.0, and seldom is anything retired. Rather, periphery applications can be left to 'tick over' and eventually run into disrepair, out of support status, or simply become untenable for future digital estate planning. Another area to review is data capacity, both in terms of volume flows and storage, where retention and system calls can cause significant volumetrics. Similarly, licence numbers and version control, or worse, customisation, can give cause for concern on cost containment and potential future development bottlenecks.

I encourage you to take a regular, healthy dose of simplification to 'clean out the pipes'. A thorough check-through of the above-mentioned areas will find wasteful resources that can potentially hamper progress or become hardcoded into the future state. Finding and removing them will release the capacity to support change and capabilities.

The Change Tapestry

To execute a simplification programme, we need change levers to remove complexity. A programme, established by steadfast leaders, needs to be driven by Pareto insight that identifies the 20% of value destruction that will give the 80% upside. Applying the proper intervention will come down to the possession of skills and tools and also the availability of the right mindset and sponsorship.

Part of that mindset is knowing what levers to pull and when, whether that means driving one stream of simplification (e.g. one of the above) or a number simultaneously. The following is a tapestry of interchangeable change levers, which are the friend of the simplifier:

– Insights and valuation: Analyse the journey points and the product/service portfolio to pinpoint where the biggest impact can be made. The focus should be on identifying the value destroyers. These are the products, processes, customers, channels, and organisational structures that consume resources, budget, time, and oversight that cost more than the benefits derived.
– Targeted interventions: The appropriate intervention and solution need to be identified for each simplification opportunity. In some circumstances, agile proposition development to reimagine a broken situation is the right thing to do. In other circumstances, removing steps and 'killing silly rules' (a favourite pursuit of mine) may be appropriate. In the middle sits process reengineering as well as automation and digitisation. Outsourcing and offshoring options with BPO (business process

outsourcing) should also be considered, especially in sub-scale circumstances or where there are severe cultural barriers to change.

- Beyond the bookends approach: Making individual interventions is not enough. Champions continually look up and down the value chain. This includes backup into supplier steps, and downstream into post-sales service cycles.
- Standardisation and reusability: Removing or finding a means to codify 'bespoke' or custom-fit services is a must. Personalisation can be modularised. This modularisation can also facilitate the reuse of processes, methods, and applications.
- Skills and aptitude: Recognise that you need customer-centric skills that you may not have, such as experience designers, process engineers, and digital technologists. Robotics and machine learning specialists are also critical when it comes to automation and digitalisation. Efforts will need steadfast leadership that will continually force new perspectives and new ways of looking at old problems. And resilient experimentation that follows the data to kill or scale is the compass of the great.
- Continuous improvement: It is wise to adopt an "80% is good enough" attitude. Serial simplifiers prioritise pain points, find solutions but steer clear of last mile paralysis recognising that perfection is the enemy of progress. They move on to the next friction point and keep looking end to end – there are always easier wins to be had. They also apply a rule that the solution cannot add; it must subtract.

Be cautious of large simplification programmes that, through complexity of governance and over-representation, can stall progress. We all know it takes longer for committees to commit. Decision-making is key, and taking things away is not always a popular pursuit, so sponsored leadership is a must-have. Finally, technology is an enabler, which we will cover next.

Tools and Conditions to Support Execution

Investing in the tools and organisational conditions to enable teams to drive efficiency is key.

It is simply not enough to ask your teams to drive this. They will find this difficult; after all, it is not easy to ask someone to undo their work, something that has probably made them successful in the past. This investment assists in building competency as well as visibility and motivation. When I drive simplification and efficiency programmes, I work through the organisation systematically, on each of the following steps:

- Process technology: Implementing process management technologies and automated monitoring processes to speed up change, reduce downtime, and identify opportunities.
- Change management: Personal development and group coaching to help overcome resistance to change and embrace improvement and simplification.

- Value chain operating model: Mapping and analysing holistic top-level business process architectures, emphasising value, to align organisation effort with output.
- Benchmarking: Comparison with a leading competitor and parallel industries to aim for best practices and success; there is nothing like a bit of competition to motivate.
- Adaptable structure: Preparing the organisation leadership and teams to adapt structures as processes evolve to ensure resources are optimised. Simplifying processes without being willing to simplify and optimise the team structure will cause the 'red light' syndrome – progress might stall, or proposed benefits will hit red status.
- Activity-based accounting: Process-oriented recording and controlling costs from indirect areas of activity to maximise accountability and scope brings everyone into the tent of accountability.
- Rewards: Empower teams to go and simplify – sometimes that is reward enough, but be clear on expectations and make sure that remuneration structures are not set up in contradiction. My consultancy recently helped a team identify a solution for automating a critical process step that was causing friction in a journey (and losing customers), but we found a reluctance to execute. When we investigated we found out that they were targeted on completion rates of that very same step. The more they achieved, the better they were rewarded; but we were trying to kill it. You can imagine where that one was going. KPIs and rewards should be oriented around customer outcomes, and their improvement along with simplification, and self-sufficiency. I encourage you to think hard about your rewards and whether they are blocking progress.
- Ambassadorship: Identification of motivated and credible team members to play the role of ambassadors and change agents, trained in process and change methodologies. People listen to their own, and hard calls require hard calls, which are best made from within.

These tools and supports are not exhaustive, and specific approaches to eliminating waste and creating capacity will have their own means. But they are important enablers that I encourage you to consider.

Selecting the Right Interventions

When it boils down to it, there are normally six types of interventions that can be applied to drive efficiency, and enable simplification as depicted in Figure 27.

When viewed through the lens of expected impact, effort, and scope, each intervention scores differently. The selection of the right mix of interventions is important, and depending on the size of your organisation, spread of processes (which links to the breadth of products/services), a number could be used in parallel. But it may not be necessary and there may not be the capacity to adopt all.

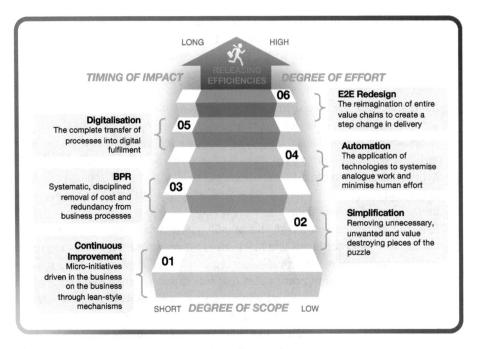

Figure 27: Intervention efficiency ladder.

Specific needs or circumstances command different options. For instance, continuous improvement is typically adopted holistically in an organisation that is perpetually committed to excellence and spans all organisational activities. Simplification and digitalisation on the other hand may be a timebound programme, with a focused scope to a particular part of the business.

Overall, the levers that are lower down the ladder have broader scopes, take less effort, and have quicker impacts. The further up the ladder, the narrower the scope and the greater the effort (for each intervention) and duration as well as impact.

Factors to consider are the degree of scope, the timing of impact, and degree of effort. The ultimate aim is to release inefficiencies across all methods; the important factor is finding the most effective route.

A Comparison of Business Process Engineering Versus Continuous Improvement

We will take a closer look at the two prime efficiency levers, business process engineering versus continuous improvement in Table 3, to highlight some important nuances between them. I encourage businesses to embed efficiency mechanics to choose the right method.

Table 3: Business process engineering versus continuous improvement.

Factors	Business process engineering	Continuous improvement
Degree of change	Radical, one off	Incremental, continuous
Goal	Dramatic improvement	Small, cumulative enhancement
Characteristics of change	Abrupt change	Gradual, constant change
Organisational impact	Higher	Lower
Relative risk	Higher	Lower
Implementation	Directive, top down	Empowered, bottom-up
Senior management involvement	Intensive throughout	Up-front and interstitial
Enablers	Technology, PMO, HR	Ground-level leadership
Potential use of technology	Very high	Incidental (short)

Case Study: Simplicity and Selectivity at L'Oréal

L'Oréal harnessed a Simplicity Programme across their c. 90,000 workforces to build a stronger health and safety culture that in turn enabled the company to be ahead of the Coronavirus curve, and play a key role in supporting the pandemic defence effort.

Life at the 90,000-strong organisations had become cluttered. Staff and management were overwhelmed with organisational complexity, too much information feeding in 24/7, and an 'always at work' culture (sound familiar?). In tandem, the business had become bloated with processes and policies to manage the chaos.

Growth had driven complexity, but these were not the spoils that the organisation was looking to glean. So the management team in Paris gathered and began to design a programme that would help the organisation take control of its well-being and productivity challenges, to build stronger internal resilience.

The programme focused on two core themes, the first being simplicity. They revamped health, safety, and well-being communications to help their teams easily consume the supports that were in place but had gone unnoticed before the programme. The response was welcoming.

In tandem, the company worked on selectivity. This involved loosening tight historical corporate controls on health, safety, and ergonomics programmes, giving teams discretion on how to implement them.

This was an interesting journey for everyone involved, and a central and facilitating aid was the publication of a simple four-step maturity model. Teams self-audited where they were on the model, and worked with published guidance provided for each level to implement local measures. The result was corporate consistency through benchmarks, coupled with local empowerment to facilitate buy-in and localisation as teams drew down from the guidelines and toolbox to build their own solution set.

One of the tools provided (called Take 2) was introduced when colleagues and teams reached stage 3 of the maturity model, which gave them the capabilities to run a dynamic risk assessment before they began a task. This, and many other tools experimented with through a carefully curated engagement programme, laid the foundations for L'Oréal to navigate the pandemic when it arrived.

The company had bred a culture of self-risk management. Teams were empowered by simplicity and selectivity, which enabled the company to maintain operations and produce millions of products such as hand sanitiser and other vital supplies for the front line.

This example illustrates how complexity can build in internal processes and structures. Process and project simplification coupled with interventions such as progressive change management and ambassadorship can turn the needle.[58]

Reflection

- To summarise, I have called this second critical capability "efficiency" instead of "simplicity" because, while simplification is undoubtedly the primary activity to reducing wasteful recourses, the aim is to be outcome-led: efficiency for your organisation, and, ultimately, your customer.
- Focus on vigorously eliminating burden and waste from the customer journey to maximise the customer experience – this is where digital businesses start with the customer.
- Digital businesses manage time, assets, people, and capital as scarce resources, as inefficient burdens in the customer journey are a waste in operations.
- A golden rule is that before you can digitalise, you must simplify and make processes lean; it is a sin to code bad or complex processes.
- Some areas to work on at front and back of house, to simplify, are:
- Product simplification: To eliminate the 80% of products that only drive 20% of the profit
- Process simplification: To remove product-level journey friction through automating processes wherever possible
- Customer and service simplification: To identify the cohort that utilises 80% of your effort to acquire and serve only deliver 20% of the value
- Distribution simplification: To identify sub-optimal routes to market and either elimination or revise them

---

58 YouTube, "Introduction to L'Oreal Simplicity Project," accessed April 7, 2023, https://youtu.be/WENLLt3C2X0.

- Budget simplification: To lower spend and increase return on investment
- Resourcing simplification: To potentially liberate and rebalance skills and resources where appropriate
- Sourcing simplification: To lower the number of sourcing partners and increase the services outsourced to achieve economies of scale and service
- Corporate entities simplification: Review legal entities and corporate structures to identify unnecessary overheads, complexity, and log jamming
- Project delivery simplification: To trim the fat, lower costs and increase impact
- Technology simplification: To assess application maintenance, development, infrastructure, and security costs, including volume flows, storage, and licences
- The above-mentioned checks are ruthless, but it is the type of dogged determination you will need to 'wipe down the decks' and eliminate bottlenecks. Efficiency creates the capacity for you to digitalise your business and to emerge from building a transformative experience.
- Ultimately, efficiency is about releasing and driving value to your end user.

Chapter 9
Digital Engagement

> The purpose of life is to live it, to taste experience to the utmost, to reach out eagerly and without fear for newer and richer experience. – Eleanor Roosevelt

We can now build on the philosophy of customer-centricity with a potentially trimmed-down organisation and newly released capacity to begin building digital experiences and be digitally engaging.

We can now uncover what you need to develop and deliver 'digital' – online and mobile solutions – for engagement, access, propositions (products and services), and ultimately meaningful value.

This capability sits at the heart of a digital business model, enabled by customer-centric leadership, and efficient processes. It also leverages data analytics and is liberated through agile, innovation, and open through partnering and ecosystems.

Channel Strategy

A good place to begin thinking about how to embrace digital as the means to drive engagement and act as the access point to deliver experience is at the engagement layer of our Digital 360°. At the engagement layer, there needs to sit a composite channel strategy, which sets out what channels you will engage your target audience, and what roles those channels will play in that regard.

To keep pace with customer adoption of digital, accelerated by the Covid-19 pandemic, and a general exponential shift in touch point management, organisations are adopting channel strategies that maximise the power of each. They are doing this by building an evolving and complimentary channel mix that blends choice and consistency for the end user, while at the same time leveraging digital (automated) access to reduce overheads.

In the top half of Figure 28 is an opening perspective of how a channel strategy could look and evolve for a business that relies on digital and physical touch points to access the market and deliver its propositions.

Across the top, you will see that I have clustered the roles channels can play:
1. business development,
2. sales and service, and
3. maintaining relationship.

https://doi.org/10.1515/9783111034713-015

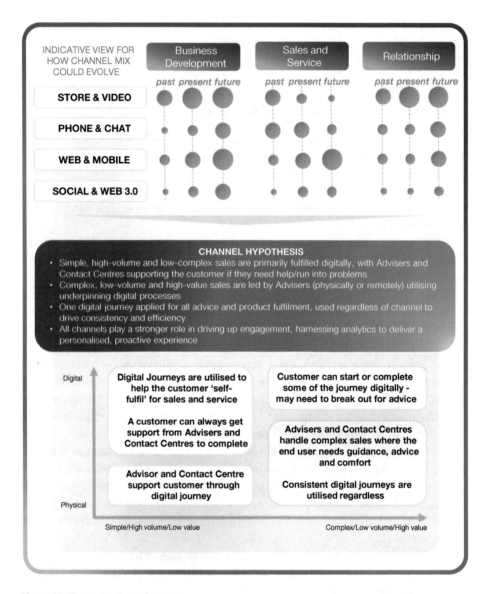

Figure 28: Illustrative channel strategy.

On the top left of the illustration, I have clustered channels into four primary classes:

(a) The physical store where salespeople and advisors engage customers (and I have extended this to include video, which of course has become a supplementary or augmented channel increasingly used through and post the impact of the 2020 pandemic)

(b) Phone and chat, where human or automated advisers (bots) are available to support end users

(c) Online and mobile channels which are digital device interfaces and will extend to include voice assistants such as Alexa

(d) Social media and Web 3.0, which are considered engagement platforms in themselves, usually accessed by online and mobile channels but in the future will also be accessed by mixed reality (virtual and augmented)

I have separated the last two categories as I believe the former is where we have 'owned' channels (e.g. we can manage and have complete responsibility for our own websites and apps) compared to the latter which we participate in but do not have full ownership.

Channel clusters (a) and (b) are usually considered physical, human channels, with channels (c) and (d) considered digital channels. However, my view is digital has an important role to play in supporting the physical and human channels, and humans should always be one step away from supporting the digital channels.

What the illustration attempts to do is bring to life the role that each channel cluster has played historically, and a suggestion as to the evolution of that role for each channel today. It also illustrates the role each of those channels could play in the future.

As you will see, there are a number of dynamics suggested, which frame my hypothesis:

- All channels will play a more significant role in future business development and relationship management as data and digital engagement tools are harnessed.
- As we digitalise propositions and their fulfilment, stores/video and the phone will play a lesser role in sales and service activities, and that traffic will primarily shift to web and mobile. Perhaps to a lesser degree social, and Web 3.0, but one could imagine a world where Web 3.0 has a much greater impact should its promise unfold.
- The primarily human channels (stores, video, phone, and chat) will become focused mainly on human-to-human business development and relationship management, albeit supplemented by the digital channels.
- At the bottom of the illustration is an underpinning channel hypothesis supporting this, which assumes in the future that simple, high-volume and low-complex engagement will primarily be fulfilled digitally, with advisers in stores and contact centres supporting the customer if they need help or encounter problems.
- Advisers (physically or remotely) lead complex, low-volume and high-value engagement, utilising underpinning digital processes.
- Digital journeys help the customer 'self-fulfil' for sales and service. A customer can always get support from advisers and contact centres to complete.
- One digital journey is applied for all advice and product fulfilment, used regardless of channel, to drive consistency and efficiency. All channels play a stronger role in driving up engagement, harnessing analytics to deliver a personalised, proactive experience.

– To bring this to life, think about the sale of clothes. You might find that fast fashion will be primarily sold online and on mobile, with customer service (such as returns) managed online or remotely on the phone. But when it comes to buying a wedding dress or morning suit, this is more likely to be handled in-store with bespoke tailoring and customisation fulfilled by the human touch. Brand awareness will be facilitated through all channels, increasingly more through digital channels, but managing relationships and ultimately delivering the product will remain primarily a human-centred activity.

What I have outlined here needs one further dimension: channel coordination. There are three primary coordination models adopted in business today, which you will, at times, see or hear used interchangeably. Each has its unique outcome when it comes to experiencing fluency.

1. Multi-channel: Present across multiple channels simultaneously and engaging the end user independently. There is no channel coordination, which is easier to build and run but you step into a challenge when the end user wants to, or needs to, hop channels and finds they need to start again. In the case of garments, this is like spotting a jacket online and then going to a store to see if they have one only finding out that it was an online-only garment.

2. Omni-channel: Designed for end users to move across channels at points in their journey. I often use the word 'seamless' experience, to signify that the client's prior history is carried across channels to maintain consistency. Using the example of a shopper buying clothes again, an omni-channel experience is akin to a shopper reviewing a suit online, checking it is available in a local store and requesting a click-and-hold service to try on the suit in-store before buying, safe in the knowledge that the right size and colour is waiting for them.

3. Opti-channel: An extension of omni-channel in that it offers channel-shifting but with the journey designed to offer the 'optimal' route for the particular client and circumstances. In opti-channel journeys, digital businesses attempt to collect more data so that journey routing can be deployed to maximise the user's experience and commercial value (by which I mean more sales and a better experience, delivered at less cost). Consider visiting a wedding dress website, browsing and saving a variety of styles to an online 'scrapbook' (similar to Pinterest), then receiving a prompt to schedule a video consultation with a concierge who can help augment the experience by sharing further insights on style, fit, and availability. The concierge takes that one step further by organising an in-store fitting where all the wedding dresses and a fitter are already waiting (perhaps with some champagne in tow).

As you will hopefully see from these examples, the more sophisticated the channel strategy, the more complex its fulfilment, but the more potentially commercially rewarding and experience rich it will be too – at least that is the idea.

Getting users into channels and engaging with experiences in whatever manner they are constructed requires digital brand and marketing. We will uncover that next.

Digital Marketing – Opening Up the Channel Doors

Digital marketing can be viewed as a proactive engagement activity which begins with a deep understanding of customer patterns, working collaboratively with product management to develop the right message for the right audience to be delivered at the right time and in the right way for impact, and executing that messaging through optimised channels, including digital.

The following are steps and sequences that you can both create and execute for digital marketing and 1:1 campaigns:

1. It all starts with insights: Marketeers start by leveraging customer segment analytics and customer experience (CX) tracking (quantitative and qualitative). They do this through digital and physical journeys and competitive and market trends to understand what drives engagement, sales, experience, and drop-off, which they then use to implement interventions across all product, marketing, sales, and servicing engagements. They gather trends and background intelligence to point them in a general direction of what their customer is doing and the best way to engage with them, including the digital and physical mix. It is a perpetual cycle of observation and general user trends.
2. Defining the proposition and target market: Marketeers then work with product and servicing teams to collaboratively develop the key proposition points that they (the business) wish to promote and to which specific customers. Business teams have a key role in developing the 'what', for 'whom' and 'why', and need to guide marketeers in the right direction. The 'why' is both for the customer (as in the benefit) and for the business (the target business benefit).
3. Audience management: At this stage, the decision is made whether the campaign will be above the line (general) or below the line to a specific audience (personalised to either the company's customers via their website or through ads on social media and mobile, etc.). Data sources, audience management techniques, and tools required are established for personalised campaigns. (Note: at this stage businesses also plan for audience building, which means gathering details and consents for ongoing engagement such as newsletters and member privileges.)
4. Segment campaign planning: Coupling the insights gathered in step 1 and the target objectives from step 2, the marketeer can begin to develop an engagement plan that is designed to deliver maximum reach, impact, and outcomes for the targeted segment categories. They also need to align to the business strategy and brand, and deliver on the commercial objectives. This will include a proposed channel mix, budget requirements, audience profile, and key messaging and content requirements. Importantly, tracking mechanisms and success measures are also defined and agreed.

5. Scheduling: At this point, the marketeer will also cross-reference the segment campaign with the overall campaign calendar to ensure there is harmony, and sign off with the product or service owner. The campaign calendar should also include top-level brand positions being taken, and any business communication themes expected or events planned so that scheduling is tightly coupled to optimise messaging in the market and to manage over-congestion of both traffic and narrative. There is nothing worse than good campaigns drowned out in the noise, or mis-stepping and out of time.

6. Content and journey design: A key part of campaign execution is the development of messaging and editorial/proprietary content in addition to micro-journey design and user experience (UX). What are the desired steps you want customers to take after they are made aware of the solution (i.e. this could be a purchase journey and on to check out, or an advisory discussion). These steps are to design the triggers and flow of building awareness, triggering interest, channel routing with efficiency measured by click-through rates, and ultimately sales or self-servicing.

7. Channel development: Development and execution of the content on digital and physical channels. This will also include technical digital marketing execution, tagging and taxonomy, search engine optimisation (SEO – identifying the key content that is required to ensure the algorithms on advertising platforms pick up and prioritise placement), display advertising, paid search, and pay-per-click placement. Here marketeers may also plan multivariant testing (showing slightly different messaging to different control groups to test the most effective) as well as remarketing and engineering personalisation as per the audience management step.

8. Technical and analytics platforming: Not necessarily coming in sequence here, marketeers will ensure that running and developing the underpinning marketing and data infrastructure enables effective digital marketing and e-commerce. The application of analytics and marketing automation and integration with external digital marketing services, e.g. Google, social channels, and data repositories, is included here, particularly in organisations that have the resources to conduct personalised campaigns.

9. Business readiness: Throughout the preparatory steps 2–8, marketeers will remain in close working partnership with product and service owners. Together, they will coordinate business readiness with channel owners, compliance, and technology to ensure that campaign risk is managed. Perhaps crucially, alert the front line to be aware and ready to support execution with messaging, tools, and, of course, targets.

10. Execution: Execution followed by campaign management is a close working relationship between the sales and servicing teams to monitor and optimise engagement, making tweaks as they go along.

Back to our shopper example and a quick walk through some marketing scenarios. A marketer managing a web platform for a high-profile fashion brand will live by their analytics dashboard every day. It helps them visualise and understand what kind of traffic hits their site and how effectively the site converts traffic into value. Value could be content consumption, such as articles or online purchases. It also includes service activities such as returns and refunds. This is step 1.

As part of the daily routine, the marketer will engage with the owner of a specific product line, for example, men's casuals, to understand their upcoming product plans and, therefore, their digital marketing asks. As a result, the marketer learns of a new line of shirts that are essential to the season's product plans. Together with the product owner, they identified the shirt as most likely to be attractive to professionals in their 30s as an accompaniment to business casual suits, who buy predominantly online but also in-store. This is step 2.

The marketeer will create a campaign plan, ensuring that it takes a prominent place on the front page carousel of the website, as it is a season highlight and a key commercial line. They will develop an above-the-line and personalised campaign plan to known purchasers of their casual suit range. This will involve quantifying the number of impressions that marketing content will need to make to satisfy the sales target requirements of the product owner; the marketeer can judge this based on their experience of funnel conversion ratios. As the below-the-line expectations should be easily quantifiable based on prior campaigns, the above-the-line impression levels will be calculated to close any gaps. This is steps 3 through 5.

After signing off of the campaign plan but before going into execution, the marketer will put in place the necessary content production, web development, and analytics requirements on the inside and bid for or book the ad space required on online and social channels externally. They will also liaise with in-store marketing and communications to ensure that parallel placement plans are in place. They will also agree targets and activities with the e-commerce team in conjunction with the product owner, and all business readiness activities prepared. This sees steps 6 to 9 concluded, and everybody will step into campaign mode, step 10. They will receive daily, if not more frequent campaign analytics. At a daily stand-up, the marketing, product, e-commerce, and channel owners will monitor progress, remove blockages and tweak ad spend, content publication, SEO and factor in 'call to action' page placements (one of many tactics that could be employed). Sometimes there is a formal stand-back review of a campaign at the end, but mostly learning and reflection is 'on the go'.

What I have outlined above is 'digital marketing on a page', a much-simplified description and flow of digital marketing execution. In practice, it is far more complex. It is highly technical and needs strategic planning to execute, probably a topic worth a book of its own. But I have hopefully given you the rudimentary steps and requirements to assess your digital marketing capabilities at least, to discern whether you can implement additional steps and, of course, to see the links between digital marketing, product, and channel management.

Engagement Strategy and Prioritising Where to Focus

As we think about digital engagement, it is important to take an end-to-end view; in other words, it begins with awareness and runs through to renewal, as depicted in Figure 29. Getting this view across the life cycle is useful in breaking down the key phases for focus and investment. Strategy, as noted earlier is about making choices. Some organisations choose to create a digital experience across the life cycle, using experience design or UX and CX techniques. You will note these phrases are inter-changeably used and I have shared a simple explainer for each further down. I also note that some organisations choose to be brilliant at certain stages of the life cycle, a strategically differentiating choice.

In some of my preparatory interviews I was struck by, in some cases, the dominance of focus on CX, and less on UX. UX, in my view, is the ultimate arbitrator of CX – the parts make the sum. I also find it interesting that some brands excel in one phase of the life cycle and prioritise their resources, design activity, and activation to build competitive advantage. Some examples are included below, but note that Amazon is an excellent example of mastery across all the phases.

The question for each digital business is where the focus should lie. It is hard to achieve everything, and factors like sector and business model as well as seasonality might inform you to push and pull your focus up and down the cycle. For instance, in the early days of a business or even product launch, building an audience and 'getting customers' will be key. This is very much the case for platform business models.

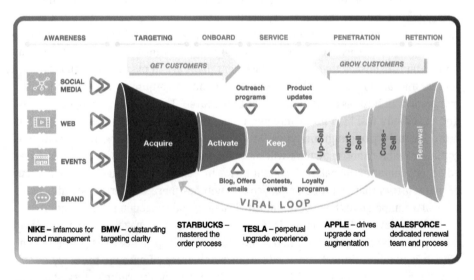

Figure 29: Customer life cycle funnel.

For more mature businesses with deeper customer bases, and comprehensive, complementary product lines, the focus will be on cross-sell and up-sell or 'growing customers'. For business models and businesses that depend on significant asset spending and long relationships with loyalty a key factor, 'keeping' customers is a big focus.

Understanding where your focus is on the life cycle allows you to channel your efforts, allocate resources, and build capability and expectations from the business. An acquisition business looks a little different from a grow or keep business. That said, all of these will need some level of mastery.

Experiences Explained

- CX results from a customer's total experience with a brand across all touch points in their lifetime with that brand and its business. It is the sum of the parts, subjective and influenced over a period of time and by multiple factors.
- UX is more concerned with how an end user feels and experiences a particular journey. It is therefore a 'part' of their overall CX.
- UX design is the art of designing experiences that will solve a job or task for an end user, and aims to deliver towards the overall CX.
- User interface (UI) design is a subset of UX, focusing on the aesthetics and visual elements of the digital experience.

An acronym for building and executing user design is 'Basic', as it should always be or have:
- Beauty: Is it aesthetically pleasing? Does it follow the style guide, is it properly aligned with business need and customer expectations?
- Accessibility: Can everyone use it? Does it comply with standards? Is it cross-platform compatible?
- Simplicity: Does it make life easier? Does it reduce the user's workload? Is its functionality necessary?
- Intuitiveness: Is it easy to use? Does it require little or no instructions? Is its outcome/output predictable?
- Consistency: Does it match the systems? Does it reuse established patterns? Is its performance consistent?

Phygital

I referred to 'phygital' in the previous chapter on efficiency. Phygital combines digital and physical to create a composite end-user experience, and is something digital businesses increasingly need to consider among the many aspects of delivering digital experiences. They must consider how digital blends with the physical world; it is seldom that this is not a major consideration across the life cycle.

As end users, consumers and equally B2B users, engage with brands, experiences, and products, they do so in the physical as well as the digital world. The IBM Institute for Business Value, in association with the National Retail Federation, conducted a global survey of more than 19,000 respondents across 28 countries in September 2021. The report found that the Covid-19 pandemic has changed consumer behaviour, and after spending much of the height of the pandemic in a 'virtual-first' world, consumers see digital tools as a necessary part of the shopping experience. They now expect to see hybrid shopping journeys. This is especially true for Gen Z, which uses hybrid shopping more than any other generation. The full report can be downloaded from IBM.[59]

While digital adoption is increasing, it is not necessarily at the detriment of physical engagement. In fact, engagement on aggregate is increasing overall, and the balance of digital to physical touch points must be considered in this context. The best digital companies track and understand the role that the many physical touch points play in the journey, and design a blended experience to create consistency, amplification, and smart resource management (omni- and opti-channel design).

Store Archetypes

The store can play one or several roles in the phygital experience. This can cover branding and sales of products or services with high physical attributes, such as cars and furniture. That said, brands like Tesla and IKEA are bypassing this to a large degree, leveraging scarcity, design and desire, as well as great e-commerce experience, designing the store or warehouse as a pick-up location. Community and creation are other big themes leveraged by brands such as Apple and Banks.

In the four corners of the illustration in Figure 30, I have shared a perspective on the different roles that physical stores and locations can play in a broader experience, and in what circumstances. For instance, luxury physical goods such as perfume, wines, and artisan coffee use physical locations as a way to 'experience' the product in a well-designed, sophisticated, and well-appointed locations. Nespresso stores are an excellent example of this.

Brands that sell an anchor product and associated services that generate cross-sales where human or product engagement ensures success use stores as community hubs to re-enforce brand and expose those cross-sell opportunities. Banks are improving at this,

---

59 IBM, "Consumers Want It All – 2022 Consumer Study," accessed April 7, 2023, https://www.ibm.com/thought-leadership/institute-business-value/en-us/report/2022-consumer-study.

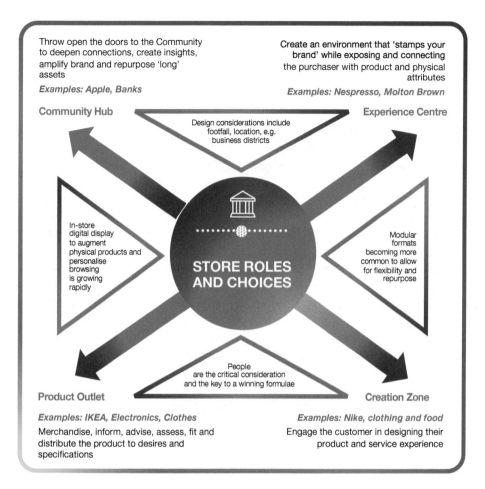

Throw open the doors to the Community to deepen connections, create insights, amplify brand and repurpose 'long' assets

Examples: Apple, Banks

Community Hub

Design considerations include footfall, location, e.g. business districts

Create an environment that 'stamps your brand' while exposing and connecting the purchaser with product and physical attributes

Examples: Nespresso, Molton Brown

Experience Centre

In-store digital display to augment physical products and personalise browsing is growing rapidly

STORE ROLES AND CHOICES

Modular formats becoming more common to allow for flexibility and repurpose

People are the critical consideration and the key to a winning formulae

Product Outlet

Creation Zone

Examples: IKEA, Electronics, Clothes

Merchandise, inform, advise, assess, fit and distribute the product to desires and specifications

Examples: Nike, clothing and food

Engage the customer in designing their product and service experience

Figure 30: The role of the store.

but Apple are the masters with exceptional locations, store design in sync with the brand feel, and the genius bar for repairs and showcase events that all lead to loyalty and upsell.

Ikea, as mentioned previously, have applied the ultimate, quintessential CX with stores that are advice and product outlets, with seamless journeys linked to online and mobile, anchored on a single, opti-channel profile. Nike has excelled at using the store as a 'creator' zone where consumers can personalise products and hang out with like-minded people.

The store is important, but not the only physical touch point to consider – as a digital business, it is incumbent to walk in the shoes of the customer to understand where they are likely to be when they are seeking a solution for their 'jobs to be done', and then architecting placement and interventions to be there for them to provide the solution.

Think about how FX booths are placed across airports, and ATM's and even portable toilet facilities are (or indeed are not) strategically places at large social events.

Digital Product Management

Product managers are the powerhouses responsible for driving ground-up change and digital transformation from within the organisation at the epicentre of a digital business and designing digital experiences.

High-impact product managers succeed in ideating, testing, and launching products by employing a near-obsessive focus on their end users and customers. They centre solutions on qualitative and quantitative data insights, developing symbiotic relationships with engineers and designers, and creating products for strategic business benefits.

Today, product managers are the glue that binds the many functions that touch a product, from vision to engineering, design to customer success through sales, marketing, operations, finance, legal, and much more. They not only own the decisions about what to build but influence every aspect of how it gets built, launched, and performs against its targeted objectives and ultimately retired.

Unlike product managers of the past, who were primarily focused on execution and measured by the delivery and performance of new products, the product manager of today is increasingly the mini-CEO of the product and experience it delivers. They wear many hats, using a broad knowledge base to make trade-off decisions and bring together cross-functional teams, ensuring alignment between diverse functions from proposition to compliance.

Modern product management shifts from tailoring marketing messages for buyers to building products for those who use them.[60] This requires rounded competencies as product management evolves, and the combination of strategy, management, business analysis, and design defines success. This is a key difference from product managers of the past, whose role more resembled project managers. That is not to say that project management is not part of the brief. It is central to it, but not the totality.

The key attributes of the digital product manager are multifaceted, with a skillset spanning CX design, commercial acumen, data-driven decisions, and technology fluency. No small feat, which is why they are hard to find, or the better ones, at least. Daily they lead cross-functional teams from manufacturing and distribution, digital, design, development, and support functions like compliance in developing and delivering digital solutions.

---

60 Deloitte, Digital Product Management accessed April 7, 2023, https://www2.deloitte.com/content/dam/insights/us/articles/5224_Digital-transformation-7/DI_Digital%20transformation%207.pdfhttps://www2.deloitte.com/content/dam/insights/us/articles/5224_Digital-transformation-7/DI_Digital%20transformation%207.pdf.

To do that, they need to be able to talk the talk of the business and translate it into technology-enabled journeys and propositions. In doing this, they always remain focused on and passionate about the customer but always balance business goals with customer outcomes and continuously blend the two for win-win propositions. They manage to straddle crafting a vision for what a digital product can achieve while diving into requirements testing and technical specificity with practitioners and deliverers.

The digital product manager is responsible for so much more than a product, and the title does not do the role justice. While building and iterating features, services, and extensions is part of the role, it is an overall experience that the digital product manager focuses on, so do not be put off by the title.[61] They are exceptional at balancing the 'why' with the 'how' and the 'what' with the 'when'. They also guide using data extracted from digital journeys and experiences and champion the cause for digital across the business. Hence, I often use the expression 'mini CEO'.

Digital product managers are strategic, customer-centric thinkers. They start and end their focus on the customer. In fact, they coordinate every aspect of digital capability and play a major role in informing overall strategy. However, their focus is on translating the overall strategy into propositions, and product-level value exchanges with customers, and end users in a B2B setting. Here is a view on what keeps them busy:

Provide strategy and direction, which include

- Understand their target customers' needs and map them to the business purpose and strategic direction
- Collect, communicate, and understand the marketplace as well as the competitive and regulatory environment
- Combine this internal and external knowledge to forge a proposition vision and strategy that delivers for all stakeholders in their chosen market

Develop propositions underpinned by products and services, which include

- Design, prototype, and pilot new products or features in line with the proposition vision and strategy
- Build a product service and feature backlog that supports a continually enhancing digital proposition

---

61 The Digital Product Manager, "What Does a Digital Product Manager Do?" Pallavi Agarwal, accessed April 7, 2023, https://theproductmanager.com/topics/digital-product-manager/.

- Continually assess the viability, feasibility, and desirability of items on the back-log to prioritise them for development
- Build engagement plans to go to market with propositions

Manage the total supply chain from design to delivery – this involves

- Plan for raw materials and production capacity, including people and technology
- Track and personally monitor activities and performance in their supply chain and intervene with empathy to remove blockages and find enhancements
- Assure product and service quality

Ensure CX and customer service are distinguishable – activities include

- Monitor and analyse delivery experience across the customer journey to identify enhancement and pain points
- Translate problems and opportunities around the organisation and back into the development teams
- Reward, recognise, and celebrate exceptional performance across the value chain and with partners

Champion their customers' needs and product solutions across the organisation by

- Spreading the good word about the customer and associated proposition vision as well as articulating the opportunity on what it will take to unlock it
- Work across the organisation to develop the skills, practices, and ultimately the confidence to support digital product management
- Understand the organisational culture and how to introduce change and drive motivation for results

Work with suppliers and partners to deliver resources, capabilities, and augmented services – key activities include

- An ecosystem strategy facilitates boosting capability or extending and augmenting proposition
- Finding and onboarding suppliers and partners, and with them, agree the development model and the benefit-sharing approach
- Defining the boundaries and managing relationships and performance with a win-win-win mindset

Work through distribution channels to maximise reach, catered for by

- Agreeing on the omni- or opti-channel framework, and the underpinning roles and responsibilities of true journey management and experience design execution
- Managing customer and end-user engagement to ensure that performance and experience are in line with agreed success measures
- Work with the front line to 'learn by doing' and bring back enhancements and improvements for prioritisation in the development backlog

Harness technology and API interfaces for efficiency and ecosystem opportunities empowered by

- Understanding the technology stack and tools that are required to support progressive digital product management, and work with engineering teams to put them in place
- Digital product managers will pay particular attention to API interfaces and microservices (which we'll cover in the Technology platform chapter) that facilitate secure data and service sharing and insight extraction (two-way: in and out) to guide the digital product portfolio and its development

Digital product managers employ a host of tools in their day-to-day work, including:

Communications and collaborations

- Google Workspace for logistics, including Gmail, Chat, Calendar, Docs, Sheets, Slides, and Forms
- Slack and Jira for inter-team communications and workflow
- Miro and FigJam are well-developed and utilised for online collaborations

Design and wireframing

- Figma for design, prototyping, and demos
- Balsamiq for building wireframes (overlaps with Figma)
- Canva for lift and drop graphics

Analytics and insight

- Google Analytics tends to be the centre of the universe on this one, and is really a powerful tool with integrators to all front-end digital platforms, including Salesforce and Adobe, which themselves provide solid insight tools
- Voice of the customer/CX platforms include Qualtrics, Medallia, and Confirmit, to name but a few (there are many)
- Mixpanel and Amplitude are useful complements for tracking

Project management

- Jira, Trello, and ProductPlan are all strong project and workflow tools, and most commonly deployed from our experience

User experience

- Hotjar and Crazy Egg are useful for recording and heatmapping activity in online journeys
- User testing (award for most apt name) is for exactly that
- Typeform for online surveys and quizzes

While digital product managers will not necessarily hold responsibility for the organisation's overarching strategy, they have a critical role in informing and aligning with it. They recognise that there are many masters to serve and constantly balance the priorities facing the front line and the rest of the organisation.

Digital Engagement Framework

We have explored several important components and enablers for building digital engagement to deliver digital experiences.

To close this chapter and bring it all together, I will leave you with a digital engagement framework which can be used to structure and assess your digital business aspirations. This is the epicentre, and, as with digital product management, should sit at the centre of your digital business.

There are, in my experience, six components that a digital business needs to have in place to excel:

1. Digital engagement strategy: Having a clear digital engagement strategy and culture, effective governance, and a roadmap for digital channels and continuous life cycle management and enhancement.

2. User experience: Designing intuitive and pleasing interactions across digital and offline touch points to enable a simple, easy, and seamless experience to drive advocacy and growth.
3. Digital marketing and execution: Capability to reach audiences in an agile fashion with processes, technology, functionality, and people for efficient delivery of customer, brand, and conversion outcomes.
4. Digital product management: Researching, designing, delivering, and continuously revitalising the proposition and underlying products, services, features, and functionality to solve end user needs while delivering commercial returns.
5. Analytics and insights: Using analytics and insight data intelligently and creatively to improve business and product outcomes and customer engagement. This includes managing analytics data efficiently, ensuring analysis is used in the strategy and design process, and the continuous improvement effort.
6. Development and deployment: Enabling the digital teams and platforms to flex and scale through skills, methodologies, and infrastructure across various devices and technology applications. This includes the management of rigorous but flexible development and deployment processes.

In the framework (Figure 31), I have collated the six components into three layers: strategic, execution, and foundation and identified the core competency under each of the components to illustrate a deep view of what is required.

Working through the organisation, digital analytics, insight development, and deployment are foundational. The marketing, sales, and service team will deliver and execute digital marketing and manage digital products. The executives and the board will govern the strategy, culture, governance, and change management.

This is an organisation's entire portfolio of skills and activities to deliver and support digital experiences. Strategy and governance will be proprietary, but in the execution and foundation layer, much can be outsourced to agencies and partners (which might be the case for smaller businesses).

Many of the skills and activities outlined here will be new to many organisations, but they are well documented and acquirable in a normative market and only those applicable to the digital experiences are required, e.g. B2B will be a subset.

Developing or utilising all the skills in particular contexts may not be necessary. Completion of a skills evaluation using red-amber-green is a useful method on several fronts, e.g.:
1. Evaluating current versus target capability (own or agency/partner)
2. Evaluating the capability required for a specific initiative

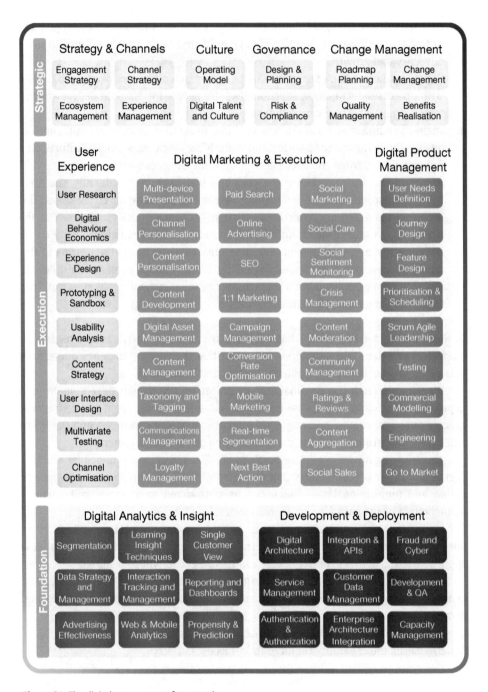

Figure 31: The digital engagement framework.

Case Study: Lululemon – Pivoting Through the Pandemic

Traditionally known for its leggings and yoga pants, Lululemon expanded significantly through the pandemic. While other brands and retailers grappled with store closures and an incredibly turbulent marketplace, Lululemon found success using digital marketing campaigns, opening seasonal stores, and creating a personalised virtual shopping experience while digitally engaging its market to deliver a soothing and successful experience.

In fact, the company increased its brand value by as much as 40% and its web traffic from 23% to 37% during the first 2 months of the pandemic. These numbers are no accident as Lululemon promptly responded to changing consumer habits with a revamped digital and in-store strategy.

Arguably, the team at Lululemon did a better job than any other at connecting with customers who were stuck at home during lockdowns. In April 2020, the brand created something unique for the community that changed its e-commerce sales dramatically: a live video-chat shopping experience.

Equipped with this feature, customers now had the option of scheduling 1:1 video meetings with Lululemon specialists to discuss product sizing, personalised recommendations, gift ideas, and footwear.

Lululemon specialists had also received additional training since the onset of the pandemic. What the brand coined as 'omni-educators' they now work in stores and throughout its digital channels so that customers have access to personalised human experiences.

Although pandemic restrictions have subsided significantly (at the time of writing anyway), roughly one out of four Americans who wear Lululemon continue to work from home. Three out of four stay-at-home workers skip the gym, and four out of ten say they're more motivated to exercise while doing it at home.

These trends played to Lululemon's strengths so much so that the brand needed to find a way to reduce congestion outside their physical stores at the height of Covid. To its benefit, the brand introduced a virtual waitlist, appointment-based visits, and opened 100 pop-up stores in 2020 that eased wait times at larger locations.

One could say that underlying consumer trends played into Lululemon's favour, as the desire for wellness increased through such a testing period. But it was only with the mindset of thinking how they could pivot as a business and redirect their proposition through a new channel strategy, underpinned by a new marketing position, that such as responsive experience was delivered and benefited their base, and as a result their business.

Reflection

– I have left you with a composite picture of what is required to design, deliver, and sustain digital experiences, which sit at the heart of your new digital organisation.
– To keep pace with your customers and their adoption of digital technology, adopt digital channels that allow you to engage with them and truly understand their behaviour.
– For compelling digital experiences, consider your channel strategy, how you will engage with your audience, and what role your channels will take, namely:
    – the physical store, if appropriate (incorporating phygital),
    – phone and chat including instant messaging,
    – online and mobile, and also voice, and
    – social media and the internet, which will extend into Web 3.0.
– Also consider:
    – multi-channels, which simultaneously engage the user across multiple channels;
    – omni-channels, which allow users to move across channels at different points in the journey; and
    – opti-channels, an extension of omni-channels that enable journey shifting and offer the optimal route for the user and the business.
– And finally, do not underestimate the critical role of the digital product manager in providing a targeted strategy for your digital products and marketing. With it, you have the potential to build powerful digital experiences, CXs across your brand, UXs on targeted journeys, complemented by user design focusing on visuals and aesthetics.

Chapter 10
Analytics

. . .design for evolution rather than creating a static design optimizing for the present. – John Hagel

Analytics sits next to digital engagement on the seven-block capability model as it flows in this sequence.

Digital creates a data footprint, with analytics and artificial intelligence (AI), the use of digital technologies to interpret that data and give us either business intelligence, or intelligent-like services that support business, services, and processes. We will uncover the span of intelligence and intelligence-like services that are available for exploitation. We will explore how to develop a strategy that enables data analytics to support business activities and the operating model. We also examine use cases, and some points of caution that go hand in hand with unleashing this perhaps most potent of the capabilities we will cover.

AI's time has come. Although with us since the early twentieth century in its rudimentary format (Alan Turing's work, for instance), it has gone through peaks and troughs of interest (Summers and Winters, respectively) to become one of the most promising, and some also say scariest, technologies of the twenty-first century.

Svetlana Sicular, VP Analyst, Gartner said of AI:

> If AI as a general concept was positioned on this year's Gartner Hype Cycle, it would be rolling off the Peak of Inflated Expectations. By that we mean that AI is starting to deliver on its potential and its benefits for businesses are becoming a reality.

According to the Stanford University 'AI Index Report, 2021',[62] AI investment increased from $12.7 billion in 2015 to $67.8 billion in 2020. Forecasts indicate that the compound annual growth rate for the 2019–2024 period will be 20.1% (source: IDC Research 2020). As for adoption, in the 2021 McKinsey State of AI Report,[63] 56% of respondents report using AI in at least one business function, and 27% of the same respondents reporting at least 5% EBIT attributable to AI, all indicating we are starting to see mass utilisation.

62 Stanford University, "Measuring Trends in Artificial Intelligence – AI Index Report," accessed April 7, 2023, https://aiindex.stanford.edu/ai-index-report-2021/.
63 McKinsey, "The State of AI in 2021 – Survey," (December 8, 2021), accessed April 7, 2023, https://www.mckinsey.com/capabilities/quantumblack/our-insights/global-survey-the-state-of-ai-in-2021.

https://doi.org/10.1515/9783111034713-016

Data Analytics Maturity Model

I have already detailed some of the history of AI; the maturity stages of AI outputs (descriptive to prescriptive); and definitions of algorithms, machine learning, and deep learning in Part I. So, we will dive into a maturity model for AI (Figure 32), which illustrates the application of services across a business panorama.

Analytics and AI, like digital, have the potential to provide value across a 360° business horizon, and as you can see in the model, there are four mega-quadrants for its application: customer, risk, people and organisation, and operations (which includes technology itself).

Data is at the centre of the AI universe (see ring 1), and from there, you can see where AI products (rings 2–5) can be deployed across the four quadrants to release value for various use cases. For example, in the customer quadrant, analytics in rings 2 and 3 can provide a business with deep insights into their customer and provide both business and customer with a single view of their holdings and transactions; these are use cases.

Radiating from there, where we shift from base analytics to AI-powered tools, trained models can provide sales propensity outputs that equip marketeers with subsequent best action recommendations to help ensure the accuracy of campaign relevance. Equally, AI can be deployed to support customers and customer-share responses from vast libraries supporting staff with bots that help to decipher questions coming in on mobile and voice channels using natural language processing, and share responses from vast libraries of potential responses to aid reply.

On the outer rim, the most recent advances in deep learning and Large Language Models (also tagged as Generative AI) help to power machines that can help make decisions, create content, and automate workflow. Examples include robot-advisors that evaluate large swathes of personal data and suggest corresponding financial plans or service bots that engage in real time with customers and end users to solve and execute transactional queries.

As indicated in the model, teams, divisions, businesses, and sectors can map their maturity using the spidergram method giving an overview of where and how AI is exploited, as well as potential use cases and opportunity paths.

As you can imagine, the opportunity for AI use is so vast, I could not possibly follow every use case route here. I can, instead, share with you the fundamental building blocks so that you feel equipped to at least explore the opportunity safely and efficiently. This leads us on to establishing a robust strategy for AI, and a supporting operating model.

Data Analytics Strategy

As we have discovered, data is at the centre and foundation of successful data analytics. Analytics and AI cannot breathe without data, and its provision and ongoing streaming in a safe and compliant way from its potential sources and origins are of

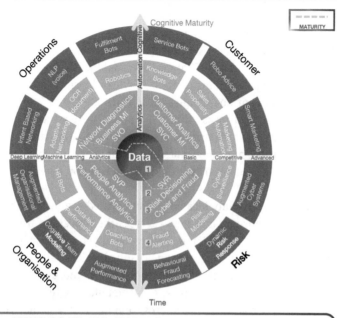

APPLYING DATA ANALYTICS TO THE OPERATING MODEL

- Any Analytics strategy needs to be built on solid data foundations - this is zone 1, the centrepiece of any AI strategy - without it you are blind
- Base case analytics spans maturity zones 2 and 3 - using analytics to describe what happened and why it happened, supporting humans to make better decisions
- Zone 4 relates to the application of machine learning, which is when we start to use the term AI, where outcomes can be predicted and decisions can be made in real time, with human pre-programming
- Zone 5, often correlating with the emerging power of Deep Learning, relates to AI taking action in either supervised or unsupervised ways to respond and act for the business

Above we use the Data Analytics Opportunity Map to illustrate the tools which use Data and Analytical technologies to enable a full spectrum of business services. In zones 2 and 3, the collection and presentation of 'single views' and business intelligence enables business insights and decisioning. This is basic Data Analytics in todays terms. Advanced businesses are using Machine and Deep Learning to augment and automate decisions, or go one step further and create new propositions and business services.

Figure 32: Data analytics opportunity map.

primary concern. This is often in 'big data' warehouses, away from its core systems, where it is busy fuelling data and analytics products. There, it will be 'cleaned' and 'labelled' and prepared for 'interrogation' by advanced algorithms.

Algorithms, for the benefit of clarity, are equations that perform calculations on data sets to derive a decision. That decision could be to present information back to the user, or to carry out an instruction. They can be small or large, and they can be strung together in enormous sequences to calculate the most complex of questions, and conduct associated tasks. Think of Amazon's Alexa as an everyday example. When you instruct Alexa, algorithms (there are quite a few) are listening and converting your speech patterns or linguistics into its language (machine code), then checking that against millions of records it holds in its reference model to correspond with instructions.

Once it has successfully located and confirmed the instruction, it carries it out, comes up with an answer, and then reverses the process to translate the answer it has been trained to locate back into language that you understand.

The same underlying steps are the building blocks of all analytics and AI, including the most recent developments in Generative AI and platforms such as ChatGPT: input a request, translate the request to a computation, find the data to solve it, extract an answer the computation requires from the data, and then report it back.

A final step for an algorithm is to learn and improve. This can happen in one of two ways:

1. An algorithm developer trains the algorithm to improve its accuracy based on the response correctness. This is called supervised learning.
2. Some algorithms are designed and developed to self-learn and correct their own levels of accuracy. This is called unsupervised learning. All algorithms are trained in either manner to a sufficient degree of accuracy to release into production use. But like us humans, self-learning algorithms continue to learn and adjust to get smarter to stay ahead of changing contexts (or we could call them data points).

Data, ingested and stored safely in dedicated warehouses commissioned by data engineers leveraged using data scientists with algorithms, is the foundation of data analytics. Before I move on to the enabling strategy components that surround data and algorithms, I want to draw attention to 'business demand'. In my experience of working with data analytics strategies and businesses on a maturity curve, one of the biggest stalling points (bar not having data) is a lack of business appreciation for what data analytics can do, and therefore, motivation to release data and resources to refine algorithms to deliver business value for specific use cases.

Therefore, I recommend that data analytics is not constructed as a lone wolf in the organisational setting, but much like we have all grown up to appreciate and understand digital, the same needs to be the case for data. Time spent on building a data DNA will be time well spent in terms of opening the eyes of opportunity, equipping your organisation on how to work with data and data analytics teams, and understanding how to mature benefit realisation while offsetting risks. This is when data and resources to translate it into value with data scientists happens, and data analytics can breathe.

Once business demand releases data and resources, and the data foundations and algorithms are in place, it is time to move on to the strategy for AI. This is where the maturity model comes in. A business needs to decide where to point the effort, identifying the most relevant use cases, and put in place enabling components, as follows:

Leadership and Talent

- AI leadership, empowered to drive innovation and make decisions
- Central coordination of strategy and execution, with use cases driven by end users to release value
- AI development plan for all key roles – incorporating developing existing talent, and onboarding new skills
- Leaders model curiosity, upskilling, and transition themselves and their teams along the change management curve

Models, Tools, and Tracking

- Standard enterprise-wide tools, frameworks, and development processes for model development and utilisation
- Automated testing tools and regular model updates
- End-to-end data science platform and computing power
- Value, ethics, and performance tracking

Data Gathering and Management

- Ensuring that a digital business is set up and motivated to gather, classify, hold, and treat data in a secure and reusable format is rudimentary. 'Rubbish in equals rubbish out'.
- Understanding the mix of structured and unstructured data available, structured data is highly specific and stored in a predefined format, whereas unstructured data is a conglomeration of many varied types of data stored in their native formats, as well as internal and external data, and recognising the benefits and limitations of each.
- Identifying the target data required to deliver on the desired holistic range of use cases (here I refer back to the data analytics maturity model as the starting point) and putting plans in place to acquire, gather, and engineer it.

Methods of Working

–   Setting risk appetite and a supportive environment for AI innovation to ensure accuracy benchmarks are met, but acceptance is not stifled by unreasonable demands.
–   A framework for AI governance covering all facets of AI development and related risks.
–   Use case development run books to ensure that business, data, and risk teams can collaborate and create value.
–   Alignment to 'one way for AI' that ensures value taking and risk management optimised – we have seen organisations spring up separate teams with segregated systems and tools that just seem like a waste of scale.
–   Many advanced AI-enabled businesses today are setting up AI centres of excellence (COEs) to provide overall enablers and governance, and particularly the development of reusable models, working hand-in-glove with AIOps (also termed MLOps), which are teams placed in the business and close to the customer who uses the COE outputs to drive AI product delivery for local use cases.
–   Processes for moving from pilots to production.
–   Value mapping and communication methods to share results and learnings.

Benefits Tracking

–   To close the loop on the investment case, digital businesses should engineer benefits tracking to ensure that the expected value identified in use case prioritisation is monitored and results used to refine the use cases, but also sharpen the broader assumption set and prioritisation process.

Ethics

While I will not deep dive into ethics, as it is a complex and much-debated theme given the rise in sophistication, I will share some do's and don'ts from my experience in this area, which should be overseen by a consequence or second-line governance mechanism.

Do:
–   Put the client or user first at all times with empathy
–   Be clear about your intent
–   Ask for and demonstrate 'return on consent'
–   Protect the brand; this is paramount
–   Test all algorithms and data sets for bias, ethics, and morality

Avoid:
- Sharing data with internal or external parties without expressed consent
- Putting commercial returns first
- Having a hidden agenda, or alternative use of data
- Using consent beyond demonstrable value
- Disregarding the value of the brand or putting it at risk
- Ignoring the risks of bias, ethics, and poorly trained algorithms

On a serious note, Epic Games, the developer of the popular video game Fortnite, was fined by the FTC, a staggering $275 million in December 2022 for collecting child data without parental consent. It was simultaneously fined $245 million for using so-called dark patterns, deceptive privacy-invasive default settings and interfaces that tricked Fortnite users, including teenagers and children, into buying in-app purchases.[64] Be warned. It is incumbent on us to understand privacy and the collection of data beyond mere tick boxes and unfortunately regulators have had to deploy rules and laws to manage such issues, so it's not just reputation that is at risk.

These are all the typical components required to launch and sustain a successful data analytics strategy. An additional key component will be a run book and a data analytics team with the business capabilities and communication skills to engage and embrace the business needs to create the demand, bringing it to fruition through analytics products.

If leaders and talent do not exist within the organisations, it is possible to find them externally from the consultancy houses and boutique providers, large and small. They can help to build the investment case and 'fast-forward' value realisation. However, I encourage you to develop a core internal competency for data analytics, given it is a critical component for commercial and competitive longevity.

Data Analytics Use Case Development

It takes a dedicated data analytics leadership team to unlock collaboration in an enterprise setting and to make progress. Developing a run book, ideally with the business, is an excellent way to lay down the tracks to follow. Such a run book needs to marry the engineering requirements with business demand and set down the steps, governance, and hurdles you need to achieve.

---

[64] The Guardian, "Fortnite Video Game Maker to Pay $520m Over Privacy and Billing Claims," (December 19, 2022), accessed April 7, 2023, https://www.theguardian.com/games/2022/dec/19/fortnite-epic-games-pay-fine-ftc-privacy-billing.

Accenture is one of the leaders in data analytics, and share some of the most consumable, instructive, often mundane work to focus on, and insightful materials on the why and how. Their 2020 'Ready. Set. Scale' Report illustrates how to go from idea to production, and then to amplification through continuous engineering and is worth reading. Accenture's research showed that 87% of respondents trying to scale AI were struggling because of a lack of or inappropriate delivery strategy.[65] From my work with clients and research on this, this reflects the reality for most, and their template is a solid place to start.

Data Analytics Benefit Categories

There is often a narrow view of the potential benefits of data analytics scaling.

Data analytics use cases can and should have measurable benefits, but often businesses only measure monetary returns. Delivering value and ROI is crucial, and often robotics process automation is one of the best means to deliver value quickly. However, I encourage data analytics scalers to define the hard and soft benefits for their business: to think of them as sitting on both sides of a benefits axis (a hard side and a soft side) and then put in place departure benchmarking and progress tracking to guide efforts illustrate progress and celebrate.

As regards hard benefits, here are the categories that sit on that side of the scale, and typically the levers I see to unlocking them.

Solving Business Needs

- Find use cases and ambassadors to embed analytics in commercial activities and drive commercial returns.
- 'Industrialise' and reuse analytics products across different use cases for speed and efficiency.
- Build talent in data science, coupled with business engagement and run books to drive more efficient use case development, and ultimately democratisation of algorithms into business teams as self-serve data products.

---

65 Accenture, "Read, Set, Scale Report: What Is the Difference Between Applied and Artificial Intelligence? What is AI?" accessed April 7, 2023, https://www.accenture.com/bg-en/insights/artificial-intelligence/scaling-enterprise-ai.

Data Analytics Operating Model Optimisation

- Develop a unified strategy and shared ownership across segregated AI initiatives, specialists, and business: the sum is always greater than the parts.
- Rationalise vendors and have a coordinated approach to extracting value.
- Cleanse the portfolio by identifying and cleaning redundant and inefficient analytics activities (simplification).

Sweat Data and Technology

- Where possible, use cross-enterprise platforms to deliver more efficient, economical data leverage with reduced maintenance costs – adopting the philosophy of 'reusability' (data, talent, algorithms).
- Build master data management practises and systems to reduce data preparation, transfer, definition, and cleanse overhead.

Productivity

- Automation: Eliminate repetitive, often mundane work to focus on higher-value activities.
- Augmentation: Deliver better quality intelligence faster with recommendations for action.
- Awareness: Provide historically unseen perspectives, opportunities, and risks.

The categories above can be measured and hard monetary value identified, but there are further 'softer' benefits on the other side of the scale that are not to be sniffed at.

Culture

- Awareness: Improved visibility and awareness of analytics as an enabler and value creator.
- Adoption: Enterprise-wide adoption of analytics to support decision-making at all levels.
- Celebration: Reward and celebrate AI-driven success to re-enforce adoption and build brand.

Innovation

- Harness data to understand the proposition, operational and market value, and destroyers.
- Data as a core value barometer of innovation value.
- Spin off analytics as a service to bolster propositions or as payback for the investment.

Solving the business needs is the destination point for scaling data analytics. This is the best and probably only way to secure motivation and the resulting data, resources, and management time. However, as is often the case, there is a maturity to realising significant gains, and often organisations need to temper those and allow the capability to build and culture and adoption to flourish. Hence, I see organisations have equal focus on soft and hard benefits at the start of their journeys and, over time, tipping the scales towards hard business value, but always keeping some degree of duality.

Value mapping is also used to categorise and extract the value of data analytics for the business and can be a critical lever and fundamental to unlocking organisational demand. In fact, I believe it should be central to the prioritisation of focus and initiatives. Value mapping is the process of breaking down where data analytics can be deployed in the organisation, and effort:impact mapping the value to be gained. On the impact side, we have seen useful benchmarking from data analytics consultancies such as McKinsey that have the use case history and expertise to give an order of magnitude. Value mapping is an excellent means to 'clear the path' and shine a light on benefits, and zones of value. Note: this approach is useful across all the digital business capabilities.

Analytics Products

So far we have covered the why, the what, and the how to leverage data analytics. We will now close the loop by connecting that effort and investment with the outputs of data analytics back to those maturity stages.

For the sake of universality and reach, I will use Disney+ again as an example. To understand the maturity of data analytics and visually bring it to life, you will see from Figure 33 that the four maturity steps of data analytics are tracked through to the core features in the Disney+ experience. The analytical sourced insights behind each are the outputs or products that analytics teams share with their digital business, which are converted to a value exchanged with us, the user.

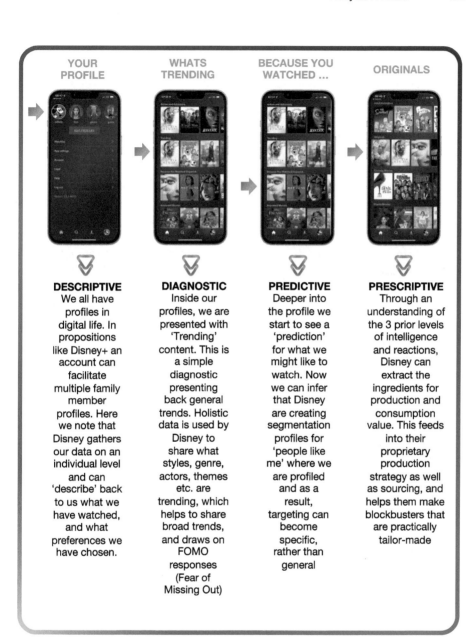

DESCRIPTIVE
We all have profiles in digital life. In propositions like Disney+ an account can facilitate multiple family member profiles. Here we note that Disney gathers our data on an individual level and can 'describe' back to us what we have watched, and what preferences we have chosen.

DIAGNOSTIC
Inside our profiles, we are presented with 'Trending' content. This is a simple diagnostic presenting back general trends. Holistic data is used by Disney to share what styles, genre, actors, themes etc. are trending, which helps to share broad trends, and draws on FOMO responses (Fear of Missing Out)

PREDICTIVE
Deeper into the profile we start to see a 'prediction' for what we might like to watch. Now we can infer that Disney are creating segmentation profiles for 'people like me' where we are profiled and as a result, targeting can become specific, rather than general

PRESCRIPTIVE
Through an understanding of the 3 prior levels of intelligence and reactions, Disney can extract the ingredients for production and consumption value. This feeds into their proprietary production strategy as well as sourcing, and helps them make blockbusters that are practically tailor-made

Figure 33: Analytics products.

Getting Started

You may already be on the journey, so I hope that the shared perspectives resonate with you and help draw out future building blocks and enablers to leverage data and analytics.

Or, you may be at the start of your journey. If so, it may be daunting as it will be very new. But as with all things in life, there is only one way to start – get started. This usually follows three steps:

1. Mobilise – Bring the key contributors together and lay down the foundations:
    -   Bring people from data and technology together with digital and business teams to define a vision for data analytics, including key objectives and outcomes.
    -   Using the likes of the data analytics maturity model, develop an initial list of use cases for prioritisation in a backlog – business areas need to be involved here as they will need to unlock the data, resources, and ultimately use analytics products to release value. Risk and compliance are vital stakeholders here too as any analytics development team will have to satisfy themselves that they are morally, legally, and regulatorily sound.
    -   Develop an agile governance run book that helps to set out the work that needs to be done, who will do it, and governance that balances risk and reward.
    -   Secure 'get going' budget and identify the target data and technologies that you need to bring into production; this is a go/no go step at this point, but once data and tools with governance are in place, it is possible to proceed.
2. Assemble – Resource up a cross-skilled team to turn intent into reality:
    -   Brief, excite, and bring together a cross-functional team from the key contributing areas mentioned above; this should be led by use case business owners (there may be multiple owners), supported by data and model specialists.
    -   Infuse data engineers and scientists with scrum/delivery capability and ensure it is underpinned by support functions, including risk, compliance, and also finance (for business case development).
3. Explore – Design and develop proof-of-concept (POC) use cases that can go on to be scaled/reused, but importantly at this early stage, learning is as or more important as a value point:
    -   Using agile methodologies, draw from the backlog of use cases.
    -   Develop POCs to test the run book, the data, and the technologies and algorithms – this may be a repeating step until the team can be happy with the first product that they are willing to trial with end users.
    -   Scale up or step out, depending on early value realisation.
    -   Use learnings to enhance the run book, data management, and algorithms and products.
    -   Build the operating model and a blueprint for industrialised data analytics.

Time, data, persistence, and a balanced view of hard and soft value are essential ingredients on the road to success.

Data analytics offers real potential for practically every business. It is a downstream beneficiary of digitalisation and, in many ways, how digital manifests in better experiences and growth through smarter business services.

I briefly mentioned agile methodologies. You will have heard or expect that agile occurs in every part of the digital business landscape. Next, we will explore what agile is and how it can be used to support creativity, velocity, and value creation.

Case Study: Marriott's Starwood – Leveraging Data to Sharpen Profit and Personalisation

Starwood Hotels (one of the brands under Marriott Hotels) use dynamic pricing. It changes based on a variety of factors, such as local and global economic situation, weather, availability and reservation behaviour, and cancellations. This tactic has resulted in a 5% revenue increase per room.

They go so deep with utilising data that they even follow if famous musicians are playing at the Madison Square Garden, so they can adjust their rates at their nearby hotels.

To create a better customer experience, they have begun testing out facial recognition check-ins. Their guests don't need to wait at the reception desk anymore, and the hotel gathers even more valuable information. Another element they have implemented to gather data is installing Amazon Echos into the rooms. This allows guests to make Alexa handle everything that was previously handled by reception staff. Now guests can get all the information they want, while Marriott gets the knowledge of their customer's preferences, needs, and potential concerns.

Case Study: Uber Eats – Leveraging Data to Optimise Logistics and a Better End User Experience

Uber entered the saturated market of food delivery and thrived, thanks to data. They wanted to be recognised as a delivery genius that delivers food while it is still warm, so they tried to model the physical world in a way that would allow them to be as accurate as possible when predicting the time of food delivery.

To make this work, they collected the data of how much time it usually takes to prepare a certain meal, so they could pinpoint the exact time when the delivery person should come and pick it up.

This action allows the drivers to pick up more meals on their way (as they don't have to wait for the food to be prepared) and Uber encourages them to carry more than one meal per trip with a bonus for each meal they collect.

This, however, is not something that has never been done before, but by using data, they are doing it better than anyone before.

What Uber Eats is doing is a textbook example of how big data and data analytics can help businesses expand their services and give them a clear advantage over their competitors.

Reflection

– Digital creates a data footprint, with analytics and AI used to interpret that data to deliver value through knowledge and action.
– It provides value across a 360° business horizon, specifically across four quadrants of the business: customer, risk, people and organisation, and operations, including technology. It is, therefore, essential and integral to your business, in supporting your processes and services.
– The data maturity model illustrates how AI can be applied throughout the business, namely:
  – leadership and talent,
  – tools and tracking,
  – data gathering,
  – methods of working, and
  – tracking benefits.
– But analytics needs to be built on strong foundations, so get the data structured and housed for leverage.
– Set up to test and learn, and don't forget the hard and soft benefits axis.
– Observe for and govern misuse, and connect products with value.
– Designing data propositions take dedication and, often, specialised teams to help unlock potential in the organisation. Developing run books with data analytics can help you get started on this part of your transformation journey, helping you align the engineering requirements with business demand.

Chapter 11
Agile

If everyone is moving forward together, then success takes care of itself. – Henry Ford

Agile is a much-flouted term, and unfortunately misunderstood given it has many variances and circumstantial applications. While we look at those variations and divergences in this chapter, it is important to retain an overarching perspective of why agile is a vital digital capability.

The pace of change, propelled by digital and driving downstream end user expectations to higher levels, demands that organisations respond fast or lose ground. Technology services (hardware, software, and cloud) enable rapid development, deployment, and analytical tracking of digital propositions.

The result of these unified complimentary forces is that businesses can adopt a newfound, rapid, and perpetuating cycle of designing, delivering, and testing end user digital value. This contrasts significantly with traditional development methods, broadly defined as waterfall or linear sequential life cycle methods to be more technical, and is a game-changer.

Agile accelerates pace and creativity, reduces risk, and increases potency by putting the end user at the centre of shortening delivery cycles.

The Back Story

At the turn of this millennium, 17 eminent software development leaders gathered to consolidate an emerging demand to reshape software development. New models were already emerging such as Extreme Programming and Scrum, but the Agile Manifesto issued in Spring 2001 was the culmination of a new philosophy and shared in Table 4.

With an overarching aim to support the software development industry, the Manifesto[66] espoused 4 key values, backed by 12 principles which we lay out below and are particularly important. They set out a well-rounded and grounded 'modus vivendi' for digital leaders and their teams. I believe that understanding and adopting these guide rails are more important than a specific method of applications, for reasons we will uncover.

Agile is often confused with terms like Scrum, Sprints, and Kanban. However, these terms relate to specific doctrines of implementing the 'Agile Way'.

---

[66] Agile Manifesto, "Manifesto for Agile Software Development," accessed April 7, 2023, https://agilemanifesto.org/.

https://doi.org/10.1515/9783111034713-017

Table 4: The Agile manifesto.

Agile manifesto	4 principles	12 principles
We are uncovering better ways of developing software by doing it and helping others do it. Through this work we have come to value.	1. Individuals and interactions over process and tools. 2. Working software over comprehensive documentation. 3. Customer collaboration over contract negotiation. 4. Responding to change over following a plan. *That is, while there is value in the items at the end, we value the items at the start more*	1. Our highest priority is to satisfy the customer through early and continuous delivery of valuable software. 2. Welcome changing requirements, even late in development. Agile processes harness change for the customer's competitive advantage. 3. Deliver working software frequently, from a couple of weeks to a couple of months, with a preference to the shorter timescale. 4. Business people and developers must work together daily throughout the project. 5. Build projects around motivated individuals. Give them the environment and support they need and trust them to get the job done. 6. The most efficient and effective method of conveying information to and within a development team is face-to-face conversation. 7. Working software is the primary measure of progress. 8. Agile processes promote sustainable development. The sponsors, developers, and users should be able to maintain a constant pace indefinitely. 9. Continuous attention to technical excellence and good design enhances agility. 10. Simplicity – the art of maximising the amount of work not done – is essential. 11. The best architectures, requirements, and designs emerge from self-organising teams. 12. At regular intervals, the team reflects on how to become more effective, then tunes and adjusts its behaviour accordingly.

The Agile Shift

Working with software has facilitated a new organisational shift. Adopting the agile philosophy has allowed organisations to break down the hierarchical structures that served businesses in the last industrial revolution, where product, certainty, and scale trumped.

Today, customer-centricity, speed to market, and digital experiences are the sought-after needs. Organising work, talent, and focus in smaller, self-empowered teams that break work up into incremental mini-developments, guided by prioritised customer-driven objectives, is at the heart of the agile shift.

Digital businesses embrace agile not just because of software development but because it aligns with modern leadership theory. Leadership theory is a complex affair. A summary of the macro-movement cites that leadership evolved from top-down styles in the 1920s, e.g. Great Man and Trait theories, to the adaptive leader in the middle of the twentieth century, for example, behavioural, situational, and contingency theories.

What then followed was the emergence of transformational leadership in the latter quarter of the twentieth century, e.g. transformational, collaborative, and servant leadership, to distributed leadership in the twenty-first century, extending into social network, and to what we see today, neuroscience-based leadership.

We see this played out in organisations today in their formation and operation. For example, whereas in the past we saw hierarchical business functions (and perhaps still see this structure in legacy organisations), today agile businesses are organised into 'sprint teams' or squads working across an organisation in a dispersed way.

In the past teams were formed slowly over time as new products and services were developed, thus creating silos, with managers overseeing departments or sections. Today, an agile organisation assembles and dismantles quickly as projects and assignments are assigned to experts for the project. 'Managers' do not manage in the traditional sense but guide the project and sponsor talent as appropriate.

Legacy silos are replaced with open spaces. Seating is arranged for cross-functional collaboration, and where people were rewarded by level or tenure, with a leader-follower culture (think, individualism, directive, competitive, and captive), agile businesses have a leader-leader culture of citizenship and empowerment. There is collective thinking with shared values, and people are rewarded by outcomes, reputation, and collaborative effort.

I have summarised the shift from traditional ways of working to the agile organisation in Figure 34.

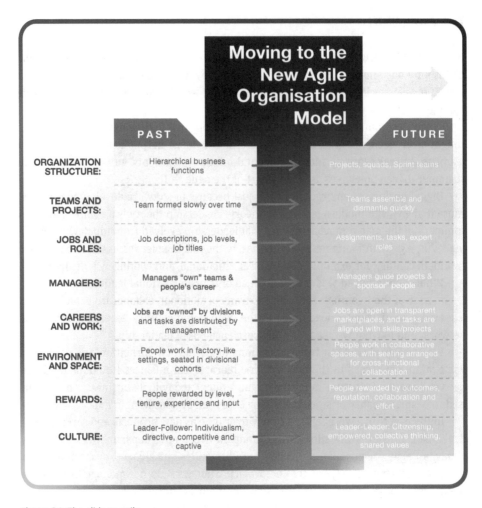

Figure 34: The glide to agile.

Scrum at the Centre

The most recognised of the agile methodologies is Scrum. It is built on empiricism, focusing on small increments of work with constant learning from end user feedback that better informs what you do next.

The work is orchestrated by a Scrum Master. Priorities are set by grooming the backlogs, and the product owner calls the priorities if needed. Ceremonies such as Sprint Planning, Daily Scrum, and Retrospectives are central to matching end user improvements with team and process improvement. The Scrum process is visualised in Table 5, but remember variations are often applied as teams iterate for their needs.

Table 5: The Scrum process.

Product backlog	Sprint backlog	The sprint	Daily scrum	Increment	Sprint review
– List of requirements for the new product can be changed and adapted at any time – Requirements are prioritised and divided into work packages	– Splitting the work package into smaller packages and allocating them to team members – Documentation of the remaining work for each package	– Current iteration – Implementation of a work package – Fixed duration (time boxed) – Results in a functional intermediate result	– Daily 15 min meeting – Information sharing and progress unblocking – Everyone always knows what each team member is working on at the moment	– Work package that is not modified during the sprint – Functional intermediate result (increment of potentially shippable functionality)	– The team presents the intermediate result to the product owner and stakeholders – Feedback is integrated into the next sprint

Headline Stages for Stepping Into Agile

What might an agile organisation look like in the context of a working project?

1. A business forms a small, focused, cross-functional, self-managed team to tackle a customer need. The product owner builds a list of ideas or features. This person typically divides time between the agile team and key stakeholders.
2. The product owner continuously ranks a list of features based on the latest estimates of value to customers, financial results, and impact. A process facilitator (Scrum Master) protects the team from distractions and puts its collective intelligence to work.
3. The team then deconstructs top-priority items into small modules and decides how much work to take on and how. They build working versions in short sprints.
4. Team members hold daily meetings to review progress and identify impediments (often called the 'Daily Scrum'). Disagreements get resolved via experimental feedback loops instead of internal debates or appeals to authority.
5. Teams test small working increments with groups of potential customers. If the customer gets excited, the increment may be released immediately, even if other stakeholders feel it is not ready.
6. The team brainstorms ways to improve future cycles through a ceremony called a retrospective. Likewise, the team prepares to go after the next top priority on the list.

You will notice that the steps I have outlined here resemble the digital product management approach outlined under digital engagement. Agile is at the centre of digital product management, and the product owner is the same as the digital product manager.

Underpinning this way of working are several enabling pillars that must take place:

- **Value:** Understanding where value is created in the industry and where the company needs to be distinctive, as well as mapping back how and where that value is released in the business. This helps to identify areas that might benefit from greater agile development.
- **Structure:** Identify the right agile methodology and tools for the company at that point in time through experimentation and defining 'our way'. This is best implemented through experimentation, collaboration, and I highly recommend writing it down, using visualisation and mini-branding to bring it to life. The focus should be on teams, not individuals, and bring in external coaches to get going if appropriate.
- **Roles:** Defining the key roles in each squad and enabling like-roles to convene regularly to knowledge share. Skills development through peer learning is implicit, and regular external education and exposure to best-in-class practices are strongly recommended.
- **North Star:** The backbone should be the core processes, people, and technology to enable agility. Identify required changes in culture and mindsets, and be sure that everyone, across all teams, is working to a North Star, adopting common practices and tools.
- **Develop a high-level roadmap:** Decide on an implementation approach. Create a backlog list and prioritise immediate next steps. Engage sponsors regularly to share progress and learning – encourage leaders to guide with questions. Sponsorship is key.

The Kanban

Kanban adopts the agile principles but is more applicable to teams with many incoming requests, as opposed to a very defined scope (e.g. a product to manage).

Using a Kanban board allows the team to review these requests and constantly prioritise them, which allows more adaptable reprioritisation. You will probably find Kanban in use where there are many product owners, a heavy operational focus, and, therefore, synonymous with DevOps (Constantly Developing while in Operation, also called CICD, Continuous Integration and Continuous Delivery), although this is also found in Scrum.

The main ceremony for Kanban teams is a daily stand-up (similar to Daily Scrum), although they also undertake stand backs. While there is sometimes an agile coach, there is no single 'product owner'. The team owns engaging end users, the stakeholders, and the organisation. Many non-software teams also use Kanban, e.g. HR and finance. Kanban and daily stand-ups can also be mobilised at the executive leadership team level. It helps with regular rhythm and strategic bind. Many teams pick and choose from both schools or borrow from others such as extreme programming and lead development to create their own 'blueprint'.

Table 6 illustrates the contrast between Scrum and Kanban as the two main houses of agile in use.

Many teams pick and choose from both schools or borrow from others such as extreme programming and lead development to create their own 'blueprint'.

Table 6: The Scrum versus Kanban process.

Scrum		Kanban
Scrum comes with three roles: product owner, Scrum master, and Scrum team.	Roles	It doesn't necessarily recommend a set of roles. Yet, sometimes there are roles such as service delivery and request managers.
Scrum involves planning before the start of each sprint.	Planning	Kanban doesn't require pre-planning, as the approach is constant planning review (other than end user research).
Each sprint lasts between 1 and 4 weeks. After the sprint, working software must be delivered.	Time delivery	There are no time-boxes and deadlines – the team is constantly releasing working software.
Velocity and capacity charts help teams track the overall Scrum progress – these are known as burndown metrics and some teams use a points system.	OKRs	Lead and cycle time help the team determine the time it takes you to finish a task, and measure performance.
Daily sprint stand-ups are encouraged, so the team is on the same page, share problems, and learn.	Meetings	Meeting are not necessarily required. Yet, many Kanban teams do daily stand-ups.
The Scrum board consists of all the tasks without having specific columns. The Scrum board is reset after each sprint.	Boards	The Kanban board features 'To-do', 'Work in progress', and 'Done', 'In Review', and 'Blocked' columns (typically).

There are at least 50 known and published agile methodologies and growing. There are likely to be many more as organisations discover, trial, and create their own 'systems' tailored to their circumstances, using their own lexicon. This is to be encouraged as the stretched-to-fit practice is much more likely to stick. But I recommend practitioner audits and constant review through retrospectives. Other software platforms support an agile approach, such as Jira and Smartsheet.

Again, teams should experiment and tailor to suit.

Many organisations come from a lineage of waterfall delivery which entails a clearly defined sequence of execution with project phases that do not advance until a phase receives final approval. Once a phase is completed, it can be difficult and costly to revisit a previous stage. While it brings a certain amount of certainty, it also has its drawbacks.[67] The shift from waterfall to agile is big, and not to be underestimated and I have outlined the big shifts in Table 7.

Table 7: Waterfall versus agile.

Waterfall		Agile
Large, functionally organised teams that work in parallel	**Team and work**	Small, cross-functional teams that work collaboratively and in coordination
Heavy at the beginning on requirements gathering, and end for testing and acceptance	**Customer and business involvement**	Constant engagement, collaboration, and inclusion
Predict and design all features up front with exhaustive documentation	**Design**	Modularised and prioritised design approach, with frequent revisions and reprioritisation
Build all features at once to exact specifications	**Development**	Iterative – build what is in scope, and proving valuable
Large, infrequent releases – integrate and test when development is complete	**Delivery, testing, and integration**	Rapid, frequent increments – continuous, real-time testing and integration
Reduced visibility, adaptability, and time to market increases risk	**Risk**	Increased visibility, adaptability, and time to market reduces risk

The risk profile is often misunderstood by businesses when they are pre-agile. Leaders are conditioned to putting their finger on a proposed delivery and date. Whereas with an agile approach to working, they need to trust the team and the process. Agile projects are reported to have double-digital benefits across metrics such as speed to market, delivery cost, customer feedback, and team engagement, including higher software quality. The ability of the organisation to blend waterfall with an agile approach and to formulate a proprietary version of agile are important enablers.

Scaling Agile When Agile Moves to the Centre

Some organisations are keen to adopt an agile approach, either through experience or observation, and seek to scale and embed it organisation wide. This is usually because of the benefits outlined so far, but it comes with a warning. As outlined in the Harvard

---

67 McKinsey, "The Five Trademarks of Agile Organisations," (March 1, 2018), accessed April 7, 2023, https://www.mckinsey.com/capabilities/people-and-organizational-performance/our-insights/the-five-trademarks-of-agile-organizations.

Business Review's article 'Agile at Scale', not every function needs an agile team, and caution must be exercised against launching organisational-wide agile teams without careful consideration, as it risks bottlenecks in collaboration.[68]

In addition to adopting an agile approach, a business needs to review and potentially evolve its budgeting process to remove friction or disturbance and align on expectations.

Scaling agile is not for the faint-hearted and is an operating model and cultural transformation. It should be approached with a transition mindset, where the effectiveness and stickiness of agile working can be tested in different areas. Figure 35 shows organisational concepts from scaled agile, which is well cited as the 'Spotify Model', and illustrates how squads, tribes, chapters, and guilds work.

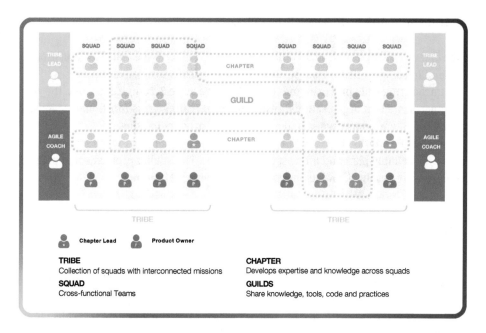

Figure 35: Scaled agile at Spotify.

SAFe® for Lean Enterprises is a knowledge base of proven, integrated principles, practices, and competencies for achieving business agility using Lean, Agile, and DevOps. The latest version, SAFe 5, is built around the seven core competencies of the Lean Enterprise that are critical to achieving and sustaining a competitive advantage.[69]

---

68 Harvard Business Review, "Agile at Scale – How to Go from a Few Teams to Hundreds," Darrell Rigby, Jeff Sutherland, and Andy Noble, accessed April 7, 2023, https://hbr.org/2018/05/agile-at-scale.
69 Scaled Agile Framework, "SAFE Scaled Agile," accessed April 7, 2023, https://www.scaledagileframework.com/.

In summary, as once said by Felix Hieronymi, a software engineer turned agile expert at Bosch where agile working has been extensively and successfully deployed, 'You cannot gain this experience by reading a book'.

As central to delivering the digital experience for the business, agile needs to be experienced. Once it is, it liberates the company. It decentralises control, allowing experts and teams within the organisation to have greater control over projects. Decisions are made quicker, and ultimately, changes are made for a better end user experience.

Now that we have unravelled agile, we will move on to innovation, another culturally and experientially steeped capability where agile nestles perfectly.

Case Study: John Deere – Sorting Out the Backlogs

John Deere wrestled with missed delivery dates, quality issues, and lack of product ownership using a release train scaling approach to software delivery.

Introducing agile practices and the LeSS (Large-Scale Scrum) framework, the company performed an organisational restructuring, creating cross-functional, co-located teams, a single product owner, and a high-quality product backlog.

Within 6 months, the company saw improvements. Teams were more focused and could reliably plan and forecast delivery dates. The quality problems that plagued releases were resolved, and teams consistently delivered on time.

Reflection

- Agile is a cultural shift in working. Originally adapted to working with software, it is now deployed across digital businesses (and other modern organisations) to executive projects rapidly.
- Digital businesses embrace an agile approach to working, not only because it enables quicker development of technology, but because it aligns with modern leadership. Adopting this style of leadership and working has allowed organisations to break down the legacy-style, product-based hierarchical structures for a decentralised, customer centricity.
- Agile teams are organised into small cross-functional groups that are self-managed and self-empowered with collective objectives using a variety of the agile schools (Scrum, Kanban, etc.)
- While caution must be exercised over implementing agile teams organisation wide (regularly reviewing to remove friction or bottlenecks), the agile approach is central to a modern digital business.

- Digital transformation is impossible if the organisation is inefficient (services, processes, and people). Similarly, efficiency is not possible if silos and bottlenecks hamper creativity and innovation.
- When implemented carefully, the agile approach will enhance the business model enabling speed to market, efficient delivery cost, customer feedback, team engagement, and higher software quality. This in turn is passed on to your end user as enhanced value.

Chapter 12
Innovation

The best way to predict the future is to invent it. – Alan Kay

In the digital age, innovation requires agility, hence the link. An agile philosophy and its associated methods should underpin innovation, whether leveraging pre-existing capability or part of establishing innovation capability, which we should recognise is a taller ask.

Innovation is often defined as a new idea, method, service, or product. But it extends to the improvement of services or products already in existence, and the acceleration of change in product development. That is a broad canvas to work on, so in this chapter, we will spend time appreciating the different 'innovation territories', how to apply them, and what it takes to drive them. We will also explore how to unlock innovation within the organisations, along with some of the pitfalls to navigate.

Innovation is implicit for businesses to compete and win in the digital age; standing still is not an option. The current competitive environment is too vigorous, the tools too potent, and the opportunity too great. It could be said that you need to innovate or die, but a more positive view is to innovate to thrive. I like to take the latter, knowing that the former is the de facto default.

According to Innosight's Biennial Corporate longevity reports, corporate longevity remains in long-term decline. Their latest analysis shows the 30- to 35-year average tenure of S&P 500 companies in the late 1970s is forecast to shrink to 15–20 years this decade.[70]

On the flip side, McKinsey reports that those who pursue innovation as a core competency see a delta in value (and, therefore returns), particularly through a crisis, which is more frequently felt.[71]

Innovation Horizons

They say that the oldies are the best, and that is the case for McKinsey's Three Horizons of Innovation first articulated in 2000. It depicts a mental model to help business leaders categorise and allocate resources to innovation[72] across:

---

[70] Innosight, "2021 Corporate Longevity Forecast," S. Patrick Viguerie, Ned Calder, and Brian Hindo (May 2021), accessed April 7, 2023, https://www.innosight.com/insight/creative-destruction/.
[71] McKinsey, "Innovation in a Crisis: Why It Is More Critical than Ever," (June 17, 2020), accessed April 7, 2023, https://www.mckinsey.com/capabilities/strategy-and-corporate-finance/our-insights/innovation-in-a-crisis-why-it-is-more-critical-than-ever.
[72] McKinsey, "Enduring Ideas: The Three Horizons of Growth," (December 1, 2009), accessed April 7, 2023, https://www.mckinsey.com/capabilities/strategy-and-corporate-finance/our-insights/enduring-ideas-the-three-horizons-of-growth.

https://doi.org/10.1515/9783111034713-018

- existing products and services,
- extension into new products and markets, and
- the creation of new markets

One of the more recent challenges with the model was the interpretation that innovation was sequential, starting with core and moving out, or that transformational innovation on Horizon 3 took a long time or happened later. The reality is that organisations today are encouraged, or required, to innovate across all three horizons simultaneously. We will call this multispeed innovation. Deloitte has done an excellent job of reinvigorating how and where to apply multiple pursuits of innovation concurrently in an organisational setting (see Figure 39 – Deloitte's Innovation Framework), and I recommend this multispeed approach.

As you will see, they suggest that product service and line of business teams should allocate resources to innovation in core activities with a near- to medium-term value realisation timeline. Through partnerships, incubators and R&D, they recommend running parallel and complementary innovation activity in adjacent lines and new territories for immediate, medium- and long-term value creation.

The idea of multimodal innovation is what I aspire to, extracting value from today, which means evolving the core. Creating opportunity for tomorrow means extending the core while defining new value or building the next core.

This links back to our jumping the S-curve and strategic portfolio management, and also correlates to the triple-tier journey mapping we covered under customer-centricity. You can read more about Deloitte's thinking on product innovation and governance at Deloitte.com.[73]

Multimodalism

Multispeed innovation requires a multispeed set-up and disposition as it means running multiple modes of innovation in parallel.

Table 8 articulates three innovation stances: exploitative, extending, and exploratory. As you can see, the focus of the business drives the degree of freedom, resulting OKRs and the type of environment required.

Also note that the proximity to the current core drives the degree of freedom of exploration, risk, and culture. But as importantly, we start to extract that running multiple modes at once results in the need to be ambidextrous (this means deploying multiple practices simultaneously). This can be a cognitive stretch and one that needs both leadership discipline and organisational engineering and tooling, which we will move on to next.

---

73 Deloitte, "Digital Product Management – A Structured Approach to Product Innovation and Governance," (October 18, 2009), accessed April 7, 2023, https://www2.deloitte.com/us/en/insights/focus/industry-4-0/product-innovation-and-governance.html.

Table 8: Multimodalism.

Multimodal – the ability to run parallel tracks at different speeds			
Stance	**Exploitative**	**Extending**	**Exploratory**
Modes of innovation	Sustaining innovation – Horizon 1	Developmental innovation – Horizon 2	Disruptive innovation – Horizon 3
Strategic intent	Cost and profit – sweating the core assets	Diversification and growth – stretching the core	Experimentation, learning, and growth – probing for new cores
Focus	Efficiency, squeeze assets, lengthen plateaus/sustainability	Renewal, new territories, defence/offence	New business models and competitive disadvantage
OKRs	Margins, productivity, and return on investment	Acquisition, market share/diversification, and payback	Learning, venture building, and brand
Culture	Lean, low risk, and incremental	Assertive, risk accepting, and flexible	Rapid, risk taking, and curious
Leadership	Authoritative, top down	Focused, stretching	Visionary, empowering

Innovation Architecture

To establish multimodal innovation muscles, there are some much-desired, and I would say, essential building blocks that need to be implemented or aimed for.

At a foundational level, both budget and focus need to be in place as part of the digitally enabled strategy and portfolio approach outlined in Part II. The former becomes evident when environments (physical space, and digital sandboxes) and an allocation of resources are in place. This could be a mix of internal willing participants and often external new thinkers. Getting the balance right is important, as ultimately a business pursuing innovation will seek to grow its own innovators. At times, they need help with new ways of working and thinking; hence the mix is ascribed.

As part of the foundations, I also mentioned focus. By focus, I mean, which of the modes are in scope and what developmental themes relate. What are the associated expectations or return on innovation envisioned, and what degree of risk is expected. We also call this risk appetite, and it increases as we move from sustaining through developmental and out to disruptive.

Regarding return on innovation, we come back to our currencies idea that commercial and knowledge return are an essential duality to manage. In the Sustaining mode, commercial is the primary currency, but some learning through experimentation, is also important. As we move out through developmental and into disruptive innovation, learning becomes more elevated on a few fronts, and are all with a view to ultimately deriving commercial value:

– Learning about what markets, problems to solve for, and what trends to embrace – whether technological, social, or political which facilitates direction setting
– Learning about new ways to innovate, whether that be through data, new technologies, or new means, for example, partnerships
– Learning through experimentation, what has promise, and what does not

Reward always needs to link to return, and should follow the sliding scale of commercial and learning currency associated with each mode. In the sustaining mode, realising immediate commercial value is the focus. In the disruptive mode, understanding, harnessing, and gleaning insight on where commercial value can be created through experimentation (but ultimately the launch of new ventures) is the focus of reward.

Sustaining Innovation

In this mode, businesses are solution oriented – they are focused on solving for pain points or seeking out incremental improvements in existing propositions to fend off competition, gain marginal momentum in the market, improve customer experience, and increase customer loyalty or take out fat. As per this last point, sustaining innovation is often the Efficiency work we walked through earlier.

The focus of sustaining innovation activities revolves around:

– The problem is well understood
– There's an existing market
– Innovation will focus on improving performance, lowering cost, and is incremental
– We know what the customer and end user want and/or need
– The market is predictable
– Traditional business methods are sufficient

Good examples include bug fixes and new features in our software and hardware (think Tesla or iOS upgrades), and prioritisation and execution for themes are extracted from tracking and extracting insights from our operations and markets today.

Lean and agile methodologies are used to execute, often within existing operational and production teams, using simple techniques such as business process re-engineering and continuous improvements as well as workouts and simplification programmes. But I am surprised that more of this activity does not ensue in this first mode. Too often, I see teams complacent and wishing if not critical that someone else is not improving things. Continuous assessment and scheduling of simple change is the hallmark of the digital business.

Developmental Innovation

Here I often find businesses becoming active on problem-solving – they have a concrete view on where threat or opportunity may lie, and have the appetite and mandate to pursue value creation (or value avoidance, or a mix, e.g. create new value to offset eroding value creation – again think of the s-curves).

The focus of developmental innovation activities revolves around:
- Problems (emulating from friction in customer jobs) that have been identified from existing propositions in market that need to be explored
- The opportunity to extend current propositions into adjacent markets
- Taking a core asset or competency into a new territory, for example, leveraging unique skills or service such as an internal manufacturing service to build an outsourcing service (think how Amazon developed its internal cloud and analytics services and then went to market as a B2B offering through Amazon Web Services)
- The customer may not know what they need, but they know what they want, for example, the form factor of the first smartphones was prohibitive for comfortable continuous streaming or office workflow, and hence the tablet was born
- The size of the market is quantifiable, albeit not proven

The business model may be evolved, and this may be the focus of the innovation. For example, in 2000, Michelin, a global leader in tyre manufacturing, made the leap from selling tyres as units to providing tyres as a service – fleet solutions.[74]

In this mode of innovation, businesses will use many of the tools we explored in our chapter on customer-centricity, such as personal development, design thinking, prototyping, journey mapping, and experience design to name a few. But a cornerstone will be data to guide on what problems are the biggest to solve, and in what markets they may have the biggest impact.

Another untapped source of potential in this space is co-creation and crowdsourcing. We are all bounded by the horizon we see, and the knowledge we bear. We all know something interesting (or scary) lives beyond the horizon but we are constrained from freeing our minds by not being able to see it. Convening, co-ideating, and collaborating with like-minded curious souls is often an accelerator and liberator for finding bold new territories and positions.

Philips,[75] the Dutch manufacturing conglomerate, identified the internet of things (IoT – connecting physical assets over the internet to share data and process tasks as a result) as a potential competitive game changer. With this opportunity, they set the task of exploring what jobs their customers were trying to do in their homes with Phi-

74 Harvard MBA Student Perspectives, "Michelin: Tires-as-a-Service," (November 17, 2016), accessed April 7, 2023, https://d3.harvard.edu/platform-rctom/submission/michelin-tires-as-a-service/.

75 Harvard MBA Student Perspective, "A Bright Future for Philips," (November 16, 2016), accessed April 7, 2023, https://d3.harvard.edu/platform-rctom/submission/a-bright-future-for-philips/.

lips products, such as light bulbs, baby monitors, and air purifiers. The insight Philips gleaned was that their customers wanted control to create a safer yet more ambient place to live and relax.

This led Philips to utilise the IoT and connect what we would call 'dumb' products such as light-bulbs, baby monitors, and air purifiers, to smartphone-enabled controls to make them smart products. This allowed customers to change the hue of the lighting, feel closer to their babies, even though they could be in the room next door, and adjust the airflow to create a cleaner living environment.

To enable Philips to move from opportunity to solution, they work with Berlin-based 'Plug&Play', which specialises in collaborating with upcoming tech start-ups to accelerate solutions to markets while it keeps its core business focused on scaled production and distribution. Plug&Play filter, host, and connect Philips with hundreds of IoT start-ups for ideation, co-creation, and joint innovation.

Disruptive Innovation

In this mode, we find curious and unbridled innovators with a 'mad but maybe' mind-set who are willing to rip it all up and start again. They are looking to create and dom-inate new markets, not compete in existing ones but rather disrupt them.

The focus of disruptive innovation activities revolves around:
- Problems that are not well understood
- Markets that do not yet exist
- Innovation is dramatic and disruptive
- The customer 'does not know what they do not know they do not have'; needs have not been truly defined – either for customers, end users, or businesses
- Market is unpredictable
- Traditional business methods fail, are mature, or are susceptible to challenge

This is often found in start-up mode, where businesses root out and hang their hat on solving a big problem, without the constraints of legacy. In the pursuit of that, they harness technology and associated business model ideas and partners. They are open to and accept failure as a way to learn and refine and ultimately land on a value crea-tion opportunity by way of that process.

Thinking and acting like this in an unconstrained and emancipated manner is ex-traordinarily difficult to achieve for leaders who are immersed in and responsible for day-to-day or run operations. This is why we have separate incubators, accelerators, and R&D functions that facilitate innovators with time, space, and experimental learn-ing opportunities without the constraints of value delivery; their job is to create it.

Discovery[76] is a South African firm formed in 1992 set to become a new vanguard in Health Insurance. The company decided to reverse-engineer the business model. Instead of insuring premium holders against the worst that could happen, they decided to build their proposition by providing their subscribers with the means to build and live a healthy life and as a result live longer to reduce premiums. This presented broader macro-benefits, such as taking pressure off the health system and increasing personal wellness.

Subscriptions to gyms with up to 80% reduction and rewards programmes built on tracked exercise (through fitness apps) and healthier eating (linked to supermarket chain loyalty cards) rewarded 'good' behaviour with lower premiums. Not satisfied with the health market they extended the idea into life assurance (becoming South Africa's largest player in 15 or so years); car insurance where trackers are installed with policyholder permissions to track and reward safe driving habits; and their latest foray is into behavioural banking with 650,000 clients already onboarded – once again a natural extension of their 'shared' value' model.

The journey for Discovery, however, is not to be underestimated; rewriting (excuse the pun) the insurance industry is an expensive and risky endeavour. However given its growth (now across 20 major markets with north of 35 million clients on their Discovery and Vitality brand) it is collating an incredible store of data and intelligence that, if leveraged, could fuel the next wave of innovation.

Looking back on the three modes of innovation, there is nothing new in what I have presented here. Multiple horizons have been around for years, as have other ways to look at the market, such as the GE Growth Matrix I shared a twist on in Part II. What is different is discipline and methods, the cognitive dexterity to run all three in parallel, and allowing each to do it is paramount. Also facilitating this is cross-pollination; the best ideas for disruptive innovation often come from work in Sustaining.

We will now unpack several key accelerants and enablers that support this discipline, starting with design thinking.

Design Thinking

Design thinking is a proven approach to identifying problems and finding innovative solutions. Variants can be used in all modes of innovation but usually exist in developmental and disruptive. Starting with an innovation trigger, the thrust is to use time, processes, and motivated creative intellect to explore all the underpinning drivers for the problem and then prioritise the top issue to be solved. Repeating the cycle, teams then

---

76 Harvard MBA Student Perspectives, "Healthier Premiums: using technology to drive positive behaviour in insurance," (November 18, 2016), accessed April 7, 2023, https://d3.harvard.edu/platform-rctom/submission/healthier-premiums-using-technology-to-drive-positive-behaviour-in-insurance/.

explore all the potential solutions and then prioritise the top solution to bring forwards for development.

This is also called the double diamond, and there is a very simple canvas available from the company What Could Be[77] that you can download from their site if you want to get started. I have augmented it with a five-step process and associated inputs or tools that can be utilised to run a design thinking initiative. My belief borne from experience, is that there is no single or perfect way to do this, other than to simply start out and get going. Use the broad thrust and use a facilitator if you do not have the skills in-house. Practice makes perfect.

Design Thinking Five-Step Framework

The basis of moving into the five-step process is that there is a trigger of a large or complex problem that you deem worthy to solve. For instance, it could be in a business-to-business world that leaders find it difficult to identify, engage, and onboard the right consultancy for the right job, which could in fact be for design thinking and we will use this to illustrate the methods and outcomes.

Step 1 – Discover (Sometimes Called Empathy)
The first thing that a design thinker might do in this instance is take a step back to learn about the business as an end user and what they are trying to achieve, using at least a number of the following means to get under their skin:
- User interviews
- Surveys
- Focus groups
- Stakeholder interviews
- Field observation – you could even sit with a business as they go online to search, recording the kind of search words and sites they attempt to visit, or watch them call peers to hear about firms they have used to get a thrust of what they are looking for and how they frame it
- In addition to the point above, we would cite data analysis from online journey tracking
- Metrics from processes and value chains if appropriate
- Competitor intelligence sites and papers

Once gathered, this should be collated under themes and presented on a 'discovery board'. In our example from interview and survey themes, we might indicate users and providers do not share a common language, or field observations note that users

---

77 What Could Be, "The Design Thinking Canvas," accessed April 7, 2023, https://www.whatcouldbe.com/.

get frustrated looking online and move to call an acquaintance for referrals to add comfort to and accelerate the search process.

Step 2 – Define

Armed with the discovery insight, the design thinker might then move to determine and crystallise the real and underpinning problems by using some of the following methods:
- Personas and journey maps which articulate the steps that users are seen to take, identifying where frustration emerges and where progress can be evident
- Storyboards and user stories, which are another means of visualising key moments, obstacles, and breakthroughs; bring the realities to life – think cartoon reels; and do not underestimate the value of visualisation
- Extract 'issue statements' supported by narratives – these start to shine a light on the focus areas for prioritisation
- Map the assumptions if any – these are always very helpful and are useful to re-visit as a source for inspiration and clarity testing
- Sometimes it is helpful to do side-by-side or comparative analysis, for example, in this case what the journey looks like online, through an acquaintance – looking at the composite and blends sometimes illuminates inspiration

At this point, we should have gathered all the influencing issues, good and bad. From there the core barriers to progress can be identified and clustered for solutioning. This can happen quite naturally through discussion or facilitation. It might require voting, or even a scoring mechanism but be warned that they are elaborate and need to be designed back into the discovery steps. They can chew up time and if incorrectly designed misdirect the effort.

In the case of our example we might have found:
- There is no single place to go and see the design thinking consultancies in my market – SEO rankings and paid ads drive a broad range of results
- It is difficult to compare providers; they all report wonderful results (we are re-minded never to judge a book by its cover), and there is no means to compare
- Pricing an initiative is difficult – nobody publishes rates
- Getting past testimonials and understanding on the ground performance is hard – there is no independent appraisal available
- It takes much work to get down to a short-list – most people call around to people they trust to get a referral, and this usually results in evaluation processes being side-stepped, and opportunity foregone

Now that we have the underlying issues driving the gnarly problem to be solved, we move on to ideating and identifying how one might solve it.

Step 3 – Ideate

Here we use an array of methods and engagements to flush out a variety of potential solutions, which include:
-   Brainstorm sessions
-   Mind maps
-   SCAMPER maps
-   Crazy 8's (8 ideas in 8 min)
-   Card sorting
-   Storyboards
-   User journeys
-   User flows

Some of the approaches here may not be familiar to you. If this is the case, a facilitator may be helpful. All roads lead to creating the right environment and approach where there is no such thing as a bad idea, so I encourage you to try out some different methods and add a little bit of time pressure which can be a helpful percolation method.

The target is to develop a long list of ideas that can then be shared and digested, and then another round can follow (called 'build up'), where members take the best ideas they have heard and take it a further step forwards. Ideas will spark more ideas, and some of the best breakthroughs happen in this zone.

It is then time to move on to prioritisation, and again there are an array of methods which include voting, categorisation (such as the rational, delightful, darling, long-shot methods illustrated below), and matrixing on axes such as attractiveness or novelty and ease of implementation.

I suggest you try different methods, and judge which might be appropriate for a particular group (e.g. if the CEO is in the room, it is hard not to go with their vote, so try matrixing).

For our example we will work on the basis that we came up with a long list, but decided to proceed with one under each of the categorisation methods as follows:
-   Rational: develop a site where clients can go and explore design thinking consultants on offer by categories, for example, region, price, size
-   Delightful: a rating system, driven by users and some central analytics, that ranks on factors such as technical prowess, value for money, and responsiveness.
-   Darling: develop a 'pitch and bid' tool to allow users to build a pitch, and then post it to on-site bidders to then select a short-list based on certain criteria and receive bids for consideration
-   Longshot: build a design thinking agency as there is clearly a gap in the market

As we move into the next stage, consideration should be given to amalgamating ideas and completing 'build up' rounds. The inclusion of the Longshot as a wild card could be useful as a provocateur to stretch the imagination and further build insights (think disruptive mode). However, it may be excluded when you get down to the business end on the basis of practicality, so be prepared for that.

Step 4 – Create a Prototype

The best way to move forwards from this point, in my experience, is to prototype and simulate the end user experience, including the underpinning requirements to deliver and build a solution. This brings the three key questions of design to the fore: If a solution is desirable and if it is feasible, and that will help inform if it is viable. Methods include:
- Questionnaires and surveys
- Paper prototypes – again think storyboards and cartoons
- Storyboard and story books
- User journeys with hi-level or detailed user flows
- Digital mock-ups – wireframes
- Low-fidelity interactive prototypes (using tools like Figma)
- High-fidelity design (e.g. Invision Studio)

While creating a prototype, you should also extract and categorise enabling requirements across the headings of people, process, systems, and data so that sizing effort can be undertaken to ascertain the important viability question.

The prototyping method will most likely be driven by factors such as time, budget and resource availability, how complex or tangible the ideas are, and the end user persona. In our case, given that we are talking about a business market but we want to get in there quickly to test for direction setting, we have chosen to build a micro-journey illustrating all three of the rational, delightful, and darling ideas. We have also supplemented it with a short questionnaire to understand what businesses want to see in a design thinking provider (teasing out the longshot option).

Now we are ready to test our ideas in the wild – the moment of truth.

Step 5 – Test

This critical evaluation stage built around testing in the real world can employ a long number of methods, and as with prototyping, the most appropriate will be based on factors such as availability, proposition depth, degree of validation required (e.g. would it be a sniff test, or a formal business case step). Methods include:
- 1:1 or group usability testing, including shadowing and SUS (System Usability Scale) surveys, including heuristic evaluation and eye tracking
- A/B testing – done when testing variants
- Focus groups and interviews incorporating desirability evaluations
- Quantitative metrics testing what is important – this could include security, health and safety, consumption, and a whole host of other operational and workability measures

This is the moment of truth, and often, we might have to go back several steps to go forwards again. But when we pass through a loop of robust and satisfactory testing and the business case is in good shape, we are ready to move into the development backlog for build.

Blue Ocean Strategy

Design thinking is applicable at a micro and proposition level, but is not always applicable at a macro or enterprise setting. For such a setting, the Blue Ocean Strategy approach is a simple but expansive frame to create competitive advantage and evolve market positioning[78] (under which propositions can be built).

The strategy map is a useful way to assess desired competitive differentiation and, as the name implies, puts a clear blue ocean between you and the competition. The opposite is to swim in a competitively crowded space where blood flows. A desktop example is presented in Figure 36, based on the gaming console market, to bring the utilisation of the map to life.

There are four zones, and each helps to direct focus. Focusing on the position taken by Oculus (now branded Meta Quest), you can observe that they have chosen to differentiate access to gaming through virtual reality (VR), and prioritised Avatars as a key attractiveness factor in addition to price differentiation to grow a user base.

The 'reduce' factors of crowd-gaming, game range, graphics, and UX are of lesser focus in the present, and deprioritised due to lack of demand or scale. Similarly, hardware dependencies are put on the back burner for later development (as we imagine is the case for Game Range). 'Eliminate' features such as memory upgrades and premium membership are excluded for current focus, but may be brought back into focus in future.

Blue Ocean in Five Steps

I encourage you to try out the strategy map to see where your blue ocean could be. Here are five simple steps to get you started:
1. Map key competitive attributes against closest/most challenging competitors.
2. Identify, through ideation and other methods (such as design thinking), features, or services that could/will create competitive differentiation and uniqueness.
3. Isolate features in market that are in high demand or enable step-change growth.
4. To make space for items that are to be prioritised in steps 2 and 3, select features or services that are to be deprioritised from development; this could be due to lacklustre demand, the market not being ready, or inability to execute.

---

78 Blue Ocean Strategy, accessed April 7, 2023, https://www.blueoceanstrategy.com/.

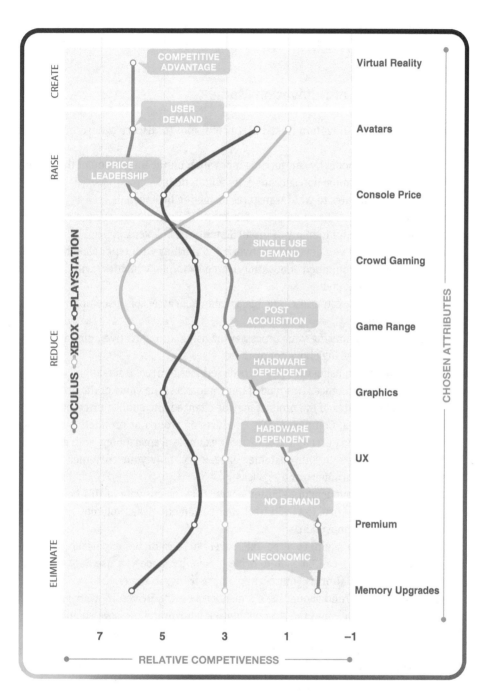

Figure 36: Blue ocean strategy map example.

5.   There are always features and services that need to be retired, go out of fashion or are commercially not viable. In line with simplification, these should be jettisoned.

Doblin's 10 Types of Innovation Model

Doblin's 10 types of innovation model is a useful tool to discern where innovation should be focused.

Doblin created a model by categorising innovation on the foundation of three main elements and further innovation subcategories within them:

1.   Configuration: Relates to what transpires inside the business
     a.   Profit: Crucial for any business for growth and includes pricing strategies, but would extend to many of the 10 Simplification levers.
     b.   Network: How you develop a network and partner with other stakeholders to drive innovation; open Innovation is one example, which we will delve into later in this chapter.
     c.   Structure: How you utilise tangible or intangible assets of the company to drive innovation.
     d.   Processes: Optimising your processes, or using an innovative approach to enhance your offering above competitors.
2.   Offering: Relates to using core products or services to drive innovation
     a.   Product performance: This type of innovation uses the value of the product, for example, features of the product may be changed, the quality, price, etc.
     b.   Product system: Complementary products or groups of products bundled so that they can be purchased together, for example, a smartphone with a sim.
3.   Experience: Relates to your customer experience, how your customer interacts with your brand, products, and services
     a.   Service: We have explored customer-centricity extensively in this book, so the subject is well-worn. How you treat your customers speaks volumes, and also be used to drive innovation.
     b.   Channel: Once again, covered extensively here in digital experience; a plethora of channels can be used to drive innovation once you use data to understand which platforms your customers are using, and why.
     c.   Brand: Your brand should have a distinct message, driven by your values (remember purpose and the strategy house); your brand message should be very clear so that your customers and end users know exactly what you stand for.
     d.   Customer engagement: Similar to digital experiences, how you engage with your customer; this type of innovation is about applying different marketing techniques and creating innovative interactions with them.

Doblins Framework[79] can be used to map back to the 'Create' zone on the strategy map and used to identify where your innovation efforts should be focused to create uniqueness. It is also a reflective frame to use in a competitive assessment; I have used some mainstream examples in Figure 37, to bring it to life. I recommend you use it to self or market reflect similarly to illicit conversations, and debate where to focus your efforts.

Innovation Canvas

Yes – there is a canvas for everything, and if you search for 'innovation canvas', you will find more than a few.

They are all worth a look, and my consultancy most often creates our own or blend some for each assignment. If you are looking for an off-the-shelf solution, the KTN website is a great resource. On there, you will find a paper canvas, but the site also enables you to build a digital one. We use the paper version when we gather people in a room to create energy as the 'ceremony' of committing pen to paper forges focus and cognitive ignition. The site has full instructional videos, and downloadable question cards and a guide that make it as easy as it gets. While these tools are designed to enable self-guidance and execution, it is hard to see around corners and know what you do not know. Try a facilitator if it is your first time. You may find them in your organisation just as quickly as externally – if you and they are brave enough.

Innovation Maturity Assessment

Innovation is nothing without people, process, and measurement.

To test how fit you are as an organisation, I suggest you consider completing a maturity assessment of your innovation prowess (sample shared in Table 9). This is a simple but expansive frame to show how ready you are to embrace innovation to create competitive disadvantage, evolve propositions, and utilise the methods shared in this book to support step change development. Involve the team in both the diagnosis and solution; as with all change and innovation, it is best to make sure it is invented 'here'. (Note: scoring and solutions are samples, and shared for guidance – don't be shy to evolve them.)

---

79 Forbes, "20 Fresh Examples of Customer Experience Innovation," Blake Morgan (October 21, 2019), accessed April 7, 2023, https://www.forbes.com/sites/blakemorgan/2019/10/21/20-fresh-examples-of-customer-experience-innovation/.

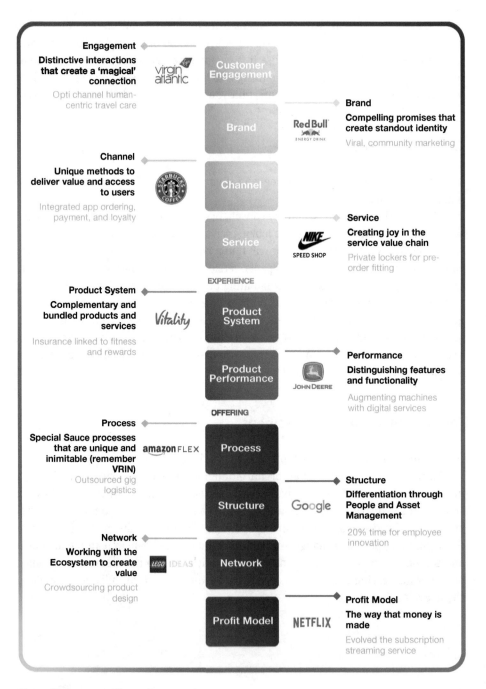

Figure 37: Ten types of innovation examples.

Table 9: Maturity assessment.

	Disagree	Partially agree	Agree	Solution
Our culture makes it easy for people to put forward novel ideas	●			Consider an initiative like Kickbox to jumpstart ideation
There is good collaboration across teams on new business opportunities			●	Recognise and reward; showcase and 'ambassadorise'
There are internal processes and supports for running innovation projects		●		Conduct an audit, codify what works, and close the gap
We have formal innovation development programmes/intrapreneur schemes	●			Include module at induction and graduation programme
We use external parties to help ideate – customer, end user, start-ups, consultants	●			Engage with incubators, academia, and customers
Colleagues are given time, space, and resources to try new things out	●	●		Consider formal '20% time' initiative
We have clear rules for investment in new projects				Review and update prioritisation mechanisms
We have a clear risk appetite for innovations		●		Agree appetite at board and communicate
We know how to measure success, and kill projects when they are not working	●			Complete audit of processes and revitalise
We have reward and incentive structures in place for innovation ideation and execution		●		Explore what more can be done to motivate
We have a regular cadence of continuous improvement initiatives (CIP)			●	Leverage CIP insights for Horizon 2/3 initiatives
Competitors quickly copy our product introduction and often make pre-emptive launches		●		Ensure that IP is protected; Patenting
We have a strong external brand and presence for innovation		●		Amplify brand to maximise credentials

Intrapreneurs – Where Do They Sit?

Intrapreneurs are the 'dark horses' among us. Too often, they are not liberated, their talents go unnoticed, wasted, and left frustrated. It is worth seeing these change-makers out and giving them an innovation platform, and an innovation

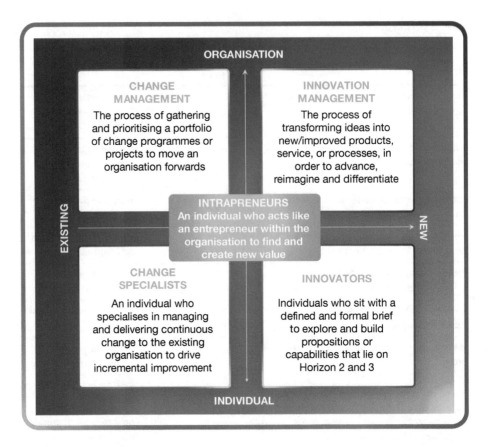

Figure 38: Where intrapreneurs sit.

mandate as outlined in Figure 38. They can often be identified as the curious, self-propelling change-makers on the left-hand side of the grid, and can be released towards the right-hand side with care and intervention.

An intrapreneur is an employee with entrepreneurial characteristics and the ambition to develop new ventures within the existing structure of an organisation. Intrapreneurship is therefore a system that allows employees to act like an entrepreneur within a company, for the benefit of the company, and a means to liberate individual skills and motivations.

They take a ground-up approach to creating and developing ideas that can enhance the competitiveness or productivity of the company. It can involve change, new products and services, or setting up new business entities. So, it is about new ventures within the existing structure of the organisation. But it can involve temporary spin-ins into external institutions (universities, research centres, etc.). Corporations may immediately or eventually even decide that the venture is better externalised, leading to formalised spin-offs.

The benefits to an organisation are manifold. With the optimal organisational culture and environment, it provides a more promising employee experience for entrepreneurial-minded staff and releases their innate talent. It shortens what might normally be lengthy design cycles by allowing intrapreneurs to create a collaborative work environment inside and out.

It builds an inherently more efficient and faster process for new product development or introduction of new propositions to the market. It empowers existing talent to champion innovation and can be more efficient and self-sustaining versus outsourcing. It finds and releases value in the internal intellectual property of an organisation that often goes untapped, and helps both the financial and vitality performance of the organisation (vitality meaning the ability to adopt and respond to market conditions).

I recently participated in a European-funded local development programme to identify the means to boost intrapreneurship in Ireland, and serve as an EU blueprint. You can see some of the research outputs, use an intrapreneurship index questionnaire and toolbox at the Intrapreneurial Index.[80]

The Innovation Journey

There is a typical growth journey that organisations make to reach innovation maturity. No two journeys are the same, but there is a road well-trodden. In our enterprise experience and our client work, we see many organisations follow a similar maturity path. Starting out with some curious doyens who believe there is more to be achieved or a defence to be made, the journey starts with exploration and moves towards education, experimentation before full scale adoption brings about mastery. This resembles a logical and easy path, but it is always easier looking back. In the heat of the battle there are many twists and turns.

The five-level innovation maturity journey and key attributes that are likely to prevail; where are you on your journey?

Level 1: Expose – Agree to Explore

- Concluded on the need to innovate, and have begun to act
- Facing some internal disbelief – there is already enough pressure in many systems and resourcing is a battleground so there will likely be some pushback
- Not sure how to get started, but curious and willing to take a first step
- Limited resources or budgets available, but willing to do what can be done
- Have begun some exploration such as reading books or trying a few workshops to identify ideas

---

80 Intrapreneurial Index, "Improve Your Intrapreneurship Activities," accessed April 7, 2023, https://intrapreneurial-index.com/.

Level 2: Educate – Opening Our Minds

- Spending time figuring out what innovation means, and where to focus
- Engaging with innovation consultants to take the first steps
- Inviting others to participate, but failing to gain momentum
- Trying some early initiatives and dedicating some part-time internal resources
- Finding out what others are doing – receiving talks, visiting incubators and accelerators

Level 3: Experiment – Early Efforts

- Have a number of innovations 'on the boil'
- Allocated medium-scale resources – often to random or unstructured innovation themes
- Harnessing external partners as accelerators
- Beginning to formulate the 'ways to innovate'
- First deployments and measuring success

Level 4: Adopt – Sharpen the Pencil

- Broadening innovation to the whole organisation
- Structured processes, prioritisation, and methods working around prioritised themes
- Formalising and industrialising open innovation
- Linking business goals and innovation activities, with a clear metric
- Innovation becomes central and no longer at the edge

Level 5: Master

- Innovation is a brand and 'what we do'
- Formal methods and even training programmes
- Innovation reaches every corner of the organisation
- Venture building and ecosystem collaborations are common course
- Extending services to external parties, even 'innovation as a service'

As with all the insights I share in this book, I have aggregated for simplicity and acknowledge that no two journeys are or will be the same. But these are the primordial steps, and while at first if you have not begun it might seem daunting, once you get moving and remain committed, the progress accelerates and achieves momentum with every new step.

Innovation Maturity Blueprint

To help you on your journey, I have detailed in the blueprint in Table 10, the critical and enabling actions across key themes that should be followed to embed innovation at each stage in the sequence. As you will see, one leads to the next in a linear building block fashion.

Table 10: Innovation blueprint.

Enabler	Expose	Educate	Experiment	Adopt	Master
Vision and strategy	Define what innovation is, and the vision for success	Develop informed, clear mission, and strategic themes	Vision and mission integrate with the business strategy	Innovation and significant informer of business strategy	Strategic focus develops beyond core business, e.g. Greenfield or M&A
Team	Early adopters invited to form first-phase operating model	Ways of working get defined, and mission shared	Ways of working extended into the business and cross-business collaboration commences	Move towards agile as the norm as innovation becomes prevalent	Self-driving agile at scale organisation
Funding	Small purse red-circled for discovery by sponsor	Continued support by executives, embedded resource allocation	Businesses carry dedicated innovation budgets and resources	Innovation moves to 'as a service' across divisions and regions	Spin-out P&L or VC dynamics adopted
Tools	Basic methodologies (Canvas's) and limited tech (front end) in place	Intermediate methodologies (design thinking) and digital architecture are developed	Advanced methodologies (ethnography) and access to enterprise technology platforms	Bespoke methodologies and full-scale technology capabilities	Methodology and technology design and consulting prowess
Business engagement	Stay one step removed to facilitate breathing space	Active alignment of activities between innovators and business on needs	Demand and supply prioritisation, driven by three mode backlog	Recycling of ideas and deliveries across multiple business lines	Parallel business models, investment, and acquisitions

Table 10 (continued)

Enabler	Expose	Educate	Experiment	Adopt	Master
Partnerships	Research willing partnerships for learning and knowledge	Early co-development to leverage partners for speed and learning	Extensive partnership research and ultilisation, coupled with co-development	Cross-entity and international partnership networks	JV's, ventures, and acquisitions
Measurement	Learning among the core team and sponsors	Focus on making an impact on core business KPIs	Range of hard and soft measure, spanning three modes with business aligned	Innovation as a service metrics complement 'embed' measurement	Return on capital and business building

I have not detailed how and where in organisational terms to house an innovation function, assuming that is the ambition. Sometimes businesses seek innovation to be instilled across or within the organisation. But organisations find that difficult – focus and success tends to be on the here and now, which coalesces well with continuous improvement. However, my experience is that developmental and disruptive innovation needs to be gestated in a traditional organisation before being ingrained.

Gestating Innovation

It is often difficult to drive developmental and disruptive innovation in business as usual. It is nobody's fault; it is simply the nature of business genetics. The host (the existing organisation) is coded to run and execute, not change, and will fight off a virus that threatens its existence. The incumbent holds the resources and as possession in nine-tenths of the law, the odds are with it. This is why it is important to consider the right approach to gestating innovation in an enterprise setting, in a way that it can achieve the duality of growing, while not being killed by the host's antibodies.

The following are three approaches to helping innovation thrive.

Business Resources are Seconded to a Central Innovation Team to Drive Out Dedicated Initiatives, and Form Innovation Approach

Pros:
–   Innovation resources and practises are honed and matured in a dedicated environment, where resources are freed up, immersed, and 'trained up'

Cons:
- Development and design are one step removed from the business, potentially missing key input
- Skills developed can dilute when going back to the business

When it works best:
- Where there is a need for full-time resources on large-scale projects
- On end-to-end development, which is being built and launched with external partners
- When there is a desire to immerse business teams in innovation ways of working

Innovation Resources (and Possibly Partners) Work in the Business to Progress Initiatives, and Instil the Innovation Approach

Pros:
- Development and design are close to the business and thus help adoption, leverage existing knowledge, and develop an internal innovation muscle

Cons:
- Pace and progressiveness can slow down
- There is usually a fiercer resistance to radical change
- Resources can be pulled and cannibalised for business as usual agenda

When it works best:
- Projects that need to be developed close to business and operations
- Where there may only be a need for part-time or mixed business representation

Innovation (Potentially with Partners) Work Separately to Business, Going to Market Directly, or Hand Back for Scaling When Production Ready

Pros:
- It maximises speed to market and learning
- Helpful in the formulation of new cultures and operating models/systems

Cons:
- Access to business resources (if necessary) may be challenging
- Opportunity to educate and develop business muscle may be diluted
- When it works best:
  - New frontier projects
  - Joint ventures
  - Projects with appropriate degrees of sensitivity or confidentiality

One factor that can kill innovation is lack of funding, or an inability to show returns on investment in metrics that are meaningful to the key stakeholders. We will take a look at that next.

Value, Discipline, and Measuring Success

Multimodal innovation requires a multimodal set-up and disposition.

The 'green box', a McKinsey model I like, isolates and evaluates the value a company currently and then needs to generate from two forms of innovation; breakthrough and incremental. It is quantified using net new revenue, earnings growth, or both. Critically, the green box represents the growth that only innovation produces, after netting out all other possible sources such as market momentum, in-year pricing adjustments, distribution and marketing activities, and M&A.

This amount is then cascaded into a set of objectives and metrics for the company's operating units, which reflect them in level-down innovation portfolios. This is a very clever way to 'ingrain' innovation as organisations head for levels 4 and 5 of the innovation journeys.

The Green Box model[81] is ideal for the commercial side of innovation, and it should be the adopted philosophical approach. If an organisation is not ready for it, it can still apply the principles at, for example, the organisational level or innovation team level targets and metrics.

Beware, however, if the business is not measured on it, it will not be resourced and prioritised, and therefore innovation will stagnate. Commercial returns are the hard side of the equation, but there is a soft or perhaps intangible side. Building capability is critical and perhaps even more important in the early phases of maturity, similar to the discussion we had on Data Analytics.

Some examples are highlighted in Table 11. Across both sides of the measurement scales, I also espouse taking a holistic view; all three modes should be included under a portfolio management approach.

The Pitfalls and Surprises to Watch Out For

From experience, interviews, and knowledge accumulated over the last 20 years, the following are some closing guidance points on building the innovation muscle.

81 McKinsey, "The Innovation Commitment," (October 24, 2019), accessed April 7, 2023, https://www.mckinsey.com/capabilities/strategy-and-corporate-finance/our-insights/the-innovation-commitment.

Table 11: Commercial and capability focus.

Commercial focus	Capability focus
Incremental return from continuous improvement in the sustaining innovation mode	The number of innovation opportunities identified and assessed
New value arising from developmental and disruptive innovation	The number of colleagues involved/trained in innovation practice
Growth through partnerships joint/open innovation	Speed to market and innovative technology foundations

Leadership Dimension

– Early-day sponsorship: It is critical that an innovation agenda, and the brave souls that vest it in an organisational setting, are backed by a sponsor with the vision to motivate and the clout to provide air cover, particularly in the early phases of maturity.

– Business acumen and empathy: Innovators, particularly if in a separate 'division' need to have and display empathy with the needs of the business and the demands that are on them – being there to help, not take, all the while pulling and pushing to create momentum and stretch.

– Avoid exclusion and bias: Be sure to avoid an innovation team mix that is 'pale, male and stale' – mix it up with new blood, diverse thinkers, and backgrounds to avoid 'reinventing the wheel' trap, and bring constructive dissatisfaction to the process and philosophy

– Partner chemistry and alignment: There are is army of partners out there just waiting to be involved and turn a buck. Make sure that you pick partners that lead on the former but are interested in both solving problems and building value. Note that the value could equally be money, but not solely.

Business Dimensions

– Alignment and impact: Innovation themes need to be anchored in what matters to the funders and the participants. If seniors do not believe that it will add value, they will pay platitudes. If initiative participants aren't motivated, then they will tyre kick and discretionary effort will go untapped.

– Resources and infrastructure: The road to hell is paved with good intentions. The road to success backs those up with committed resources. Willing, motivated, and capable are a must and do not frustrate those people, and the agenda, without access to tools and technology or efforts will be wasted.

- Discipline and measurement: To knit innovation into business strategy, ensure that the themes and metrics are aligned with what people get measured on. Follow up and track progress, interrogating to unearth the real insights. Forget, fail, often – we live by the kill fast mandate – if it is not working, drop it and move on. Do not flog dead horses.
- Brand depth: Some firms practice cosmetic innovation – appearance without having true substance. This superficiality will be found wanting, and those that you attract will quickly smell out shallowness. This will be at the long-term detriment of the intended undertaking and be brand counterproductive.
- Risk philosophy and practise: Risk tolerances in day-to-day business are understandably tight – businesses trade on trust and accuracy. In innovation, there needs to be a different philosophy – retaining trust and executing with accuracy should not be diluted, but there does need to be an acceptance that returns are not guaranteed and that efforts are experimental.

Reflection

- Digital businesses are inherently innovative.
- Innovation is implicit for your business to compete and win in this digital era. The landscape is too competitive, with the pace of technology increasing exponentially, so not innovating is tantamount to failure.
- But before you can allocate resources to innovate, you need to determine how you will innovate, and there are various modes with specific focuses:
    - Exploitative – cost and profit
    - Extending – diversification and growth
    - Exploratory – experimentation, probing for possibilities
    - Sustaining – solution-oriented, with. focus on cost and profit
    - Developmental – problem-solving, with a focus on diversification and growth
    - Disruptive – unbridled innovation, with a focus on experimentation and probing for new possibilities
- Digital businesses drive innovation across all 3 modes in parallel, which we call multimodal or ambidextrous innovation management
- Other frameworks you can draw inspiration from are; Doblin's 10 types of innovation, and innovation canvases (see references).
- But innovation is nothing without people, process, and measurement. To test how fit you are as an organisation, consider completing a maturity assessment of your innovation maturity to test your competitive disadvantage, propositions, and how you will develop accordingly.

Chapter 13
Open Through Partnering and Ecosystems

> Teamwork is the ability to work together toward a common vision. The ability to direct individual accomplishments toward organisational objectives. It is the fuel that allows common people to attain uncommon results. – Andrew Carnegie

One of the perhaps most formidable armaments that organisations have been able to employ in the digital age is that of ecosystems and adopting an open business model through partnering.

We spent time in Part I introducing two primary types of platforms (technology and end user), which are business arrangements that leverage an ecosystem of partners to bring collective value. This 'open' approach to working in partnership to build value for both the end user and the enterprises involved is not new. People and business have been in partnerships for centuries, but they were bounded by the analogue medium of communication, commerce, and law of the time.

An Open through Partnering and Ecosystems business model serves to extend and flex the business model muscle – expanding the ways in which to produce products or goods, or get them into market and monetise them. Specifically, application programme interfaces, or APIs, which are the means to connect digital systems and therefore businesses, have spawned a revolution of partnership business models that we will unravel in this chapter.

To anchor our thinking, I have presented the four quadrants of stretch in Figure 39 that are enabled by partnerships to illustrate how a business can:
- enhance its existing proposition by ingesting third-party services (top left)
- extend its core proposition into new markets (top right)
- enhance existing capability to help it serve its existing markets better (lower left)
- extend capability as a service to build new revenue and business lines (bottom right)

All of these positions are utilised in an 'open' business stance.

Partnership Archetypes

Figure 40 illustrates how we think about partnerships. A base principle of participating in an ecosystem is engaging in partnership to create a proposition or capability with joint value as a result. But as there are different types of partnership arrangements that exist which result in different types of ecosystems, we want to unpack them so that we can delineate between the variants, for there are many. This, as a result, will help us frame a clearer picture of what an ecosystem is and how we can

https://doi.org/10.1515/9783111034713-019

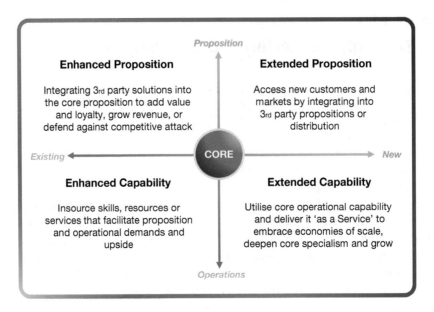

Figure 39: Four quadrants of stretch.

apply different approaches to working with or in partnerships in ecosystems, which is what we use as our basis for being 'open'.

To help us frame the different types of partnerships that there are and, therefore, different types of ecosystems that exist, there are two axes that we will use: Value Share (where participants share value arising from the partnership) and proposition (the range of propositions available as a result of the partnership(s)).

In the bottom left sits a closed position where a business works towards the market independently and with no partnerships; these are what we will call the solo artists. This is not to say that they do not consume services provided to them by 'service partners'; they do and this is where outsourcing 'as a service' consumption takes place, which facilitates the bottom left-hand side of the quadrants of stretch to enhance capabilities. Vendors such as Salesforce who provide significant CRM and digital asset management capabilities sit here. Partnerships that support joint value creation and proposition sit in the other three quadrants.

Beyond the solo artists, we start to get into joint partnerships which are illustrated by collaborations, joint ventures, and distribution agreements. We will call these 'closed' ecosystems. However, a business needs to adopt an open stance to participate in them. We do not include the outsourcing or 'as a service' vendors because they do not directly participate in the proposition domains of partnerships, albeit they do serve and support them. Let's now take a look at the three joint partnership categories.

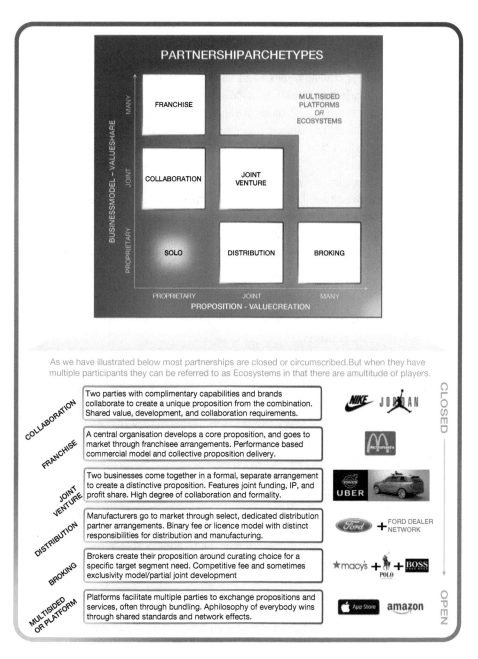

Figure 40: Partnership archetypes.

- Collaborations exist where two businesses with complimentary capabilities come together to create a unique and proprietary proposition. They usually agree who does what in terms of design, manufacturing, and distribution; the Air Jordan range of footwear created by Nike and Michael Jordan are a good example.
- Joint ventures are an extension of collaborations and where two businesses (sometimes but rarely more) come together in a formal, separate arrangement to create a distinctive proposition. Together they bring that proposition to market under a new brand that is separate from their existing businesses. It features joint funding, intellectual property, and profit share with a high level of collaboration and formality. Volvo and Uber have created a separate joint venture to build a new genre of autonomous vehicles, which is a good example
- In distribution arrangements, manufacturers go to market through select, dedicated distribution partners. This features a binary fee or licence model, with distinct formal responsibilities for manufacturing and distribution and rarely any joint proposition development (occasional at best). How Ford operates as a car manufacturer and distributes through independent dealers illustrates this.

There are then three broad categories of multi-party partnerships; franchises, broking, and multi-sided platforms.
- Brokers differ from agents in distribution agreements in that they act as a distributor for many manufacturers and create their proposition by curating exclusive choice under one roof for a specific target segment need. Competitive fees and sometimes exclusivity model/partial joint development feature – exclusive department stores such as Macy's that sell multiple luxury brands such as Ralph Lauren and Hugo Boss are a good example
- Franchises are a unique business model where a central organisation develops a core proposition, and establish a franchise of distribution through independent franchise owners. Like brokers, they are closely aligned to distribution arrangements with the primary difference being the franchisee is involved in the manufacturing as well as the distribution activities. McDonald's is a good example, and a performance-based commercial model and some degree of collective proposition delivery are normal features.

Both the broking and the franchise models are ecosystems as they involve multiple parties collaborating and individual success is dependent on the whole, albeit they are what we would call 'circumscribed' ecosystems, meaning they have distinct limits and boundaries.

Finally, we have multi-sided platforms, which are perhaps the most notable and familiar and where we can refer back to the technology and end-user platforms we discussed in Part I. These are truly 'open' ecosystems where a central platform acts as the conduit to intermediate buyers and sellers. Amazon and Apple's app store are relevant examples here, and we will unpack them next.

It is not just multi-sided platforms that create and enable ecosystems – as you can see, there are a number of variants, each with their own characteristics, advantages, and limitations. But all partnerships facilitate an open business stance, meaning you are engaging in a partnership arrangement to solve business problems or capture value opportunity, even within closed loops. Hence all the above archetypes are applicable for our open capability.

I have chosen to take a primarily outside-in view here by categorising proposition development and value sharing. I will include operations later in the chapter, which is another important dimension, but let's look at some examples first.

Multi-sided Platforms – Ryanair Is a 'Host'

Given there is much interest in multi-sided platforms and that if we understand them we can understand all ecosystems as they are usually sub-sets, we will spend some time unpacking a number of them to get a flavour of the variants by examining some well-known examples.

Ryanair, the European low fares airline, is a multisided platform that hosts an ecosystem to deliver value to its travelling customers, depicted in Figure 41. It achieves this by presenting multiple travel-specific propositions in multiple value-sharing arrangements to its customers by hosting complementary services. It is distinctive from broking because it facilitates access to, rather than control or advise on the propositions, and through its open stance, it allows customers of one to access all others across the ecosystem. Ryanair understands that shared value creates stronger partnership collaborations, and the sum of the collective proposition is better for everyone. It is also efficient for Ryanair as it allows the customer and its partners to connect and directly solve for the jobs to be done, rather than doing it for them.

Ryanair's core proposition sits in the 'Solo' territory. Its arrangements with its individual partners populate a number of the partnership positions as indicated in Figure 46, and its central role is to 'host' the ecosystem through facilitated win-win-win intermediation or introduction instead of playing the middleman when it comes to execution.

Multi-sided Platforms – Amazon Is the 'Hero'

Amazon operates a different ecosystem approach, which we call the 'Hero' model (see Figure 42). Amazon is renowned for putting the customer at the heart of its service proposition and delivering services to remedy needs. Here, though, its business models differ from Ryanair as it provides and orchestrates a marketplace between buyers and sellers by commanding ease, supply chain optimisation, and scaled delivery excel-

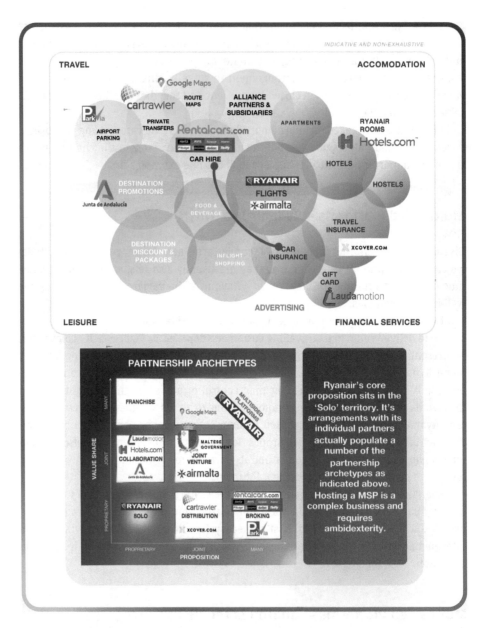

Figure 41: Ryanair ecosystem.

lence leveraging digital tools and data analytics. So it takes a much more active role in solving for the jobs to be done, and creates differentiation in service delivery.

After leveraging network effects to build the western world's largest multisided platform, Amazon then extended its business model and developed market leading supply chain services, including wholesale B2B arrangements in publishing, logistics, and cloud and data services (Amazon Web Services). It has also acquired and integrated partnerships in areas such as Financial Services, Healthcare, and Fashion. We call it the hero as it takes the lead and heavily commands the ecosystem to adhere to Amazon standards and meet the needs of the customer – owning the customer experience is front and centre.

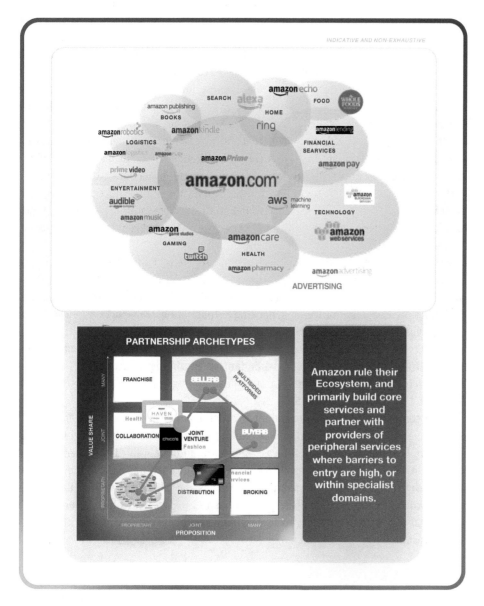

Figure 42: Amazon ecosystem.

Multi-sided Platforms – KBC Is 'The Ambient Integrator'

KBC is a leading European Banking and Insurance group renowned for its digital prowess. In Belgium, the Czech Republic, and other European states where it is active, it has developed an open service architecture for its digital and predominantly mobile services. Its approach is that of two-way integration, and it embodies the concept of ambient finance.

The concept behind 'ambience' is to deeply embed services within external or parallel value chains and become implicitly dependent. If you think about it, banks and card companies have been embedding their services into commerce since their genesis. The subtlety here is that the banking service is no longer positioned as a concluding method of settling a trade, which is where money and finance normally appear. The service is engineered to facilitate the tasks at hand, and not just to pay for it.

In applying this, KBC has embedded its proprietary banking services into day-to-day customer jobs to be done, such as car park ticketing such that it solves the whole job, and not just part of it. Drivers simply connect their mobile banking app to the car parks service so that when they are entering or exiting the providers car parks, payment is automatically settled (usually through number plate reading). This even extends to refuelling at forecourts and renting transportation. This makes their role embedded, seamless, and sticky, much as Apple Pay has.

The other dimension to the ambient approach is to make the bank's digital estate a one-stop-shop for all the day-to-day activities and administration tasks, so that it becomes the home of convenience, much as Tencent's WeChat is in China. This includes the bank's own payment processing, parking authorisation, transport hire, tickets purchase (events, travel, etc.), a digital safe, and correspondence vault; all using the bank's services with third-party integration. Some services are even available to non-bank customers, but full access is dependent on becoming a customer. These additional services compliment a mature day-to-day banking app and KBC Brussels engage the market for development ideas.

In a comparative study, independent international research agency, Sia Partners,[82] has crowned KBC Mobile the best mobile banking app in the world. It highlights various factors in its analysis, including the vast amount of additional third-party services, the simulation tools, full online capabilities for many types of transactions, the excellent hassle-free user experience, connectivity (wearables, digital identity verifier items, cash withdrawals at ATMs, etc.), and the possibilities to interact with KBC's other physical and digital distribution channels including the central role of 'Kate', KBC's digital personal assistant.

---

82 Sia Partners, "Sia Partners 2021 International Mobile Banking Benchmark," (September 2021), accessed April 7, 2023, https://www.sia-partners.com/en/insights/publications/sia-partners-2021-international-mobile-banking-benchmark.

One of the central themes of KBC's strategy is to be 'digital with a human touch', which relates to the phygital stance I discussed earlier. This stance is embodied in the philosophy that digital is rudimentary in the delivery of efficient, yet compelling, end user experience whether a customer is self-serving, or with the assistance of a human. Both the design of the user flow needs to be emphatic (hence, the great UX), and digital and physical need to work in symphony to be there 'when I want, for what I want, how I want' (with 'I' in the scenario meaning your customer).

Multi-sided Platforms – Some Other Examples

Let us now look at some other variations of the multi-sided platform (see Figure 43) before we move to unpacking how to think and act on the options and variations we have outlined.

– The mediator: Airbnb is the classic mediator ecosystem, facilitating a supply:demand marketplace for people with accommodation looking to let it to people looking for accommodation. As well as facilitating this connection and settling transactions through a ratings and reviews system of property and hosts, they add value by plugging in categorisation, insights, traveller experiences. The company also creates value for property letting logistics, e.g. cleaners.

– The web: The health ecosystem is perhaps one of the most complex known. An interconnected, but often loosely coordinated (at best), mesh of services. Its intricateness results from an almost infinite multiplicity of conditions and associated treatments across a plethora of public and private care providers and insurers. This is referred to as a web as it spins out from the patient with multiple strains and intersections.

Other examples of ecosystems include the social platforms that intermediate user engagement and infiltrate it with advertising and sometimes direct access to services to liberate a revenue model. These ecosystems mediate, or intermediate, and extract value through advertising, access fees, and premium services where participation is often free of advertising and presents enhanced benefits you know who they are, and there are many.

Where to Play – Choosing the Right Departure Point

Open through Partnering and Ecosystems sits at the apex of the capability triangle for digital businesses, as it can bolster digital business prowess through extended capability, proposition, and distribution options. How to adopt an open stance and participate in Ecosystems begs three primary questions – 'where to play', 'who to play with', and 'how to play'.

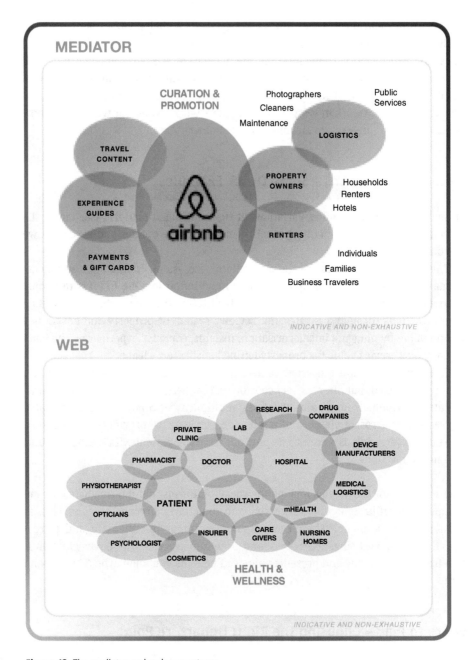

Figure 43: The mediator and web ecosystems.

Where to Play

Depending on the business strategy which is defined by market dynamics taking into account what ecosystem forces are at play including competitive circumstances, you may wish to consider participating in or leveraging one of a number of ecosystems and their inherent partnerships.

Doing so may be to enhance market position and revenue – that is where you utilise ecosystems to strengthen the business and compete in the market you are already in. Ryanair has embraced partnerships to build a composite travel proposition by hosting an ecosystem of complementary service providers in its digital business.

Equally, you may wish to integrate third-party services and be the hero of your own ecosystem, or you may choose to mediate an ecosystem and like Amazon you could choose to combine both. Instead of or in addition to, you may also wish to extend your proprietary or ecosystem-enabled proposition into other ecosystems; for example, Ryanair presents itself in travel aggregator sites as a destination for flights and travel complements.

And to add one more, you may wish to extend your capabilities into other ecosystems as an enabler to capture service-oriented value. KBC and WeChat have implemented this by ambiently integrating its payments processing into car parking and other day-to-day services.

This 'where to play' question looks to determine which of the Quadrants of Stretch one wishes to utilise, noting that several or all can be adopted in combination.

Who to Play With

The partners or ecosystems you will ultimately work and collaborate with will ultimately be defined by the kind of ecosystem play you wish to pursue. However, partner choice is not automatic and we encourage you to separate the where and the who, and as you'll see in the next question, specific partners can also be informed by the 'how to play' question.

How to Play

Following the logic, the where and who will drive the how, and it may in turn reverse inform the who.

To bring this down into more pragmatic terms, or at least make it actionable, Table 12 is a choice matrix for open business strategies.

The matrix helps to flush and flesh out the dimensions that need to be considered when opening up the debate on open collaborations. Not all dimensions may be appropriate, and context-specific additions may be required, but this is a good starter for 10 based on my experience. Crucially, these are not a set of binary choices – they are intended to illicit debate, and positioning could be easily in the centre of the choice vectors presented, for example, on the offence:defence vector, one could seek to capture value from an unfulfilled need in the market (offence) while getting ahead of potential forays by competitors (defence).

Table 12: Choice matrix for open business strategies.

Dimension vectors	Consideration
Host:contribute	One of the most important decisions an organisation needs to make is to lead or participate in ecosystems, and the stance will inherently inform the choices to be taken.
Purpose:profit	As simple as it sounds, being really clear on the intent of collaborative initiatives is crucial from the outset as it sets down the guiding principle of any venture – profit and/or purpose is a cornerstone.
Offence:defence	Understanding the competitive perspective of your situation is a prime requirement, and the resulting need will inform what kind of partnership or platform participation is appropriate. For example, an acquisition of a new target segment could lead to a very different approach compared to defending existing customer territory.
Innovation: efficiency	The mode of innovation being pursued will inform what kind of talent and collaborators you are seeking. Continuous improvement under a sustaining innovation brief may require a capability partnership, whereas developmental and disruptive innovation may require breakthrough proposition partners or ecosystem plays.
Serving:creating	Finding and presenting new propositions to existing customers (serving them) could look different from partnerships where the objective is to build and create new value (new propositions, new markets etc.).
Narrow:broad	An important strategic decision is the scope of your strategy and therefore ecosystem approach – are you focusing on going deep into a specialist area, or broadening the agenda and owning a new category or territory.
Bundled:parallel	An aspiration to combine propositions or capabilities to create a bundle 'sum of the parts' proposition, or go to market in parallel with a complimentary range of solutions around a mega need will have important choice points.
Fixed:adaptable	Some organisations have a time or intent bound reason for considering partnerships and platforms, for example, a seasonal theme, or a specific product launch, whereas others are focused on exploring new territories and adapting through learning to find their sweet spot.
End user: community	Picking a partnership approach that focuses on creating value from end users presents a different criteria set as opposed to building an ecosystem around facilitating value add to a community or network of participants and contributors.

Table 12 (continued)

Dimension vectors	Consideration
Existing:new	Analysing whether parties to a collaboration (self and collaborators) have and will use existing muscle within an initiative, or whether new capability needs to be built will need to be taken into account, with a sliding scale of risk and confidence applying.
Few:many	The scope and intent of the collaboration (which takes into account the dimensions above) will derive key determinants for the breath of partnership(s) and/or ecosystem membership
Open:closed	Linked to the few:many dimension, partnerships and ecosystems need to decide of they are open for participation and governed by intent and standards, or whether there is controlled criteria for membership.
Partner:platform	Based on the above and other dynamics such as competitive mapping, commercialisation, and availability, organisations need to define whether partnership, platform or a hybrid arrangement is optimal.

As you will have garnered from what we have uncovered so far, and the choice considerations I have set out here, participating in partnerships and ecosystems is a complex business. Time, consideration, and debate need to be applied – I have hosted many a conversation with brow-frowning participants as they work their way through the choice architecture, but always to good results if patience and logic are applied. The dimensions and options presented will help break down the many options and choices that can be made. BCG presents an excellent series of analysis on ecosystem strategies, including a framework for stepping through the consideration for ecosystem strategies, built on 3 years of global research, which is peppered with examples.[83]

Next, we will move on to operational and execution considerations.

How to Win – Preparing the Operational Model

In parallel with the strategy considerations set out above, we should also be getting to grips with the operating model implications and requirements to conclude decisions and prepare for execution. As we have started to extract, working in collaborative arrangements brings with it a new level of complexity.

Usually a collaboration requires you to maintain your existing businesses and operations, while working on stepping into a new collaborative venture, and as part of

---

83 BGC, "What Is Your Business Ecosystem Strategy?" Ulrich Pidun, Martin Reeves, and Balázs Zoletnik (March 11, 2022), accessed April 7, 2023, https://www.bcg.com/publications/2022/what-is-your-business-ecosystem-strategy.

that understand and successfully work alongside a partner's organisation or platform. In Figure 44, I share the operating model considerations for how to think about this, noting that we have only 'opened the lid' here, but we do find looking at the 'layers' a solid starting point.

Participating in ecosystems and partnerships have considerations across all five layers of our Digital 360° model, and they range from:

- Proposition and distribution (engagement layer) back to
- Partnerships and platforms (proposition layer), down into
- Manufacturing and operations (process layer)
- Technology and data (technology and operations layer)
- With people and skill considerations running throughout

As you can see, there are new dimensions to be handled and, importantly, co-existence considerations to be solved. Breaking these down by looking through the 'architecture' of the organisation is helpful and can lay the ground for full and frank implication and response planning.

Critical Success Factors

Regardless of the choices made and territories executed against, we have extracted our learnings and insights on what makes partnerships through ecosystems work, and present them for your consideration below.

Pre-requisites

These are the table stakes going into any multi-party engagement:

- Making sure that the right mix of collaborators is present, and everybody has the right philosophy, resources, and can commit to the duration of the venture.
- Agreeing who owns what, including the customer – we have seen this turn things sour, particularly when there is a lack of clarity around cross-sale or Intellectual Property (IP) rights.
- Getting the governance right and early, including decision rights and dispute mechanisms, is critical to heading issues off at the pass.
- Agreeing on success factors including what comes first, for example, acquisition or revenue, how it will be measured, and how it will be rewarded – 'skin in the game'. commitment and incentives that drive collaborative behaviours are important to design.
- Sharing data and learning together should be key, with enablers to do both strong formation points.

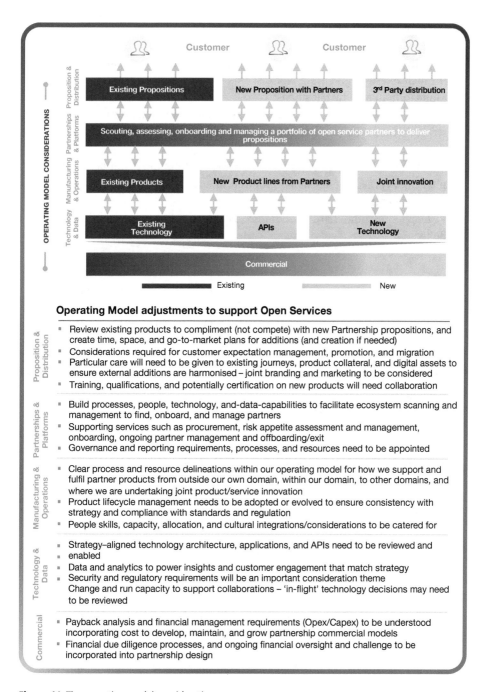

Operating Model adjustments to support Open Services

Proposition & Distribution
- Review existing products to compliment (not compete) with new Partnership propositions, and create time, space, and go-to-market plans for additions (and creation if needed)
- Considerations required for customer expectation management, promotion, and migration
- Particular care will need to be given to existing journeys, product collateral, and digital assets to ensure external additions are harmonised – joint branding and marketing to be considered
- Training, qualifications, and potentially certification on new products will need collaboration

Partnerships & Platforms
- Build processes, people, technology, and-data-capabilities to facilitate ecosystem scanning and management to find, onboard, and manage partners
- Supporting services such as procurement, risk appetite assessment and management, onboarding, ongoing partner management and offboarding/exit
- Governance and reporting requirements, processes, and resources need to be appointed

Manufacturing & Operations
- Clear process and resource delineations within our operating model for how we support and fulfil partner products from outside our own domain, within our domain, to other domains, and where we are undertaking joint product/service innovation
- Product lifecycle management needs to be adopted or evolved to ensure consistency with strategy and compliance with standards and regulation
- People skills, capacity, allocation, and cultural integrations/considerations to be catered for

Technology & Data
- Strategy–aligned technology architecture, applications, and APIs need to be reviewed and enabled
- Data and analytics to power insights and customer engagement that match strategy
- Security and regulatory requirements will be an important consideration theme
  Change and run capacity to support collaborations – 'in-flight' technology decisions may need to be reviewed

Commercial
- Payback analysis and financial management requirements (Opex/Capex) to be understood incorporating cost to develop, maintain, and grow partnership commercial models
- Financial due diligence processes, and ongoing financial oversight and challenge to be incorporated into partnership design

Figure 44: The operating model considerations.

Cautions – What to Watch Out for

- Due diligence both on partners and platforms is essential, particularly a look-through exercise given the weakest link threads across its entirety, and is the foundation upon which it stands.
- Understanding boundaries is essential, which usually comes down to both known strategic intent across the partners and platforms, and ongoing monitoring as that inevitably shifts in the market dynamics.
- Chemistry and culture are critical – if minds are not alike and behaviours complementary, then the harmony required to achieve great things can be soiled – this starts at the top.
- Risk appetites, often hard to crystallise, need to be aligned to ensure strategy does be too.

Non-negotiables – These Are the Potential 'Deal Breakers' or Walk-Away Criteria

- Lack of good old-fashioned communication and transparency can kill progress – getting the right cadence from the start is paramount.
- Straying beyond the bounds of the agreed venture is a death knell, and collaborations need to have clear mechanisms to negotiate dynamics that can play out, including walking away.
- Over-the-top moves where collaborators replicate and move to competitors.
- Tangential plays where collaborators step into other partnerships or platforms that are damaging.
- Gouging or imbalanced participation – taking more, giving less.

Accessing the Start-up Ecosystem

Many organisations look outwards to open innovation and start-up networks with sector-specific focal points (e.g. medtech, agritech, and fintech) to tap an ecosystem of new capability and proposition with the intention of partnering, co-creating, and often acquisition.

This is especially the case when they lack the belief that they can build this capability on the inside, in a reasonable or required period. There is a typical maturity path that organisations organically follow in engaging the start-up ecosystem to help understand what the road might look like and to inspire taking on multiple levels at once to fast-track.

Community Building and Scanning the Ecosystem – Level 1

Engaging with the local start-up ecosystem; this can be through existing meetup groups, incubators, accelerators, the angel community and venture capital firms, or other funding sources (such as Government) to understand the focus of start-ups, identify potential partners, and to build a presence to attract talent, collaborators, and customers.

Incubation Through Co-working Space and Mentoring – Level 2

Provision of co-working space for start-ups that share a common or complementary proposition to one's own business strategy to achieve 'innovation by association'. Mentoring support can also be provided to boost the start-ups and, therefore the local community (so there are brand and economic benefits as well as it being the right thing to do) but also, this provides an opportunity to open the door and build internal knowledge and innovation/mentor skills.

Acceleration Through Focused Support and Mini-ventures – Level 3

Sponsoring a select number of best-performing/most aligned start-ups through an accelerator programme deepens the benefits outlined on levels 1 and 2. Here it is important to curate partnerships or commercial relationships that help the start-up commercialise, and often firms co-create at this level to bolster the sponsoring company's capability or proposition needs. Typically, accelerators are run as an 8- to 12-week program, with in-residence support structures, to push the start-up from prototype to MVP through to first clients and ready to secure outside funding. Here the benefits are a mix of capability, brand, and capability/proposition building.

Venture Building With Targeted Investment – Level 4

Undertaking joint venture building with start-ups to 'create likely winners' by partnering with either a fledgling start-up team or an existing business to create a new venture with joint ownership. Significantly higher expectations get set at this stage in terms of investment (money, systems, IP, and people) and also returns. Sometimes this focus has the result of narrowing the engagement and tracking of the start-up ecosystem, but is balanced out by the sponsoring business becoming part of the ecosystem.

Corporate Venture Capital and Strategic Portfolio Building – Level 5

This is very similar to participating in traditional venture capital programmes. The investment thesis is geared not only towards the core business, but also exploratory themes (usually identified in developmental and disruptive innovation modes), with investment criteria split between potential to support strategy, exploration, and maximising ROI. The intent is to maximise investment, strategic alignment, brand, knowledge building, and risk diversification.

The opportunity pursued, as highlighted in level 5, is often to support the innovation focus of a business by tapping partners in the start-up ecosystem, so these two capabilities are interlinked here and more generally. It is important to note that maturity needs to be matched by investment/resource commitment, and a commitment to longevity is required. The start-up ecosystem has seen many corporates come and go, and mentally split mature businesses into givers and takers – businesses that are committed to investing and co-creation or businesses that are curious with the primary goal of building knowledge.

Acquisition by Extension

Acquisition may just as easily sit in the Innovation capability, but it makes sense to present it here as it flows from the last start-up ecosystem theme.

Some organisations add a sixth level to engaging with the start-up and indeed scale up ecosystem, which is to acquire. They pursue this because they believe they need to acquire capability or proposition as an innovation booster and ultimately make it core for strategic growth purposes, or sometimes to eliminate upcoming strategic threat and own a new territory.

There is unlikely to be any tangible assets of note at these stages, and they are buying into the promise of the venture, market space, the team, and the technology. The following are some of the drivers for acquisition we see out there:

- Grow target customer base – Acquisition opportunities that present a means to grow products, services, or propositions in chosen target markets
- Build economies of scale – Book acquisitions that leverage synergies between buyer and target to facilitate efficiency, scale, and data leverage
- Revenue plays – Business or book acquisitions that present an opportunity to lift revenues through efficient capital outlay
- Capability building – Buying or targeting parts of a business, operation or team that meet a capability gap identified to support strategy execution
- Data opportunities – A business or book where the inherent data could facilitate business opportunities
- Value play – Opportunistic acquisition or merger that presents value in terms of business, book, assets or capabilities at a 'steal'

- Innovation booster – A deal to develop innovation and adjacent business lines/propositions, acquire innovation talent, or build research capabilities
- Pre-emptive strike – Take out a competitor, or offset a strategic risk event

While we have covered a lot of the strategic and operational considerations of Open through Partnering and Ecosystems in this chapter, there is a fundamental enabler we have not come to yet, and that is Application Programme Interfaces or APIs. APIs are the technological connectors that enable businesses to connect digitally in consistent and safe ways, facilitating developers to connect, test, and deliver integrated digital solutions. We will cover that in more detail as we now start to move into the next chapter on technology (where it more naturally sits).

Reflection

- An open business model extends and flexes opportunity by opening it up and expanding the ways it can product products or services to bring them to market.
- Leveraging open opportunities with partnerships and ecosystems can unlock new paths to growth, capability, and efficiencies. But it is important to understand the different type of partnerships you can leverage. Some highlighted are:
    - Collaborations where two businesses with complementary capabilities come together to create a unique and proprietary proposition
    - Joint ventures are an extension of collaborations and where businesses come together in a formal, separate arrangement to create a distinctive proposition, bringing it to market under their respective brands
    - Distribution arrangements where manufacturers go to market through select, dedicated distribution partners
    - Participation in or the hosting of multi-sided platforms
- However, leveraging partnerships and ecosystems is complex. The choice matrix for open business strategies (Table 12) will help to help you interrogate and determine what needs to be considered and how to proceed with the many choices available.
- Very importantly, which is why we have Open through Partnering and Ecosystems as our last core competency, the other six are required to embrace being an Open business, as are the three enabling capability platforms we move to next.

The Three Enabling Platforms

You've got to start with the customer experience and work back toward the technology, not the other way around. – Steve Job.

We will now dive into the foundational conductors for the seven core competencies – the three enabling platforms of technology, risk, and people.

These three underpinning and enabling platforms surround and solidify digital competencies to deliver digital-fuelled strategies.

Together all 10 manifest in composite digital capability. The seven core competencies are essentially the 'what' of digital business – what we want to harness and leverage to execute in the pursuit of a digital strategy to deliver a business ambition.

Technology, people, and risk underpin and create the platform for execution:

- how – the technology that powers digital capability
- who – the people that design strategy, propositions, systems, and so on to drive results
- hazards – the risk issues, mitigation, and appetite necessary to pursue digital business ventures

Think of the seven competencies as the instruments in an orchestra, and the three enabling platforms as the music, musicians, and production plan to create the symphony.

Chapter 14
Technology

Don't be fooled by some of the digital transformation buzz out there, digital transformation is a business discipline or company philosophy not a project.–Katherine Kostareva

You might find it odd that we are exploring technology later in this book and that it was not amongst the first areas to cover. It is entirely intentional because as any digital CTO, CIO, or engineer worth their salt will say – the technology solutions always start with the strategy and the customer experience we are aiming to build.

In this chapter we will look at the technology components, architecture, principles, and approaches required to support a digital business. We will not be getting very technical, but at the same time we will not be straying into the conceptual. Our focus here is on giving you an understanding of how strategy translates into technology, and what technology solutions and operations are required to enable a digital business.

Digital Technology – Balancing Supply and Demand

The technology requirements for a digital business should be set out in a demand:supply equation, where the desired objectives and outcomes are translated into an overarching technology strategy, and underpinning design of hardware, software, and operating model enablers.

In Figure 45, I have set out a high-level, indicative technology architecture for a digital business, and dig deeper into each 'layer'. From the start, it is important to keep in mind that a demand:supply equation is driven by demand, but ultimately reconciled by availability, feasibility, and affordability – the supply side. Therefore a balancing act needs to be struck between desire and doability.

The other early flag to raise here is co-existence. While it is aspirational to define and desire a digital technology stack, many organisations are caught in or with legacy and need to craft a transition plan where old and new need to live together and, over time, rebalance – we will come back to this point shortly.

Figure 45 illustrates what a capability map could look like to define the 'jobs to be done' by a digital stack of technologies (capabilities to the left, technology layers to the right). As you can see, the components identified across the layers reflect what needs to be in place to enable a digital business and experiences. They are essentially the top-line functional requirements. To avoid confusion, let's explain the difference between business, functional, and non-functional requirements.

Business requirements describe an ambition, for example, acquire customers. Functional requirements describe a function, job, or feature that a technology delivers against that ambition, for example, the targeting of customers on social platforms.

https://doi.org/10.1515/9783111034713-020

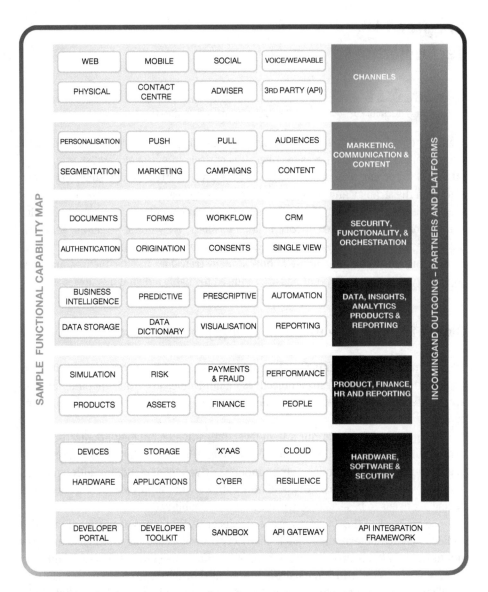

Figure 45: Target Capability Map for Digital Technology.

Non-functional requirements describe how the function should be performed, or how the system should behave; for example, customers should be able to complete the on-boarding journey within five clicks of being engaged.

Linking Requirements to Outcomes – A Method to Ensure That There Is a Linkage Between Intent and Applications

One way to flush out critical functional (and non-functional) requirements is to utilise the customer journeys mentioned earlier in the customer-centricity chapter. As shown in Figure 46, there are 10 journeys in this illustrative use case for a money aggregation proposition. Each journey had its specific journey map and combined service blueprints that articulated the technology required to execute each step. The total and top (linked to the key journey moments) digital functional capabilities were identified to deliver the experience. This closes the loop on ambition to enabler, and from that, a digital capability map can be built.

Application Assessment

Building digital businesses and their underpinning technology stacks invariably involves the selection of new software applications and products. Or the assessment and validation or replacement of existing tools.

In the past two decades, we have seen a proliferation of new products come to market, and thankfully there are many free resources such as www.captera.com that assess and rank the 'freeware' and most prevalent paid applications. However, while these may be useful as initial guides, a systematic and robust evaluation is required of any software to ensure it will do the job it is asked to do.

One can also utilise the excellent work of Gartner and other research firms to assess technology strength and suitability, but again only ever to a generic level. I always strongly suggest identifying the requirements to support the job and journeys at hand as outlined on the prior pages to glean the 'shopping list' against which to assess application suitability. And our big callout is never to start with the software pitch and try to work backwards – that is the world of solutions looking for problems.

Design Principles – How to Pull It All Together

As leaders, we need to sufficiently understand how to define what technologies we need, how to amalgamate and 'stitch' the technologies together in a way that enables the digital business and capabilities we have been describing.

Design Principles that a digital technology strategy should aspire to are detailed below, including the Success Factors that enable execution.

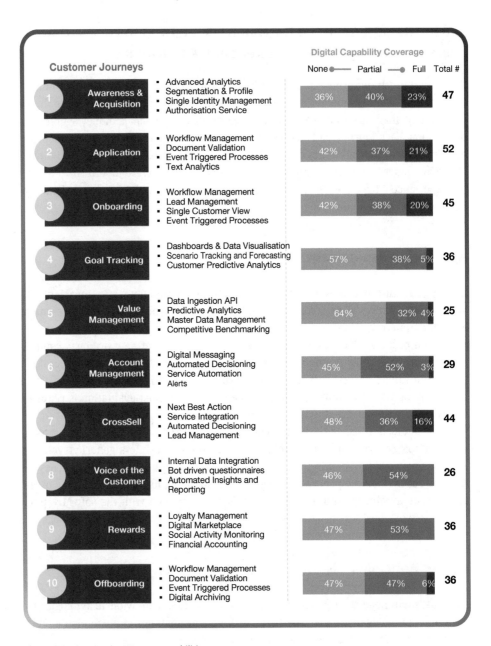

Figure 46: Mapping journeys to capabilities.

Design Principles

Discreet and Componentised
End-to-end services are assembled through dedicated applications performing discreet tasks called microservices. Each microservice runs on its own virtualised infrastructure, called containers, that are infinitely scalable in the cloud.

Accessible and Consumable
Microservices architecture facilitates scope-specific utilisation due to their containerisation, and, therefore, more frequent or multiple deployment as well as easier scaling. This needs to be enabled through a robust API strategy and capability (more on that a little later).

Scalable and Elastic
Digital architectures leverage cloud infrastructure and security services to avoid undue capital and resource (people, time, etc.) being tied up. They should benefit from consumption-based, on-demand utilisation, which is 'made to measure' and responsive or elastic.

Ecosystem Ready
Infrastructure, applications, and their teams are provisioned, designed, and architected to consume and serve partnerships and platforms, in line with our Open through Partnering and Ecosystems capability covered earlier. This includes old systems where that is a factor, and ensuring that they are fit for purpose is critical – a train will only move as fast as it's slowest carriage.

Agile, Automated, and Secure
Release automation and security requirements are embedded into the software development life cycle of agile teams (refer back to Agile) which enables services to be built and operated by the same DevSecOps Teams for continuous development.

Success Factors for Deploying the Design Principles

Emphasis on experience and value
Leaders should set the bar of execution expectation around delivering customer-centric experiences which as a result add value back to the enterprise. If the experience is poor, or if the effort will not glean rewards, then it should not cut the mustard.

Constant collaboration and iteration
Technology cannot work in isolation, nor can business. In the operating model there needs to be a 'round-table' mentality with joint responsibility for the development and life cycle improvement.

Risk appetite and nimble governance
These collaborative teams need to be bestowed with and embrace a risk appetite and tolerances that facilitate agile development and experimentation. Tracking and constant reprioritisation are required to enable continuous testing and learning.

Talent and operating model development
Technologies themselves, and how they are architected, integrated, and developed constantly evolve, and therefore so will talent. Technology talent should get to know commerce, and vice versa, and new talent is often required to stay ahead.

Lean mindset
Exuberance needs to be kept in check, and a mindset of scarcity needs to be instilled in a more decentralised operating model or complexity and cost can creep in. Fat always builds unless a self-regulating regime is embraced.

Building Bridges With APIs

To enable the technology principles and success factors, you should work on the assumption that APIs are an integral component of technology strategy and operations. Equally, when we unravel Open through Partnering and Ecosystems as a core digital capability, by extension, we are entirely dependent on APIs to open the gateways or build the technology bridges to successfully and safely integrate with partners and platforms. This means that a digital business requires an API-centric footing.

An API Strategy at Its Core Needs to Deliver on Four Key Objectives

- be able to unpack internal services for developers and product owners to innovate at speed
- serve as the means to connect and package up internal services and applications to create comprehensive propositions
- act as a means to package up services and propositions when participating with partners and platforms
- integrate with and ingest external services from partners to bolster proprietary systems, propositions, and platforms

API Product Management

Based on these four objectives, APIs are not just 'connectors'. This is their function, but they are products in themselves, given their proficiency, efficiency, and solidity (security), as they deliver a proposition to an end user. The end user, whether an internal developer, a partner, or an ecosystem, consumes what is on the APIs other end: the API product.

On top of technical and compliance management protocols that can be understood in separate technical deep dives, the API product management levers are key for successful API product management, and are set out in Table 13.

Table 13: API product management.

User mapping	Build personas to under the needs of end users, and design API services, tools, formats, and governance to enable adoption
API marketplace	Maintain an inventory of API services, quality documentation, diagnostics, and access supports such as sandbox's which enables promotion and utilisation
Developer experience	Design to minimise developer friction and create an ambassador community – this assists in both API marketability and improvement insights
Embedded security	Given APIs facilitate an open door to key systems and data, a security-first development philosophy should always be adopted
Reuse and value planning	Product managers and developers should target reuse to drive 'ROAPI', and assign OKRs to drive experience, commercial, and risk metrics
Life cycle management	A 'development to sunsetting' approach should be adopted, with robust governance to maintain standards, and improvement programmes

Data Analytics Architecture

"Behind every great leader . . ." is an often reused quotation docking point, and in our case, behind every great technology stack there needs to be a great data architecture and operation.

All too often, we have seen a biased focus towards the technologies, architecture and operations without due consideration to the data flow and leverage. To ensure that the stack can not just execute its functional and non-functional responsibilities, but also empower the Data Analytics products as covered earlier, a conscious and strategic data architecture is necessary.

In the same way that I presented a reference model for the holistic technology stack, here is the data analytics stack, which essentially sits behind or more aptly inside the main architecture. I will not detail a double click here, but I have included guidance on what to expect from each layer in Table 14, from both requirements and an operational perspective.

The design principles and success factors presented earlier are also applicable here. In particular, a harmonised cloud strategy is needed to ensure that a mix of data from often 'on premise' systems can be blended with modern cloud processing and extraction applications.

Table 14: Data analytics stack.

Value extraction		
	Requirements	**Operations**
Data analytics utilisation	Adoption and utilisation of the data analytics products such as decisioning, engagement, and reward	Business and technology leaders working together to ensure product adoption and improvement loops
Data analytics services	Analytics services that deliver descriptive, diagnostic, predictive, and prescriptive data analytics products	Data science and business consumers collaborate to define use cases and extract end user value
Data storage and compliance	Data warehouse and data lakes that host and prepare data (through cleansing) for consumption by services	Master data management teams sit at the intersection of the data topography to channel and categorise data for analytics production and compliance
Ingestion and processing	Streaming and capture (live or batch) of internal and external data for allocation to data storage	Data engineering design data capture journeys to fulfil use cases, and data analytics end deliverables
Source systems and data streams	Scope and outward flow of key data points for transfer from host systems to data analytics storage systems	Data owners and their engineering teams prepare and transfer demand-side data to defined destinations
Infrastructure and security	Hardware, protocols, and security that facilitate the safe flow of data across the topology	Data infrastructure and security specialists provision, deploy, and monitor data analytics environments

Untangling Legacy

Many long-standing organisations have large estates of complex technology legacy hosted 'on premise', including core customer, product, and financial records. In the worst cases a spaghetti of complex interdependencies exists, often as a result of well-intended progressive investment strategies in the pre-digital Industry 3.0 era.

As technology philosophy and engineering, with significant benefits accruing, has moved considerably in the last 40 years and continues to accelerate (exponentially!), those organisations are caught in a Sophie's choice. The effort, cost, and cultural change required to migrate from now burdensome stacks is so significant that appetite is low, and rightly so as failure is high. On the other hand, organisations see the necessity for a transition given not doing so will result in missing end user expectations, avoidable cost, and speed as well as declining skills and systems integrity as those systems drift into retirement or decay.

Often the core technology used comprises very old mainframe or other monolithic types of server infrastructure which is expensive to maintain and difficult to change. Some organisations have attempted to wrap old systems with new technology to keep pace with the market and benefits. I have seen this mostly to launch new distribution channels, improve customer experiences, and bolt on new data analytics capabilities. But this strategy has often added further complexity, cost, and operational commitment and constraint, counteracting the intent.

Maintaining and adding further to 'technical debt' places an immense burden on organisations as the time and effort required to sustain these technology platforms for business as usual is not then available for innovation and proposition development, never mind harnessing new modern architectures and agile methodologies. A further exaggeration is the need to maintain skills on older platforms, which are in decline and no longer supported in terms of education, patching, and integration.

Other organisations have outsourced their core IT to external vendors using the application service provider (ASP) model to try and benefit from economies of scale, external acceleration muscle, and know-how. For some this has transpired to an effective lock-in to a platform (and a partner), again exacerbating the pain-points that the organisation is trying to alleviate. This can be offset by hooking up to a shared services model, with the trade-off being change and features are decided by the ASP vendor for common consumption, leaving differentiation and agility hard to secure.

These pathways have put organisations at a distinct disadvantage over those newer and more nimble companies born into the modern architectures we prescribe. The ability to leverage agile development, digital data, and analytics capabilities as well as APIs and benefits of the cloud are sadly missed. And so too are the resulting benefits for end users, colleagues, businesses, partners, and, ultimately, commercials.

Organisations must move from monolithic application architectures to those which allow for more flexibility and agility. This can be achieved with a gradual decoupling of the core application components and over time then adopting modern hybrid cloud application architectures including utilisation of microservices and interconnecting into wider cloud ecosystems as they emerge.

It is important to plan for and execute this change agenda as quickly as possible but on a tested timeline born out of realism rather than pure ambition, and on the understanding that this takes multiple years, is expensive and will deflect resources and money in the short term. In order to assess what is the best route to modernisation, businesses need to assess two axes – the technology and the business pain points. The diagnostic in Figure 47 illustrates how this might be done, and the resulting interventions that usually ensue.

The State of the Nation

We will explore technology risk management when we move into the next chapter, but a pre-emptive move is to understand the 'state' of the technology estate so that strategic decisions can be made.

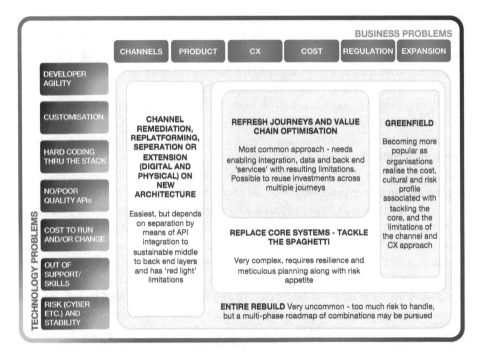

Figure 47: Framework for untangling legacy.

To that end, I like to use the FURPS+ diagnostic, originally developed by Hewlett Packard, extended to include the '+' dimensions and widely used. It enables users to assess the functional and non-functional attributes of installed software. Using the FURPS headings, architects, engineers, and operators assess the strength and weaknesses of the applications in their stack to illuminate the 'currency' of the estate:

- Functionality – The main operational functions or requirements of the system or release. Essentially what the system does for the user.
- Usability (UX) – The aesthetics and accessibility across the human and machine interfaces. This looks at how do other systems, processes, or human users interact and use the functionality.
- Reliability – The availability, robustness, and fault tolerance of the system. Uptime and accuracy are important determinants here.
- Performance – Speed, efficiency, resource consumption, throughput, capacity, and scalability are measured, and link to meeting delivery expectations.
- Supportability – The maintainability of the system, its modularity, and how easily it may be upgraded enhanced and repaired. This helps to define extendibility.
- Plus – This facilitates the discovery of additional constraints that need to be factored in such as external interfaces and legal needs but can also capture design, physical, and implementation factors.

I often see the results presented in a spidergram visual, which in turn spurs a retention and remediation plan that can be linked back to informing an overall technology strategy and coexistence planning.

The one aspect that is for me missing in this model is an evaluation of the climate impact, and broader ESG performance of a technology – one which I would implore you to add.

Agile Developments

DevOps is a collaborative way of working between IT development and operations teams to extend the principles of agile development to the IT software deployment process. It facilitates the thrust of agile vision centricity, with continuous iterative technology development and deployment. Software code is released, tested, security assessed, and deployed into production using automated methods to allow for rapid continuous change at high frequency. Fused Agile DevOps is critical to enable a modern digital and data stack.

Agile DevOps merges two great schools by facilitating cross-functional teams to collaborate and work in an iterative fashion to allow for continuous product development cycles. Breaking down development and delivery into small packages allows continual progression and meaningful delivery in reasonable timeframes, which can meet the demands of the rapidly changing world.

Constant feedback loops used throughout the cycle permitting continuous updates and constant re-evaluation and re-prioritisation are key dynamics within an agile project/programme, particularly helpful for the delivery of minimum viable propositions (MVPs). But the approach also promotes cultural transformation in traditional environments by blurring lines of demarcation, forcing greater collaboration, and promoting common purpose and objectives. This is often achieved through working to user-centric goals and values articulated by 'User Stories' (used to describe desired outcomes and granular requirements and covered earlier).

Some of the promises of agile methodology are higher team productivity and morale, faster time to market for new products and product features, improved quality, and lower risk. Underpinning this is creating the conditions for multi-disciplinary teams to develop close personal working relationships and work toward a common agenda supported by the constant availability and presence of required subject matter experts.

As mentioned earlier, agile teams work in scrums with scrum masters managing day-to-day activities and removing blockers to progress. However, overarching project/ programme management is even more critical in larger agile projects to ensure overall objectives are being realised and accurate planning and reporting are made available to sponsors and other stakeholders. However, within agile delivery programmes, leadership, facilitation, support, oversight, and problem-solving are what managers and senior SMEs should concern themselves with.

Tools are essential for managing an agile project, especially in IT development. Tools such as Atlassian Jira and Confluence and Microsoft DevOps are commonly used.

You do not have to automatically adopt agile for everything. It may be less suited to certain project types where a high degree of upfront certainty of requirements and planning is needed or where fixed external dependencies exist and would not allow for continuous agile-style development. For example, in projects requiring advanced or specialist engineering disciplines, such as in healthcare systems or passenger travel where a high degree of certainty is required throughout the development and deployment life cycle.

Harnessing the Cloud

We discussed Cloud in the opening of this book as one of the forbears of Industry 4.0, and it is only fitting that we visit it again, and in the context of it being a lightning conductor of digital technology strategies.

Cloud technology enables a business to outsource and acquire state-of-the-art IT infrastructure and operations services using an external provider to deliver flexibility, scalability, and efficiency. Here is a more practical view of the Cloud, and a reminder of the three main cloud models:
- SaaS (software as a service) – distribution of specific software applications over the internet, and central development model (e.g. Salesforce)
- PaaS (platform as a service) – software, development tools, and hardware (a technology platform) provided from virtual environment (e.g. Oracle)
- IaaS (infrastructure as a service) – provision of server, storage, and computing infrastructure from virtual centres delivered via the internet (e.g. Amazon Web Services)

Depending on the organisational type and context, cloud technology may involve all of or only selected IT infrastructure and operations. Virtually all start-ups and small to mid-size greenfield organisations founded over recent years will largely or exclusively use cloud-provided IT services. Whereas larger and more established organisations will typically use a mix of 'on–premise' hosted infrastructure and cloud services, called a hybrid cloud arrangement.

It has always been an option for organisations to use an external provider to manage IT infrastructure and operations. However, (public) cloud providers have brought the truly mega-scale enabling acquisition of services immediately, on-demand, and on a pay-as-you-go basis. The ability to subscribe and unsubscribe on demand to advanced

IT infrastructure services like this has levelled the playing field for smaller organisations regarding affordable IT investment.

Cloud providers use a custom-developed cloud management 'fabric' to enable customers to draw from a massive pool of services and infrastructure. The big three providers (at the time of writing) are Amazon Web Services (AWS), Microsoft Azure, and Google Cloud Platform (GGP), with a lot of smaller providers following suit and often providing more specialised services. Oracle Cloud is also worth mentioning for larger businesses.

There are different variants to the cloud model. These are primarily:

- A public cloud, where all the services are made available and publicly accessible to all users by large cloud providers, is what most people mean when they talk of cloud computing
- A private cloud is effectively more like the traditional model of exclusively providing and managing IT infrastructure and services private to a specific organisation, albeit using shared data centres and with modern service management tools and systems more akin to public cloud management
- A hybrid cloud is where an organisation bridges both public cloud services and its own on-site (or externally hosted and managed) private infrastructure and services. This model is the most typical employed of larger more longstanding organisations as it has allowed them to adopt the benefits or public cloud gradually while maintaining their existing estate or migrating it to the cloud incrementally

The Benefits of the Cloud

Agility, flexibility, and the rapid provision of a wide range of IT infrastructure and software services on demand are at the heart. This allows for rapid execution of proof of concepts, prototyping, customer/usability testing, and rapid setup of environments which are typically in IT development projects (e.g. Dev, QA, UAT, Pre-Prod, and production environments) which traditionally would have a significant lead-in time to realise.

Moving from fixed or inflexible variable cost arrangements to completely flexible variable pay-as-you-go and pay-only-for-what-you-use cost models is another significant claimed benefit. Services are selectable on a la carte basis and at various performance and service levels and corresponding pricing tiers. This offers enormous advantages if appropriately managed.

Best in class cybersecurity protection at a low cost arising from massive economies of scale inherent in some of the shared services made available through public cloud platforms is a further promoted benefit.

Data backup is provided reliably, cheaply, and usually automatically, thus reducing costs, stress and risks associated with the management of a large estate of applications with significant databases and storage requirements. High availability and disaster recovery options available and easily accessible usually is an add-on services but at low cost and easily arranged. Many out-of-the-box standard services offer robust service-level agreements without purchasing additional capability.

Disaster recovery is usually provided via regional data centres spread across the world. State-of-the-art and technology constantly being updated is available on tap. Cloud computing offers a virtuous circle where the more people use it, the more investment goes, creating more demand (a network effect). Access to high-end AI processing, big data analytics, high-performance computing, and other types of advanced computing would otherwise be inaccessible to all but large organisations.

Demonstrable compliance with a variety of international security and data privacy compliance standards, including ISO 27001, IS 27018, PCI DSS, SOC 2/3, HIPPA, and Cloud Security Alliance CCM is another important benefit.

That said, Cloud, while having many proclaimed benefits, is a challenging journey for many organisations, and comes with warnings – here are a few to watch out for:

–   Governance is critical and even more so than for managing internal infrastructure as public clouds are internet-facing and access security must be very tightly controlled.
–   Costs for IaaS services are high and may be higher than running on-premise. A large migration of servers from on-premise data centres to cloud hosting is unlikely to yield savings. It may even cost more unless substantial staff and other significant fixed costs other than data centre management can be eliminated.
–   European data centres must be used for complete and easily verifiable GDPR compliance.
–   Some regions and sectors where there is a high regulatory bar can be more conservative on Cloud adoption – think Financial Services and Medicine (money and health). Although this has largely been alleviated as we turn through the 2020s.

Case Study: Aldo – A 360 Technology Stack to Support Digital Ambitions

Aldo's inflexible back-office systems were unable to support business needs. Having experienced rapid growth on a global scale, the company eventually outgrew its rigid legacy environment.

Aldo transitioned from an on-premise legacy system with manual touch points to a single cloud-native solution. The HR IS/IT role has evolved from system maintenance and report creation to strategic projects and innovation. Aldo gained ease of use, better performance, scalability, reduced risk of downtime, and compliance in areas such as GDPR.

In addition to eliminating paper forms and driving payroll, benefits, and audit efficiency, key improvements include faster onboarding for new hires, internal reorganisations, and completion of year-end payroll cycle.

Aldo has delivered an intuitive UX/UI. New hires use the tool for pre-onboarding, a process that streamlines the onboarding cycle and enables cost savings.

Existing employees use a one-stop, self-service tool to initiate and execute HR tasks, reducing the burden on HR. Store managers have increased productivity with access to real-time data about their teams and ability to execute transactions on the go.

Case Study: San Diego County Office of Emergency Services – Cloud Services Making a Real-World Difference

The San Diego County Office of Emergency Services coordinates the county's response to disasters and is the designated organisation that residents turn to for disaster updates such as floods and wildfires. The OES is also responsible for notifying and coordinating agencies when a disaster strikes, ensuring all needed resources are available and mobilised efficiently.

To efficiently serve the whole community, the OES developed a cloud-based portal that could send notifications to San Diego residents on their mobile devices, with information being available in Spanish, and formats for blind or deaf citizens.

During disasters prior to deployment to a cloud-based platform, the country's on-premises servers could not handle the huge flood of visitors to their official website, resulting in the site crashing. That experience led them to look for a better web hosting solution, which made them turn to the Microsoft Azure cloud platform, reducing their costs by 78%.

With these improvements and updates in place, the OES agency is now meeting its goal of efficiently serving more country residents during times of crisis, providing information in real time with push notifications, allowing them to make the right decisions to ensure their safety.

Reflection

In summary, technology is the engine of digital, and the businesses that thrive on it; data is the fuel. However, the technologies that are leveraged in the digital age are different from those that powered Industry 3.0.

A new set of design principles, architecture, development, and operational rhythm are required to leverage them, crafted to enable the seven core competencies and the three enabling platforms of risk, people, and platforms.

Chapter 15
Risk

In an ancient anecdote, Damocles was offered a day on the throne of his king Dionysius to taste the true meaning of power. But above the throne of Dionysius hung a sword, held only by the single hair of a horse's tail, to serve as a constant reminder that amassing power and riches brought envy, enemies, and ever-present threat. Despite his original delight at the prospect of tasting such greatness, Damocles soon turned to beg the king that he descended the throne and acknowledged that with great power comes great responsibility.

We might interpret a negative connotation from Damocles' U-turn, that we are under constant threat from rivals and/or the envious. Or that those who hold power live in constant fear. We do draw on that a little, as there are dark forces in the digital world that we do need to be fearful of and act accordingly to protect our domains, or we could extend that sentiment to the threat of digitally enabled market disruptors.

But we can also muse that Damocles learned that living in terror is an unhappy place, and hence we need to find and focus on creation not destruction to find contentment. We could also say that there is the lesson of walking in the shoes of another to truly understand the state and desires of those around us, a topic we explored in our customer-centric capability.

This ancient adage rings true when we consider the power that digital technology impels. Digital is technology-grounded, but it is so much more than that. It is a way of thinking and acting. It is the ability to create experiences, to build businesses, to create, liberate, and democratise value.

The inverse is, therefore, always true, as logic theory denotes when there is a conditional element. The misuse of digital has the power to undo experiences, dismantle businesses, and misdirect or even destroy value. We therefore need to take a lens of care, balance, and respect for that power into our thinking and execution.

Technology Risk

Every temple needs formidable foundations. You will recall that in earlier parts of this book, we visited the nine customer expectations of today, and we placed trust at the centre. Trust manifests itself in many ways, including how we treat data for the end user and for commercial reasons (which we also visited in the Data Analytics chapter). But at a much more elementary level is the maintenance of trust in our business models and systems. This extends to meeting the regulatory requirements imposed by oversight mechanisms to ensure minimum standards are met, and therefore trust is maintained.

https://doi.org/10.1515/9783111034713-021

Table 15: Technology risk spectrum.

Technology risk spectrum	
Architecture and strategy	The ability of the technology 'system' to deliver strategic outcomes that are affordable, reliant, and elastic
Business continuity	Maintaining continuity, growth, and resilience of core processes alongside disaster recovery
Data assurance	Managing the quality, accuracy, and coherence of data, and data management governance
Cyber security	Protection of systems, data, and stakeholders from external threats
Change management	Delivering technology development, implementation, integration, and change within time, cost, and quality standards
Legal and compliance	Ensuring that technologies, data, processes, and people meet regulatory and legislative requirements
Vendors and partnerships	Managing the end-to-end technology supply chain to mitigate the weakest link across an open ecosystem

When it comes to managing technology risk, which is at the core of maintaining business model and system-level trust, there are a number of facets that we want to pay attention to which are summarised in Table 15.

The National Institute of Standards and Technology, a standard-setting agency of the US Department of Commerce, has developed a Risk Management Framework (RMF) that integrates security, privacy, and cyber-supply chain risk management activities into the system development life cycle. Developed for leverage by any enterprise, it is a good place to start for guidance and structure.

The RMF provides a dynamic and flexible approach to effectively manage security and privacy risks in diverse environments with complex and sophisticated threats, evolving missions and business functions, and changing system and organisational vulnerabilities. The framework is policy- and technology-neutral, which facilitates ongoing upgrades to IT resources and IT modernisation efforts to support and help ensure essential missions and services are provided during such transition periods.

Executing the RMF requires close collaboration between information security programmes and privacy programmes. While information security programmes and privacy programmes have different objectives, those objectives are overlapping and complementary. Information security programmes are responsible for protecting information and information systems from unauthorised access, use, disclosure, disruption, modification, or destruction (i.e. unauthorised system activity or behaviour) in order to provide confidentiality, integrity, and availability.

Privacy programmes are responsible for ensuring compliance with applicable privacy requirements and for managing the risks to individuals associated with the creation, collection, use, processing, dissemination, storage, maintenance, disclosure, or disposal (collectively referred to as 'processing') of Personal Identifiable Information (PII).

Building Moats

Cybersecurity is not optional – it is a tablestake. As we digitalise our world and as adoption, touch points, and ecosystems grow and expand, the attack surface grows and extends concurrently. The Covid pandemic accelerated this as we went online to shop and work, perhaps without all the necessary measures. At the same time, end users expect protection from the brands they engage with, and it is harder to deliver that these days. Phishing, hacking, malware, and ransomware attacks are all on the rise as bad actors feed off our forays; and it is not just proprietary systems that we need to think about. In 2021, a direct attack on Microsoft affected more than 30,000 businesses large and small – size does not matter. Cybercrime costs $6 trillion in 2021 and is estimated to drain $10 trillion in 2025, up from $3 trillion in 2015.[84]

A response needs to be comprehensive, starting with understanding the assets, actors, and rules that need to be taken into account, and building measures to stop, track, and respond to threats and attacks.

Deloitte's cyber-strategy framework encapsulates the core elements of a cyber-defence[85] and as a complement we would draw your attention to the USA's National Institute of Standards and Technology Cybersecurity Framework[86] which leverages the world's largest defence network's knowledge and tactics and makes them available for individuals and businesses to leverage. Both present excellent starting points for cyber-defence strategies.

I have seen different organisations manage cyber-defence in many different ways. Some organisations hide it under lock and key, almost subscribing to the clandestine nature of the theme itself. Others make it much more transparent and seek to make cyber-management a part of everyday business across their teams, and even out to customers and clients. I support the latter school of thinking. According to the World Economic Forum,[87] 95% of cybersecurity breaches are as a result of human

84 Cybercrime Magazine – "Cybercrime to Cost the World $10.5 Trillion Annually by 2025," accessed April 7, 2023, https://cybersecurityventures.com/hackerpocalypse-cybercrime-report-2016/.

85 SIFMA.org – "SOC for Cybersecurity – An Overview of the AICPA's Cybersecurity Attestation Reporting Framework," accessed April 7, 2023, https://www.sifma.org/wp-content/uploads/2018/03/SOC-for-Cybersecurity.pdf.

86 NIST Risk Management Framework, accessed April 7, 2023, https://csrc.nist.gov/projects/risk-management/about-rmf.

87 World Economic Forum – "Global Risks Report 2023," accessed April 7, 2023, https://www.weforum.org/reports/global-risks-report-2023.

error, so defence management needs to manifest itself in and carry responsibility for every system, team, partner, and end user.

MITRE ATT&CK® is a globally accessible knowledge base of adversary tactics and techniques based on real-world observations of cybersecurity threats. The ATT&CK knowledge base is used as a foundation for the development of specific threat models and methodologies in the private sector, in government, and in the cybersecurity product and service community. MITRE have developed and shared the knowledge base to fulfil its mission to solve problems for a safer world by bringing communities together to develop more effective cybersecurity. ATT&CK is open and available to any person or organisation for use at no charge, and it is an enlightening resource to explore.

The Knowledge Base is displayed in matrices that are arranged by attack stages, from initial system access to data theft or machine control. There are matrices for common desktop platforms such as Linux, macOS, and Windows and technologies like cloud, containers, networks, and mobile platforms. ATT&CK stands for 'adversarial tactics, techniques, and common knowledge'. The tactics are a modern way of uncovering cyberattacks.

Rather than looking at the results of an attack, which is also called an 'indicator of compromise' (IoC), it identifies tactics that indicate an attack is in progress. Tactics are the 'why' of an attack technique. In the Enterprise ATT&CK matrix there are currently 14 tactics, with each tactic correlated to an assigned set of techniques that have been used by bad actors.

There are 185 techniques and 367 sub-techniques in the Enterprise model, but that extends further with 2 congruent matrices:
- the Mobile ATT&CK, which covers mobile devices
- the PRE-ATT&CK matrices aimed at arming security specialists with the knowledge to understand how bad actors operate pre-attack, e.g. reconnaissance and target selection – MITRE continuously adds updates to its matrices and is a free resource

However, many organisations want to, and should, employ specialists to operate cyber-defences. Organisations such as MITRE and Lockheed Martin are global leaders in this space. You can learn more and explore the matrices at Mitre.org.[88]

There are many free resources available to support organisations in getting to grips with technology risk and cyberthreats. But this is a complex area, which is continually evolving, so it needs dedicated support and management time to ensure that the Damocles responsibility is in check.

---

88 Mitre, "ATT&CK," accessed April 7, 2023, https://attack.mitre.org/.

It is also, unfortunately, a growing area which is natural given the growth of the digital market. And resources are tight, with reports citing that there might be as many as 3.5 million unfilled cybersecurity roles worldwide through 2025.[89]

Risk Identification

As we broaden our lens beyond technology and data into the full digital sphere to interrogate the business and identify the potential risks for consideration and treatment, I suggest a two-step approach, namely, identification and calibration.

The first step is an important one as it is where we 'cast the net' to ensure that the full spectrum of risks is gathered and considered. Table 16 shows what a typical Identification Grid could look like, including some sample entries, but note both the dimensions and the sample entries are illustrative and not exhaustive. Businesses should run this exercise on a recurring basis, e.g. quarterly.

Table 16: Risk identification – asking the right questions.

Risk identification grid	How could risk emerge?	How would we recognise it?	How vulnerable are we?	What are the effects of risk?
End users	System downtime or latency	End user complaints; system outage	X systems that scored low on our FURPS+ analysis are indicating sub-SLA performance	Reputation, loss of customers, and complaints/redress
Staff	Staff fraud	Embezzlement of customer/client funds	A number of operational systems have inefficient automated monitoring and system controls	Reputation, loss of customers, and significant financial exposure
Sales and service	Lack of data and permission capture to engage customers/clients	Unable to contact customers or breach of data compliance	Inability of data capture in x product lines	Inability to capture latent growth; Regulatory breach

89 EIN Press Wire, "Cybersecurity Jobs Report: 3.5 Million Openings Through 2025," (November 11, 2021), accessed April 7, 2023, https://www.einpresswire.com/article/556075599/cybersecurity-jobs-report-3-5-millionopenings-through-2025.

Table 16 (continued)

Risk identification grid	How could risk emerge?	How would we recognise it?	How vulnerable are we?	What are the effects of risk?
Partners	Break down in the ecosystem value chain	Customer complaints; system outage	As the orchestrator, we hold significant brand and service delivery responsibility	Reputation, loss of customers, complaints/redress and financial exposure
Processes and systems	Theft of end user credentials	Embezzlement of customer/client funds	Perpetual risk – always on	Reputation, loss of customers, complaints/redress, and financial exposure
Data and analytics	Incomplete data sets used in training channel AI models	Incomplete or poor end user experience in search or automated chat	Existing user data may not extend to train the AI for all potential use cases	Reputation, loss of customers, complaints/redress, and financial exposure
Strategy and change	Inability to deliver strategic change agenda due to legacy technology architecture	Expensive change profile, or incomplete delivery of intended journey design	Modular, micro-service system design with modern API strategy in place, so risk should be low	While we have the architecture in place, some inflexible legacy or third-party systems may present a bottleneck

Risk Calibration – Response Strategies

Once the risks have been identified and examined using the risk identification questions above, it is time to calibrate them.

I suggest doing this through a probability:impact lens, and I have used an alteration of the 5 × 5 approach often seen in risk classification, of which I am a fan, in Figure 48. However, I extend to calibration particularly, on the impact side to include headings such as Performance, Cost, and Time impacts. This is harder to navigate when it comes to crystallising risk realities and their prioritisation, so it is with good intent that I introduce and encourage this.

Type of Risk	Description of Risk	Probability			Impact			Risk Response Strategy	Risk Owner
		H	**M**	**L**	**Perf**	**Cost**	**Time**		
Customer Experience Delivery	Latency and intermittent system performance result in poor availability for customers and CX		●		Poor End User Experience			System remediation roadmap to address low scoring availability systems	Chief Technology Officer
Fraud	Staff could manipulate systems (EUC or End User Computing) to embezzle customer finds			●		10% of customer balances		Implement EUC Governance Framework	Chief Information Security Officer (CISO)
End User Consents	Lack of data consent capture inhibits proactive customer engagement		●			5% of cross sales targets		Enable consent capture in journeys, and launch proactive customer consent capture campaign	Product Owner(s)
3rd Party	Ecosystem partners fail to deliver on service promise		●		Reputational damage	Cost of brand defense plan		Partner SLA Management and Tracking	Product Owner(s)
Cyber Theft	Theft of end user credentials	●			Reputational damage	10% of customer balances and cost of brand defense plan		Employ Cyber specialists to perpetually advise and test perimeter defenses, coupled with ongoing end user knowledge and alerting campaigns	CISO and Product Owner
AI Bias	Existing business data sets prohibit AI models to properly train for all go forward use cases			●	Reputational damage		Slower than expected deployment	Restrict use case deployment and release when human in the loop controls and synthetic data set training satisfy test criteria	Chief Analytics Offices (CAO)
Strategic Change	Technology architectural deficiencies strangles change ambition			●	Competitive disadvantage	10% increased cost to acquire and fulfil	Drag on speed to market	Strategic architecture Roadmap	CEO and CIO

Figure 48: Risk calibration response categories.

The Broader Digital Risk Spectrum – The Hard Risks

Extending to the full business setting, there are other associated 'hard' risks that we have seen manifest. If not now, soon all business engagements will mostly, if not entirely, be executed using digital tools to deliver digital propositions or processes. Therefore we need to identify what those holistic risks are, and where they surface, before we can think about what they mean and how we can mitigate them. In Table 17 the primary themes are observed. However, note that this is not an exhaustive list.

Table 17: Risk spectrum, the hard risks.

Risk dimension		Impact zone
More and more we are using cloud and freeware to support our day-to-day tasks and workflow, which inherently includes document repositories and proprietary record	**Code and file sharing**	Incorrect guidance, lack of awareness and controls or human error can lead to sensitive documents resting in easily accessible but uncontrollable environments
The availability of easily installed 'business-side' SaaS can be advantageous, and easily provisioned and integrated, resulting in data and processes resting outside the core	**Shadow IT**	While it is attractive to businesses teams to 'drive on', creating standalone or softly integrated pools of data and/or processes can pose significant control and exposure risks
Internal resourcing and skill supply is being outstripped/overstretched by demand as organisations both take on digital transformation but also seek to keep pace with regulation etc.	**Capacity and knowledge**	Undersupply can potentially be solved by augmented people and training, but is costly, time sensitive and the risk can persist if self-sufficiency is not catered for
Inherent biases can exist in data sets being used in or for training AI models, and many automation and AI tools and users can lack the methods to interrogate/validate/remove bias	**Bias**	Lack of awareness, processes, and oversight of bias and improper automation can lead to inherent/systemic risk
Digitisation and digitalisation through online/mobile journey development, robotics, and AI could lose critical process and risk requirements in the transition/migration	**Automation**	Without due diligence in the design, test, and release cycle, diluted risk measures could be codified and remain undetected
Rising complexity and demand in the change portfolio, as well as transition to digital business models (e.g. open), requires governance to evolve and adapt	old	Lack of review and refinement of the governance model to keep pace with digital business methods and means could have a counter risk impact – governance needs governance

In addition to the extended business risk themes above, digital risk also pushes all the way through to the end user and particularly the customer, with strong linkage to meeting their minimum expectations. Service delivery, and how that is discussed on social media, is a perpetual risk to be managed. Supporting end users to adopt digital solutions (not forcing them), and giving them comfort on how their data is being stored and treated also features. Finally, making sure that end users know and support the business model seeing it as fair and transparent, and how the organisation thinks about how they are integrating ESG dimensions into their digital business are important if not paramount risk considerations (particularly the last one).

The Broader Digital Risk Spectrum – The Softer Risks

When it comes to building a digital business, which is really what is termed as digital transformation, we have tried and failed a few times ourselves, and observed others also fall into the traps. But learning those lessons gives us resolve and guidance. Some of these traps are unforeseeable, which is why traditional risk assessment techniques do not work, and why lessons learnt from those that have gone before can be so valuable. I have captured the main, avoidable pitfalls that may need to be negotiated in Table 18.

These risks have arisen repeatedly in the strive for digital business building, and the solutions offer guidance on how to avoid them.

Table 18: Digital risk spectrum – soft risks.

1 **DON'T CODE THE PAST – TAKE OUT THE TRASH:** In the development of new digital service and journeys it is critical to look forwards, and not backwards. That means taking the opportunity to remove complexity and simplify the experience from junk that just builds up over time. The important thing is do not hard code imperfection.
2 **A DEFINING NORTH STAR – THE GUIDING LIGHT:** This helps everyone work towards a guiding vision, which should always be the genesis or departure point while also remains the touchstone to check progress. The North Star needs to be enlightening and motivational, calling on a common purpose that unlocks discretion, but also provides guiderails and scope-creep boundaries.
3 **BREAK SILOS – AVOID THE STOVEPIPE SYNDROME:** In a transformation setting, do not underestimate power structures and the default to protect the 'status' quo. A pre-departure success condition is to get everyone pointing in the same direction through time, talk, and logic which are great healers. These are the hard, vital yards
4 **CREATE CAPACITY – LESS IS MORE:** To do more, you need to do less – capacity is finite, whether that is money, operations, people, or systems. New ventures need new skills and new mindsets, which do not grow on trees. Transformation is not a straight line, so build in time and patience to go backwards in order to go forwards.

Table 18 (continued)

5	**EAT THE ELEPHANT – ONE STEP AT A TIME:** Avoid the Big Bang Theory – mass matters and will weigh you down. Eat the elephant in bite sizes and remember that agile reduces not increases risk – it does this by focusing on the immediate, important, and impactful, but does so in line with the North Star to stay aligned
6	**FAILURE = FEEDBACK AND IS THE BREAKFAST OF CHAMPIONS:** Failure is the process of eliminating what doesn't work in the pursuit of what does. It therefore requires risk tolerance and an acceptance that will typically rail in any organisation that is designed for perfection. It also requires an openness to pivoting – great discoveries can often unfold in unplanned ways, and that is innovation.
7	**KILL DISTRACTIONS – DISCIPLINE RULES:** As while great things can come unexpectedly, terrible things can come with distractions. Maintaining focus on the 'currencies of success' and sticking to it requires you to kill nice but not needed initiatives with empathy. Stick to the course and continually recalibrate to keep straying off the field.
8	**CLOSE THE CIRCLE – BY OPENING IT UP:** Bias and homogeneity are dangerous bedfellows and can lead to dilution, misdirection, and plainly getting it wrong. Simple rule – make your participants and focus reflect the market and balance participation through inclusion, diversity, and equity.
9	**MEASUREMENT = DONE AND QUESTIONS TRUMP ANSWERS:** Sometimes we defy measurement for the fear of failure. But we have already established that failure = feedback, so measure and even reward it. In data we trust – do not fight with it. Also asking the right question will get to the right outcome so encourage inquisition and investigation.

Anchoring Digital in Enterprise Risk Management

Risk is defined as the effect of uncertainty on objectives, and risk management itself is defined as the creation and protection of value. As a practice, it aims to improve performance, encourage innovation, and support the achievement of objectives. Sometimes this runs counter to an experience of 'business preventers' on the ground, who understandably, with risk as their only metric, opine and sometime veto projects and practices to minimise risk as the prime objective.

Underneath, however, risk management is about a trade-off between opportunity and threat in the pursuit of strategy, and an organisation needs to set out a risk appetite in that regard. This is seldom done as sometimes digital is not seen as part of the cost strategy (counter to my belief from Part II), or risk management is not seen as a core strategic requirement. An integrated approach to digital, strategy and risk is essential.

Risk Appetite and Tracking

One of the hardest and probably least common aspects of risk management I have witnessed organisations work on is the development of risk appetite. To strike the re-ward:risk trade-off I referred to previously, and to guide teams on what level of risk is acceptable in their thinking and pursuits, risk appetites and risk-associated tolerance can be beneficial. Risk tolerance is the degree to which risk appetite should be stretched and remain acceptable, given risk needs to be elastic to facilitate strategic execution dynamics in the real world. Embedding risk monitoring and perpetual risk management is thereafter critical to maintaining the right balance of expectation and acknowledgment.

Case Study: Save the Children – Blocking the Cyberthreat

As a well-known global NGO, Save the Children faced a high level of cyberthreat. Charity organisations are a popular target for cyber-criminals and are particularly vulnerable to disruptive attacks such as ransomware due to the critical nature of their work.

Cybersecurity is a high priority for Save the Children. The organisation safeguards sensitive information relating to vulnerable children, as well as the personal and financial details of its staff, volunteers, and donors.

In line with wider efforts to establish a more centralised approach to IT and security management, the organisation needed a solution with a high level of functionality that could administer a large number of endpoints from a single point.

Its position as an NGO also meant that ethical concerns play a greater role than they do for most private sector companies.

Through various cybersecurity protection measures, more than 100,000 attempted malware infections were identified and resolved across Save the Children's global infrastructure in an average month.

The solutions continually block thousands of attempts by worms designed to hide in the system and download further malicious software.

Case Study: JPL – Active, Inclusive Risk Management

JPL, a division of NASA, face high intrinsic risk as they pursue long, complex, and expensive product-development projects.

But since much of the risk arises from coping with known laws of nature, the risk changes slowly over time. For these organisations, risk management can be handled at the project level.

JPL, for example, has established a risk review board made up of independent technical experts whose role is to challenge project engineers' design, risk-assessment, and risk-mitigation decisions. The experts ensure that evaluations of risk take place periodically throughout the product-development cycle. Because the risks are relatively unchanging, the review board needs to meet only once or twice a year, with the project leader and the head of the review board meeting quarterly.

The risk review board meetings are intense, creating what Gentry Lee calls 'a culture of intellectual confrontation'.

As board member Chris Lewicki says, 'We tear each other apart, throwing stones and giving very critical commentary about everything that's going on'. In the process, project engineers see their work from another perspective. 'It lifts their noses away from the grindstone', Lewicki adds.

Reflection

Risk is at the core of maintaining the business model, and developing trust.
Factors to consider for technology risk are:
- Ensuring technology systems can deliver strategic outcomes that are affordable and reliant
- Maintaining business continuity of core processes alongside disaster recovery
- Managing the quality, accuracy, and coherence of data
- Protecting data, systems, and people from cyberattacks and external threat
- Developing and integrating technology in a timely, cost-effective manner maintaining quality standards
- Ensuring technology and data meet regulatory and legislative requirements
- Effectively manage supply chains to mitigate weak links across an open ecosystem

Summary – Part III

Finally, we move on to people, without whom any plan is just an empty shell. People are the spark that ignites possibility and opportunity. They are the stokers of the flame that illuminates the way, and they are the kindle that fuels the fire of enterprise and value.

For this final enabling platform, we will begin with a new and dedicated part of the book. This allows us to delve into, expand, and explore a rounded set of dimensions which allow us to comprehend and map an approach to building what we will term Digital DNA.

Before making that departure, let's summarise the nine dimensions we covered in this part.

Customer centricity: Industry 3.0 gave us the tools to pivot from manufacturing to experiences, and digital leaders leverage technologies to deliver them. We now understand customer-centricity as the state of being perpetually obsessed with delivering a job-solving solution, through a great experience. Gartner defines it as 'the ability of people in an organisation to understand customers' situations, perceptions, and expectations. Customer centricity demands that the customer is the focal point of all decisions related to delivering products, services and experiences to create customer satisfaction, loyalty and advocacy'.

Efficiency: To pave the way to build these experiences, and create capacity to do so, simplification is a foundational endeavour. Focus on vigorously eliminating burden and waste from the customer journey to maximise the customer experience – this is where digital businesses start, with the customer. The aim with efficiency is to manage time, assets, people, and capital as scarce resources, as inefficient burdens in the customer journey are a waste in operation.

Digital experiences: Digital Product Management sits at the centre of defining, designing, and executing composite value-adding experiences. To keep pace with your customers and their adoption of digital technology, adopt digital channels that allow you to engage with them and truly understand their behaviour. For compelling digital experiences, consider your channel strategy, how you will engage with your audience, and what role your channels will take organisation wide.

Data analytics: Digital businesses leverage data and AI to deliver intelligence services to serve the end user proposition, partners, and the enterprise. Digital creates a data footprint, with analytics and artificial intelligence (AI) leveraged to interpret that data to create value. It provides value across a 360° business horizon, specifically across four quadrants of the business: customer, risk, people and organisation, and operations, including technology. It is, therefore, essential and integral to your business, in supporting your processes and services aligned with your strategy.

https://doi.org/10.1515/9783111034713-022

Agile: To deliver at pace, harness talent, reduce risk, and put the end user in the centre, an agile philosophy and methods are essential. Digital businesses embrace an agile approach to working, not only because it enables quicker development of technology, but because it aligns with modern leadership. Adopting this style of leadership and working allows you to break down the legacy-style, product-based hierarchical structures for a decentralised, more customer-centric business.

Innovation: Value leaders employ innovation across multiple levels to extract value today, while building the value platform for tomorrow. Innovation is implicit for your business to compete and win in this digital era. The landscape is too competitive, with the pace of technology increasing exponentially, so not innovating is tantamount to failure. Before you can allocate resources to innovate, however, determine how you will innovate, using frameworks and models to help you target your efforts.

Open through partnering and ecosystems: Technologies and modern business ambitions have created a new era of open partnerships and ecosystem platforms to extend growth and capability. An open business model extends and flexes the business by opening it up and expanding the ways it can create products or services to bring to market. Leveraging open opportunities with partnerships and ecosystems can unlock new paths to growth, capability, and efficiencies. But it is important to understand the different type of partnerships you can leverage.

Technology: Digital capability requires digital technology architectures, applications, integration APIs, and operations. Technology must be set out in a demand and supply equation, where objectives and outcomes are translated into the overarching technology strategy, underpinning design of hardware, software, and operating model enablers.

Risk: Risk increases as we introduce complexity and ambition, and our digital efforts need to be monitored and mitigated accordingly.

We should not, and cannot, expect to operate at peak maturity and performance across these 9 and the 10th element to come, people. Getting there will be an endeavour, and later in the book we will focus on establishing staged execution. But first, let us move to the People platform, and Digital DNA.

Part IV: **People, Culture, and Digital DNA**

We talk about automating operations, about people, and about new business models. Wrapped inside those topics are data analytics, technologies, and software – all of which are enablers, not drivers. At the center of it all, are leadership and culture. Understanding what digital means to your company – whether you are financial, agricultural, pharmaceutical, or a retail institution – is essential. – Jim Swanson

We have garnered the complexity of building a digital business. Engineering an organisation and culture to execute across these intricacies requires a delicate balance across themes such as artistry, precision, safety, risk-taking, commerce, and purpose.

Creating the environment for these often-competing forces to coexist and in fact cross-pollinate to thrive off one another can only be achieved by leadership that possesses clarity, dexterity, resilience, focus, and empathy. The tone is always set from the top, and particularly in the cycles of change and transformation we are determining.

In this part, we will spend time exploring and assembling the components that are required to define and develop a digital culture – digital DNA. This includes digital leadership that is required to set and drive this tone, as well as the skills, behaviours, and mechanics of a digital business's operating model and the system that drives it.

https://doi.org/10.1515/9783111034713-023

Chapter 16
Breaking Down and Building Up Culture

What We See and What Is Harder to Fathom

In 1976, Andrew T. Hall, an American anthropologist, presented a model for understanding culture in his book *Beyond Culture*, and he used an iceberg as a befitting analogy. At its simplest, Halls' approach cited that there are facets of culture that we can 'see', which is the tip of the iceberg that sits above the water line. In the business context this equates to behaviours, customs, structures, and skills, but only accounts for 10% of the total picture. Ninety per cent of the influences that drive and anchor culture are out of view, or below the water line and under the surface. This includes attitudes, beliefs, and assumptions, and, most deep of all, values.

Iceberg Models have been stretched into multiple other spaces such as strategy, social exploration, and brand – so you will see them in several similar ways on your travels. I think that they work very well for helping us frame culture, and in this part I will use an abstract of Halls 'Iceberg'[90] to unpack what a desirable digital culture looks like, and how to navigate an organisation towards it.

In Figure 49, I have illustrated the digital DNA iceberg, an adaptation of Halls and numerous other's work. Above the 'water line' sit **Behaviours, Skills, and Practices** – these are the conscious dimensions that we see every day, are explainable and they are the most easily changed as well as being directly attributable to what sits on and below the 'water line'.

Jumping to below the 'water line' we find **Values, Attitudes, and Beliefs** – these are the unconscious dimensions, are what are implicitly learned as a result of observation, have deep lineage and are often difficult to observe and articulate. This in many ways is the culmination of the entities philosophy, and these dimensions are very slow to change, if they do at all.

Connecting and then manifesting what sits below the waterline into the everyday behaviours we see and feel above the water line are **Structure and Customs**. This is how people are formally organised, and how power is informally distributed and wielded in a business – the structural and organisational dimensions. Change tends to be evolutionary here, but can be revolutionary with the right interventions as this layer is the lightening conductor for culture.

---

90 Edward Hall, *Beyond Culture* (Anchor Books; Anchor Books ed edition, June 1, 1997).

https://doi.org/10.1515/9783111034713-024

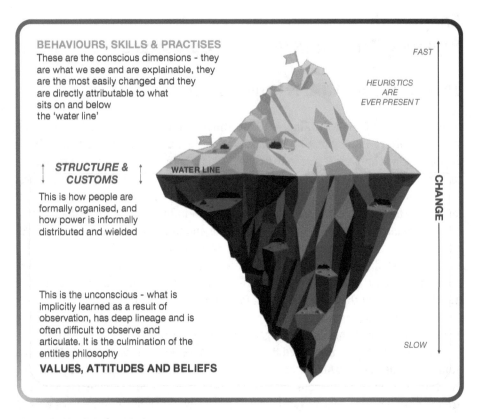

BEHAVIOURS, SKILLS & PRACTISES
These are the conscious dimensions - they are what we see and are explainable, they are the most easily changed and they are directly attributable to what sits on and below the 'water line'

↑ **STRUCTURE &** ↑
↓ **CUSTOMS** ↓

This is how people are formally organised, and how power is informally distributed and wielded

This is the unconscious - what is implicitly learned as a result of observation, has deep lineage and is often difficult to observe and articulate. It is the culmination of the entities philosophy
VALUES, ATTITUDES AND BELIEFS

WATER LINE

FAST

HEURISTICS ARE EVER PRESENT

CHANGE

SLOW

Figure 49: The digital DNA iceberg.

The Nine Dimensions of Digital DNA

Corresponding with the conscious, unconscious, and structural dimensions of the digital DNA iceberg, we use a nine-dimensional digital DNA system to help us frame, develop, and hone the digital culture required to enable a digital business. You can see this in Figure 50 and will note that digital leadership sits at the heart of the model, and the digital business. On the waterline along with structure and customs, leaders anchor the digital culture through the formal structure of their organisations and importantly also through the informal customs, which are the unwritten 'rules' in which power is observed and plied.

The other key components that shape and empower a value-driven digital operating rhythm are methods, policy, and rewards. Methods relate to working practices such as agile covered in the last part but should also include tools and work systems. Policy relates to the 'harder' HR protocols and procedures that are necessary to establish guiderails and operational-level support. Rewards, never to be overlooked, ensure that desired outcomes and compensation are aligned.

Pinning down the DNA model, we have the trilogy of behaviours, values, and skills. Values sit below the waterline and surface as behaviours. These behaviours are at the 'tip of the iceberg' and result in the actions and activities we see every day to build digital businesses. Behaviours are also informed by the maturity of skills and confidence in abilities.

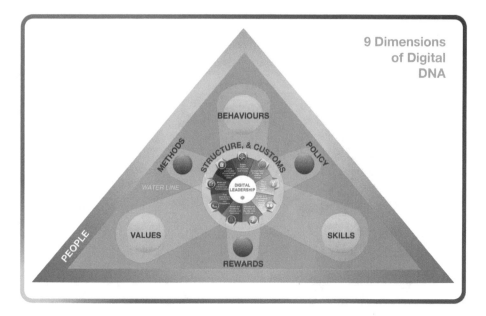

Figure 50: The nine dimensions of digital DNA.

I will go forwards now to break down each of the nine dimensions as a means to help guide on how to host and hone a digital culture that is facilitating of, and a driver for a digital business.

The Epicentre – Digital Leadership Flywheel

Digital leadership can be defined as having the dexterity, courage, and conviction to create a culture of creativity by applying modern digital practices, tools, technology with insights, and drive to create value for the customer, the organisation, and the community at large – the stakeholders.

Digital Leadership is not about technology – it is about harnessing technology for a better world, pointing it at jobs to be done, trying and failing and trying again with strategic nous and persistence. It is about executing, ambidextrously, as the execution often defines the strategy with conviction and adaptability. Digital leaders see the path, walk ahead, and bring the organisation on what is often a difficult journey.

They also drive perpetual change by establishing and accelerating (in pace with the law of accelerating returns) a flywheel of action, engagement, organisational engineering, and connectivity. As illustrated in Figure 50, they sit at the epicentre of a digital business to anchor and connect the digital agenda with the purpose of the business, to underpin that purpose through an empowering digital strategy, built on a rich perspective of the inside and outside world. And they take the lead in developing digital culture.

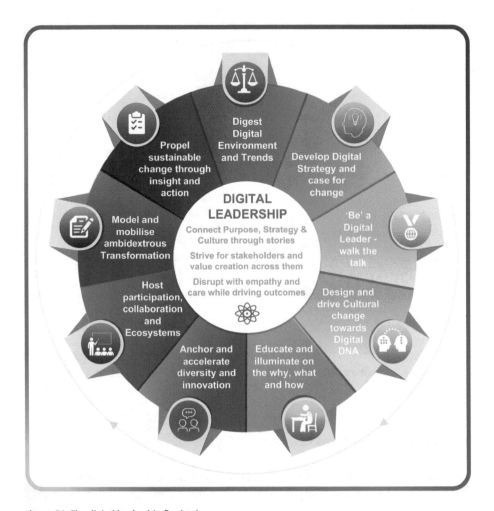

Figure 51: The digital leadership flywheel.

This requires them to role model what it takes to be digital – they walk the talk. They incessantly drive to understand the stakeholder, and build solutions to solve for their needs. But they understand that this is hard. It means change – and change is always hard. Therefore they understand the culture iceberg, and work above and more importantly below the waterline to instil the nine components of digital DNA.

Digital leaders believe that education is important – you cannot change when you do not know why, nor how. They spend time crafting stories, understanding emotions and constraints, and help their corporate companions to deal with ambiguity while seeing a bigger and better future.

To instil real change, step change, they accelerate innovation over and beyond continuous improvement and into new horizons. To do this, they understand the importance of cross-representation and an inclusive approach which can unlock a more equitable and also a more substantial solution. To do this, they gather and engage, hosting collaboration across an internal and external ecosystem of participation. This is at the core of mobilising ambidextrous transformation programmes, and it is done with care and empathy, but the eye is always on the prize of driving sustainable value.

Most importantly, digital leaders set the tone, and embody the core and true values of a digital business – this is where culture gets fused and is the true digital DNA.

Values of Digital Businesses

Under the water line sit the anchor points that embed and foundationalise culture. This is the system of ideas, the philosophies, and the edicts to and through which culture is formulated. In a sense it is the 'source code'. By this, I mean the very fibre of our belief system, and essence by which we think, act, and engage. I think of this as the DNA, in the same way that every living organism contains DNA or the genetic code that makes you or I the person that we are. DNA carries the instructions for the development, growth, reproduction, and functioning of all life.

And culture is that – life. It empowers, guides, fuels, and drives the life we lead and the way we apply our resources to think, work, and act. While it would be impossible for me to illustrate a 26 double chromosome DNA model similar to human DNA, I believe there are nine core strains of digital DNA underpinning a true digital culture as illustrated in Figure 52.

Nine Core Strains of Digital DNA

- Design 4 digital: Digital is the default method to deliver solutions and is applied 720° – the first 360° for looking out to solve for and with end users, and the second 360° for looking in to solve for and with colleagues
- Defining North Star: A compelling, motivational and expansive purpose, crafted with the end user in mind (and ideally in the room) guides and drives inputs, processes and outputs
- Data-led ambition: Ambition built around stakeholder outcomes drives what is measured, as opposed to measures such as profit or margin defining our ambitions. Data is our source of honesty and progress, used to reward, correct and direct

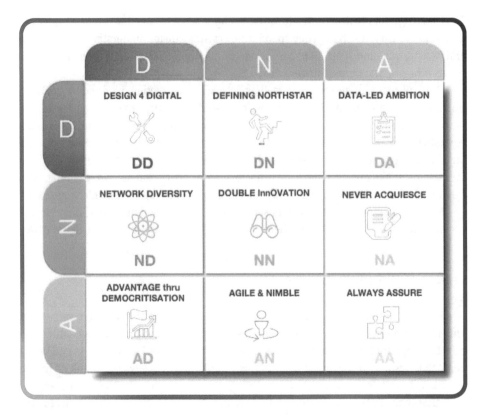

Figure 52: The core strains of digital DNA.

- Network diversity: Networks of partners, colleagues, and thought leaders and inspirators are used to diversify propositions, capabilities, and reach, and done in a value-sharing and equitable and inclusive way
- Double innovation: Innovation is a way of being, and within that there is a mandate to liberate innovators – one cannot happen without the other. Intrapreneurs are the innovation tribe
- Never acquiesce: An insatiable appetite to do better, and a curiosity to seek out new ways and means lead to a stance of continuous, constructive dissatisfaction and fire in the belly. We do not look back other than to learn – we look forwards with a growth mindset to create value
- Advantage through democratisation: Insights, invention, and inventory are shared with the world, on the basis that it makes it a better place, and that from a better place we can stand taller, see further and reach for new heights in a symbiotic relationship with the ecosystem
- Agile and nimble: Build for adaptability, continuous learning, and recalibration which facilitates fluidity and a means to shape-shift and match focus to what's right in front. Not being hard-wired to an irreversible track, following value with agility

- Always assure: Empathy, safe passage, and trust-building are inherent traits. Recognising and responding to fears and distress, and putting in place the knowledge and means to protect and secure what is important

I suggest a test on these nine core strains. Without them, the chance of building a digital business that uses the capabilities outlined in Part III, to drive a strategy as demonstrated in Part II for the reasons of our pace of technological change and innovation shared in Part I, will diminish significantly. In the words of Aristotle:

> Excellence is never an accident. It is always the result of high intention, sincere effort, and intelligent execution; it represents the wise choice of many alternatives – choice, not chance, determines your destiny.

We will now see how these values surface through the organisation and stakeholders to emerge as behaviours.

How Values Drive Behaviours

Corresponding to each of the values above, we should expect and need to curate a set of corresponding behaviours that shape how a digital business thinks and acts day to day. They are as follows:

- Design 4 digital – to apply Digital 720°, protagonists start with the end user in mind, and in their processes. They understand the job the customer is trying to do, and they use design skills and digital/data as means to solve for them, and so connect demand with supply
- Defining North Star – Advocates strive towards a common purpose, and connect with colleagues/partners as well as their own internal motivations in that pursuit. They talk about 'here we believe in …' and they ask the question 'is this in line with our purpose' when designing or decisioning
- Data-led ambition – to be ambition-led means digital businesses are not afraid to take on BHAGs (big, hairy, audacious goals), in fact that is what they get out of bed for. This is what defines and motivates them – success is an outcome, but they define what it will take to get there, track it and pivot as and when data dictates
- Network diversity – to leverage the crowd, as role models for Diversity, Equity and Inclusion, they agitate to engage diversity of thought, inclusion, challenge, and solutions. They balance viewpoints, and seek to find equitable resolutions. They embrace difference as a means to stretch the possibilities, but always work to coalition and cogency
- Double innovation – to liberate innovation, exponents make time, use resources and prioritise 'making it better', 'finding a new way' or 'thinking about the alternatives'. Organisations find these people, and liberate their attitude and ambition (intrapreneurs as innovators)

– Never acquiesce – to seek out opportunities, proponents are constant learners, building knowledge both within and outside their domains, and spend time experimenting and learning about new ways to do things. They do not act with fear of regret, they embrace failure as feedback, and are energised by their next iteration

– Advantage through democratisation – to reap rewards from sharing, champions share their successes and failures, but also their resources and innovations with those who will treat them with respect, and parallel ambition. They talk about 'leaving it in better shape than we found it' and open their arms to collaborations

– Agile and nimble – to exist with permanent adaptability, there are no fixed mindsets here – the default stance is evolution, if not revolution. They are ready for change, understanding it is hard but willing to push forwards. They let go of the old in the pursuit of better, and move forwards to learn and understand

– Always assure – to be the stewards of trust, and champions of emotion and surety, they look around corners and ask 'what could go wrong here', 'what are or should we be worried about' and 'how do we take fear and anxiety away' to make digital a thing that people can embrace, prosper from, and enjoy

Reward Spine

Extending onwards from values and behaviours are **reward, recognition, and opportunity**, three central themes that are behavioural but strike to the heart of motivation and are as a result of the correct motivation structures. They are inextricably linked but each play an important role, and together they are complimentary. Reward is an extrinsic motivator, whereas recognition and opportunity are intrinsic motivators, and together they inform a 'rewards spine' that is the ideal mix of motivational levers a digital business should manage and monitor.

The levers that sit on the Reward Spine broken down into extrinsic and intrinsic to reflect the two dimensions. Base salary and perks are foundational and are the centre arc of a reward structure around which these levers are anchored. By perks I include factors such as holiday entitlements, insurance and pension, annual salary inflation – all essentially 'pay in lieu' reward features. Base pay and perks need to be role, sector, and market specific, but can be adjusted as can all the levers and together they can concoct a competitive, attractive and strategically conducive reward fabric.

We will start with the extrinsic levers as they knit closest to base salary and perks, and then move to the intrinsic levers:

– OKR-related bonus incentives that tie in to OKRs around customer metrics (e.g. NPS), innovation, velocity, and commercial growth to name a few, can be architected through money and other valued currencies, e.g. stock and annual leave. Careful consideration should be given to ensuring that the OKRs are connected with and drive the right activity and behaviours to support the purpose and strategy of the business.

– The same is the case for issuing equity, which is the opportunity to participate in the value growth story. This opportunity to participate in the core value that an organisation or venture is building, through share allocation, favourable share purchase, and profit distribution is attractive to all parties and if constructed correctly it is a win-win-win for the employee, employer and also the stakeholders. The subtle word here is stakeholders and not shareholders – the latter being just one of the former, which also include the customer, partners, the sectors, economies, and ultimately the planet.

– Recognition and celebration is motivating and achieved through identifying, acknowledging, commemorating, and praising performance and excellence both behind the scenes, inside and also on the outside of the firm. A firm with strong foundational values and the right behaviours which are supported by a well-architected reward model should have more confidence in doing this so it doesn't backfire.

– As we start to move towards the intrinsic motivators now, the build up of knowledge and learning through paid for and formal education, coaching and mentoring is a valued reward level, and cross-beneficial. Talent and skills mapping are essential in developing attentive programmes that diagnose potential and personal development needs to support personal and organisational excellence and growth. Applied learning should be a central philosophy, ensuring that academic learning is applicable and applied to the organisational strategy and setting. Mentoring and coaching should be complementary to formal education programmes, but also offered as standalone supports for key talent and career transition windows.

– Going deeper now into the intrinsic motivators, connecting employees with the purpose or North Star of an organisation that is a higher order intent and aligned with a personal cause is attractive and unlocks loyalty, energy, and discretionary effort. The opportunity to make a difference on a theme that innately resonates with a personal mission can be deeply motivating and aligning. We have probably all read or heard of the NASA janitor who responded to the question 'what do you do around here' from JFK on a campus visit as the epitome of this – 'we're sending man to the moon sir'. The breakthroughs that NASA as an organisation made in the mid-nineteenth century were perhaps some of the greatest known to date, and that uniting Purpose was a central tenet.

– This extends into connecting with the values of the business, and the core culture – open and pronounced discussion around values, with an opportunity to feed into their creation and articulation is a deeply connecting activity, that harnesses discretionary intent, but unfortunately is not pursued by many organisations in a meaningful and inclusional way.

– Often part of or indeed a personal north star is gaining exposure to new projects, cultures, territories, and stimulating innovation pursuits or ventures, and is valued as a means to support personal growth but also to create new value for all as well as build profile. This exposure also opens mindsets and prepares for adaptability and resilience which benefits all parties

– Freedom to choose when to work, where to work, what projects to work on and to what degree of time is committed to work is an increasingly valued motivator. The responsibility to take control of the schedule, decisions and resources is an incredibly effective motivation, and with the right boundaries in place which include clear OKRs and connectivity to purpose, can see discretionary output. The opportunity to take on more responsibility, stretch projects and/or establish new programmes or teams facilitates loyalty and employer brand recognition.

A final and encompassing part of the employee proposition that I often see companies employing are **wellness programmes**. The full gamut of wellness extends into:
–   Financial – planning services to support financial literacy, decision-making, and planning
–   Physical – health and lifestyle supports to nurture a better body
–   Mental – psychological and counselling services to support extreme mental challenges
–   Emotional – content and coaching on life skills and habit formation to nurture a better mind
–   Intellectual – stimulation and learning of new skills, in parallel with those in the occupational stream
–   Social – programmes that tackle bias, and increase an environment of belonging for all walks of life – this is often where we see diversity, equity, and inclusion as an agenda
–   Spiritual – supports that help connect with and celebrate the broader meaning of life
–   Sustainable – the ability to participate in activities that have a positive, meaningful impact on the world we inhabit, and can span across the UN's 17 sustainable development goals

Organisations use a mix of all or some of the above levers to create a compelling reward proposition that will drive the behaviours and underpin the values we have outlined, but also support retention and recruitment of the necessary talent for a digital business – something that is increasingly more demanding. What is right for each company will depend on the nature of work, the market, importantly the purpose and values of the organisation as well as what is deemed motivating in the local economy and regime. Benchmarking and primary research are good places to start on what will be required to build an alluring proposition. Thereafter much like the 6D strategy model it is a case of picking a mix of core enablers and constructing a model that is reviewed and refined over time.

Advantages and Best Practice of OKRs

I extolled the benefits of OKRs (objective key results) when we uncovered strategy, and again under Rewards, encouraging leaders to use the approach to stitch strategy to execution, while building motivation and reward as a means to ensure that strategy carries through to delivery. OKRs can help to triangulate day-to-day work with strategy, but also to reward strategically aligned cultural activity once the correct linkages are made between the OKRs and culture.

Rewards should be aligned to the achievement of OKRs and ratio's need to be assessed and set in accordance with factors such as market-level pay, experience, etc. (in line with pay and reward allocation models). The broader benefits of OKRs are outlined below, as well as the best practice methods for implementation.

Advantages

- Alignment – connect team performance to shared objectives so everyone moves in the same direction
- Prioritisation – the three to five objectives for each level of organisation drives us to tasks that carry the most impact
- Transparency – OKRs enable the whole business to be aware of how everyone involved plans to make an impact
- Empowerment – Increased visibility gives everyone the context they need to make the best decision
- Measurement – Illustrate how far along individual, team, and the overall company are in their goals
- Accomplishment – OKRs are meant to be stretched, just beyond the threshold of what seems possible

Best Practice

- Overall the objective level should be Objective, Bracing, Judicious, Exact, Clear, Tangible (OBJECT)
- The associated key results should be – Reachable, Exponent, Significant, Understandable, Limited number, Trackable (RESULT)
- In practices there should be between three and four objectives per business, division, team or person and an associated three to five key result max per objective
- The OKRs of the business should cascade down to an individual level through divisional and team structures – the sum should equal the parts, if not more. OKRs started with Peter Drucker's movement towards success measure management in 1954 after he published *The Practice of Management*, which was the first book at

the act of management as a discreet responsibility, and by extension MBO, or 'management by objectives'[91]

One of the most common challenges I see when developing OKRs (or indeed any set of KPIs) is the trap of imprecision. All too often, leaders and organisations assign immeasurable and ambiguous objectives. This makes it more difficult for the potential recipient of rewards to be able to track and prove accomplishment, and for the allocator to do the same. There is great merit in the application of specificity, exactness, and source of proof. This makes OKR setting and associate reward allocation transparent and fair, aligning with the general culture of digital.

Here are some examples of imprecise versus precise (see Table 19).

Table 19: Imprecise versus precise OKRs.

Imprecise	Precise
I want to finish more projects on budget	I will get involved in the estimation process, track budget daily, and communicate budget concerns to my teams in our daily meeting to get my next three projects to finish within a +/− 10% range of original estimate
Improve the site's user experience	We will reduce the number of clicks it takes a user to reach the highest traffic page that the majority of our website users regularly visit from any point on the site to two clicks or less by end of our design phase on June 1
More form completes	We will increase the number of qualified leads (as confirmed by Salesforce) by 5%, by reducing the required fields in the form by the end of Q3
Accessible website	We will build the website to meet WCAG 2.1 AA standards that will be thoroughly tested against the criteria and is deployed to production by the middle of the year

Linking Investment With Commercial and Capability Success Factors

Another dynamic I frequently come across in organisations is how to set and reward the act and art of innovation. In my view, the allocation of clearly parameterised commercial and capabilities objectives to investment allocations is a robust mechanism. This approach borrows on the 'Green Box' model put forward by McKinsey[92] (covered

91 Plai Team, "A History of Objectives and Key Results (OKRs)," accessed April 7, 2023, https://www.plai.team/blog/history-of-objectives-and-key-results.

92 McKinsey, "The Innovation Commitment," (October 24, 2019), accessed April 7, 2023, https://www.mckinsey.com/capabilities/strategy-and-corporate-finance/our-insights/the-innovation-commitment?cid=app.

under the Innovation Capability), but stretches it to suggest that return on total innovation (ROTI) can and should be measured by value created in the form of money (commercial) but also in the form of knowledge and skills (capability).

The 'green box', is the value the company generates from all forms of innovation – breakthrough and incremental – over a finite planning period (perhaps 5 years), quantified using metrics such as net new revenue, earnings growth, or both. Critically, the green box represents the amount of growth that only innovation can produce, after netting out all other possible sources (including market momentum, in-year pricing adjustments, distribution and marketing activities, and M&A). This amount is then cascaded into a set of objectives and metrics for the company's operating units, which reflect them in their own innovation portfolios.

To find new opportunities and determine the appropriate number and mix of initiatives, leaders need to do the following:
– Confirm the total value of the portfolio needed (use the green box)
– Evaluate existing innovation projects based on incremental value delivered, risk (recognising that not all projects will succeed), and alignment with strategic priorities
– Determine portfolio sufficiency (the degree to which the existing mix of projects could plausibly deliver the green box)
– Be comfortable with saying 'no': stop projects that are dilutive, and resist the siren song of incremental initiatives (perhaps requested by a customer or two) that are unlikely to pay for themselves
– Reallocate those resources – including competencies and skills – to new initiatives or to current ones that additional support can accelerate or amplify
– Identify portfolio gaps and define new initiatives to close them

I recommend extending the green box model for innovation to incorporate capability and not just commercial metrics. In essence this means as we set return hurdles and to ensure innovation maturity is rewarded, in the short term these hurdles need to straddle commercial and capability return on spend, as in less mature environments capability comes before commerciality.

An appropriate mix for the level of maturity needs to be business specific, but can draw from the following:

Commercial

– Incremental return from continuous improvement in the Sustaining innovation mode
– New value arising from developmental and disruptive innovation
– Greenfield/new business model growth
– Growth through acquisition and joint/open innovation

Capability

- The number of opportunities identified and assessed.
- The number of colleagues involved/trained in innovation practices.
- Speed to market and innovative technology foundations.

As innovation maturity grows, a shift from capability to commercial begins and over-time the latter starts to index higher, but should never be over-dominant. These measurement and motivation factors just covered are or should be part of the policies of a digital business.

Policy and Defining the Guiderails for a Digital Business

When it comes to policy, I am not going to rehash the basic people policies that any or-ganisation should have today such as Health and Safety, Conduct, Disciplinary, etc. These are table stakes, and I suggest an overlay of the principles which I have outlined below alongside guidance on how they can be implemented in practice in Table 20.

It is the role of HR alongside digital leaders to develop people policies in line with these principles, and to role-model them. It is also critical that systems, data-gathering, and insight delivery are central to shaping, designing interventions, execution, and fre-quent policy renewal.

Digital Skills Embolden Values and Facilitate the Digital Operating System

I have shared with you my view of the baseline digital skills required to support a digital business in Figure 53. While the list will appear lean to many, and perhaps na-scent, my suggestion would be to evaluate your leaders and their teams as to how they might score on a benchmark exercise – I think you will find that many will score well on many of the dimensions, but many will score low or be absent. To build and sustain a digital enterprise one needs to push the skills quota much past 50% and closer to 80% coverage (whether that be on an individual or proportionately distrib-uted team basis), with a basic proficiency across all components.

This will perhaps feel like a tall order, but it is in my experience what is re-quired – these skills are one of three anchors of the nine dimensions of digital DNA, enable fluency and throughput, and are the basic engineering of digital teams.

Table 20: Principle guiderails for a digital business.

The principle	The definition	The practice
Purpose and values	Embed the purpose through values so that it becomes intrinsic, implicit and implied in day-to-day work	Decisions such as investment, hires, as well as communications and branding are tested against and guided by the values at all times
Mix and balance	Ensure the teams demographic resembles that of the market and continually rebalanced to ensure biases are eradicated, and opportunity is maximised	When hiring, promoting, establishing projects, and governance (decision-making), ensure that representation is properly mixed and balanced
Access and flexibility	Enable teams and leaders to access talent within and without in accordance with needs, duration and collective good	Access to colleagues across an organisation (with the appropriate permissions and backfills) and in the contract economy should be facilitated
Champions	Find out what makes people shine, and help them to fulfil their innate desires and potential, aligning them with the organisations needs	Talent planning should marry the needs of the organisation with those of the individual, creating equilibrium of potential and opportunity
Self-direction	Tapping into intrinsic motivation, facilitate self-direction and self-determination for individuals and teams	Empower individuals, and their teams, to set their own agendas and rhythm through guidance, mentoring, and OKR management thus limiting overhead
Lifelong learning	Enable the learning organisation to continually refresh its skills, knowledge, and methods	Continually refresh talent needs, knowledge and methods through perpetual demand: supply planning informed by local and central experts
Rotation and dexterity	To enable dexterity, broaden the talent pool and continually seek to strategically rotate talent	Employ systematic rotation that balances team needs and individual growth pathways through talent planning panels
Collaboration	Engineer work practices, expectation and rewards to harness the creative power of many, connect agendas and eliminate waste	Team, project, and corporate cadence should facilitate 360-degree stakeholder inclusion, outcome management, and reporting
Data-driven decisioning	Counteract the potential bias of opinion (anecdotal) decisioning by balancing quant and qual data input	Shape decision-making methods and behaviours to balance decision making through the use of balanced cross-informing hard and soft data

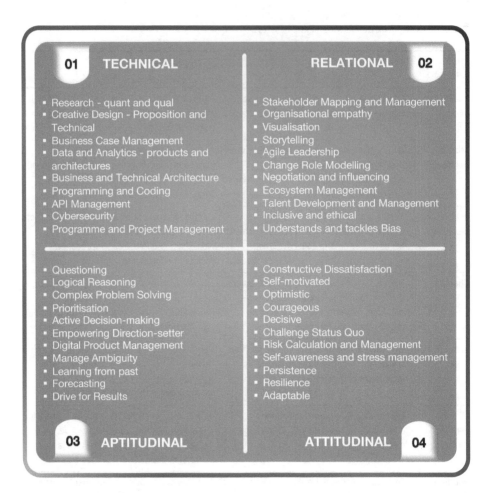

Figure 53: Digital skills matrix.

A Perpetual Cycle of Data-Driven Curiosity

I believe that the practice of Digital Product Management (covered under the Agile Capability) is the central method around which an ongoing cycle of exploration and development sits. While it is natural to think that this is just for the teams that drive out proposition, it can and should extend to every facet of the business. That is through collective participation in propositions for end users (compliance, finance, etc.) but it is also the core methodology to be applied to continuous improvement in operations, people development, etc.

The core activities from digital product management that should be considered in all walks of digital business life are as follows:

- Data every day: Every discussion, design and decision, every day, should start with data and resulting insights, and every action results in gathering the data about the result so that there is a perpetual data-informed cycle
- Framing: Digital businesses frame problems and opportunities to solve, extracting direction from data insights. They use linear, disciplined thought processes: data-insight-question-rationale-benefit-action
- Ruthless prioritisation: Through the ongoing cycle of insight gathering and interpretation, many questions will arise that need to be answered. Product Leaders hold the business to clear account on what's important to solve, and ruthlessly prioritise accordingly
- Visualisation: Once the priorities have been set (the backlog), good practice is to visualise the outcome – lo-fi prototypes, storyboards, etc. clarify ideas, organise information, depict outcomes, and calculate inputs
- Code-centric: In line with the agile manifesto, working code trumps documentation, as it inherently is! Coding solutions is the go-to – building product, deploying, cleaning, testing, refining
- Crowd power: Collaborating with the product team to debate, define, and design solutions anchors every day, followed by stakeholder testing and working with domain compeers
- Change management: Pushing product into market, ensuring quality through continuous development and improvement. The human change cycle is observed, and implementation caters for ease of passage through change curves
- Learn before you leap: Every deployment is an experiment, and so they are treated with anticipation while reactions are observed for failures, successes, and learnings. This fuels the next chapter of development.

There is no single-fit and standard approach to digital product management, just like there is no one way to 'do agile'.

Every team, shaped by the experience and preference of their Digital Product Leader, will bend and shape the patterns and philosophies to fit the setting, inherent preferences and mood of their business. It is, however, the central tenet for how a digital business needs to think and act.

Chapter 17
Structures and Customs of a Digital Business

The Hard and Soft Decrees

In this central component of the nine dimensions of digital DNA, we will surface two complimentary dimensions for how an organisation translates it values and also its strategy into operations and ultimately into behaviours and everyday tasks. These are:
- The optimal way to organise resources around 'work to be done' where that work is in the pursuit of strategy – this is what is known as the operating model and relates to the structures of a business
- The day-to-day routines and practises that happen within the structure, and how to set the right rhythm for the organisation to run – that is what we will term the operating system (OS), and relates to the customs of a business

Combined, they are the means and methods through which businesses conduct and orchestrate capital, including but not only human capital, to deliver a strategy in line with a purpose and in the pursuit of value. They are, therefore, how a business organises itself and employs capital and people to achieve it is goals.

We refer to these as decrees given that they are formal means by which an organisation establishes itself, but note that the operating model is a 'hard' decree given it is the formal structures and relationships (e.g. with partners, customers) and has legal status (company, partnership, etc.), whereas the OS is 'soft' in that it is informal and relates to the flow and norms of how the operating model goes about its daily business.

Bill Gates, co-founder of Microsoft, was once quoted as saying 'Like a human being, a company has to have an internal communication mechanism, a "nervous system", to coordinate its actions'. Using the human is a good analogy in that the operating model is like the body, and the OS is like the mind. Equally we could say the operating model is the hardware that delivers outcomes, and the OS is the software that guides the hardware on how to deliver the outcomes.

We see that culture and therefore digital DNA comes to life in both. The operating model essentially illustrates the way in which work is carried out and governed to deliver the outcomes of the business. So, it utilises human and other capital (money, raw material, and assets) to produce products and services, which are packaged in a value proposition and sold in the value exchange with the customer or end user. This is where skills are structured and employed, using methods to do the work required – this relates to the Skills-Methods axis of our nine Dimensions.

The other axes of Value-Policy and Behaviours-Rewards come to life in the OS, as this is how those structures, skills, and methods are guided, by leadership. Combined they are therefore the structures and customs with digital DNA straddling both. Let's move forwards to use the two dimensions and to help us break down both the Model and System.

https://doi.org/10.1515/9783111034713-025

Orchestrating the Hard and Soft Dimension of the Organisation

The Operating Model Canvas is an excellent tool for defining the work required to deliver value and how to 'organise' resources optimally to deliver that value. But that model needs to run on an OS as we mentioned, which is not covered sufficiently in the Operating Model Canvas, so here we use and fuse it with the OS Canvas which we borrow from The Ready. The OS Canvas defines the customs by which people work in the Model, and if they are collectively harmonised value is not just delivered, but done so optimally for all participants.

The Operating Model Canvas[93] was created by Andrew Campbell and colleagues at Ashridge Business School to help organisations understand the 'as is' of how they are organised to create value, and to define a 'go to' if required (in the case of say a new business, or a new strategy requiring a new structure). We will look at an example in a few moments.

The OS Canvas[94] was created by Aaron Dignan's The Ready, a specialist consultancy firm which helps organisations transition to a new world of work. It supports leaders and teams to understand how they work within the constructs of a business, and how that can be evolved to optimise resources and drive value and cohesion.

Using the Operating Model Canvas – Building Structure Around Value

It is difficult to create an Operating Model 'Blueprint' for how a business should operate, for a number of reasons. Firstly, complexity and extent. Secondly, time and motivation (working in and not on the business), and thirdly, there are often different interpretations of what operating model means, usually a limited one (how many people are in each team, and what they generally are responsible for).

The Operating Model Canvas helps to go beyond general and get to specifics, capturing people resources to work tasks and extending it to suppliers (partners), and then how collaboration should happen and what information and management oversight is required.

Figure 54 shows an example of the operating model for a learning organisation, based on work we do across a number of institutions and academically oriented organisations.

This is what we might term a 'simplex' overview meaning that it captures an enterprise overview on a single page, which like strategy on a page can be very helpful.

---

93 The Operating Model Canvas, accessed April 7, 2023, https://ashridgeonoperatingmodels.com/book-operating-model-canvas/.

94 Medium, "The Operating System Canvas," Aaron Dignan (February 9, 2019), accessed April 7, 2023, https://medium.com/the-ready/the-operating-system-canvas-420b8b4df062.

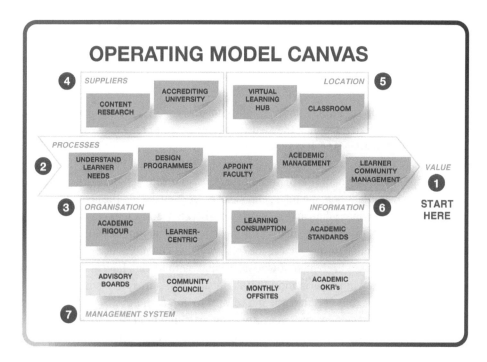

Figure 54: Operating model example.

The Canvas also works to help teams see how they work within their own confines and with others, and is extremely helpful when establishing new collaborative ways of working.

I have used the Operating Model Canvas on a page as illustrated with smaller organisations and their teams, and in larger entities, have created documents with hundreds of pages describing strategy, how that strategy translates into the 'work to be done', how to organise the skills to do the work and what supports they require (processes, technologies, data, etc.) including, of course, every kind of variation in between.

Just like strategy, there is no single way to go about building an operating model – personalities, size, and context all inform the approach. That said, we believe that the Operating Model Canvas is a good starting point, and just like we are proposing to do with the fusion of the OS Canvas, it can be extended and modified.

The following are the guiding steps that I use when helping teams work through the Operating Model Canvas to build up a picture of who they need to do what, with whom and how that will be supported, measured and managed. Each step relates back to the Canvas component highlighted in Figure 54 (Note: this is a summarised version – you can read and view more on the Operating Model Canvas site cited).

1. The operating model always starts with the outcome or value that is the desired delivery for an end user – that needs to be clearly stated, understood, and measurable.

2. Next we set out the steps of sequential work, or processes, that need to be taken and executed in order to deliver the target value – this can be defined at a high level or at an operational level and is a value chain.

3. Understanding the work and tasks required then leads to defining the skills needed – in complex or large businesses, those skills are usually organised by competency or sometimes location. The objective here is to give competency-based teams clarity on when they work with other teams on what – this is usually done via structure and RACI (Responsible, Accountable, Consulted, Informed) charts.

4. If suppliers or partners are required to support the value chain work, their role needs to be understood, included, and clear agreements made through SLAs.

5. As well as who does what, and how they collaborate via RACI, the canvas also captures the location or where they do the work – this is important when it comes to hard goods/manufacturing but also for collaborations and multi-location businesses.

6. Once the blueprint is created of who does what, with whom, how and where, it is time to define what information (data and insights) and systems is required to enable the work, but also to track and reward its completion.

7. Finally the management system captures an articulation of how governance and decisioning making work. As you will have seen on the previous page, for this component we use the OS Canvas.

One of the most challenging dynamics that pre-digital organisations find on their transformation journey is putting the customer at the heart of their operating model, with digital a key enabler to drive better experiences (two of our key capabilities). These traditional businesses grew up around product being the centre spine of the organisations' value chain and margin with a solid return on capital being the key value outcome. Today, digital businesses put the customer's jobs at the centre, and the key value driver is experience (from which commercial value is derived).

Traditional businesses have mostly developed in silos, drawn along functional lines, which have been a barrier to collaboration and working as one towards those customer centric outcomes, as well as agility and sharing.

Digital businesses do not work in traditional matrix structures with rigid functional boundaries but rather imbue a network structure and organise around outcomes and value, with product managers empowered to make decisions with implications that cut across functions. Teams are often not permanent, but adapt and flex as the market and strategy pursuits dictate.

This new way of organising means moving the power structures, most often wielded by resource allocation and change budgets, from product teams who drive for margin to customer-focused digital teams who drive for outcome. Using steps 1 to 3 in the guidelines for the Operating Model Canvas above is a very powerful means to help an organisation to see the need to re-engineer in this way.

Steps 2 and 3 then outlines what work needs to be done and by whom, with the Responsible and Accountable allocations signalling clear demarcation and decision-making. Organisations who use the Operating Model Canvas to reorientate their structures towards customers and outcomes do this by rationally setting down how that is done, and digital product management should be at the heart of the value chain processes.

The operating model may in itself be sufficient to help articulate how to organise (structure) and run (customs) a business in that the final step (management system) then facilitates the articulation of the Value-Policy and Behaviours-Rewards axes we propose.

However, in my experience that is not always the case. Many organisations need a deeper and more thorough assessment of the softer and 'customary' aspects of their business as this is where culture really lies. That is why we fuse the OS Canvas with the Operating Model Canvas as it helps us to do just that.

Using the Operating System (OS) Canvas – Understanding How the Organisation Really Works

I use the OS Canvas to help teams detect and describe how their organisations tick – what I call their customs. These are the unwritten ways in which the business itself and as a whole thinks and acts. The method of using it is quite simple. A team simply picks all or usually a number of important components from the canvas and works through the questions outlined to assess the 'as is' and define a 'go to' that supports the evaluating endeavour, for example, strategy execution, cultural development etc.

The following are the 12 components and their correlating questions for ease of reference, and fuller instructions for using the OS Canvas can be found at The Ready website.[95]

1. PURPOSE
–   How we orient and steer: the reason for being at the heart of any organisation, team, or individual?
–   What is our reason for being?
–   What is meaningful about our work?
–   How does our purpose help us make decisions?

2. AUTHORITY
–   How we share power and make decisions: the right to make decisions and take action or compel others to do the same?
–   Who can tell others what to do?

---

95 The Ready, accessed 7th April 2023, https://theready.com.

- How do we make important decisions?
- What is safe to try? What is not?

3. STRUCTURE
- How we organise and team: the anatomy of the organisation; formal, informal, and value-creation networks?
- What is centralised/decentralised?
- Within teams, how do we approach roles and accountabilities?
- How does our structure learn or change over time?

4. STRATEGY
- How we plan and prioritise: the process of identifying critical factors or challenges and the means to overcome them?
- What are the critical factors between success and failure?
- How do we develop, refine, and refresh our strategy?
- How do we use strategy to filter and steer day-to-day?

5. RESOURCES
- How we invest our time and money: the allocation of capital, effort, space, and other assets?
- How do we allocate funds, effort, space, and other assets?
- How do strategy and planning influence resource allocation?
- How does our approach enable us to respond to emergent events?

6. INNOVATION
- How we learn and evolve: the creation of something new; the evolution of what already exists?
- Who participates in innovation? Who has the right to innovate?
- What is the role of failure and learning in innovation?
- How do we balance the short term and the long term?

7. WORKFLOW
- How we divide and do the work; the path and process of value creation.
- What is the relationship between our workflow and our structure?
- How do we maintain visibility across all our projects?
- How are projects initiated, cancelled, or completed?

8. MEETINGS
- How we convene and coordinate: the many ways members and teams come together?
- Does each of our meetings have a clear purpose and structure?
- How are meetings facilitated and documented?
- How do we improve or eliminate meetings that are no longer serving us?

9. INFORMATION
- How we share and use data: the flow of data, insight, and knowledge across the organisation?
- What information is shared freely?
- What information is contained or controlled?
- What tools, systems, or forums support storing and sharing?

10. MEMBERSHIP
- How we define and cultivate relationships: the boundaries and conditions for entering, inhabiting, and leaving teams and organisations?
- How is membership (in the org/team) gained? How is it relinquished?
- What do all members expect of one another?
- How do members move between teams and other boundaries?

11. MASTERY
- How we grow and mature; the journey of self-discovery and development; our approach to nurturing talent, skills, and competence.
- What is our approach to learning and development?
- How do we give and receive feedback?
- How does competence influence the roles we inhabit?

12. COMPENSATION
- How we pay and provide; the wages, salaries, bonuses, commissions, benefits, prerequisites, profits, and equity exchanged for participation in the organisation.
- What is our approach to compensation?
- What mechanisms have we put into place to reduce bias in compensation?
- How are changes in compensation triggered and conducted?

I have shared both the Operating Model and OS Canvas as they are good starting points, are proven by many, and are easy to get started with. That said, they are not to be thought of as the silver bullet both in terms of being complete and fully comprehensive (as mentioned previously, we should start with them and augment). More importantly, they are merely tools. It is the human endeavour and openness to succeed that defines their effectiveness. Be mindful that facilitation is your friend, and to give these pursuits patience, time, and empathy.

Diagnosing and Navigating Culture

While the amalgamation of the Operating Model and OS Canvas are solid starting points for diagnosing and ultimately setting out a pathway for a digital business structure and culture, we have encountered a number of other useful tools on our journey. The Unite Culture Canvas from Swiss firm Digital Leadership is a comprehensive framework to identify both the contributors to and connections between culture components. It loosely correlates with the headings we have shared in our nine-point model, but helps to look through an 'as is' and 'boots on the ground' perspectives.

You can find downloads of and instructions for how to use the Unite Culture Canvas, including copies of the canvas, and a number of variations that help to gather team perspectives, complete diagnosis through a bank of questions as well as a 'contextualised' version that helps identify what needs to be done to redefine a culture that is required to deliver a new strategy here: https://digitalleadership.com/unite/operating-model/

The eight-point Culture Framework presented by Boris Groysberg, Jeremiah Lee, Jesse Price, and J. Yo-Jud Cheng in the 2018 HBR article 'The Leaders Guide to Corporate Culture' is a comprehensive model, anchored around how people interact (the x axis), and their response to change (the y axis). The resulting 'eight types' of organisations are then presented as 'archetypes', and facilitate determining the dominant cultural amalgam that exist.

In the five-series publication the authors present a guide to understanding and navigating the framework, as well as a very helpful (albeit rudimentary) online assessment tool which you can find here: https://hbr.org/2018/01/the-leaders-guide-to-corporate-culture.

The article also espouses four levers for evolving culture which we find useful and align with our own thinking and experiences – they are as follows:

- **Articulate the aspiration** for cultural change in tangible terms that helps to baseline the desire in the current context
- Leaders are the **catalysts for change**, and need to be 'with the programme' acting as role models
- **Facilitate culture conversations** by making time and space for the organisation to discuss where it is and where it needs to be
- Understand and **reform organisational structures** to ensure that are conducive for change

Within the above points (as anyone with experience of driving significant organisational change will attest), lie the truth that simultaneous structural and cultural change is a very difficult gauntlet to run. Widely reported, recognised, and regarded as the major impediment to transformational change, culture is and should remain a top priority for digital business leaders. According to McKinsey,[96] transformation efforts fail 70% of the time, with contributing factors including insufficiently high

---

[96] McKinsey, "Why Do Most Transformations Fail?" Harry Robinson (July 10, 2019), accessed April 7, 2023, https://www.mckinsey.com/capabilities/transformation/our-insights/why-do-most-transformations-fail-a-conversation-with-harry-robinson.

aspirations, a lack of engagement within the organisation, and insufficient invest-ment in building capabilities across the organisation to sustain the change.

This is why I have embellished it as the final and all-encompassing of the core capabilities of a digital business. Failure to craft and curate a facilitating culture is surely the most likely point of demise.

We have seen what the desired state should be, and shared some perspectives on methods and tools to diagnose existing culture such that a path can be deciphered and navigated in building digital DNA. Given that culture is the most important and perhaps hardest facet of digital transformation, it is just as important to know what hurdles get in the way, which we call the culture traps and can be summarised as follows:

- Lack of a common purpose and a clearly aligned strategy, different parts of a business pursuing different goals that leads to friction and disagreement.
- Traditional business silos restrict the kind of open collaboration and common mission work that is required to change holistically
- Lack of accountability and a blame culture, often amplified by silos
- Hierarchical power structures where decisions flow into bottlenecks, are often bi-ased, and impede empowered innovation
- The 'not invented here' syndrome that blocks creativity and pace
- KPIs and reward structures that do not align with the desired state and strategy, causing resistance

These are just some of the barriers. But probably the most significant in my experi-ence of navigating these traps and running the gauntlet of cultural and structural change. Before this sentence, insert a new one as follows 'While execution is ever-dependent on culture and structure, it too is dependent on how to organise for signifi-cant change, capability building and strategy execution – this is the other side of the gauntlet run.' We will address these and other key components of running the gauntlet in our next part on roadmapping. For now, it is enough to identify and reflect on whether you have the right Digital DNA in your organisation.

Case Study: DBS Bank

When Asian Bank DBS embarked upon its digital transition, Chief Information Officer David Gledhill knew the bank had to focus on three core elements; how it would embed digital transformation at the very core of the organisation, how to embed the customer journey (and instil customer-centric thinking) throughout, and how to trans-form its culture so that it felt and operated like a fresh-thinking start-up.

On becoming digitally transformed, the bank learned how to build, operate, and act like a technology company, learning from some of the technology giants I men-tioned at the outset of this book – Google, Amazon, Netflix, Apple, LinkedIn, and Meta. Learning how to operate like a technology company and not 'like any other bank' meant they could learn how to be nimble, build agile teams, automate, and practice agile at scale (22,000-strong, to be exact).

The bank's outcomes, as Gledhill states, were 'speed to market, scalability, experimentation, and [all the things you expect to see in] technology companies', such as in DBS' case, innovative offerings such as mobile-only banking in India.

Gledhill's advice? 'Test and learn, test, and learn, test and learn'. You can read more about DBS' transformation at DBS.com,[97] and on their video.[98]

A Final Word on Education

As we now get ready to move on to delivery and dexterity, the final of the 6Ds and where we bring the components of strategy, capability, and culture together, we want to mention education. We believe wholeheartedly in the most important human capital investment of education, and while experience is worth its weight in gold, learning and knowledge are complimentary bed-fellows and encourage digital businesses leaders and students to search out and partake in a holistic journey of wisdom.

Learning can be achieved in many ways as articulated below, and we encourage digital businesses leaders and participants to seek out and utilise at least a number of the methods. I have organised these into the three primary types of education – formal (academic, structured, and planned), non-formal (non- or part-academic and complimentary to formal), and informal (unstructured and loosely planned).

Formal

- Domain-specific and general leadership programmes carrying certification from universities and colleges
- In-house education programmes, sometimes also carrying certification from universities and colleges
- Minimum competency frameworks and content
- Graduate programmes
- Apprenticeships

---

97 DBS.com, "Ransforming a Bank by Becoming Digital to the Core," accessed April 7, 2023, https://www.dbs.com/media/digital-transformation/dbs-cio-david-gledhill-on-transforming-a-bank-by-becoming-digital-to-the-core.page.
98 YouTube, "How DBS Transformed Its Culture to Become the World's Best Bank," accessed April 7, 2023, https://www.youtube.com/watch?v=THrxDjO4KD4.

Non-formal

- Training and guidance by internal and external facilitators
- On-the-job training by senior and experienced practitioners
- Rotations either in or across teams, division, and regions
- Seminars and events – internal and external
- Mentoring and coaching, either by internal or by external peers, sponsors, and facilitators

Informal

- Observation and exchange both inside and outside
- Reading and references
- We would put a particular emphasis on immersive rotation and stretch-mentoring as a means to open the minds, as often seen in large corporates as a good compliment to a rhythm of lifelong learning, and formal and informal knowledge building

Summary – Part IV

Let's bring our thoughts on Digital DNA to a close reminding ourselves why it is the most critical and all encompassing in the words of Josh Bersin,[99] the global thought leader on people in work: 'Digital transformation is not about technology at all. It is about people.', which encapsulates our belief that the most important capability to make an investment in is the enveloping platform of people".

The following are the reflection points from People chapters to help underpin that message:

Above the line: Culture is visible above the waterline through the behaviours, skills, and practices that we see every day.

Below the line: But culture is formed and uniquely shaped below the line by the values, attitudes, and beliefs of business leaders.

Culture prism: Those values, attitudes, and beliefs are brought to life through structure and customs, shaping behaviours and the way we do things.

Digital leadership: Strikes the match for digital culture by leading the way, defining vision, and orchestrating the flywheel of connectivity and ambidexterity.

Anchor points: Values, skills, and behaviours we believe are the anchor points of a digital culture, and give life to the 10 core capabilities.

Guidewires: Methods, policies, and rewards help to put shape on the patterns of work every day, and point it towards creating value with digital.

Operating model: While strategy should define value, the operating model should define the set-up to release that value.

Operating system: How people engage and interact within the operating model is defined through the operating system – the customs and norms.

Diagnosis: Culture can be diagnosed using some modular reflection tools, and can guide organisations through the culture jaws.

As we said at the end of the last part, culture is the spark and the flame that ignites and fuels a digital business. If it is not carefully curated that flame will famish and results will be sombre at best – culture is the defining capability of designing, building, and sustaining a digital business.

---

99 Josh Bershin, accessed April 7, 2023, https://joshbersin.com.

https://doi.org/10.1515/9783111034713-026

Part V: **Delivering Value Through Ambidexterity and Roadmapping**

Execution is a specific set of behaviours and techniques that companies need to master in order to have competitive advantage. It's a discipline of its own – Ram Charan and Larry Bossidy, *Execution: The Discipline of Getting Things Done*

After spending considerable time on the seven core competencies and three platforms of a digital business in the last two parts, we now come back round to close out on the 6D model for strategy and its final two dimensions – delivery and dexterity. This is where we pull everything together into a comprehensive and cogent programme of execution.

While we are spending time in this part on execution, we will keep ourselves at a strategic level rather than an operational level. This means we will think about programmes and not projects, platforming for success rather than detailed processes and plans. We will break out the philosophies, models, methods, and success factors that are required for developing and executing complex transformation programmes of work to either build or evolve a digital business.

Project plans are, of course, important, and as I learned quickly in a career in retail, the devil is in the detail. But when we think about the breadth and scale of what becoming and living as a digital business entails, it encompasses entire programmes of projects. Without a top-down programmatic approach, correctly architected, the basics of good project management will not be sufficient to get the job done. Project management will not be absent, however, and throughout this part we will incorporate how large transformation programmes of change wrap around good project management.

Thriving digital businesses are inherently competent and prolific at building and executing project plans. This often entails clear scoping and sizing, mile-stoning, resource and dependency planning, and disciplined adherence to solving problems, collaboration, timelines, resources, and goal delivery. Most organisations have strong capabilities in this space. Transforming into a digital business or transforming outcomes requires a superset of capabilities and an approach that sits above, around, and underneath excellent project delivery.

While we will focus on what it takes to execute building and/or evolving a digital business, I have called this part of the book roadmapping as it is about setting out a path of transformational change, maintaining adaptability to recalibrate and adjust activities, expected outcomes, and the application of resources given that this fluency and flexibility is often what makes the difference.

Let's start with our underpinning model – the five foundational pillars of execution.

https://doi.org/10.1515/9783111034713-027

Chapter 18
Five Pillars of Execution

As illustrated in Figure 55, the four enabling pillars of philosophy, models, prerequisites, and execution revolve around a central, coordinating fifth pillar – refine and reflect.

Programmes to build and mature digital businesses require the ability to continually evaluate purpose, strategy, capability building, and delivery. They involve using that knowledge and information, as well as ever-changing market conditions, to calibrate and evolve forwards looking focus, directed by backwards-looking execution learning. That is why we have a central co-ordinating pillar and within that sit the right methods to direct, measure, govern, and ultimately extract the value aspired to in the purpose and strategy. This central pillar is connected to, informs, and co-ordinates the four enabling pillars.

Philosophy is closely linked with purpose as it anchors around the mindset required for transformational change and delivery. Models facilitate the establishment of significant programmes and the right top-down approach being adopted to deliver strategic outcomes. Pre-requisites ensure that the correct preparations and capabilities are in place to facilitate delivery. Finally, execution accommodates the culture necessary to drive outcomes in the face of complexity and strain.

We will now go on to dive into each of the pillars in more detail.

Philosophy – The Right Mindset

Ambidextrous Leadership

In Part II, I made reference to Joseph Schumpeter's model of ambidexterity where he espoused that business leaders need to live in a perpetual state of duality, meaning that they need to exploit the business they have today to extract near-term value, while exploring new horizons of growth and future potential in order to create value for tomorrow.

Digital business leaders are required to live this concept, balancing productivity and creativity, which relates to the portfolio approach covered in Part II. The cognitive stretch and management challenge associated with this is not to be underestimated. A hallmark of today's great leaders is the ability to context switch; on the one hand optimise and drive an operational agenda for immediate delivery, while on the other, thinking and acting like a start-up to disrupt the existing business, and transition from old to new.

To do this, leaders must develop a vision for the future, communicate it passionately and encourage the business that they are leading to aspire and drive towards

https://doi.org/10.1515/9783111034713-028

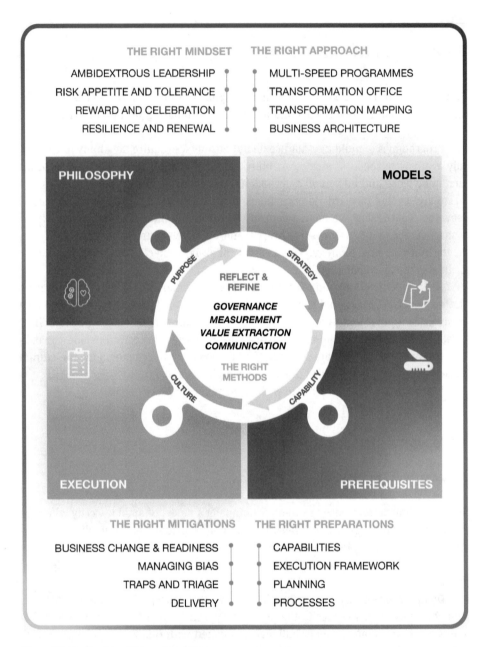

Figure 55: The five foundations of execution.

that vision. In parallel with this visionary leadership, proponents need to embrace operational planning and ensure that today's results are delivered to fund tomorrow's pursuit. This involves commanding and managing tension and isn't the job of just the leader. In fact, ambidextrous leaders articulate friction, explain it to their business, then both guide and structure the organisation to handle tension, where possible utilising them for good effect.

For instance, leaders get the balance right when they articulate that they need operational excellence to drive smarter utilisation of resources to deliver a better customer experience today while utilising some of the efficiency to be spent on testing new innovations for tomorrow. They can also throttle what is often the scarcest resource, people, to respective agendas, for example, customer experience improvements and proposition innovation. They maintain the ability to observe and migrate threats or opportunities to the correct agenda and capability to solve for them. This might mean that a potential breakthrough proposition idea identified in 'business as usual' is elevated and enabled by innovation accelerators or pulling those specialist innovation resources away from continuous improvement activities that should be managed in the core.

Ambidextrous leaders, therefore, master the ability to utilise two contradictory, yet complementary, leadership styles, blending them and applying them in the appropriate way and right organisational context, namely:

– transformational leadership: using encouragement guidance and the challenger mentality to think differently, to experiment and to innovate, ultimately challenging the status quo on mindsets to capture latent or value not yet created (linked to Schumpeter's Explore)
– transactional leadership: planning, objective setting, disciplined monitoring, course correcting, managing risk, and controlling resources tightly to ensure committed results are delivered (linked to Schumpeter's Exploit)

This kind of multi-disciplined leadership does not necessarily come naturally to everyone, but with the right structures and desire, it can be developed and honed. One of the most important structurally enabling mechanisms to facilitate ambidexterity is that of setting appropriate risk appetites and tolerances across the digital business portfolio. Getting this balance right is also an important risk mitigation activity.

Risk Appetite and Tolerance

Risk appetite is the amount of risk an organisation is willing to accept to achieve its objectives and ultimately its strategy. Risk tolerance is the acceptable deviation from the risk appetite. To help put this in context, think of road speed limits. The speed limit is the risk appetite that is applied to travelling on the particular road and reflects the correlation between speed and danger. The lower the speed limit the higher the correlation between speed and danger. In recognising that the world is neither finite nor perfect, risk tolerance is reflected when authorities may not enforce speed limits in the absolute strictest manner. That might mean roadside police may not stop travellers who are, say, less than 10% above the status speed limit, but will do at greater than 10% above.

Ambidextrous leaders therefore set different risk appetites across the portfolio of their organisation and will also apply risk tolerance to further set and enable the right conditions for success. A good example would be setting a zero-tolerance risk appetite for a regulated activity within an operational function; so that might be acquiring safety permits for construction projects. Given the exposure to serious injury or loss of life, the risk tolerance would understandably be very tight, and assumed to only be acceptable in the case of say dormant sites that have no human activity.

At the same time, a construction firm may be undertaking an experiment with a new digitally enabled, automated construction process that shows good promise, e.g. is more sustainable. In this instance, there may actually be no pre-existing safety regulations, so the construction firm may seek to establish the appropriate regulations. To do that, they may undertake rounds of testing to establish the risk to health and safety, and therefore, may need to accept that there is a greater degree of exposure to harm. In such circumstances, they would also control the environment and limit human exposure, only allowing such exposure with the right degree of insurance and permissions in place.

Ambidextrous leaders understand that the pursuit of value necessitates degrees of risk, and in fact, the greater the pursuit the greater the risk. But as they manage a portfolio, they quantify risk acceptance in different parts of the portfolio and communicate what risks they are willing to take or what tolerance they have against that risk appetite. This allows for explore and exploit activities to be boundaried or unbounded such that the balance of risk and reward is appropriately set.

Reward structures should be inextricably linked to risk appetite, and should be both enabling and guiding. Equally, celebration is an important component, even of failure once that is acceptable failure. Let's take a look at that next.

Reward and Celebration

We covered reward mechanisms for digital businesses in Part IV, so there's no need to revisit that specifically. However, I do want to point out that reward and risk should be complementary in their construction. This means that both incentives and disincentives should be aligned to, guide and enable adherence to risk appetites.

Carrying the example of construction forwards, a firm may set incentives and rewards that are triggered when zero tolerance on safety permits on operational sites is achieved. In the case of the exploratory activity, both the risk appetite and the reward mechanisms will of course need to be different. In this case, the company will incentivise achieving both failure and success rates for the new automated construction process, such that they understand and can ultimately approve the process in the knowledge that there is an acceptable operational risk appetite. In this case the failures are just as, if not more important than the successes, as they identify safety limitations.

The nuance is important here. Being crystal clear on why failure is really a success helps to articulate the risk appetite and its rationale. The accompanying reward further bolsters that situation and provides the necessary motivation of delivery. Following on from that, celebration (which, remember, is a strong motivational lever), should also be utilised to articulate and affirm risk appetite and tolerances. Communication and celebration are crucial in rewarding tolerance as they allow for degrees of freedom that can't be catered for in linear appetites.

Beyond that, however, I see celebration (whether it be of tolerated 'failures' or notable achievements) as a very significant tool for digital businesses and their transformations. Often, an organisation can become significantly consumed by its capability building or proposition delivery, given the scale and complexity, as you can now probably appreciate having read the previous parts.

In this consumption, the toil and effort undertaken by the body of the organisation in delivering digital business initiatives can be overlooked, and if not acknowledged, weaken or destroy this important intrinsic motivation lever. Effort, learning, controlled failure (within risk appetites and tolerances), and willingness should all be monitored, acknowledged, and, where exemplary, celebrated to set the tone of expectation and success definition.

Resilience and Renewal

Acknowledging, celebrating, and even rewarding failure will surely seem counterintuitive, but, given the earlier declaration that some 70% or more of transformation efforts fail, should illuminate the necessity to expect failure. As in life and especially in traditional businesses, we are not programmed for failure or rewarded for it; quite the opposite.

Therefore, ambidextrous leaders and organisations that are on the journey of digital transformation must embrace the likelihood of failure. They need to build resilience, the ability to reset and renew effort, and the determination and the spirit to go again. Digital, despite having been around for quite a number of years now, is still new to most and therefore, there was no predefined playbook. It is only to be expected that failure facilitates learning, which breeds success. Is that not the way we all achieve greatness? In the words of Thomas Edison, on being posed the question what it felt like to fail 1000 times when trying to invent the light bulb, 'I didn't fail 1,000 times. The light bulb was an invention that took 1,000 steps'.

Creating the new nearly always takes longer, and is harder than one expects. That is why resilience and renewal are important features of enabling roadmapping towards digital maturity. Resilience can be built by:

- returning to the purpose for energy and motivation
- managing emotions, and maintaining a stance of realistic optimism
- constant reminders that course changing is necessary
- focusing energy not on the failure, but on the reason for failure and the mitigants or corrective actions that should be learned
- stepping away and taking a break, or rotating towards other activities for perspective and renewal
- leveraging relationships and empathetic sponsors

The adaptability inherent in resilience and renewal is a great reminder of why we have the central fifth pillar that allows for systematic evolution. It is also a good time for us to move on to models that allow for flexibility and reduce the risk of complexity and misadventure.

Models – The Right Approach

Multispeed Programmes

As I explained in the strategy part of this book, modern digital businesses are likely to need to execute multiple speeds of the change to manage a digital portfolio and s-curves. By this, I mean it may be necessary to drive change that is continuous and sustaining in the core business of today (also called exploit), while at the same time set up programmes that are aligned with developmental and disruptive innovation (aligned with explore). This needs ambidextrous leadership with the structure and mechanisms that allow a single, aligning approach to multiple streams or speeds of change to ensure that overall, any speed-specific requirements, risk or resources are managed in harmony.

A model for 'harmonising' multiple speeds of change is illustrated in Figure 56, and is premised on applying a consistent methodology running from intent to delivery. The ultimate goal is to work towards a single view of change or roadmap, which is enabled by initiatives following a diagnose-dissect-design set of steps, with alignment and migration checkpoints at the end of each stage.

Once an initiative is identified for strategic delivery, it should go through a diagnose stage. This allows the business to discover what the intention is, define requirements and ensure it is on the right speed. At this point, the business can additionally ensure that adequate resources, budgets, and so on are in place. By making those checks at this point of initiative maturity, the intent (demand) and the requirements (supply) can be communicated, then catered to the entire portfolio, with prioritisation/de-prioritisation calls made.

At this point, I suggest initiatives go through a challenge step that allows the business to complete a collaborative assessment by a cross-speed team (or a Programme

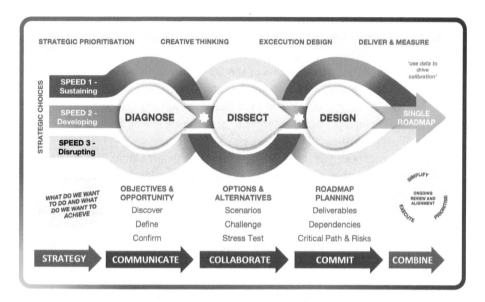

Figure 56: Harmonising multispeed programmes.

Office – more on that later) to assess the likelihood of success and alternative scenarios. This is where the programme can evaluate critical success factors, cross-speed dependencies, and opportunities, as well as ascertain success probabilities and risk appetites. Again at this point, initiatives can be calibrated for resources and dependencies with any resulting requirements or effects calibrated across the portfolio. The inclusion of the cross-stream resources is important for alignment as well as idea and risk generation.

The final stage is delivery design, where once armed with the knowledge gained in the prior two steps, detailed project planning takes place and deliverables (milestones), along with all dependencies and critical path (sequencing) are worked through, include a final risk assessment. The final portfolio alignment is completed at this point before the initiative goes on to the single roadmap.

From there, initiatives move into programme portfolio governance, where there is continuous review and alignment through the delivery stages and the portfolio is perpetually simplified, prioritised, and managed for execution. Measurement is ongoing throughout delivery to enable this calibration; the docking point with the central reflect and refine pillar.

Transformation Offices

I have worked with and established multispeed roadmaps under the remit of CEO Offices, those of the COO, heads of strategy, CIOs, chief digital officers, and chief transformation officers (CTOs). The latter role is becoming more prevalent in larger organisations, to cope with the effects of spin out syndromes, multispeed programmes, relentless acceleration of change velocity and transformation in general. Research from McKinsey[100] published in December 2022 cites that 23% of the US top 100 CPG and retail organisations now have enterprise-level CTOs that span across three typical archetypes:

– Responders: CTOs that are drafted in to deal with burning platform and crisis circumstances, who focus on near-term financial improvement with a heavy emphasis on driving coordinated execution.

– Revitalisers: These CTOs are more medium-term focused than Responders, who put a greater emphasis on enabling a change and building new leadership and capabilities for emerging or impending change dynamics.

– Reinventors: This archetype leads an organisation through a significant strategic shift over a number of years, and are often associated with digital and business transformation in sectors and regions undergoing significant market or competitive disruption.

There is a fourth archetype identified called Reports, who unsurprisingly act as a PMO and report back to the organisations on the effort and outcome of change, but typically have a hands off, passive role with little impact on changing 'change'. I have also witnessed Strategic Execution Offices that are more akin to Reporters, but play a heavier emphasis on coordinating the strategic phase of change (the first 4 Ds in our 6D model – discover, detect, diagnose, and direct) and although they have a more influential role on the what, they have a limited remit on the how.

Although referenced as in the minority, I have also worked with a fifth archetype that attempts to straddle a composite of McKinsey's first three archetypes – the All-Rounder. These leaders are the epitome of ambidexterity but a rare enough find. All of the archetypes and transformation leaders mentioned typically are managing a transformation roadmap of sorts that resembles the multispeed roadmap outlined earlier, or a transformation roadmap that we will come to next (the difference is subtle, but worth calling out).

But before we do go to Transformation Roadmaps, let's just note that McKinsey has done a nice job of extracting the universal aptitudes and competencies of the effective CTO, which I have summarised as follows:

– Business Thinker – has experience and understands what makes the business tick, how to extract value and the cycle of markets and competition

– Enterprise Acumen – has the ability to join the dots from strategy and external forces with operations and organisational forces

---

100 McKinsey, "Meet the Newest Member of the Consumer C-suite: The Chief Transformation Officer," (December 5, 2022), accessed April 7, 2023, https://www.mckinsey.com/capabilities/transformation/our-insights/meet-the-newest-member-of-the-consumer-csuite-the-chief-transformation-officer.

- Trust Broker – leverages experience and applies it with empathy and good communications skills to build credibility for insight and influence
- Challenger – with insight and earned authority, plays the role of the helpful antagonist to help the organisation to 'think outside the box', and see the unseen
- Understander – uses all the senses and empathy to understand how an organisation works and feels so that it can deal with hard (process, structure) and soft (fear, lack of understanding) dynamics
- Enabler – as the chief influencer, works through people to deliver results with weighty communications and compelling storytelling backed up by data
- Energiser – feels the mood of the organisation and helps to regulate it by elongating the highs, and navigate the lows

Transformation Offices and Officers, regardless of where they sit play an instrumental role, should apply the attributes outlined above and be the conduit for translating strategy to execution through multispeed programmes or transformation planning. The latter is often articulated through Transformation Mapping which we will use next.

Transformation Mapping

The difference between multispeed programmes and transformation mapping is that they:
- have a longer term, elongated vista;
- incorporate building capabilities as well as delivering business change;
- factor in structural change; and
- align change with business goals.

In Figure 57, I have shared an indicative transformation map, which is based on a generalisation and amalgamation of a number of transformation programmes we have worked on. This version is based on what is traditionally known as a T-Map (T for Transformation), which I have extended to include a line of sight on both critical path and business value, hence we call it a transcendence map.

As you will see, the map gives you a perspective across a 5-year time horizon, and is broken into four streams all leading to a desired outcome at the top right (in this instance, building an enterprise fit for ongoing transformation and evolution); the first three being the contributory streams of technology and systems, customer and proposition and business and people capabilities which all lead to delivering the business benefits in the final value stream.

The streams work in parallel, and the roadmap items articulated are significant programmes of work in themselves. But the map also indicates another degree of sophistication that illustrates how an enterprise level transformation is cross-dependent and cross-enabling. This is indicated by the colour coding and numbering, which signals in what domain the programmes of work sit and how they are linked. For instance, building digital prowess is done by developing Web Services and Robotics, User Experience, and eCommerce which sit across the respective domains of technology, customer and capability and are all indicated by the number 1. In this case, building that digital prowess is in response to findings in a Voice of the Customer programme which identified demand for digital, and led to a new proposition roadmap, which then dictated an App refresh – these items are indicated by the number 2.

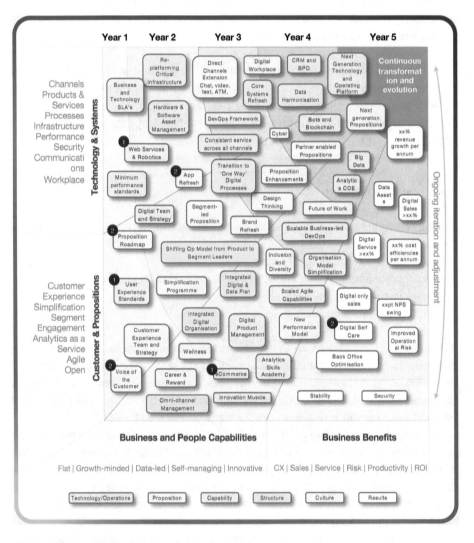

Figure 57: Transcendence map.

Much like a strategy on a page this view gives us transformation on a page. As with all 'on a page' visualisations, it is not possible to show all the linkages, dependencies and critical paths on the medium we are working with here, but those items are captured in detail on supplementary artefacts and facilitate cross-programme planning and alignment.

The transcendence map also facilitates connecting effort with value – as you'll see the building of digital prowess (items 1), identified in the customer demand and response planning (items 2), lead to delivering digital self-care for customers which resulted in reduced transactional demand on human operations (e.g. the call centre). Customers were happier, and operations were able to redirect resources to value capture activities such as sales and further change.

These kind of transformation mapping techniques are closely linked to Business Architecture, which we will move to next.

Business Architecture

Business architecture as a discipline can be a critical enabler of transformation programmes in the right circumstances. Let's take a moment to give ourselves a quick definition.

Object Management Group, the global open standards body, host a Business Architecture Working Group[101] that have defined Business Architecture as the 'blueprint of the enterprise that provides a common understanding of the organisation and is used to align strategic objectives and tactical demands'. In truth, this means it is a means to capture and portray what the business does, how it does it, how it is organised, and how it creates value.

In Part IV under operating model we covered the benefits of breaking down and visualising the work required to deliver on the jobs to be done and to help design the optimal way to organise people. Business architecture takes us one step further in that it helps to create an enterprise blueprint that stretches from the customer or end-user and the channels that they use back into the propositions and operating model where value is created, and then connecting that through to the systems and data needed to facilitate delivery. This Business Architecture is therefore the articulation of business strategy that corresponds with and informs the Enterprise Architecture, which as we learned in Part III is the technology (and data) strategy. These two architectures are the yin and yang of an organisation and how the 'front' marries to the 'back'. Together they provide the glue.

There are plenty of examples of Business Architecture online and at your nearest consultancy, but an approach that we have come across and have been inspired by is

---

101 OMG – Standards Development Organization, accessed April 7, 2023, https://www.omg.org/.

the Exploded View by the Swiss-based consulting firm foryouandyourcustomers.[102] Their white paper illustrates how an organisation can unbundle and layer how it is organised, and provide visibility between how value is created with customers/end users and the corresponding moving parts behind the scenes, for example, in the product, process, and technical layers. This has the benefit of pointing all effort towards customer-centricity, understanding the cause and effect correlation of resources (people, data, technology) and visualise what needs to change when change is being planned. The whitepaper is worth a read as a good accompaniment to this chapter.

In many ways creating business architecture and enterprise blueprints is the visual manifestation of what the CTOs vision for the combined business, data, and technology capabilities and solutions required to deliver proposition, value, and ultimately the strategy.

What I like about business architecture blueprints is that they visually connect the dots of what is required to succeed from front to back of a business. This helps people as both actors for customer engagement, drivers of operational tasks and also designers and deliverers of projects and change understand what the implications and indeed opportunities for digital are. It also helps engineers, whether they be technical, structural, process, or data in nature comprehend and be guided towards building the optimal model.

A few words of caution. Employing and building business architecture blueprints can be a costly task so if a business is not set up to use them to derive opportunity, foresight, and value, a little bit like customer journey maps, they can sit on shelves or in folders gathering dust.

The secret sauce and antidote is the right kind of business architects, whose role is to:
–   Develop blueprints that match the strategic objectives of the business with the operational, process, data, and technology foundations
–   Act as a consultant, orchestrator, inspirer, and indeed reconciler between leaders and strategists, engineers, and ultimately the people who run the business
–   Use comprehension, influence, and visual storytelling capabilities to join the dots and triangulates intent with cause-and-effect at an operational level
–   Provide triage mechanisms and solution finding when the very natural conflicts arise between desire and reality

So, business architecture is a friend of the CTO, but while I believe that business architects and architecture can play an instrumental role in defining and equipping an organisation to understand the implications of go-to strategic requirements, the effort

---

102 Foryouandyourcustomers, "The Exploded View," accessed April 7, 2023, https://foryouandyourcus tomers.com/posts/whitepaper/exploded-view/?lang=en.

and the skill required need to be in place, as does the organisations willingness to work with business architects and their craft.

Service Blueprints which we referenced in both customer-centricity and technology are the tools of business architecture – just think of them as a micro and macro lens of design and dependency capture. Technology and process perspectives are common to both, as are capabilities which are a key elements of transformation mapping as we have seen. Let's move on now to talk about capability planning.

Prerequisites – The Right Preparations

Capabilities

At the beginning of the book, I pointed to the fact that building digital business universally requires new capabilities, or at least their maturity. As a result, I have attempted to illuminate the processes (strategy, which is a capability in itself), the ten capabilities (seven core competencies and three enabling platforms) that are required to be a digital business, and under each of these, what dimensions to consider and cater for. For instance, under the people platform in the last part, I presented the nine-dimension digital DNA model for building digital culture, and for each dimension, presented a subset of drivers; for example, under digital leadership, nine segments, in the Digital Leadership Flywheel under Values, nine core strains.

When it comes to capability planning, which should constitute a central place on a Roadmap, I suggest utilisation of the 10 capabilities and their underpinning dimensions and drivers to assess current maturity. In parallel, required and go-to requirements under the 10 capabilities, dimensions, and drivers can be ascertained from the strategic planning work. Resulting gaps are then assessed for effort and impact and included as deliverables on the roadmap, and treated similarly as other initiatives in the multispeed programme approach – diagnosis of requirements, dissection, and challenge of optimal options and design for delivery.

My experience is that there is no one-size-fits-all approach to be followed here, and business sector, size, strategic ambition, and resource availability will determine the level of capability assessment and planning.

Some organisations use the 10 capabilities as a barometer, and drill in to make progress on a prioritised number of big-impact areas. Other businesses let strategy dictate the priorities, and where gaps exist go down to a dimension or even driver level. Some organisations create a diagnostic and capability maturity plan across all 10 and at all three levels (capability, dimension, and driver) which spans a multi-year roadmap with sequenced alignment, e.g. customer-centricity, digital engagement, and technology go hand-in-hand, and are progressed as one.

My default position is to assess all 10 at a dimension level to get departure bearings, assess those that present the greatest strategic gap, and then go to a driver level to identify a first batch of prioritised capability building needs. As the capability is matured, continually test and recalibrate the plan as new capability rolls out, and new needs are identified.

Whether it be for capability, initiative level (e.g. multispeed programme) or overall transformation planning, there are a core set of execution prerequisites that we have identified on our travels, and which we share with you next.

Execution Framework and Planning

To ensure that any programme of work spanning all or some capability building and change initiatives are platformed for success, I have assembled the key ingredients of an execution framework, which I call the Execution Heartbeat given this sets the pulse and pace for fruition. These are based on my experience across digital business building programmes large and small, and are articulated in Figure 58.

Starting with clarity and alignment on purpose and strategy, where choices and outcomes are communicated and understood, ownership is a catalyst for aligning a programme and organisation to move into delivery mode. In particular, leadership from the front is vital, and on the ground ambassadors are often engaged in support.

Project teams, understanding role accountability and taking into account the needs of stakeholders, assemble the necessary plans with tested, yet stretching, milestones that are made in the context of dependencies and resources being clear and catered for.

Clear outcome planning and tracking is critical, as is employing not just the right number of resources, but also those with the right skills. Attributes such as collaborative problem-solving and data-driven decisioning are key. So too is access to leadership and sponsors for decisioning and guidance, and the correct governance structures and decision-making protocols help facilitate speed and clarity.

Programmes should also be thought of as digital operations in themselves, and subject to the same treatment around design, continuous improvement and agile ceremonies such as retrospectives. Data as we mentioned should be a lightening conductor for decision-making, monitoring the achievement of OKRs, and creating an environment of transparency and learning.

As with a digital business, the culture of change should be in line with the overall DNA of the business, or model which is desired. Programme and transformation leadership should pay good attention to building the right culture, and our nine-dimension digital DNA model is a good place to start.

Planning is a core competency of any business, and particularly a proficient digital business in order to handle the span and tempo of change usually associated. But planning needs to happen at two levels, at a project level, and at a programme or transformation level. This requires an additional degree of dexterity and coordination that we will close out on in our central coordinating pillar – Reflect and Refine.

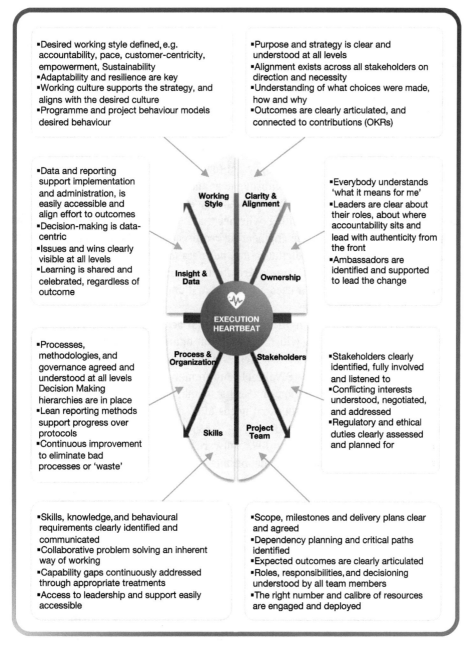

- Desired working style defined, e.g. accountability, pace, customer-centricity, empowerment, Sustainability
- Adaptability and resilience are key
- Working culture supports the strategy, and aligns with the desired culture
- Programme and project behaviour models desired behaviour

- Purpose and strategy is clear and understood at all levels
- Alignment exists across all stakeholders on direction and necessity
- Understanding of what choices were made, how and why
- Outcomes are clearly articulated, and connected to contributions (OKRs)

- Data and reporting support implementation and administration, is easily accessible and align effort to outcomes
- Decision-making is data-centric
- Issues and wins clearly visible at all levels
- Learning is shared and celebrated, regardless of outcome

Working Style

Clarity & Alignment

Insight & Data

Ownership

- Everybody understands 'what it means for me'
- Leaders are clear about their roles, about where accountability sits and lead with authenticity from the front
- Ambassadors are identified and supported to lead the change

EXECUTION HEARTBEAT

- Processes, methodologies, and governance agreed and understood at all levels Decision Making hierarchies are in place
- Lean reporting methods support progress over protocols
- Continuous improvement to eliminate bad processes or 'waste'

Process & Organization

Stakeholders

Skills

Project Team

- Stakeholders clearly identified, fully involved and listened to
- Conflicting interests understood, negotiated, and addressed
- Regulatory and ethical duties clearly assessed and planned for

- Skills, knowledge, and behavioural requirements clearly identified and communicated
- Collaborative problem solving an inherent way of working
- Capability gaps continuously addressed through appropriate treatments
- Access to leadership and support easily accessible

- Scope, milestones and delivery plans clear and agreed
- Dependency planning and critical paths identified
- Expected outcomes are clearly articulated
- Roles, responsibilities, and decisioning understood by all team members
- The right number and calibre of resources are engaged and deployed

Figure 58: Execution heartbeat.

Processes

Process are the rails on which any business runs, and are central to the governance and the Transformation Heartbeat. They are also at the centre of our Digital 360, and form the largest slice of that pie. So here we want to check in on business process management given that criticality, and that it is often a weak departure or delivery point in building digital businesses roadmaps. Many programmes have been frustrated and progress stifled by the lack of business process documentation and management. Business processes are the means by which to capture the as-is and go-to operational perspective, critically important for initiatives such as Simplification but also customer-centric proposition improvement and design.

All too often, I see businesses initiate change and sometimes build new propositions without properly documenting, whether that be through process maps, journey maps, or service blueprints, the engineering required. Critically, for existing process improvement, digitisation, or digitalisation, business process mapping equates to the entry fee. And compared to Business Architecture or Journey Mapping, it is a relatively easy skill to attain, and if used correctly can illuminate opportunity to capitalise on, but also waste to eradicate.

Many organisations coming from a non-digital departure point have no or sporadic process documentation which can prohibit opportunity, and also cause:effect planning never mind audit and risk activities. Many organisations are now employing Business Process Management (BPM) tools and frameworks to assist on both continuous improvement and automation and scenario analysis, and let's not forget that to automate or digitally code a process, it needs to be documented (that's what code in essence is).

There are a host of cloud-based BPM software tools such as Camunda and Appian that help to capture, monitor, and model business processes which are worth exploring. As we accelerate our use of software to execute business processes, the good news is that process maps come as standard fare and 'out of the box', but be cautioned that they are prepared for out-of-the-box processes and need to be adjusted for configuration, integration, cross-application processes and adaptions. We won't get in to the adopt, don't adapt lesson in detail, other than to say it is highly recommended that organisations adopt out-of-the-box processes when implementing new applications as adapting can lead to significant chock points down the road if technology upgrades cannot be scheduled because of or in addition to bespoke maintenance demands.

There are also useful reference frameworks including the BPM Capability Framework from BPM in the digital age,[103] available online and which are worth a look at for further inspiration, and every good consultancy should have one. This area is a

---

103 digital-bpm, "BPM in the Digital Age," accessed April 7, 2023, https://digital-bpm.com/bpm-capability-framework/.

table stake for a modern, sustainable business and sometimes gets overlooked hence our stop by here.

Let's now move on to close out the enabling pillars of our five-pillar model – Execution.

Execution – The Right Mitigations

Business Change and Readiness

One of the most unfortunate but yet absolutely remediable issues on roadmapping and delivery is preparing businesses for change. It happens for many reasons, mainly due to cocooned project teams, responsibility, and reward focused on deployment as opposed to value delivery and often times simply due to capacity constraints and competing priorities. There are, however, mature processes and approaches which help guide and connect delivery teams with business teams to ensure that deployments are maximised and they generally follow a Ready, Willing, and Able set of checkpoints, initiatives, and engagements.

I have shared my approach in Figure 59, and as you will see, the sequential steps serve as a means to direct the correct preparatory activities towards ensuring that friction from change is minimised, and capability adopted and as a result value maximised.

In the first instance, it starts with getting the business ready. This entails making sure that the organisation structures, resourcing, and capacity are in place, and as a follow up that the organisation has access to the systems and tools that are required. This often involves a training, testing, and release cycle, whether that be for the launch of new capabilities, or modifications to old systems. Systems and operations require processes, and in line with our earlier messages, business processes should be prepared, tested, approved, and trained out as part of the systems readiness.

Next we typically move to the Willing phase. This is by nature a more emotional and culturally focused phase which starts and ends with communication, engagement, and leadership. Sharing the rationale and case for change, illustrating the benefits for customers, end users and the business (as a whole and the employees within it) is the departure point. Building on that, colleagues should be engaged to ascertain the impact of the change proposed, resulting support requirements and a communications and feedback loop should be established along with the necessary response supports in place to smooth the path through the delivery to deployment cycle. The role of managers as change leaders is critical here in modelling behaviours that support ambition for change, accountability, and benefits realisation but also employing empathy and triage whether that be at a process or human level.

Finally comes the Able phase, and that begins with setting agreed performance metrics and KPIs (that can be rolled up into OKR mechanisms), and supported by

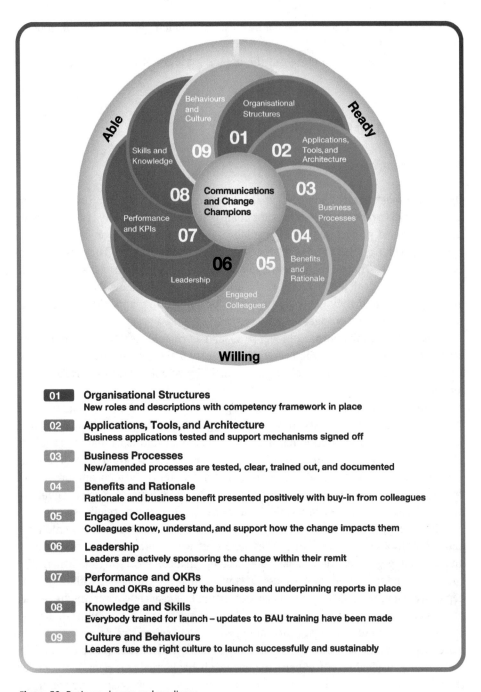

01 **Organisational Structures**
New roles and descriptions with competency framework in place

02 **Applications, Tools, and Architecture**
Business applications tested and support mechanisms signed off

03 **Business Processes**
New/amended processes are tested, clear, trained out, and documented

04 **Benefits and Rationale**
Rationale and business benefit presented positively with buy-in from colleagues

05 **Engaged Colleagues**
Colleagues know, understand, and support how the change impacts them

06 **Leadership**
Leaders are actively sponsoring the change within their remit

07 **Performance and OKRs**
SLAs and OKRs agreed by the business and underpinning reports in place

08 **Knowledge and Skills**
Everybody trained for launch – updates to BAU training have been made

09 **Culture and Behaviours**
Leaders fuse the right culture to launch successfully and sustainably

Figure 59: Business change and readiness.

training and learning evaluation to ensure colleagues are both clear on what's expected and equipped to deliver it. The final step is to ensure that a cultural overlay is applied with the articulation of desired and required behaviours which should marry back to the overall values and cultural stance,

We could delve deeper on this cycle, and depending on the complexity of the change initiatives at hand, that may be a requirement but we believe that what we have set out here offers a sufficiently robust methodology to construct change management and preparedness to suit roadmaps large and small. Taking a systemic, inclusive, and holistic approach such as this facilitates the smooth transition from change to operations, and is a bedrock for benefits realisation.

Before closing the enabling pillars, we will take a broader look at the cultural barriers that inhibit change at scale, and roadmap success.

Managing Bias

Digitally led transformations are often holistic, spanning an entire organisational architecture and therefore require a holistic response and one that caters for herd traits that we have often witnessed across an organisations tapestry. Having recently spent some time studying behavioural economics and the role that human phycology plays in the success (or not) of transformation, I believe there is an important role for behavioural economics to assist organisations and transformation leaders in designing the organisational and people change component of transformation programmes.

This in my experience is in fact the most important component of such programmes. Without an understanding for the need to transform, without creating the desired motivation to transform and without forecasting the fears, doubts, and behavioural challenges and making the appropriate interventions, failure levels can run much higher than needs be.

Were transformation programme designers to harness the lens of behavioural economics and apply it to the organisational change journey, I believe there is the potential to increase transformational success. Let me give you an example. We learned earlier that intrinsic motivation is a much greater store of motivation that extrinsic. Tapping into motivations like pride, learning opportunities, and care for colleagues is much more likely to be a motivator to go on transformation journeys compared to commercial and shareholder threats. In addition, positive, honest, and well-designed engagements and interventions can offset biases, procrastination, and fear.

The following are some biases and behavioural dynamics that play out in transformations, along with some suggested treatments:

– 'Blind spot bias': The bias that we are not biased, yet others are – address the 'we are safe' syndrome through open communications, using data and storytelling

– 'Optimism bias': Over-optimism about the potential of good outcomes – ensure to test the realities of commitments and expectations, and use scenario planning

– 'Bystander effect': The more people are around, the less likely individuals are to help a victim – communicate and engender the need for personal actions, and not leaving it to colleagues

– 'IKEA effect': Getting involved is more likely to facilitate ownership – get people involved in transformation design through engagement and storytelling, in addition to design and testing as well as business change and readiness activity

– 'Zeigarnik effect': Remembering failed or interrupted tasks more than successfully completed ones – offset the bias to focus on and report failure by balancing it with celebration of good tasks, and very importantly learning which is a critical currency of change

– 'Law of triviality': Putting disproportionate weight on trivial issues – stop people focusing time and energy on lots of small stuff that won't make a difference, rather than the small number of big things that will make a big difference

– 'Placebo effect': If we believe a treatment will work, it will have a positive physiological effect – show how others have done it, and that it can be done, is rewarding and yields positive benefits that outweigh the challenges. Also remember to share early success stories

– 'Framing bias': Draw different conclusions from the same information depending on how it is presented – dial up attention to consistent, inclusive communications

– 'Gambler's fallacy': Thinking that future possibilities are affected by past events – address the risk of believing that we will be successful in the future, because we have been successful in the past and the complacency that comes with that through a compelling and data-led case for change communications

– 'Sunk cost fallacy': Investing more in things that have already cost us, rather than redirecting effort elsewhere, even if that means negative outcomes – address the gravitational pull to hold on to the past through engagement and storytelling, and the case for change using data and relevant case studies

– 'Status quo bias': The tendency to prefer things to stay the same, as change to the baseline feels like a loss – painting the picture of the current vs the alternative, transformation pathways and very importantly painting the picture of success at the end

– 'Diclinism': Romanticising that the past has been more positive than the current, believing that society and systems are declining in value; for example, kids have less respect these days – storytell about what the past v the present holds (it is usually a positive story), and the need for personal ownership

– 'Backfire effect': Disproving evidence sometimes has the unwarranted effect of confirming our beliefs – ensure that there is fair representation of references and case studies, and seek to avoid 'Confirmation Bias' – choosing to believe and recall evidence that supports our beliefs

– 'Reactance': Doing the opposite of what we're told when it's perceived as a personal threat – ensure communications are fair, rational, balanced, and non-threatening, and give people and teams the mechanisms for feedback, engagement, and debate

– The 'Dunning-Kruger effect': The more you know, the less confident you will be – ensure that communications are not overwhelming, and maintain balance in outlook

– 'Naïve realism': Believing that we are objective, and that others are irrational, uninformed, or biased – use reflective techniques in engagement strategies to evaluate self-bias and 'eye opening', and bring outsiders in to challenge and share 'realities'

– 'Curse of knowledge': Assuming that because we know something, everyone else does too – transformation leaders need to bring their audience with them, and frequently double back

– 'False consensus': Believing that more people agree with us than is actually the case – transformation leaders need to recognise that agreement doesn't always mean willingness

– 'Groupthink': Making irrational decisions to maintain harmony – transformation leaders need to observe and intervene with communications and data to avoid this trait, which can manifest when there are unwilling or reluctant participants

There are more than 180 cognitive biases[104] that affect how we process information and act, and behavioural economics is a relatively new field. Yet with some research and diligence, transformation leaders can identify those that are at play in their context, and apply the kind of treatments I have suggested here. Much of what I believe the field can greatly assist with is designing and applying interventions, communications, and engagements to facilitate better outcomes.

I believe that behavioural economics has an important role to play in the design of our futures. What I have covered here relates to professional applications, but I also see the power of behavioural economics in social and community pursuits, as well as in our individual personal lives.

---

104 weforum.org, "24 Cognitive Biases that are Warping your Perception of Reality," (November 30, 2021) accessed April 7, 2023, https://www.weforum.org/agenda/2021/11/humans-cognitive-bias-mistake/.

Traps and Triage

The biases and their treatments above frame a significant proportion of what blocks or slows down transformational roadmap execution. That said, there are a number of other organisational and operational traps that I would like to call out, again with corresponding treatments that can help triage:

– Tug of War: I often observe the friction between change and operational resource, and capacity planning. With possession being nine tenths of the law, business leaders who hold the resource strings are often reluctant to transfer the best people to transformation and change programmes for fear of missing BAU (business as usual) budgets and responsibilities. This is best alleviated with a mix of engagement and buy-in messaging from the top, role modelling from the executive level and backed up by the right OKRs such as targets for rotations, and rewards balanced across change as well as operations.

– Bureaucracy: if design, decisioning and triage itself is not efficient and effectively structured, complexity will breed complexity and both slow down progress, as well as lead to committee-based and compromised solutions. Clear decision rights, behavioural retrospectives, and harder measures are helpful here. To give an example of the latter, I have been involved in setting hard metrics to limit adaption of software applications as teams are (because of their inherent biases, not necessarily extrinsic resistance) prone to reverse-engineering new software processes to the old ways, as opposed to adopting the new 'pre-configured' ways, which are usually the culmination of collective design.

– Over-agility: Some businesses, and eager executives with a point to prove in particular, have been caught out on over-extending empowerment by not putting in place the counter-measures to limit budget and time drift, scope creep, and misaligned adventures. Measures such as the Green Box called out earlier, and active sponsorship and short evaluation and retrospective cycles help here.

– Politeness: While always appreciated, it can be the enemy of progress, and having worked in multiple cultures, I have observed some where the first 90% of meeting time is spent dealing with easier discussions, and only opening up the hard conversations near the end of allocated time when there is inevitably too little time to engage on tough decisioning. This results in a cycle of deferral, procrastination, and a snowball effect can take place. I have, however, also worked in environments where the tough topics are first thing on the agenda, and nobody leaves until a resolution emerges. There is nothing like prioritisation and getting to the heart of matters, so you can imagine where I sit on this one.

– Reticence: Bob Igor, the long-standing CEO of Walt Disney recounts that he went all in on the need to transform the go-to-market strategy of the content division of the organisation, and shift from a model that sold to channel partners such as Netflix to creating its own platform, which we now know as Disney+. In engaging the board and the investor community, he cited that this would see income and profits fall, and costs increase. Supported by the credibility of transforming the animation division some years earlier, the board, investors, and markets all responded with a supportive vote and ratified the 'all in' position. The approach has at the time of writing turned out well with Disney+ becoming one of the most successful platforms by subscriber numbers. In interviews, Igor recalls that too many organisations are, and remain, half-hearted to drive self-disruption, which he believes results in failure. I have also observed this dynamic at a programme and client level. I strongly advocate courage and conviction; there has to be skin in the game, and this is only remedied by bold, informed, and supported leadership.

– Accountability: Accountability and dedication borne through alignment at the top of the organisational is fundamental – without it failure looms. Time and debate, often best facilitated, can help to remove bias, misunderstanding, fear, and ego, although I have seen some hard calls being made when conciliation or even congruence does not emerge.

A final thought relates to having fun. Change of the magnitude needed or desired to be a digital business is quite frankly enormous, and often the consequences of failure bear heavily. It is therefore natural that fun can get left behind. It's okay to have fun when doing serious work. In fact, I believe it's a necessity. Transformation is hard, don't make it harder by not balancing out the hard yards with some humour and humility – it takes 17 muscles to smile, and 43 to frown, so need I say more.

Delivery

I have spoken sufficiently about the factors that affect delivery of change in this part to now move on and close out this last enabling pillar by talking about the desired outcome of delivery and that's value.

I believe that there are three forms of value:
- Value that is created by new digital propositions and ventures including ecosystem engagement
- Value that is latent and unlocked by digital, e.g. channel enhancements and personalised nudges open up new opportunities in the existing customer base and operations
- Value that is protected; this is harder to measure, but more and more critical in the age of increased digitally enabled competition, this relates to the defence of existing value already being captured from current operations

Establishing which type of value that an endeavour is focusing on, and applying a common measurement approach is a cornerstone for driving, refining, and ultimately proving any roadmap and transformation plan. In the words of Dr W. Edwards Deming, the management theorist, 'In God we trust. All others must bring data'.

Required steps should include:

- Forecasting: Using financial methods as covered under our strategy chapters, measure the return on transformation overall, but also at an initiative and capability level, return on initiative, and return on capability.
- Stress testing such forecasts to flush out aggressive or misinformed assumptions, and remove factors such as Optimise Bias and the Gamblers Fallacy.
- Rigid, disciplined tracking of quantitative and qualitative measures that are inextricably linked to the desired outcomes but that also work in the context, for example, when launching a new proposition in a new market, measure customer feedback, adoption, and failure rates rather than margin or profit – often it's too early to tell in a launch phase that a product is actually profitable, and benchmarks do not exist, so it's practically impossible to give it a fair hearing.
- Think about vitality measures: Vitality is looking at the inherent capability in an organisation to create downstream value. For instance in a sales division, don't look at how many leads were generated for sales teams, that's a lag measure. Don't even look at how many customers were engaged to create leads, that's a lead measure. The corresponding vitality measure would be how many new proposition features were tried and launched in the period that results in opportunities to engage with and wow customers that would result in the lead and lag measures of engagement and leads. Go upstream to root cause, or perhaps we would be better calling it root reason.
- Calibrate: Particularly important in innovation or all new endeavours as digital tends to be, avoid the trap of setting and sticking with the first forecast as the hard perpetual target. It was built on assumptions, so take the approach to test and measure the assumptions thus fine tuning the targets and building up a calibrated position. Too many organisations 'anchor' good ideas with untested and unproven targets too early in their life cycle and they can lose their shine (and therefore focus and belief) before they got a decent chance to get tested.

With these closing thoughts in mind let's move on now to cover the final pillar and some summary reflections.

Refine and Reflect – The Right Methods

We have already implicitly covered many of the components of the fifth central reflect and refine pillar as we have worked through the other four enabling pillars of philosophy, models, prerequisites, and execution given its an integrated model. So let's summarise the key components and how it interlocks with the roadmapping approach I have shared.

Governance

Governance is at its simplest the act of putting in place all the key frameworks, functions, and processes that are necessary to make roadmap delivery successful. Governance should span the change life cycle and facilitate a structured way to deliver repeatable results, efficiently and in line with strategy. It is sometimes a little oblique and many but no single definition appears; that's because like strategy, the ambition, and context should drive the structure and application.

The Transformation Heartbeat holds the key to many of the practices of good governance, and that's the key interlink. But surrounding that we believe that there are a number of governance enabling structures that are required to empower complex roadmap delivery.

- Direction setting and strategic alignment – this is usually actioned by a Steering or Direction Group that reports to a senior business level such as the executive and has accountability ultimately to the board.
- Programme and change management – this is usually carried out by a programme board, with formalities including a chair, stakeholder representation, and a programme office that runs the processes behind good governance including coordination, planning, documentation, reporting, control, issue management, escalation, risk, and assurance (please note this is not an exhaustive list).
- Delivery – this is the project level of a programme, and where plans are developed and delivered, and coordinated with an overall programme of work.
- Governance style – the degree of communication, transparency, oversight, and control will be set by a number of factors including board expectations, as well as business culture, size, and complexity on top of external factors such as stakeholders and regulation. Understanding these factors facilitate governance design and it's an area we often find lacking in large change efforts.
- Alignment – it is also critical that change governance interlocks with a business's overall governance model, including oversight by the board, conformity with financial and budgetary requirements, adherence with risk and compliance requirements and interrogation by audit to name but a few of the key connection points. Failure to do this will cause friction and result in waste and risk.
- Evaluation and calibration – while the governance model, style, and alignment should wrap around the Transformation Heartbeat to provide a platform for execution, constant strategic evaluation of how change is being managed, how it is delivering on strategic objectives, and what learning and results should be taken into account to refine either strategy overall or roadmap focus is recommended.

This is often a missing component of change delivery and in line with the agile philosophies covered earlier and we believe such a cadence and supporting mechanisms should exist.

This can be carried out by including strategic review and alignment checkpoints in the formalities at each level of the governance model (at the formal project, programme, and oversight meetings), and taking review and alignment into reporting and escalation structures. Ultimately, the board or at least the executive level of a business should have the responsibility of driving and facilitating that strategic review and alignment, ensuring that design and delivery match purpose and strategy.

Measurement and Value Extraction

To facilitate the evaluation and calibration component set out above, a business needs to ensure that the measures of success are in place so that insight drives intelligence and trumps instinct. We have covered value measurement in the Delivery part, and the measurement of delivery itself should be catered for in Governance model, with strategic alignment also baked in.

Value, delivery, and strategic alignment measures should be the foundation for measuring and guiding overall roadmap success with one further addition – culture. Roadmaps and change initiatives of the nature outlined in this book define the forward focus, structure, and operations of a business (the transition to a digital business) and as we know, culture always trumps. Therefore, businesses should also monitor and guide the culture of roadmap delivery, using the nine dimensions of digital DNA to ensure that roadmaps extend to the totality of value.

Communication

It is fitting that we finish the five foundations for execution and indeed close this part of the book with Communication. This domain is without doubt one of the top factors that can make or break any endeavour be that in business, politics, or relationships. And across all those realms it becomes more and most important when the stakes are at their highest, and the circumstances are at their most complex. Investing and spending time and diligence on communication throughout the strategy, capability assessment, and particularly the cultural and roadmapping phases of digital business building will be one of the best made.

In a seminal 2018 report from McKinsey Institute, 'Unlocking Success in Digital Transformation',[105] communication was identified as a critical success factor, with success rates for transformation increasing up to three times when done well. Crucially, organisations succeed when leaders communicate a change story, that is, where employees clearly understand the direction the organisation is headed, why it's taking that direction, how it is changing, and how people and teams are being asked to support.

The study found that elements that most supported success were:
- Clearly communicated targets (with a sense of urgency)
- Clearly communicated key digital initiatives (with goals set for implementation)
- Goals set for utilising new technology
- New processes for how employees will collaborate with each other
- A clear explanation of how digital will impact the organisation, and how it enables the organisation to achieve business goals
- Clearly communicated approaches to new customer-centric needs

Additionally, using digital methods and channels to communicate these elements resulted in higher success rates (up to three times as much) over communication through traditional methods.

As indicated in the transformation heartbeat prerequisite the purpose, strategy, and intent need to be clearly communicated and in a way that elicits motivation, common understanding, and builds a willingness across all participants to want to take on the job at hand.

But as Aidan McCullen, author of the book *Undisruptable*,[106] often says, 'message sent does not equal message received'. What Aidan means by this is that it is wrong to assume that when we communicate once the job is done. Exemplary businesses consistently and compellingly remind themselves of what they're trying to achieve and why to ensure that both design and delivery are directed towards the proper intent and at the pace required.

The methods of communication, storytelling, and I would go on to say broader engagement is an art in itself. Communication tactics such as storytelling, multimedia delivery, facilitated discovery, prototyping, and simulation are all part of the communication toolbox. The communication stance or style is also important and supports some of our earlier points around reward and celebration. It is important to establish and enable a drum beat of information, evaluation, celebration, and learning in a manner that balances openness and transparency with objectivity and humble realism.

105 McKinsey, "Unlocking Success in Digital Transformations," (October 28, 2019), accessed April 7, 2023, https://www.mckinsey.com/capabilities/people-and-organizational-performance/our-insights/unlocking-success-in-digital-transformations.
106 Aidan McCullen, Undisruptable, accessed April 7, 2023, https://www.wiley.com/en-ie/Undisruptable:+A+Mindset+of+Permanent+Reinvention+for+Individuals,+Organisations+and+Life-p-9781119770480.

Communication and engagement is a two-way thing, and successful roadmaps and transformations should encompass listening, debate, consideration, and allow for the stakeholders of change to help direct the effort – much like we espoused in customer-centricity. I would also go on to say that it is a three-way thing – one of the greatest tools for businesses to unlock is visiting other regions and businesses that have already travelled the journey and learn from their effort. I have done this, and do today with clients and students – the knowledge, insight but importantly the belief and motivation that is unlocked through peer and exemplar visits is second to none, and should form part of any engagement and transformation planning.

B2B – A Different Story?

Before we conclude, I want to take a short reflection on whether designing strategy, building capability, or roadmapping for business-to-business (B2B) endeavours is any different from business-to-consumer (B2C), as it's a question I'm often asked and where there is sometimes much debate on. My default position is that we should not think fundamentally differently when looking at this context. Customers are end users, and end users are customers. Strategy is strategy. Building the 10 core capabilities we have outlined in this book is equally as important to B2B endeavours. And roadmapping and transformation delivery tends to be the same.

But there are nuanced differences, mainly around the stakeholder and the user landscape, which is generally more complex as are the buying and servicing cycle. Therefore the application of capability building and roadmapping need to cater for that more complex user landscape and the cyclical nature of B2B proposition and business models.

In Figure 60, I have laid out those nuances by looking through the lens of the 10 core capabilities, identifying those nuances and how they should be treated.

	What it means for B2C	What it means for B2B
Customer	Designing end-to-end journeys that remove friction, solve 'jobs to be done', build trust, and deliver differentiated delight	Apply to the E2E (through to end user) or B2B journeys encapsulating and solving for multiple users and cyclical relationships
Digital (Phygital)	Providing access to journeys through opti-channel flows, a great UX and the ability to get the job done in real time	Apply digital capability throughout the B2B value chain to increase speed, accuracy, automation, and access; jump to B2C or new business models
Analytics	Delivering personalised engagement, sales propensity, service and business efficiency, risk enhancement, and people augmentation	Apply to the E2E (through to end user) or B2B journeys to achieve the same multi-dimensional benefits across target users and business lines
Efficiency	Simplification, waste reduction, and continuous improvement applied as levers for increasing change capacity and cost reduction	Apply to the E2E (through to end user) or B2B journeys to achieve the same multi-dimensional benefits across target users and business lines
Innovation	Identifying, testing, and accelerating adjacent and transformative propositions and capabilities to build sustainable value	Apply to the E2E (through to end user) or B2B journeys to achieve the same multi-dimensional benefits across target users and business lines
Agile	Empowered teams driving iterative, mission–critical change leveraging insights, digital and collaborative work practises	Universally applicable
Open	Identifying and harnessing value chain partners to enhance and extend proposition, capability, and commercial value	Apply to the E2E (through to end user) or B2B journeys to achieve the same multi-dimensional benefits across target users and business lines
Technology	Building or refurbishing the technology stack, levering cloud, to power efficient and accelerated business capabilities	Universally applicable, but aligned to the context, journeys, and business model
People	Developing the mindset, skills, motivation, and focus to undertake transformation and deliver ambidextrous change	Universally applicable, but aligned to the context, journeys, and business model
Risk	Setting the risk appetite, tolerances, and framework to ensure risk/reward is balanced, calculated, and navigated	Universally applicable, adjusted for the context, journeys, and business model

Figure 60: B2C versus B2B nuances.

Summary – Part V

Where does that leave us? We started this book by covering what's driving digital, how that has manifested in business, and the necessity to respond. Then we learned why, and how to build strategy with digital as its centre, before moving on to the ten core capabilities required to be digital. Now we have uncovered how to establish a programme of change and roadmaps that facilitates the transition to execution and value extraction.

The following are the key reflection points we'll conclude on before moving on to our final part on how to prepare for what's coming next:

Delivery at scale and pace: Digital businesses deliver at scale, and at pace; that is the hallmark of success, it's how they get ahead and what makes them stand out. Delivery is not just projects, it's a roadmap of change spanning all facets of the business that takes a comprehensive and sophisticated approach to achieve – that is why we talk about transformation.

Multiple speeds: To deliver on strategy today, and digital ambition, businesses need to deliver an intertwined programme at multiple speeds and reconcile to handle scarcity while also balancing between value today and opportunity tomorrow.

Ambidexterity: To deliver this complexity at scale and to continually refine and recalibrate transformation roadmaps, businesses and particularly their leaders need to learn, live with, and embody ambidexterity.

Mindset: Applying the right philosophies around risk, reward, celebration, and renewal are important departure points for the transformation journey.

Approach: Establishing the right models for multispeed initiative and capability building roadmaps are important for managing complexity at scale.

Architecture: Drilling down to detail and joining the dots between vision, intent, and engineering helps to visualise and contextualise what needs to be down where, and the cause:effect dynamics.

Preparations: Putting in place the prerequisites of capabilities, such as a transformation heartbeat, and governance and communication foundations are success bedrocks.

Execution: Getting ahead on business change, bias, and blockers with behavioural and structural triage techniques can make or break progress.

https://doi.org/10.1515/9783111034713-029

Value: Extracting value needs to span commercial and cultural dimensions, and refers to creating new value, unlocking latent value, and defending value already beholden.

Calibration: Evaluating, refining, and replanning are perpetual activities to ensure that roadmaps continually stay on the efficient frontier of delivering against strategy, for stakeholders and the culture required to win.

Part VI: **Preparing for the Next Wave of Innovation**

If you don't think about the future, you cannot have one. – John Galsworthy

Chapter 19
Getting Ready to Look Forwards

I hope you have enjoyed working through this book and that it has equipped you with an overarching approach, insights, and tools to help you design and deliver a strategy, capabilities, and culture fit for the digital age to extract and sustain multi-stakeholder value.

But one thing that I presented in the opening was the notion of exponentialism, and that the pace of change is predicted to continue accelerating, so to truly sustain digital prowess it is incumbent to maintain a perpetual view on the future and plan accordingly.

Peter Diamandis, co-founder of Singularity University, Founder and Chairman of the XPRIZE Foundation, and a well-known tech-optimist, based his 2020 book *The Future Is Faster Than You Think* around the idea that we will experience more change in the coming decade than in the previous 100 years – a 10× acceleration.

Given what we have experienced in terms of technology-fuelled innovation, globalisation, and prosperity in the past 100 years, the unwavering proof of exponential development first predicted by Gordon Moore, and the endeavour of humans to make their world a better place (better being a subjective description) I urge you to look forwards on the basis that this will be the case.

This is not something new. Milton Friedman is quoted as saying:

> When the United States was formed in 1776, it took 19 people on the farm to produce enough food for 20 people. So most of the people had to spend their time and efforts on growing food. Today, it's down to 1% or 2% to produce that food. Now just consider the vast amount of supposed unemployment that was produced by that. But there wasn't really any unemployment produced. What happened was that people who had formerly been tied up working in agriculture were freed by technological developments and improvements to do something else. That enabled us to have a better standard of living and a more extensive range of products.

The difference between the latter 1700s and today is the speed of this change. What was once gradual is now rapid. Accepting this presents an uncomfortable truth. Earlier, I cited Steve Jobs, who said, 'You can't connect the dots looking forward, you can only connect them looking backwards'. That is the case, but we often miss the point that the space, or time intervals, between the dots are getting exponentially shorter.

Many, if not all of us, are often experiencing indescribable incredulity at the pace of life today. Need we look any further that how Generative AI and solutions such as ChatGPT have stirred the world into a frenzy of both fear and imagination, as the advances in LLM's have exploded and the potential of assisted intelligence now becoming very real. For many it does not feel like technology is making life easier, as life seems to have gotten harder. It is paradoxical, but in my view comes down to the

https://doi.org/10.1515/9783111034713-030

expectations from life and the freedom to pursue all that it has to offer is evolving just as fast as technology itself.

I am, however, an eternal optimist, and put store in probably Diamandis' favourite saying, 'The best way to predict the future is to create it yourself'.[107] I believe we can use tools and foresight to get a handle on what the future is likely to bring so that we can be ready for it, and indeed create it within our own realms. Harnessing insight and applying a mindset of optimistic construction of our future is the best remedy to the friction that I have described.

Therefore, we are going to look forwards now by presenting a framework to help you think about how that future could unfold in the context of your business, and how to harness anticipated change to build a better and, if possible, more controlled future.

Futurescoping

In order to build for the future, you have to develop of view of what it is going to look like, and then work out how to get there. An approach for doing this is called Backcasting, which is essentially a planning method that starts with defining a desirable future and then working backwards to identify the initiatives, policies, and programs of work that will connect that future to the present.

In Figure 61, I share my '3 Continuums of Change' model, which facilitates selecting an informed future point or points that one believes in and/or desires to be the case, then crafting the path to get there. It is a practice called Futurescoping.

Let's break down how to use the model into its three steps also called continuums given that they are perpetually evolving as individual contributors to a future state, but also shaping one another as we will bring to life.

Continuum 1 – The 6 Lenses of Life

Working towards the future always begins with trying to predict what it will look like. There are many methods for doing this, and which we use, including:

- **The Future Today Institute's 11 Macro Sources of Disruption**[108]: This is an expansive approach, and involves taking the prescribed 11 'sources' which include wealth, demographics, politics, environment, etc. and over a prescribed time horizon plotting which trends are likely to emerge, and to what degree they are hot or cold. Interestingly and appropriately, technology is not a discreet source, it applies

---

107 Peter Diamndis, https://www.diamandis.com.
108 The Future Today Institute, "The 11 Macro Sources of Disruption," accessed April 7, 2023, https://futuretodayinstitute.com/wp-content/uploads/2023/02/Wheel-1.pdf.

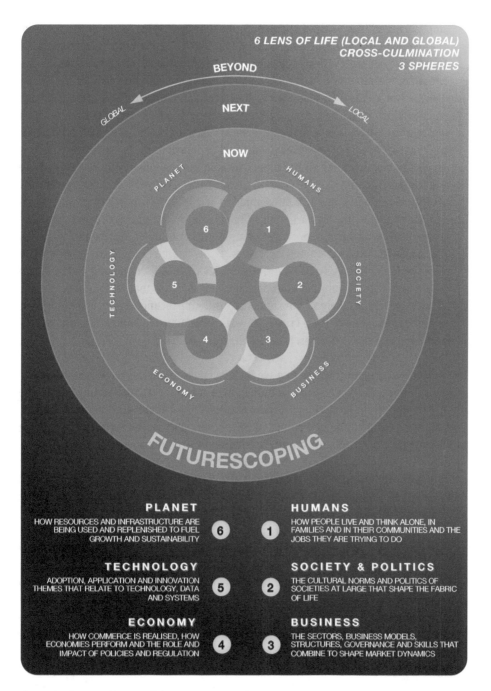

Figure 61: Three continuums of change – Futurescoping.

implicitly to all the Sources and overall the approach helps to break the potential future down into consumable and detectable vistas, and the hot v cold debates help to separate conjecture from evidence, or at least assumed certainty. I like this approach but feel it misses the human element, which we will come to later.

- **The Delphi Method**[109]: This is an engagement approach which involves picking a theme (which could be the future itself, or, say, one of the 11 Sources), building a series of questions about that theme such as what are the fact-based hot trends, and then surveying or interviewing a panel of contributors. From the responses, a consensus should emerge but it often takes multiple rounds of questioning (akin to the 5 why's approach) and therefore it can be an elongated process, specifically with broader topics, and it is susceptible to bias given it is qualitative and expert-led; for example, the Anchoring Bias can play out in that the first expert response or prediction can anchor conclusions around early presented viewpoints.

- **Future-Oriented Technology Analysis**[110]: This is a method of predicting the future world on the basis of how technology advances will define that future. Again it is a very helpful approach but perhaps 'one-sided' in that factors beyond technology are just as likely to inform the pathway for technology development itself (e.g. the impending climate crisis is diverting resources, IP, and effort into Greentech) and like the 11 sources, it misses the human factor.

In my Model, I present 6 lenses that we believe encapsulate the 11 sources as well as technology but extend it to include human-driven influences on the future as these are just as important. We will go further into what we believe are the pertinent current themes as of the time of writing (Q1 2023) under each of the six lenses, and bring to life how they are brought into the second and third continuums, but for the moment we suggest that defining what is likely to emerge across these six vistas is a good balance between being holistic, yet also being manageable for the next step which is cross-culmination. That said we encourage flexibility with this and all models we present, therefore feel free to dial up or down the lens you use, making sure that they are context-right for your size, region, and sector.

You will notice on the diagram that I have placed planet, technology, and economy to the left and indicating that they are global. This is to indicate that these three lens then prescribe a round of what I call are more likely to need a global viewpoint given the interconnected world we live in, e.g. what's happening across our planet in terms of climate will ripple across all regions, as is the case for technology advances and also economic cycles. The world is too connected to rest solely on local trends relating to these themes, but the local results of global forces are what we should aim to capture.

---

109 RAND, "Delphi Method," accessed April 7, 2023, https://www.rand.org/topics/delphi-method.html.
110 Springer, "Future-Oriented Technology Analysis: A Classification Framework," V. M. Urbano et al. (May 30, 2021), accessed April 7, 2023, https://link.springer.com/chapter/10.1007/978-3-030-69380-0_2.

And that's not to say that trends in how humans behave, how societies and politics develop as well as how businesses evolve will not also be globally pervasive; no doubt they will, but we have placed them on the right-hand side under a local heading to indicate that they are more likely to have a local twist, influenced by historic, cultural, and even geophysical factors. For instance, all-in consumer platforms such as WeChat have flourished much more quickly in Asia compared to the West, and we could perhaps construe that crime, conflict, and poverty are much more dominant themes in under-developed economies.

Continuum 2 – Cross-Culmination

Once we have identified the trends and start to crystallise what is likely to emerge under each of the six lenses, I then prescribe a round of what I call 'cross-culmination'. Put more simply, this is the process of joining the dots, both in each lens but very importantly across them to see what factors have a cause:effect relationship. This step helps to make the leap from trends to forecasting, and as with The Waltzer effect and the spin-out syndrome, it is very seldom one single strain of change has significant impact – it is much more likely that the culmination of multiple developments will bring about new world order dynamics. For instance, 20 years ago could we have predicted that 10 years forwards we would see global co-working spaces such as WeWork?[111] Perhaps if we had predicted:

– citizens would adopt a sharing economy mindset (human lens),
– spurred by the need for scarcity management (planet lens),
– that entrepreneurialism would flourish from newfound confidence as a result of prosperity (economy lens) and education (society and politics lens),
– fuelled by Industry 4.0 technologies spanning the IMPACT pillars (technology lens), and
– big business would look to harness the gig economy for new, and flexible talent solutions as the pace for innovation fastened and the need for efficient resourcing became more necessary (business lens).

It would be hard to predict such a development as co-working space when thinking about the future as a whole, but when thinking of it through multiple funnels such as the six lenses, and then cross-referencing them, it is possible to have more clarity.

This is an optional step, as you may not have the capacity or necessity for it indeed the time, but it is a step we do encourage as it helps to reconcile and create a big picture view informed from a more bottom-up approach.

---

111 We Work, accessed April 7, 2023, https://www.wework.com/.

The conclusion of cross-culmination should be picking a number of forecasts that you believe are going to be true, or which you believe you wish to make true, and then staking the associated future-point positions you wish to take and will plan back from. There are two approaches here – sometimes you will take a future-point position because you believe what will be become true is out of your control or influence and therefore you will work towards that as an assumption, either creating an opportunistic plan, or a defence plan. The forecast that says lifespans will increase as they get healthier is largely determinable by no single person or organisation – it is a long-term mega trend fuelled by prosperity, technology, self-care, governments, and businesses who serve the desire of humans to do so (all factors identifiable using the six lenses starting point themes). A life insurance company, for instance, will accordingly evolve their products, risk-parameters, and pricing to reflect future life expectancy.

On the other hand, there are future-point positions that we might wish to create as a result of forecasts, such as the WeWork example just used. In this case the backwards planning that you will endeavour to take is not an assumptive one, but an aspirational one (albeit it is based on assumptions that are in fact the inherent risks). Assumption versus aspiration is the nuance.

Continuum 3 – Three Spheres: Now, Next, and Beyond

Regardless of whether you are taking an assumptive or aspirational approach, the backwards planning in Step 3 is applicable. This simply is the method of asking 'what needs to be true to (insert your future-point position)' and doing that repeatedly but backwards until you get a step that is possible to take from the present-day forwards. This approach is in perfect symmetry with the Transcendence Mapping we shared in Part V, only backwards.

Again, in our WeWork example, the team who may have developed the position that 'there will be a global need to provide flexible co-working space for the growing gig and start-up economy' from their forecasting might have said and responded as follows:
- 'What needs to be true to deliver flexible co-working space for the growing gig and start-up economy' – well-located, and well-appointed office space that is modular and can accommodate single and multi-party person short-term office lettings.
- 'What needs to be true to provide this' – leased vibrant, downtown office spaces with expansive transport infrastructure, and designed practically and aesthetically to support migrant teams and workers.
- 'What needs to be true to find and design appealing office space' – engage real estate agents to identify the areas and buildings that suit this brief, and develop a workspace design blueprint that is repeatable and lean to fit out and migrate.

You'll get the point at this stage, and the step back planning will continue until you come back to and identify the first step, which in this case might be identifying the key countries and cities where demand will be strongest coupled with testing and building the business model and investment case (and of course finding capital).

Once this backwards planning has been concluded, it can then be reversed and projected forwards in the form of a plan and parsed up into waves under the headings of now, next, and beyond with decision points, dependency planning, and so on. In multispeed or complex situations, as mentioned, transcendence maps can be formulated to identify those dependencies and perhaps even more layered waves of development – you don't have to stick with the three prescribed.

Chapter 20
Themes and Trends That Will Shape the Next Waves of Innovation

We hope that this gives you an understandable approach to comprehensive backcasting, and future-point planning. It might sound simple, and it is designed to be as when the process starts the variables will undoubtably introduce as much complexity as you can handle. Facilitation is a helpful support for these kinds of exercises to make sure that you neither get stuck in the weeds nor drift into the obtuse. Picking facilitators with a perspective of what future trends are appropriate, and managing energy are important determinants and helpful supports.

The other 'facilitator' for success is pre-work research to help seed the six lenses with likely and pertinent trends that are appropriate to ones' context and circumstances. While we can't cover all the bases, I have shared with you below a sample of the kind of trend themes we bring into and/or expect to find in the Futurescoping work that we do and again, there are as of the time of writing and subject to renewal, refinement, and of course resignation as the fads emerge and fade.

Humans: *How people live and think alone, in families and in their communities and the jobs they are trying to do*

– Demographics: We are definitely living longer due to a general rise in prosperity, health care, and awareness, but within that longevity we are, I suggest, younger longer (leaving home later), working longer (as a direct consequence of living longer, but also due to an eroding hard stop in retirement) and older younger as life expectancy outstrips general retirement age.

– Divides: The gaps between the 'haves' and the 'have nots' could be seen to be widening, and not just in terms of money and assets, but in terms of opportunities and skills, access to services through the digitalisation of everything and geopolitical drift.

– Meaning: As we become better educated, and have more means, for example, affluence and social influence, we are questioning the meaning of modern life and its trapping (a word we use on purpose given its double-edged connotations) and seeking to connect with a broader reason for being in a Maslowesque sort of way.

– Liberation: Linked to meaning and underpinned by the rise of entrepreneurialism and movements like the Gig Economy, I observe a glide to self-determined life and particularly professional pursuits but this also extends into a demand for individualism and equity.

– Transparency: Access to democratised knowledge, but also the unfortunate emergence of fake news, has left many people seeking out if not demanding transparency,

https://doi.org/10.1515/9783111034713-031

which even stretches into a duality of privacy where people are paying more attention to the permissions that they give, but when satisfied are happy to give it in the return for knowledge and inspiration.

– Fatigue: Digital has equipped us to do, know, and learn so much that it could for some become debilitating, with choice so crippling to the extent that retreating from the 'always on' life would become a pursuit. This is definitely the case for professional life, as much as it is for our children, as companies and parents are throttling back access to screens, platforms, and content in order to limit stress and burnout.

Society and politics: *The cultural norms and politics of societies at large that shape the fabric of life*

– Citification: We are becoming urban dwellers and as we leave the land, as there is less of it, and as infrastructure, work, and social endeavour and outlet draws us there. Equally virtual work and connectivity means that we may need to travel less and therefore can be happier in urban centres.

– Enlightenment: The internet has democratised all knowledge, but also discourse, opinion, and debate so we are becoming more intelligent through awareness and multi-sided perspectives. Generative AI and assisted intelligence services emerging will further accelerate this dynamic, but equally could quell creativity as we 'outsource' to the machines.

– Activism: As we become more enlightened, because of the themes under humans (liberations, transparency, etc.), and because we have platforms for speaking up we are seeing a rise in activism which means taking a strong position on social and business themes to then create a conversation to influence an outcome that benefits that position.

– Swing left and right: As we become more active, as the divides mentioned above are growing, and we become more dissatisfied with the Institutions around us (whether that be political parties, health systems, etc.), we may be seeing movement away from the middle in some territories to the extremes of the political spectrum – left and right.

– Care: While this includes health and pandemics which are now squarely back on our radars, as we become more conscious of the broader contributors of well-being which include financial, physical, mental, social, professional, personal identity, intellectual, and environmental drivers, we are becoming more emphatic, open and active in acknowledging and facilitating care for betterment across all dimensions.

– Universal benefits: As work gets automated, as policy makers respect the right to equality, choice and social wellness, there is a growing conversation towards Universal Basic Income (UBI), the 4-day week and the Durham Proposal (UBI for select populations, e.g. ex-felons) which was partly in place through the coronavirus pandemic, despite some economists' concerns of inflated inflation!

– Human:machine: The broader discussion of how AI will change the nature of life, work, and decision-making is perhaps one of the most important of our time, as it the role of resulting ethics in corporate, political, and social circles. This also includes smart and autonomous living, transport, and infrastructure.

– Climate consciousness: By no means the last on this heading and I believe personally the most poignant, as fears of our planets negative response to industrialisation will bite us in the backside and accelerated impacts prevail, we will search and become demanding that our businesses, our systems, and our societies act to halt and even (hopefully, if it's not too late) reverse the glide path that we are on.

Business: *The sectors, business models, structures, governance, and skills that combine to shape market dynamics*

– Decentralisation: Most notable in the world of money and currencies (and let's not limit this to Bitcoin), there is a trend towards the unshackling of our commerce, information, and identities and the way we go about getting things done from control by central so-called authorities to decentralised crowd-driven mechanisms. Distrust and desires for self-actualisation are fuelling this shift.

– Innovation and renewal: As exponentialism manifests, and innovation cycles shorten and paradigm shifts deepen, the necessity for perpetual innovation to enable business longevity will emerge – we are already seeing innovation moving to the centre of strategy as leaders recognise the renewal and differentiation are key yet harder to achieve in the world liberated by IMPACT.

– Flexible work: In the pursuit of freedom, self-direction, and stimulation we are seeing a rise in the freelance and contract workers (Gig Economy) as well as choice being provided by businesses on flexible patterns, pay, and pursuits. We also expect to see a tilting of how organisations resource from permanent (on-balance sheet) to migrant (off-balance-sheet).

– Pursuing meaning and responsibility: Workers are shifting to believe that they are not winning employment, but selling services and as they do so they are taking the reins on reversing the forces and interviewing employers for pay and conditions as table-stakes, but more and more on culture and purpose as they pursue meaning, growth, and impact, and as the necessity for climate action grows, how responsible businesses are.

– Web 3.0: While ill-defined, immature, and actually no one thing (rather an amalgamation of decentralisation, virtual identities, extreme personalisation (I am my segment) and XR (extended reality which covers virtual, augmented, or mixed reality experiences), no one can deny that the likelihood of a new internet to play, consume, learn and engage in is a reality in the making.

– New sectors: New sectors and business models will arrive in anger as technology and big problems seek innovation and the next generation of entrepreneurs seek to make an impact and live to their purposes. Expect to see Green, Space, Nano, Wellness, and others move to mainstream.

– Life-long learning: To support these new sectors, and Industry 4.0 and 5.0 in general, there is expected to be a shift in both how work gets done, and the type of work itself. This will require constant retraining, and the development of new skills – furthermore as people seek out changes of careers and perspectives on a grander scale, life-long learning will be alive and well.

Economy: *How commerce is realised, how economies perform and the role and impact of policies and regulation*

– Scarcity and supply: Supply and demand have always been driving forces of commerce and economics, and as the world gets richer, more inhabited, and more demanding we could expect to see and feel scarcity and supply becoming a power tool of control and prosperity.

– Geo-protectionism: As the world gets hungrier and the battlegrounds move with climate, political, and demographic forces we could see a significant shift in the economic powers, similar to that which have emerged in Asia but expect Africa and South America to feature.

– Green rebalance: Responding to the climate challenge will need a collective response across individuals voting for conscious brands and products, businesses shifting to a circular economy and authorities putting in place the infrastructure, policy, and tax. This degree of disruption will likely require significant change, capital, and consequences in the short to medium term.

– Digital and decentralised: As economies move to become digitally powered and potentially decentralised or at least platformised, power-shifts are to be expected that could change the course of trade, capital, and decisioning.

– Re-innovation and rejuvenation: The circular and sharing economies are likely to gain more attention and capital as consumers and suppliers realise the necessity and opportunity to recycle. This potentially could have a double-innovation effect in that businesses will need to innovate the old, while innovating for the new and presents an interesting business and economic condition.

– Stretching the S-curves: As re-innovation and rejuvenation bite, we may see the necessity to balance effort towards reinvention of sustainable reconfiguration as opposed to breaking new grounds. Or economies could be restructured in this way – the old and the new innovating in parallel.

– Wealth redistribution: Despite a decline in population growth in mature economies, they are likely to remain stable, but emerging economies will catch up fast, and although the collective boat will rise, emerging economies will have a greater slice of the pie. As we live and work longer, the need to disperse wealth over a longer time frame will become prevalent, and will necessitate new methods of financial and intergenerational planning.

– Regulation: Without doubt, regulators and policy makers will be busy catering for all the shifts we forecast, and perhaps there will be a necessity to rethink the fundamentals of regulation itself following the shift from rules to decentralised, with technology as the potential enabler.

– Nudging: One area of commerce that is likely to receive increasingly regular attention is nudging, or the application of the relatively new field of behavioural economics to shape micro- and macro-decisioning and outcomes. As we understand the architecture of behaviour more and more, it is easy to see how intervention will increasingly be used for good but unfortunately also less good outcomes.

Technology: *Adoption, application, and innovation themes that relate to technology, data and systems*

– AI: The dawn of AI (after multiple winters and springs) is surely upon us as the digitalisation of everything creates the data that ever-accelerating computational machines can turn into automated insights, task-completion and decisioning to do many of the jobs we do today with human effort (e.g. driving), or jobs we didn't realise we could do, for example, solving major diseases.

– Quantum: As the demand for storage, speed, and sophistication multiplies, we can expect to see computational processing seek and break new ground in terms of size and structure, elongating Moore's law, and laying the foundations for continued if not accelerating software and device innovation.

– Connected (internet of) things: As hardware engineering is pushed to its boundaries for quantum, it will derive a spectrum of nanosensors and edge-computing in parallel that will allow for the vision of a connected everything to flourish.

– XR: Already mentioned, the potential to power Extended Reality experiences at work, home and in social settings will see a new dawn of ambient devices that will interact with us in new and tightly coupled ways. Think of it as the internet of senses.

– No-code: Software design and cloud enablement will develop to the point where code will become invisible, and tools will empower creators and operators to put digital and intelligent (AI) solutions to work – also known as the move to citizen development.

– Micromechanics: The race to not just build sensors and edge devices but nano-robots and micromachines that will go to places to date unattainable, e.g. inside our bodies, or that of any living organism is a pursuit underway, particularly in the medical field as the opportunity for automated and even autonomous microsurgery beckons.

– Bioengineering: The ultimate machine you could say is the living body and with the amalgamation of quantum, AI, and the medical sciences, the pursuit of understanding it to re-engineer it has already begun with gene and genome sequencing/editing and sNRA advancements that brought us coronavirus vaccines.

– Greentech: The application of all technologies to undo climate damage, enable current and new technologies to operate carbon-neutral/positive and therefore foster a technology-enabled sustainable future in commerce, society, consumerism, etc. should be anticipated.

Planet: *How resources and infrastructure are being used and replenished to fuel growth and sustainability*

– Energy: How energy (including fuel and food) is grown, sourced, converted, distributed, and stored is already going through fundamental change, and we could expect to see capital redirected to renewability as the climate bites and consciousness kicks in (which could cause scarcity in other areas) as well as friction in the transition given we know change is hard, and expensive at the receiving end.

– Travel: AI, IoT, mega-computing, and engineering are already colliding to bring us autonomous ground transport and get us traveling more in the air above which will necessitate a rethink of infrastructure, policy and law, and the patterns of life as things and places become more accessible faster.

– Resources: The mining and extraction of the beyond fuel 'lubricants' of life and economy such as metals, wood, and stone are also likely to experience upheaval as scarcity and sustainable methods enabled by automation and autonomous processes seek efficiency, but in parallel synthetic substitute innovation is probably one of the largest emerging innovation themes.

– Space: The final frontier could be the next one as we seek out new sources of resources, particularly minerals, but also tourism and perhaps even the start of either the next new frontiers for habitation because we enjoy the adventure, or we need to get out of/off our own.

– Meridianisation: If earth's temperatures continue to climb, we could see extreme heat and water rise force mass migration north and south towards more temperate and sheltered median-circling locations.

– Climate illness: The impacts of heat and the sun and the consumption of synthetic resources could bring new waves of illness that need mass treatment.

– Regenerative living: New, secular ways of living could start to emerge to support self-sustainable communities (eco-colonies) that also are a protected environment to retain resources, relics, and ways of life that are being disrupted yet sacred to their inhabitants.

The thoughts above are shared as a scholar of life and active observations from watching the world around me – they aren't to be confused with any great oracle-like claims, but merely the invisible movements and shifts I observe in the world. They are neither conclusive nor deeply researched, but they are intended to stimulate for the pursuit of your Futurescoping activities, and your own debates and exploration.

The specifics are not the reason to share them, rather I hope that they provide you with examples of the kinds of considerations to take into your own exercises, and are there for discovery, elimination, and adjustment or perhaps just to get the conversations started.

They are though some of the big themes I will be watching over the period ahead and will continue to appraise and ameliorate. Here we haven't drawn out the 'so what's, and that's because that's the job for you to do in your Futurescoping.

Microtrends

While Megatrends are significant overarching trends that change societies and industries, Microtrends are the patterns you notice in the detail. They are small shifts but have the potential to cause significant change. An example of a Macrotrend would be the potential for rapidly spreading global pandemics (which we have unfortunately had to endure) and associated microtrends would be the secular adoption of vaccines due to faith or anti-authority sentiment, and declining utilisation of vaccines due to the (potential) bias of Naïve Realism – where we have a tendency to believe our perception of the world exactly as it is, e.g. for those that got vaccinated and suffered Covid, while not so pleasant, it wasn't so bad and therefore it won't be so bad again.

As intimated, we can look for microtrends in research, in daily headlines and by following thought leaders. Another good example from early 2023 was the dominance of ChatGPT from the OpenAI organisation in the media circles of the world, and how through its easy access, user-friendly interface and surprisingly intelligent responses and solutions, it captured the imagination of so many. A sub-theme or microtrend of AI as the macrotrend, this also helps us to say that microtrends are in the now, and also more evidential in their availability and access (e.g. you can see and use them) whereas macrotrends are beyond our reach, in the future and yet to be defined and tangible.

The punchline – both should feature in your Futurescoping.

Joining the Dots

As promised, I return to connecting the dots and looking across the six lenses to illustrate how cross-contemplation may lead to future-point positions that are the result of cross-culmination. Let's take an example to help, borrowing from the suggested starting points above, and I have picked an easy one that perhaps is already playing out to help make it accessible.

We are witnessing an historic rise and acceleration of global temperatures, the culmination of increased consumption from a larger population and prosperity. We are have also experienced major industrial revolutions spurred by an open free market economy. As these are all set to continue increasing, we are likely to see a sharp increase in sustainable business and citizen response to halt decline and turn the ship around. They will be the driver of a political response that is currently lacking.

Our conscious enlightenment and purpose-seeking as citizens is likely to collide with the witnessing of accelerated climate impacts like floods, fires, heatwaves (due to a Waltzer effect gain in momentum), creating demand for solutions from sustainability innovators and force infringers (carbon and climate negative businesses) to U-turn rapidly as consumers vote with their feet, and as scarcity is impending.

This will create the political platform for leaders who are playing to near-term populism today, which is increasingly forceful in a more activist world, and put the emphasis on longer-term sustainability above immediate, damaging consumption.

Digital transformation has the potential to help us achieve a more sustainable world. Already, for example, digitally smart cities can reduce energy consumption, enabled by the IoT. Imagine the possibilities as we adopt Industry 4.0 solutions to create ecosystems that look far beyond corporate gain, to solve some of the world's most pressing problems and challenges, which in fact is what Industry 5.0 is defined as. The emphasis will be on a more cohesive world, we hope without boundaries, where we look to share and exchange ideas.

Autonomous vehicles have already proven to be successful, showing possibility for safer freight. As more people turn to a plant-based diet, innovation that we would have not thought possible shows promise for the future, potentially disrupting traditional farming methods and, by extension, saving finite resources. Sustainability is one of the most pressing topics that affect each and every one of us, and digitally savvy companies who embrace the challenge will end up disrupting and leading.

Conclusion

Rounding It All Up

I hope that the Futurescoping method, the starting point themes for the six lens shared, and the examples of backcasting and cross-culmination are helpful. As I said, it is over to you from here to make this your own, but before we close it's important to join one final dot, and that is back to our 6D strategy approach.

The Futurescoping model presented in this part is a very helpful method for informing the Detect component of the 6D model presented in our Strategy discussions where we suggest looking far out to identify impending or possible trends that could shape the future market and one's place in it.

Please remember the importance of this step, which is increasingly more critical in the accelerating world we are living in, and the resulting brave actions which define winners and losers – to that end we leave you with the words of Harriet Beecher Stowe, the American author and Abolitionist of the 1800s, to encourage that you take or make positions, and act like there is no tomorrow: 'The past, the present and the future are really one: they are today'.

Longevity, Resilience, and Stewardship

My closing words are on the three final themes of longevity, resilience, and stewardship, which are interconnected and cross-pollinating.

For a business to evolve in the face of the enormity and exponentiality of forecast change cycles we have opened up, and to sustain that evolution to enjoy continued benefits and value creation, we need to have a plan for longevity. To maintain longevity, in the face of the pace of change that is demanded of us will require resilience and fortitude. Resilience forges longevity, and longevity begets resilience. And to ensure what we design and create is sustainable in all facets, we need to act as the stewards of business, value, and knowledge.

Creating Space and Time for Longevity

Corporate longevity remains in long-term decline, according to Innosight's biennial corporate longevity reports. Their latest analysis shows the 30- to 35-year average tenure of S&P 500 companies in the late 1970s is forecast to shrink to 15–20 years this decade as we mentioned already. Innosight comment that creative destruction is at play with digital facilitating new players and platforms to achieve immense scale in short periods through network effects, and pushing out old players who are unable to

https://doi.org/10.1515/9783111034713-032

respond as they are anchored to old ways. This supports my view that we need to transition to becoming a digital business, and the brave pace at which I urge you to do so.

As I think about such demise and equally promise, I am struck by the Japanese concept of ikigai, which is strongly linked with the nation's renown for longevity (they have the highest number of centenarians). Ikigai is a code that guides Japanese culture to harness and blend everything that makes life special, enjoyable, and productive. While it is a complex topic, and needs its own book, I have extracted six strains below that I believe are useful to reflect on to facilitate longevity.

Exercise the Mind: The importance of regular, positive mental stimulation to keep the mind fresh and cognitive juices flowing can be tracked back to the suggestion to maintain learning and testing of thought and strategy.

Imperfection (Wabi Sabi): Wabi Sabi encourages not just acceptance but celebration of imperfection in the physical world, and this can be translated into an acceptance that there is beauty in failure through learning and evolution in any world, including the digital one.

Community (Moai): Japanese centenarians are known for habitually gathering in groups with lifelong friends who provide each other emotional and financial support, grow together, and hold each other accountable – this bond should be replicated in business.

Time, space, flow: As well as exercising the mind, the Japanese are known for rising early to get ahead of the day and declutter their minds to allow ikigai to flow. Teams, leaders, and practitioners would do well to carve out time in a hectic world.

Morita therapy: When life does get the better, the code dictates complete extraction from the source of stress and a period of isolation to allow for sustainable recovery – detox and extractive responses are sometimes necessary when flow gets just too fast.

Lean diet (nuci gusui): The Japanese diet is known to include variety (all the colours of the rainbow), but the underpin is balance and ingesting antioxidants – digital businesses should ensure variety and a good dollop of reality and challenge.

Resilience

As I said, resilience forges longevity, and longevity begets resilience. Here I am not referring to organisational or operation resilience, but personal resilience, the ability to withstand challenges with your face to the wind. Now more so than ever where we are faced with complexity and overwhelmingness.

As I have been prone to do, and now no more so than ever, I want to use a quote from Niccolò Machiavelli and his sixteenth-century political prose on the necessity for resilience in innovation and transformational change to illustrate the recall and mindset required:

> There is nothing more difficult to take in hand, more perilous to conduct, or more uncertain in its success, than to take the lead in the introduction of a new order of things. For the innovator has enemies in all those who profit by the old order, and only lukewarm defenders in all those who would profit by the new order, this lukewarmness arising partly from fear of their adversaries . . . and partly from the incredulity of mankind, who do not truly believe in anything new until they have had actual experience of it.

Four centuries later this could hardly be truer, and is a stoic reminder that change and adoption is a human endeavour, not a technological feat. Resilience requires us to observe and strive for personal wellness, to expect setbacks and treat them as temporary, to maintain adaptability as a consequence, and to build a coalition of the willing that will act as a sounding board and work together to maintain focus on a purpose-driven pursuit.

Stewardship

It is incumbent on us as leaders to be good stewards: stewards of our organisation (the structure and mechanics of it, after all the purpose of good business practice is to drive profitability and growth), our employees, partners, and stakeholders, and our planet as one of those major stakeholders. Good stewardship of our organisation must, by extension, include digital transformation.

I explained extensively at the outset of this book that the pace of technological change and innovation will not wait for laggards. Harnessing digital and undergoing transformation is not just good for business, it is the *only* way to do business, and crucially, the only way to leave a lasting legacy of value for our future generations.

We have been, and will undoubtedly continue to be, inspired by our pioneers – Babbage, Lovelace, Turing, Boolean, Hollerith, Packard Bell, IBM, Google, Amazon, Rynnair, IKEA, Tesla – and of course, they are just a handful, I could continue. They have left a legacy, one that we can look back on and learn valuable lessons from. What will be your legacy? What inspiration lessons would you want future generations to look back on and learn from? The future is rapidly hurtling towards us. Yes, it is scary, complex, and incredibly challenging, but much like the Waltzer Ride I referred to, it is also exciting and exhilarating.

My hope is that you will embark on this exhilarating digital transformation journey with me, and the time to act is now.

> Transformation can only take place immediately; the revolution is now, not tomorrow – Jiddu Krishnamurti, *The First and Last Freedom.*

Bibliography

Fortune 500. 2022. "Amazon." Accessed April 7, 2023. https://fortune.com/company/amazon-com/fortune500/.

Fortune 500. 2022. "Alphabet." Accessed April 7, 2023. https://fortune.com/company/alphabet/fortune500/.

Fortune 500. 2022. "Facebook." Accessed April 7, 2023. https://fortune.com/company/facebook/fortune500/.

Salesforce. "Salesforce Launches Global Digital Skills Index: In-Depth Insights from 23,000 Workers." (January 27, 2022). Accessed April 7, 2023. https://investor.salesforce.com/press-releases/press-release-details/2022/New-Digital-Skills-Index-from-Salesforce-Reveals-76-of-Global-Workers-Say-They-Are-Unequipped-for-the-Future-of-Work/.

Fabric. "Warby Parker's Retail Playbook to Reach 900+ Stores", Patrick Young. (March 8, 2022). Accessed April 7, 2023. https://fabric.inc/blog/warby-parker-retail/.

Forbes. "15 min Mortgages? Meet Molo – The New Fintech Aiming to Shake Up the Market." Tiffany Young. (February 5, 2019). Accessed April 7, 2023. https://www.forbes.com/sites/tiffanyyoung1/2019/02/05/15-minute-mortgages-meet-molo-the-new-fintech-aiming-to-shake-up-the-market/.

TechCrunch. "Fueling the Future of Sports: How the NFL Is Using Data to Change the Game on the Field, in the Stands, and in Your Home." Accessed April 7, 2023. https://techcrunch.com/sponsor/aws/fueling-the-future-of-sports-how-the-nfl-is-using-data-to-change-the-game-on-the-field-in-the-stands-and-in-your-home.

JP Morgan. "Opportunities in the Metaverse – How Businesses Can Explore the Metaverse and Navigate the Hype vs. Reality." Accessed April 7, 2023. https://www.jpmorgan.com/content/dam/jpm/treasury-services/documents/opportunities-in-the-metaverse.pdf.

Accenture. "Fjord Trends 2022." The new fabric of life. Accessed April 7, 2023. https://www.accenture.com/content/dam/accenture/final/a-com-migration/r3-3/pdf/pdf-169/accenture-fjord-trends-2022-full-report.pdf.

Forbes. "Replacing Legacy Core Banking Systems – SAP Has Limited Success." Tom Goroenfedlt. (December 18, 2012). Accessed April 7, 2023. https://www.forbes.com/sites/tomgroenfeldt/2012/12/18/replacing-legacy-core-banking-systems-sap-has-limited-success.

The Co-operative Bank. "The Kelly Review, an Independent Review of the Co-Operative Bank." Accessed April 7, 2023. https://www.co-operative.coop/investors/kelly-review.

Raconteur. "How Five Brands Learned from Digital Transformation Failure." Finbarr Toesland. (September 26, 2018). Accessed April 7, 2023. https://www.raconteur.net/digital/digital-transformation-failure/.

Christensen, Clayton M., Hall, Taddy, Dillon, Karen, Duncan, David S. "Know Your Customers." Jobs to Be Done (Harvard Business Review September 2016). Accessed April 7, 2023. https://hbr.org/2016/09/know-your-customers-jobs-to-be-done.

Allen, Robert C. The British Industrial Revolution in Global Perspective. Cambridge University Press, 2009.

Computer History Museum. "The Babbage Machine." Accessed April 7, 2023. https://www.computerhistory.org/babbage/.

The National Museum of Computer. "The Turing-Welchmen Bombe." Accessed April 7, 2023. https://www.tnmoc.org/bombe.

The Alan Turing Institute. "Artificial Intelligence." Accessed April 7, 2023. https://www.turing.ac.uk/.

Britannica. "Gordon Moore." Accessed April 7, 2023. https://www.britannica.com/biography/Gordon-Moore.

Intel. "The Store of the Intel 4004 – Intel's First Microprocessor." Accessed April 7, 2023. https://www.intel.com/content/www/us/en/history/museum-story-of-intel-4004.html.

https://doi.org/10.1515/9783111034713-033

Apple. "Apple Unveils M1 Ultra, the World's Most Powerful Chip for a Personal Computer." Apple Press Release. (March 8, 2022). Accessed April 7, 2023. https://www.apple.com/newsroom/2022/03/apple-unveils-m1-ultra-the-worlds-most-powerful-chip-for-a-personal-computer/.

Exploding Topics. "How Many People Own Smartphone." Josh Howarth. (January 26, 2023). Accessed April 7, 2023. https://explodingtopics.com/blog/smartphone-stats.

Statista. "Number of Internet and Social Media Users Worldwide as of July 2022." Accessed April 7, 2023. https://www.statista.com/statistics/617136/digital-population-worldwide/.

Techjury. "How Many IoT Devices Are There in 2023?" Accessed April 7, 2023. https://techjury.net/blog/how-many-iot-devices-are-there/.

Backlinko. "Social Network Usage & Growth Statistics: How Many People Use Social Media in 2022?" Brian Dean. (October 10, 2021). Accessed April 7, 2023. https://backlinko.com/social-media-users.

Seed Scientific. "How Much Data Is Created Every Day? + 27 Staggering Stats." Branka Vuleta. (October 28, 2021). Accessed April 7, 2023. https://seedscientific.com/how-much-data-is-created-every-day/.

Pointless Large Number Stuff. "One Quintillion." Accessed April 7, 2023. https://sites.google.com/site/pointlesslargenumberstuff/.

TechCrunch. "TuSimple Completes Its First Driverless Autonomous Truck Run on Public Roads." Rebecca Bellan. (December 29, 2021). Accessed April 7, 2023. https://techcrunch.com/2021/12/29/tusimple-completes-its-first-driverless-autonomous-truck-run-on-public-roads/.

Forbes. "Apple's Stunning $10 Blow to Facebook." Kate O' Flaherty. (November 6, 2021). Accessed April 7, 2023. https://www.forbes.com/sites/kateoflahertyuk/2021/11/06/apples-new-iphone-privacy-features-cost-facebook-10-billion/.

Apple Insider. "Apple Debuts New High-Security Lockdown Mode, $10 M Cybersecurity Grant." Mike Peterson. (July 6, 2022). Accessed April 7, 2023. https://appleinsider.com/articles/22/07/06/apple-debuts-new-high-security-lockdown-mode-10m-cybersecurity-grant.

Forbes. "Apple Offers $2 M to Hackers Who Can Break Its New Lockdown Mode." John Koetsier. (July 7, 2022). Accessed April 7, 2023. https://www.forbes.com/sites/johnkoetsier/2022/07/07/apple-offers-2m-to-hackers-who-can-break-its-new-lockdown-mode/.

HubSpot. "What Is Omni-Channel? 20 Top Omni-Channel Experience Examples." Clint Fontanella. (December 13, 2022). Accessed April 7, 2023. https://blog.hubspot.com/service/omni-channel-experience.

Hexnode. "Android Seamless Updates: Everything You Need to Know." Lizzie Warren. (November 9, 2022). Accessed April 7, 2023. https://www.hexnode.com/blogs/android-seamless-update-everything-you-need-to-know/.

LinkedIn. "No Need to Wait: 5 Examples of Instant Gratification." Blake Morgan. (November 18, 2021). Accessed April 7, 2023. https://www.linkedin.com/pulse/need-wait-5-examples-instant-gratification-blake-morgan.

Hubspot.com. "The Creator Economy Market Size Is Growing: How Brands Can Leverage It." Erica Santiago. (January 21, 2023). Accessed April 7, 2023. https://blog.hubspot.com/marketing/creator-economy-market-size.

The Harvard Business Review. "The Project Economy Has Arrived – Use these skills and tools to make the most of it." Antonio Nieto-Rodriguez. (December 2021). Accessed April 7, 2023. https://hbr.org/2021/11/the-project-economy-has-arrived.

The Law of Accelerating Returns. "Kurzweil, Tracking the Acceleration of Intelligence." Accessed April 7, 2023. https://www.kurzweilai.net/the-law-of-accelerating-returns.

BCG. "Flipping the Odds of Digital Transformation." Patrick Forth, Tom Reichert, Romain de Laubier, and Saibal Chakraborty. (October 29, 2020). Accessed April 7, 2023. https://www.bcg.com/publications/2020/increasing-odds-of-success-in-digital-transformation.

Covey, Stephen R, The 7 Habits of Highly Effective People: Restoring the Character Ethic. [Rev. ed.]. Free Press, 2004.

Drucker Institute. "About Peter Drucker." Accessed April 7, 2023. https://www.drucker.institute/about/.

Mintzberg, Henry et al. *Strategy Safari – A Guided Tour Through the Wilds of Strategic Management.* Free Press, 1st Edition, September 25, 1998.

Harvard Health Publishing, Harvard Medical School. "Will a Purpose-Driven Life Help You Live Longer?" Kelly Bilodeau. (November 28, 2019). Accessed April 7, 2023. https://www.health.harvard.edu/blog/will-a-purpose-driven-life-help-you-live-longer-2019112818378.

Accenture Strategy. "From Me to We: The Rise of the Purpose-Led Brand." Rachel Barton, Kevin Quiring, Bill Theofilou. (December 5, 2018). Accessed April 7, 2023. https://www.accenture.com/gb-en/insights/strategy/brand-purpose.

Ernst & Young. "How Purpose Can Help You Transcend Disruption." Ernst & Young Global. (March 10, 2020). Accessed April 7, 2023. https://www.ey.com/en_gl/purpose/how-purpose-can-help-you-transcend-disruption.

Christensen, Clayton M. et al. "Competing Against Luck: The Story of Innovation and Customer Choice." HarperBus. (November 3, 2016).

IKEA. "The IKEA Vision, Values and Business Idea." Accessed April 7, 2023. https://www.ikea.com/ie/en/this-is-ikea/about-us/the-ikea-vision-and-values-pub9aa779d0.

Future's Today Institute 'What we Create'. Accessed April 7, 2023. https://futuretodayinstitute.com/tools/.

London School of Economics. "How Tesla Is Changing Product Life Cycle in the Car Industry." Antti Lyyra and Kari Koskinen. (February 5, 2018). Accessed April 7, 2023. https://blogs.lse.ac.uk/management/2018/02/05/how-tesla-is-changing-product-life-cycle-in-the-car-industry/.

CB Insights. "How Fintechs Are Tapping Insurtechs to Bundle Services." (December 10, 2020). Accessed April 7, 2023. https://www.cbinsights.com/research/insurtech-fintech-business–relationships/.

Schumpeter, Joseph A. 1883–1950. *Capitalism, Socialism, and Democracy.* New York: Harper & Row, 1962.

May, Matthew E. "Play to Win Strategy Canvas." Accessed April 7, 2023. https://matthewemay.com/wp-content/uploads/2015/08/A3-P2WCanvas.pdf.

Cogapp. "Digital Strategy for Museums." Accessed April 7, 2023. https://www.cogapp.com/r-d/digital-strategy.

Digital Marketing Canvas. "The Digital Marketing Canvas." Accessed April 7, 2023. https://digitalmarketingcanvas.co.

Gartner Glossary, Customer Centricity. Accessed April 7, 2023. https://www.gartner.com/en/marketing/glossary/customer-centricity.

Forbes. "50 Stats That Prove the Value of Customer Experience." Blake Morgan. (September 24, 2019). Accessed April 7, 2023. https://www.forbes.com/sites/blakemorgan/2019/09/24/50-stats-that-prove-the-value-of-customer-experience/.

Strategyzer. "Business Model Canvas." Accessed April 7, 2023. https://www.strategyzer.com/business-model-canvas/key-resources.

YouTube. "Introduction to L'Oreal Simplicity Project." Accessed April 7, 2023. https://youtu.be/WENLLt3C2X0.

IBM. "Consumers Want It All – 2022 Consumer Study." Accessed April 7, 2023. https://www.ibm.com/thought-leadership/institute-business-value/en-us/report/2022-consumer-study.

Deloitte. 'Deloitte Digital Product Management' Accessed April 7, 2023. https://www2.deloitte.com/content/dam/insights/us/articles/5224_Digital-transformation-7/DI_Digital%20transformation%207.pdfhttps://www2.deloitte.com/content/dam/insights/us/articles/5224_Digital-transformation-7/DI_Digital%20transformation%207.pdf.

The Digital Product Manager. "What Does a Digital Product Manager Do?" Pallavi Agarwal. Accessed April 7, 2023. https://theproductmanager.com/topics/digital-product-manager/.

Stanford University. "Measuring Trends in Artificial Intelligence – AI Index Report." Accessed April 7, 2023. https://aiindex.stanford.edu/ai-index-report-2021/.

McKinsey. "The State of AI in 2021 – Survey." (December 8, 2021). Accessed April 7, 2023. https://www.mckinsey.com/capabilities/quantumblack/our-insights/global-survey-the-state-of-ai-in-2021.

The Guardian. "Fortnite Video Game Maker to Pay $520 m Over Privacy and Billing Claims." (December 19, 2022). Accessed April 7, 2023. https://www.theguardian.com/games/2022/dec/19/fortnite-epic-games-pay-fine-ftc-privacy-billing.

Accenture. "Read, Set, Scale Report: What Is the Difference Between Applied and Artificial Intelligence? What Is AI?" Accessed April 7, 2023. https://www.accenture.com/bg-en/insights/artificial-intelligence/scaling-enterprise-ai.

Agile Manifesto. "Manifesto for Agile Software Development." Accessed April 7, 2023. https://agilemanifesto.org/.

McKinsey. "The Five Trademarks of Agile Organisations." (March 1, 2018). Accessed April 7, 2023. https://www.mckinsey.com/capabilities/people-and-organizational-performance/our-insights/the-five-trademarks-of-agile-organizations.

Harvard Business Review. "Agile at Scale – How to Go From a Few Teams to Hundreds." Darrell Rigby, Jeff Sutherland, and Andy Noble. Accessed April 7, 2023. https://hbr.org/2018/05/agile-at-scale.

Scaled Agile Framework. "SAFE Scaled Agile." Accessed April 7, 2023. https://www.scaledagileframework.com/.

Innosight. "2021 Corporate Longevity Forecast." S. Patrick Viguerie, Ned Calder, and Brian Hindo. (May 2021). Accessed April 7, 2023. https://www.innosight.com/insight/creative-destruction/.

McKinsey. "Innovation in a Crisis: Why It Is More Critical than Ever." (June 17, 2020). Accessed April 7, 2023. https://www.mckinsey.com/capabilities/strategy-and-corporate-finance/our-insights/innovation-in-a-crisis-why-it-is-more-critical-than-ever.

McKinsey. "Enduring Ideas: The Three Horizons of Growth." (December 1, 2009). Accessed April 7, 2023. https://www.mckinsey.com/capabilities/strategy-and-corporate-finance/our-insights/enduring-ideas-the-three-horizons-of-growth.

Deloitte. "Digital Product Management – A Structured Approach to Product Innovation and Governance." (October 18, 2009). Accessed April 7, 2023. https://www2.deloitte.com/us/en/insights/focus/industry-4-0/product-innovation-and-governance.html.

Harvard MBA Student Perspectives. "Michelin: Tires-as-a-Service." (November 17, 2016). Accessed April 7, 2023. https://d3.harvard.edu/platform-rctom/submission/michelin-tires-as-a-service/.

Harvard MBA Student Perspective – "A Bright Future for Philips." (November 16, 2016). Accessed April 7, 2023. https://d3.harvard.edu/platform-rctom/submission/a-bright-future-for-philips/.

Harvard MBA Student Perspectives. "Healthier Premiums: Using Technology to Drive Positive Behaviour in Insurance." (November 18, 2016). Accessed April 7, 2023. https://d3.harvard.edu/platform-rctom/submission/healthier-premiums-using-technology-to-drive-positive-behaviour-in-insurance/.

What Could Be. "The Design Thinking Canvas." Accessed April 7, 2023. https://www.whatcouldbe.com/.

Blue Ocean Strategy. Accessed April 7, 2023. https://www.blueoceanstrategy.com/.

Forbes. "20 Fresh Examples of Customer Experience Innovation." Blake Morgan. (October 21, 2019). Accessed April 7, 2023. https://www.forbes.com/sites/blakemorgan/2019/10/21/20-fresh-examples-of-customer-experience-innovation/.

Intrapreneurial Index. "Improve Your Intrapreneurship Activities." Accessed April 7, 2023. https://intrapreneurial-index.com/.

McKinsey. "The Innovation Commitment." (October 24, 2019). Accessed April 7, 2023. https://www.mckinsey.com/capabilities/strategy-and-corporate-finance/our-insights/the-innovation-commitment.

Sia Partners. "Sia Partners 2021 International Mobile Banking Benchmark." (September, 2021). Accessed April 7, 2023. https://www.sia-partners.com/en/insights/publications/sia-partners-2021-international-mobile-banking-benchmark.

BGC. "What Is Your Business Ecosystem Strategy?" Ulrich Pidun, Martin Reeves, and Balázs Zoletnik. (March 11, 2022). Accessed April 7, 2023. https://www.bcg.com/publications/2022/what-is-your-business-ecosystem-strategy

Cybercrime Magazine. "Cybercrime to Cost the World $10.5 Trillion Annually by 2025." Accessed April 7, 2023. https://cybersecurityventures.com/hackerpocalypse-cybercrime-report-2016/.

SIFMA.org. "SOC for Cybersecurity – An Overview of the AICPA's Cybersecurity Attestation Reporting Framework." Accessed April 7, 2023. https://www.sifma.org/wp-content/uploads/2018/03/SOC-for-Cybersecurity.pdf.

NIST Risk Management Framework. Accessed April 7, 2023. https://csrc.nist.gov/projects/risk-management/about-rmf.

World Economic Forum. "Global Risks Report 2023." Accessed April 7, 2023. https://www.weforum.org/reports/global-risks-report-2023.

Mitre. "ATT&CK." Accessed April 7, 2023. https://attack.mitre.org/.

EIN Press Wire. "Cybersecurity Jobs Report: 3.5 Million Openings Through 2025." (November 11, 2021). Accessed April 7, 2023. https://www.einpresswire.com/article/556075599/cybersecurity-jobs-report-3-5-millionopenings-through-2025.

Edward Hall. *Beyond Culture*. Anchor Books; Anchor Books Edition, 1 June 1997.

Plai Team. "A History of Objectives and Key Results (OKRs)." Accessed April 7, 2023. https://www.plai.team/blog/history-of-objectives-and-key-results.

McKinsey. "The Innovation Commitment." (October 24, 2019). Accessed April 7, 2023. https://www.mckinsey.com/capabilities/strategy-and-corporate-finance/our-insights/the-innovation-commitment?cid=app.

The Operating Model Canvas. Accessed April 7, 2023. https://ashridgeonoperatingmodels.com/book-operating-model-canvas/.

Medium. "The Operating System Canvas," Aaron Dignan. (February 9, 2019). Accessed April 7, 2023. https://medium.com/the-ready/the-operating-system-canvas-420b8b4df062.

The Ready. Accessed April 7, 2023. https://theready.com.

McKinsey. "Why Do Most Transformations Fail?" Harry Robinson. (July 10, 2019). Accessed April 7, 2023. https://www.mckinsey.com/capabilities/transformation/our-insights/why-do-most-transformations-fail-a-conversation-with-harry-robinson.

DBS.com. "Transforming a Bank by Becoming Digital to the Core." Accessed April 7, 2023. https://www.dbs.com/media/digital-transformation/dbs-cio-david-gledhill-on-transforming-a-bank-by-becoming-digital-to-the-core.page.

YouTube. "How DBS Transformed Its Culture to Become "The World's Best Bank." Accessed April 7, 2023. https://www.youtube.com/watch?v=THrxDjO4KD4.

Bershin, Josh. Accessed April 7, 2023. https://joshbersin.com.

OMG – Standards Development Organization. Accessed April 7, 2023. https://www.omg.org/.

Foryouandyourcustomers. "The Exploded View." Accessed April 7, 2023. https://foryouandyourcustomers.com/posts/whitepaper/exploded-view/?lang=en.

digital-bpm. "BPM in the Digital Age." Accessed April 7, 2023. https://digital-bpm.com/bpm-capability-framework/.

weforum.org. "24 Cognitive Biases That Are Warping Your Perception of Reality." (November 30, 2021) Accessed April 7, 2023. https://www.weforum.org/agenda/2021/11/humans-cognitive-bias-mistake/.

McKinsey. "Unlocking Success in Digital Transformations." (October 28, 2019). Accessed April 7, 2023. https://www.mckinsey.com/capabilities/people-and-organizational-performance/our-insights/unlocking-success-in-digital-transformations.

McCullen, Aidan. "Undisruptable." Accessed April 7, 2023. https://www.wiley.com/en-ie/Undisruptable:+A+Mindset+of+Permanent+Reinvention+for+Individuals,+Organisations+and+Life-p-9781119770480.

Diamandis, Peter. Accessed April 7, 2023. https://www.diamandis.com.

The Future Today Institute. "The 11 Macro Sources of Disruption," Accessed April 7, 2023.
    https://futuretodayinstitute.com/wp-content/uploads/2023/02/Wheel-1.pdf.
RAND. "Delphi Method." Accessed April 7, 2023. https://www.rand.org/topics/delphi-method.html.
Springer. "Future-Oriented Technology Analysis: A Classification Framework." V. M. Urbano et al.
    (May 30, 2021). Accessed April 7, 2023. https://link.springer.com/chapter/10.1007/978-3-030-69380-0_2.
We Work. Accessed April 7, 2023. https://www.wework.com/.

List of Figures

https://doi.org/10.1515/9783111034713-34

List of Tables

https://doi.org/10.1515/9783111034713-035

Index

adversarial tactics, techniques, and common
    knowledge (ATT&CK) 274
agile
– Agile Manifesto 197, 198
– John Deere 206
– Kanban 202–203
– scaling 204–206
– Scrum process 200, 201
– shift 199–200
– stages 201–202
– waterfall *vs.* 204
Agile DevOps 265–266
AI. *See* artificial intelligence (AI)
Airbnb 243
Aldo 268–269
Alexa 2, 186
algorithms 32
Amazon 28, 186,
– ecosystem 239–241
– platforms 28
ambidexterity 118
ambidextrous leadership 325–327, 330
analytical machine 19
analytics and AI 183,
– algorithms 186
– benefits tracking 188
– business demand 186, 187
– ChatGPT 186
– culture 191
– data gathering and management 187
– emancipation, digital data 29–32
– ethics 188–189
– innovation 192
– investment 183
– leadership and talent 187
– maturity model 184, 185
– methods of working 188
– mobilise, assemble and explore 194
– models, tools, and tracking 187
– operating model optimisation 191
– opportunity map 185
– productivity 191
– products 192–193
– solving business needs 190
– sweat data and technology 191
– use case development 189–190

Android 40
API product management 260–261
Apple 1, 39
– ARKit 4
– iPhone 27
– iPod 3, 6
– M1 Ultra microprocessor 22
– protection 39
– True-Depth camera 4
archetypes 314, 332
ARPANET (Advanced Research Projects Agency
    Network) 25
artificial intelligence (AI) 29–32, 37, 183. *See also*
    analytics and AI
ATT&CK. *See* adversarial tactics, techniques, and
    common knowledge (ATT&CK)
attributes of digital organisation 50–51
Audi 49–50
autonomous vehicles 37

B2B. *See* business-to-business (B2B)
B2C. *See* business-to-consumer (B2C)
Babbage, C. 18, 19
backcasting 360
backfire effect 345
behavioural economics 345
behaviours, values 295–296
Beyond Culture (Hall) 289
big data 30, 186, 268
blind spot bias 344
Blue Ocean Strategy 220–222
blueprint, innovation 229–230
Boolean, G. 19
BPM. *See* business process management (BPM)
Brownie Camera 5
budget simplification 153
business analysis test card
– business and operations 98
– core pillars of performance 98–99
– develop the business (innovation) 97
– grow the business (core) 97
– internal and external analyses 100
– overarching strategy (and purpose) 95
– resourcing the business (funding and
    resourcing) 97
business architecture 335–337

https://doi.org/10.1515/9783111034713-036

About the Author

Garvan is an executive adviser day-to-day and, through his practice ONEZERO1, works with business leaders to develop and execute ambitious transformations with particular focus on commercial, customer, and cultural strategies. He is active across a range of sectors including banking, insurance, education, logistics, technology, health, medicine, and public sector.

Working as a strategy and execution guide with boards, C-suite leaders, and their teams, his insights and methods are built on 18 years of executive-level experience in financial services across strategy and execution, transformation leadership, and deep domain experience in customer, digital, data, and innovation. He brings fresh perspectives, ambitious thinking, and transformational change management to dynamic market and organisational challenges with a mandate to unlock opportunities, solve enterprise-level problems, and drive execution for results.

In addition to his advisory practice, Garvan is resident faculty with the Institute of Banking where he designs and delivers education programmes at all levels of the academic framework. He also guest lectures at a number of business schools, is a regular keynote speaker, moderator, and panellist on key strategic trends and future-focused topics. He also provides pro bono support to a number of charities and public good initiatives such as Digital Identity and has served as a working member of the WEF Digital Identity Coalition.

Garvan is a learning advocate given his work in education, having spent over 10 years as a member of council of the Institute of Banking and completing numerous educational opportunities including executive programmes at MIT, IMD, Harvard Business School, Oxford Said Business School, Chicago Booth, and Singularity University. He has also attained a Diploma in Company Directorship with the Institute of Directors and serves as a Non-executive Director.

To find out more, visit him and supporting resources to this book at www.onezero1.ie

https://doi.org/10.1515/9783111034713-037